Contents

PREFACE		**IX**
1	**INTRODUCTION TO DIGITAL SYSTEMS**	**1**
	1.1 Explanation of Terms	2
	1.2 Design Levels	4
	1.3 Combinational vs. Sequential Systems	4
	1.4 Digital Circuits	5
	1.4.1 Diodes	5
	1.4.2 Transistors	5
	1.4.3 MOS Transistors	11
	1.5 Integrated Circuits (ICs)	14
	1.6 CAD (Computer-Aided Design)	16
	1.7 Evolution of Digital Logic, Microprocessors, and Microcontrollers	16
	1.8 A Typical Application of a Digital System such as a Microcontroller	18
2	**NUMBER SYSTEMS, ARITHMETIC/LOGIC OPERATIONS, AND CODES**	**21**
	2.1 Number Systems	21
	2.1.1 General Number Representation	21
	2.1.2 Converting Numbers from One Base to Another	23
	2.2 Unsigned and Signed Binary Numbers	27
	2.3 Codes	30
	2.3.1 Binary-Coded-Decimal Code (8421 Code)	30
	2.3.2 Alphanumeric Codes	31
	2.3.3 Excess-3 Code	31
	2.3.4 Gray Code	33
	2.3.5 Unicode	35
	2.4 Fixed-Point and Floating-Point Representations	35
	2.5 Arithmetic Operations	36
	2.5.1 Binary Arithmetic	36
	2.5.2 BCD Arithmetic	44
	2.5.3 Multiword Binary Addition and Subtraction	45
	2.5.4 Binary Multiplication and Division by Shift Operations	46
	2.6 Error Correction and Detection	48
	QUESTIONS AND PROBLEMS	50
3	**DIGITAL LOGIC GATES, BOOLEAN ALGEBRA, AND SIMPLIFICATION**	**53**
	3.1 Basic Logic Operations	53
	3.1.1 NOT Operation	53
	3.1.2 OR operation	54
	3.1.3 AND operation	56
	3.2 Other Logic Operations	57
	3.2.1 NOR operation	57
	3.2.2 NAND operation	58
	3.2.3 Exclusive-OR operation (XOR)	59
	3.2.4 Exclusive-NOR Operation (XNOR)	61

	3.3	Positive and Negative Logic	62
	3.4	Boolean Algebra	63
		3.4.1 Boolean Identities	64
		3.4.2 Simplification Using Boolean Identities	65
		3.4.3 Consensus Theorem	69
		3.4.4 Getting Rid of Glitches or Hazards in Combinational Circuits	70
		3.4.5 Complement of a Boolean Function	71
	3.5	XOR / XNOR Implementations	71
		QUESTIONS AND PROBLEMS	74
4	**MINTERMS, MAXTERMS, AND KARNAUGH MAP**		**77**
	4.1	Standard Representations	77
	4.2	Karnaugh Maps	81
		4.2.1 Two-Variable K-map	81
		4.2.2 Three-Variable K-map	82
		4.2.3 Four-Variable K-map	84
		4.2.4 Prime Implicants	87
		4.2.5 Expressing a Boolean function in Product-of-sums (POS) form using a K-map	89
		4.2.6 Don't Care Conditions	90
		4.2.7 Five-Variable K-map	94
	4.3	Quine–McCluskey Method	95
	4.4	Implementation of Digital Circuits with NAND, and NOR Gates	96
		4.4.1 NAND Gate Implementation	97
		4.4.2 NOR Gate Implementation	98
		QUESTIONS AND PROBLEMS	103
5	**ANALYSIS AND DESIGN OF COMBINATIONAL CIRCUITS USING GATES**		**107**
	5.1	Basic Concepts	107
	5.2	Analysis of a Combinational Logic Circuit	107
	5.3	Design of Combinational Circuits Using Logic Gates	108
	5.4	Multiple-Output Combinational Circuits	113
		QUESTIONS AND PROBLEMS	118
6	**DESIGN OF TYPICAL COMBINATIONAL LOGIC COMPONENTS**		**121**
	6.1	Design of Typical Combinational Logic Components	121
	6.2	Comparators	121
	6.3	Decoders	124
	6.4	Encoders	130
	6.5	Multiplexers	133
	6.6	Demultiplexers	137
	6.7	Binary Adder/Subtractor and BCD Adder	139
		QUESTIONS AND PROBLEMS	148
7	**COMBINATIONAL SHIFTER, FAST ADDERS, ARRAY MULTIPLIERS, ALU, & PLDS**		**151**
	7.1	Combinational Shifter	151
	7.2	Central Processing Unit (CPU)	152
	7.3	Arithmetic Logic Unit (ALU)	154
	7.4	Read-Only Memories (ROMs)	165
	7.5	Programmable Logic Devices (PLDs)	167
	7.6	Commercially Available Field Programmable Devices (FPDs)	170
		QUESTIONS AND PROBLEMS	172
8	**COMBINATIONAL LOGIC USING VERILOG**		**175**
	8.1	Hardware Description Languages (HDLs)	175
	8.2	Basics of Verilog	176
		8.2.1 Verilog keywords	176
		8.2.2 Representing numbers in Verilog	176
		8.2.3 A typical Verilog Segment	177

DIGITAL LOGIC
WITH
AN INTRODUCTION TO
VERILOG AND FPGA-
BASED DESIGN

M. RAFIQUZZAMAN, Ph.D., P.E.
Professor
California State Polytechnic University
Pomona, California
and
President
Rafi Systems, Inc.
Diamond Bar, California.

STEVEN A. McNINCH, M.S.
R & D Test Engineer
Broadcom Inc.
Irvine, California

SENIOR DIRECTOR	Donald Fowley
VICE PRESIDENT & DIRECTOR	Laurie Rosatone
EDITOR	Jennifer Brady
MARKETING MANAGER	Michele Szczesniak
SENIOR CONTENT MANAGER	Valerie Zaborski
SENIOR PRODUCTION EDITOR	Ashley Patterson
COVER DESIGN	Nicholas Wehrkamp

This book was prepared in InDesign by CJ Media and printed and bound by Quad Graphics/Versailles. The cover was printed by Quad Graphics/Versailles.

Founded in 1807, John Wiley & Sons, Inc. has been a valued source of knowledge and understanding for more than 200 years, helping people around the world meet their needs and fulfill their aspirations. Our company is built on a foundation of principles that include responsibility to the communities we serve and where we live and work. In 2008, we launched a Corporate Citizenship Initiative, a global effort to address the environmental, social, economic, and ethical challenges we face in our business. Among the issues we are addressing are carbon impact, paper specifications and procurement, ethical conduct within our business and among our vendors, and community and charitable support. For more information, please visit our website: www.wiley.com/go/citizenship.

Evaluation copies are provided to qualified academics and professionals for review purposes only, for use in their courses during the next academic year. These copies are licensed and may not be sold or transferred to a third party. Upon completion of the review period, please return the evaluation copy to Wiley. Return instructions and a free of charge return shipping label are available at: www.wiley.com/go/returnlabel. If you have chosen to adopt this textbook for use in your course, please accept this book as your complimentary desk copy. Outside of the United States, please contact your local sales representative.

The inside back cover will contain printing identification and country of origin if omitted from this page. In addition, if the ISBN on the back cover differs from the ISBN on this page, the one on the back cover is correct.

Cataloging-in-Publication Data is on file at the Library of Congress

ISBN-13: 978-1-119-62154-6

Printed in the United States of America

SKY10081747_080924

Dedication

To my wife, Kusum, and our grandsons (triplets), Ayaaz, Adyan, and Safir

-- M. Rafiquzzaman

To my parents, Bill and Susan, and my wife to be, Brittaney

-- Steven A. McNinch

8.3   Structural Modeling   182
8.4   Dataflow Modeling   189
8.5   Behavioral modeling   195
    8.5.1 if-else block   197
    8.5.2 Modeling logical conditions in a circuit   198
    8.5.3 Case-endcase construct   198
    8.5.4 Conditional Operator   200
8.6   Simulation   201
QUESTIONS AND PROBLEMS   207

9   LATCHES AND FLIP-FLOPS   211
9.1   Latches and Flip-Flops   211
    9.1.1 SR Latch   211
    9.1.2 Gated SR Latch   213
    9.1.3 Gated D Latch   213
    9.1.4 Edge-Trigerred D Flip-Flop   214
    9.1.5 JK Flip-Flop   216
    9.1.6 T Flip-Flop   217
9.2   Timing parameters for edge-triggered flip-flops   218
9.3   Preset and Clear Inputs   219
9.4   Summary of Flip-Flops   220
QUESTIONS AND PROBLEMS   224

10   ANALYSIS AND DESIGN OF SEQUENTIAL CIRCUITS   227
10.1   Introduction   227
10.2   Analysis of Synchronous Sequential Circuits   228
10.3   Types of Synchronous Sequential Circuits   233
10.4   Minimization of States   235
10.5   Design of Synchronous Sequential Circuits   237
10.6   Serial Adder   240
10.7   Sequence Generator/Detector   242
10.8   Random-Access Memory (RAM)   245
10.9   Algorithmic State Machines (ASM) Chart   246
10.10 Asynchronous Sequential Circuits   254
QUESTIONS AND PROBLEMS   258

11   COUNTERS AND REGISTERS   263
11.1   Design of Counters   263
11.2   Design of Registers   268
    11.2.1 Shift Register   268
    11.2.2 "Shift register" Counters   271
    11.2.3 General-Purpose Register (GPR)   275
QUESTIONS AND PROBLEMS   277

12   SEQUENTIAL LOGIC DESIGN USING VERILOG   281
12.1   Basics   281
12.2   Examples Illustrating Non-blocking and Blocking Assignments   283
12.3   RTL (Register Transfer Level) modeling   289
QUESTIONS AND PROBLEMS   298

13   IMPLEMENTATION OF DIGITAL DESIGN USING FPGA   301
13.1   Basics of FPGA   301
    13.1.1 LUTs (Look-Up Tables)   302
    13.1.2 Programmable Switch Matrix   308
    13.1.3 Configurable Logic Blocks (CLBs)   308
    13.1.4 FPGA Architecture   311
    13.1.5 FPGA Programming   311
13.2   A Typical FPGA Chip   312

13.2.1 Configuration Pins   314
13.2.2 User I/O Pins   315
13.2.3 Power/Ground Pins   315
13.3   A Typical FPGA Board   315
13.4   FPGA-based Design and Implementation   320
13.4.1 Design   320
13.4.2 Synthesis   320
13.4.3 Implementation, Programming, and Verification   320
13.5   FPGA Examples   322
QUESTIONS AND PROBLEMS   374

APPENDIX A: ANSWERS TO SELECTED PROBLEMS   **379**

APPENDIX B: GLOSSARY   **389**

APPENDIX C: STEP-BY-STEP TUTORIAL FOR DOWNLOADING AND
INSTALLING XILINX VIVADO IDE   **395**

APPENDIX D: STEP-BY-STEP TUTORIAL FOR CREATING & SIMULATING A
VERILOG DESIGN USING XILINX VIVADO IDE   **399**
I   COMBINATIONAL CIRCUIT   399
II   SEQUENTIAL CIRCUIT   407

APPENDIX E: STEP-BY-STEP PROCEDURE FOR IMPLEMENTING FPGA-BASED
DESIGN USING VIVADO IDE & NEXYS A7 FPGA BOARD   **419**
I   COMBINATIONAL CIRCUIT   419
II   FPGA IMPLEMENTATION OF SEQUENTIAL CIRCUIT   426

BIBLIOGRAPHY   **437**
INDEX   **439**

PREFACE

This book provides the basics of digital logic with an introduction to Verilog and FPGA-based design. Emphasis is given to the basic concepts. To cite an example, we clearly point out that computers understand only 0's and 1's. It is, therefore, important that students be familiar with binary numbers. Furthermore, we focus on the fact that computers can normally only add. Hence, all other operations such as subtraction are performed via addition. This can be accomplished via two's-complement arithmetic for binary numbers. This topic is, therefore, also included along with a clear explanation of signed and unsigned binary numbers. Basic concepts such as these are illustrated using simple examples throughout this book.

Two design levels are covered in this book: device level and logic level. Device-level design using simple devices such as transistors is included. Logic-level design is the design technique in which logic gates are used; design of digital components such as an adder is also incuded. Detailed coverage of logic level design is provided in this book. Since students are familiar with C-language, emphasis is given on a popular HDL (Hardware Description Language) such as Verilog from an introductory point of view.

Digital systems at the logic level are classified into two types of circuits: combinational and sequential. Combinational circuits have no memory whereas sequential circuits contain memory. Microcontrollers and microprocessors are designed using both combinational and sequential circuits. Therefore, these topics are covered in detail. This book contains details of synthesizing digital logic circuits using Verilog. Emphasis is given on contemporary digital circuit implementation using a popular programmable logic device (PLD) such as field programmable gate array (FPGA). Basic concepts associated with the use of Verilog for specifying, designing and implementing FPGA-based digital logic circuits with modern CAD (computer aided design) tools are provided. The authors took a practical approach to implement FPGA-based design with Verilog using simple examples. Numerous meaningful examples are provided. Coverage of all these topics in a simplified manner will make this book very unique.

The book is divided into 13 chapters.

Chapter 1 presents an explanation of basic terminologies; fundamental concepts of digital integrated circuits using transistors; a comparison of LSTTL, HC, and HCT IC characteristics; the evolution of computers; and technological forecasts.

Chapter 2 provides various number systems and codes suitable for representing information in typical digital systems.

Chapter 3 covers Boolean algebra along with simplification of Boolean functions using identities. The basic characteristics of digital logic gates are also presented.

Chapter 4 includes minterms, maxterms, and Karnaugh-map simplification.

Chapter 5 contains analysis and design of combinational circuits using logic gates. Design procedure for combinational circuits is standardized into three steps. This will make it easier to design combinational circuits.

Chapter 6 includes design of typical combinational logic components such as comparator, decoder, encoder, multiplexer, demultiplexer, and binary adder and subtractor.

Chapter 7 describes design of combinational shifter, fast adders, array multipliers, and ALU. Topics such as ROM, PLD, and CPLD with an introduction to FPGA are also included. It has been pointed out that CPLDs are typically used in smaller applications while FPGAs are used in larger applications. Both CPLDs and FPGAs may be used in a single application. In such a system, CPLDs usually perform "glue logic" functions, including booting the FPGA and controlling the reset and boot sequence of the complete circuit board.

Chapter 8 covers an introduction to combinational logic design using Hardware Description Languages such as Verilog.

Chapter 9 includes various types of latches and flip-flops. Topics such as flip-flop set-up time, hold time, and metastability are also covered. It is pointed out that the JK flip-flop was popular during the 1970's when small scale integrated circuits with flip-flops using TTL were available. The JK flip-flops are now replaced by D flip-flops. This is because equations for D flip-flops are simpler and they are widely used by FPGA.

Chapter 10 contains analysis and design of sequential circuits using logic gates. Design procedure for synchronous sequential circuit is standardized into three steps. This will make it easier to design sequential circuits. Also, design of sequence detectors using three-step procedure of sequential circuits is included. It has been pointed out that sequence detectors are used in a remote control for TV or remote for garage door opener.

An ASM (Algorithmic State Machine) chart was widely used in the past along with the state diagram for designing a synchronous sequential circuit. However, with the popularity of hardware description languages, use of ASM chart has reduced significantly. Note that HDLs provide a lot more structured features including C-constructs. Hence, a brief coverage of ASM is provided in this chapter.

Chapter 11 describes design of registers and counters. Ring counters and Johnson counters are designed using the three-step process of sequential design. It is mentioned that ring counters are used for generating timing signals for the CPU. Also, it is pointed out that Johnson counters are used to divide the frequency of a clock by an integer. Since the speed of a stepper motor depends mainly on the clock frequency, Johnson counter is typically used in stepper motor control.

Chapter 12 covers sequential logic design using Verilog. Both non-blocking and blocking assignments are compared using simulation results.

Chapter 13 introduces basic concepts associated with FPGA-based implementation using CAD tools. Xilinx Vivado ide, and Digilent Nexys A7 FPGA board are used for this purpose. Several meaningful examples are implemented using simple devices such as switches, LEDs, and seven-segment displays. Thus, the concept of FPGA can easily be included in an introductory course in digital logic.

The book can easily be adopted as a text for "digital logic design" at the undergraduate level in electrical/computer engineering and computer science. A basic background in C language programming and DC circuits is essential. The audience for this book can also be practicing engineers and scientists in the industry. Practitioners of digital system design in the industry will find more simplified explanations, together with examples and comparison considerations, than are found in manufacturers' manuals.

The authors are indebted to Dr. R. Chandra of California State Polytechnic University, Pomona for his valuable input. The authors wish to express their sincere appreciation to Chris and Connie Jacobs of CJ Media for preparing the final version of the manuscript. Finally, the authors are grateful to Mary Vang for her hard work and dedication in bringing this book to production.

M. RAFIQUZZAMAN
Pomona, California

STEVEN A. McNINCH
Irvine, California

1

INTRODUCTION TO DIGITAL SYSTEMS

Digital systems are designed to store, process, and communicate information in digital form. They are found in a wide range of applications, including process control, communication systems, digital instruments, and consumer products. The digital computer, more commonly called the "computer," is an example of a typical digital system.

A computer manipulates information in digital, or more precisely, binary form. A binary number has only two discrete values — zero or one. Each of these discrete values is represented by the OFF and ON status of an electronic switch called a "transistor." All computers, therefore, only understand binary numbers. Any decimal number (base 10, with ten digits from 0 to 9) can be represented by a binary number (base 2, with digits 0 and 1).

The basic blocks of a computer are the central processing unit (CPU), the memory, and the input/output (I/O). The CPU of the computer is basically the same as the brain of a human being. Computer memory is conceptually similar to human memory. A question asked to a human being is analogous to entering a program into the computer using an input device such as the keyboard, and answering the question by the human is similar in concept to outputting the result required by the program to a computer output device such as the printer. The main difference is that human beings can think independently, whereas computers can only answer questions that they are programmed for. Computer hardware refers to components of a computer such as memory, CPU, transistors, nuts, bolts, and so on. Programs can perform a specific task such as addition if the computer has an electronic circuit capable of adding two numbers. Programmers cannot change these electronic circuits but can perform tasks on them using instructions.

Computer software, on the other hand, consists of a collection of programs. Programs contain instructions and data for performing a specific task. These programs, written using any programming language such as C, must be translated into binary prior to execution by the computer. This is because the computer only understands binary numbers.

Therefore, a translator for converting such a program into binary is necessary. Hence, a translator program called the *compiler* is used for translating programs written in a programming language such as C into binary. These programs in binary form are then stored in the computer memory for execution because computers only understand 0's and 1's. Furthermore, computers can only add. This means that all operations such as subtraction, multiplication, and division are performed by addition.

Due to advances in semiconductor technology, it is possible to fabricate the CPU in a single chip. The result is the *microprocessor*. Both Metal Oxide Semiconductor (MOS) and Bipolar technologies were used in the fabrication process. The CPU can be placed on a single chip when MOS technology is used. However, several chips are required with the bipolar technology. HCMOS (High Speed Complementary MOS) or BICMOS (Combination of Bipolar and HCMOS) technology (to be discussed later in this chapter) is normally used these days to fabricate the microprocessor in a single chip. Along with the microprocessor chip, appropriate memory and I/O chips can be used to design a *microcomputer*. The pins on each one of these chips can be connected to the proper lines on the system bus, which consists of address, data, and control lines. In the past, some manufacturers have designed a complete microcomputer on a single chip with limited capabilities. Single-chip microcomputers were used in a wide range of industrial and home applications.

Digital Logic with an Introduction to Verilog and FPGA-Based Design. First Edition. M. Rafiquzzaman and Steven A. McNinch.
© 2019 John Wiley & Sons, Inc. Published 2019 by John Wiley & Sons, Inc.

"Microcontrollers" evolved from single-chip microcomputers. The microcontrollers are typically used for dedicated applications such as automotive systems, home appliances, and home entertainment systems. Typical microcontrollers, therefore, include a microcomputer, timers, and A/D (analog to digital) and D/A (digital to analog) converters — all in a single chip. Examples of typical microcontrollers are Intel 8751 (8-bit) / 8096 (16-bit) and Microchip PIC18F (8-bit) / PIC24F (16-bit).

In this chapter, we first define some basic terms associated with digital systems such as computers. We then describe briefly the basics of transistors, digital circuits, evolution of digital logic, microprocessors, and microcontrollers. Finally, a typical practical application is included.

1.1   Explanation of Terms

Before we go on, it is necessary to understand some basic terms (arranged in alphabetical order).

- *Address* is a pattern of 0's and 1's that represents a specific location in memory or a particular I/O device. An 8-bit microcontroller with 16 address bits can produce 2^{16} unique 16-bit patterns from 0000000000000000 to 1111111111111111, representing 65,536 different address combinations (addresses 0 to 65,535).

- *Arithmetic-logic unit* (ALU) is a digital circuit that performs arithmetic and logic operations on two n-bit digital words. The value of *n* for microcontrollers can be 8-bit or 16-bit. Typical operations performed by an ALU are addition, subtraction, ANDing, ORing, and comparison of two n-bit digital words. The size of the ALU defines the size of the microcontroller. For example, an 8-bit microcontroller contains an 8-bit ALU.

- *Bit* is an abbreviation for the term *binary digit*. A binary digit can have only two values, which are represented by the symbols 0 and 1, whereas a decimal digit can have 10 values, represented by the symbols 0 through 9. The bit values are easily implemented in electronic and magnetic media by two-state devices whose states portray either of the binary digits 0 and 1. Examples of such two-state devices are a transistor that is conducting or not conducting, a capacitor that is charged or discharged, and a magnetic material that is magnetized north to south or south to north.

- *Bit size* refers to the number of bits that can be processed simultaneously by the basic arithmetic circuits of a computer. A number of bits taken as a group in this manner is called a *word*. For example, an 8-bit microcontroller can process an 8-bit word. An 8-bit word is referred to as a *byte*, and a 4-bit word is known as a *nibble*.

- *Bus* consists of a number of conductors (wires) organized to provide a means of communication among different elements in a computer system. The conductors in a bus can be grouped in terms of their functions. A computer normally has an address bus, a data bus, and a control bus. Address bits are sent to memory or to an external device on the *address bus*. Instructions from memory, and data to/from memory or external devices, normally travel on the *data bus*. Control signals for the other buses and among system elements are transmitted on the control bus. Buses are sometimes *bidirectional*; that is, information can be transmitted in either direction on the bus, but normally in only one direction at a time.

- *Clock* is analogous to human heart beats. Computers require synchronization among its components, and this is provided by a *clock* or timing circuits.

- The *chip* is an integrated circuit (IC) package containing digital circuits.

- *CPU* (Central Processing Unit) contains several registers (memory elements), an ALU, and a control unit. Note that the control unit translates instructions and performs the desired task. The number of peripheral devices depends on the particular application involved and may even vary within an application.

- *EEPROM* or *E²PROM* (Electrically Erasable Programmable ROM) is nonvolatile. EEPROMs can be programmed without removing the chip from the socket. EEPROMs are called Read Most Memories (RMMs), because they have much slower write times than read times. Therefore, these memories are usually suited for applications when mostly reading rather than writing is performed.

An example of EEPROM is the 28C64 (8K × 8).

- *EPROM* (Erasable Programmable ROM) is nonvolatile. EPROMs can be programmed and erased. The EPROM chip must be removed from the socket for programming. This memory is erased by exposing the chip to ultraviolet light via a lid or window on the chip. Typical erase times vary between 10 and 30 minutes. The EPROM is programmed by inserting the chip into a socket of the EPROM programmer, and providing proper addresses and voltage pulses at the appropriate pins of the chip. An example of EPROM is the 2764 (8K × 8).

- *Flash memory* is designed using a combination of EPROM and EEPROM technologies. Flash memory is nonvolatile and was invented by Toshiba in mid 1980s. Flash memory can be programmed electrically while embedded on the board. One can change multiple bytes at a time. An example of flash memory is the Intel 28F020 (256K × 8). Flash memory is typically used in cell phones and digital cameras.

- An *FPGA* (Field Programmable Gate Array) chip contains an array of digital logic blocks along with input and output blocks which can be connected together via programming using a Hardware Description Language (HDL) such as Verilog or VHDL. There are three types of components inside an FPGA. These are lookup table (stored in SRAM), flip-flops, and switch matrices. The concept of FPGA is based on the fact that a combinational circuit can be implemented using memory. In the past, digital logic circuits were built using all hardware (logic gates). It was a time-consuming task to debug the circuits. However, digital circuits implemented using FPGA's are faster to debug since they are programmable. Note that it is much faster to debug software than hardware. Hence, products can be developed using FPGA from conceptual design via prototype to production in a very short time. Note that FPGAs are primarily used for a product before mass production.

- The term *gate* refers to digital circuits which perform logic operations such as AND, OR, and NOT. In an AND operation, the output of the AND gate is one if all inputs are one; the output is zero if one or more inputs are zero. The OR gate, on the other hand, provides a zero output if all inputs are zero; the output is one if one or more inputs are one. Finally, a NOT gate (also called an inverter) has one input and one output. The NOT gate produces one if the input is zero; the output is zero if the input is one.

- *Microcomputer* typically consists of a microprocessor (CPU) chip, input and output chips, and memory chips in which programs (instructions and data) are stored.

- *Microcontroller* is implemented on a single chip typically containing a CPU, memory, Input/Output (I/O), timers, A/D (Analog-to-Digital) converter, and serial I/O.

- *Microprocessor* is the CPU of a microcomputer contained on a single chip, and must be interfaced with peripheral support chips in order to function.

- *Program* contains instructions and data.

- *Random-access memory* (RAM) is a storage medium for groups of bits or words whose contents cannot only be read but can also be altered at specific addresses. A RAM normally provides volatile storage, which means that its contents are lost in case power is turned off. There are two types of RAM: static RAM (SRAM), and dynamic RAM (DRAM). *Static RAM* stores data in flip-flops. Therefore, this memory does not need to be refreshed. An example of SRAM is 6116 (2K × 8). *Dynamic RAM*, on the other hand, stores data in capacitors. That is, it can hold data for a few milliseconds. Hence, DRAMs are refreshed typically by using external refresh circuitry. DRAMs are used in applications requiring large memory. DRAMs have higher densities than SRAMs. Typical examples of DRAMs are the 4464 (64K × 4), 44256 (256K × 4), and 41000 (1M × 1). DRAMs are inexpensive, occupy less space, and dissipate less power than SRAMs.

- *Read-only memory* (ROM) is a storage medium for the groups of bits called words, and its contents cannot normally be altered once programmed. A typical ROM is fabricated on a chip and can store, for example, 2048 eight-bit words, which can be accessed individually by presenting to it one of 2048 addresses. This ROM is referred to as a 2K by 8-bit ROM. 10110111 is an example of an 8-bit word that might be stored in one location in this memory. A ROM is a *nonvolatile storage device,* which means that its contents are retained in case power is turned off. Because of this characteristic, ROMs are used to store permanent programs (instructions and data).

- *Register* can be considered as volatile storage for a number of bits. These bits may be entered into the register simultaneously (in parallel) or sequentially (serially) from right to left or from left to right, 1 bit at a time. An 8-bit register storing the bits 11110000 is represented as follows:

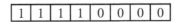

- The *speed power product* (SPP) is a measure of performance of a logic gate. It is expressed in picojoules (pJ). SPP is obtained by multiplying the speed (in ns) by the power dissipation (in mW) of a gate.

- *Transistors* are basically electronic switching devices. There are two types of transistors. These are *Bipolar Junction Transistors* (*BJTs*) and *Metal-Oxide Semiconductor* (*MOS*) transistors. The operation of the BJT depends on the flow of two types of carriers: electrons (n-channel) and holes (p-channel), whereas the MOS transistor is unipolar and its operation depends on the flow of only one type of carrier, either electrons (n-channel) or holes (p-channel).

1.2   Design Levels

Three design levels can be defined for digital systems: systems level, logic level, and device level.

- *Systems level* is the type of design in which CPU, memory, and I/O chips are interfaced to build a computer.

- *Logic level*, on the other hand, is the design technique in which chips containing logic gates such as AND, OR, and NOT are used to design a digital component such as an ALU. Emphasis is given on logic level design in this book.

- Finally, *device level* utilizes transistors to design logic gates.

1.3   Combinational vs. Sequential Systems

Digital systems at the logic level can be classified into two types. These are *combinational* and *sequential.*

   Combinational systems contain no memory whereas sequential systems require memory to remember the present state in order to go to the next state. A binary adder capable of providing the sum upon application of the numbers to be added is an example of a combinational system. For example, consider a 4-bit adder. The inputs to this adder will be two 4-bit numbers; the output will be the 4-bit sum. In this case, the adder will generate the 4-bit sum output upon application of the two 4-bit inputs.

   Sequential systems, on the other hand, require memory. The counter is an example of a sequential system. For instance, suppose that the counter is required to count in the sequence 0, 1, 2 and then repeat the sequence. In this case, the counter must have memory to remember the present count in order to go to the next. The counter must remember that it is at count 0 in order to go to the next count, 1. In order to count to 2, the counter must remember that it is counting 1 at the present state. In order to repeat the sequence, the counter must count back to 0 based on the present count, 2, and the process continues. A chip containing sequential circuit such as the counter will have a clock input pin.

   In general, all computers contain both combinational and sequential circuits. However, most computers are regarded as clocked sequential systems. In these computers, almost all activities pertaining to instruction execution are synchronized with clocks.

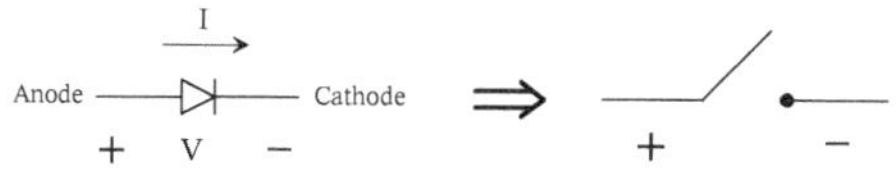

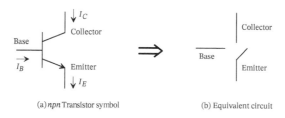

FIGURE 1.1   Symbolic representations of a diode

(a) *npn* Transistor symbol   (b) Equivalent circuit

FIGURE 1.2   Symbolic representations of a *npn* transistor

1.4   Digital Circuits

Circuits which understand 0's and 1's (binary numbers) are called "Digital Circuits". Transistors are used to design digital circuits. The transistor can be considered as an electronic switch. The ON and OFF states of a transistor are used to represent binary digits. Transistors, therefore, play an important role in the design of digital systems. This section describes the basic characteristics of digital devices and logic families. These include diodes, transistors, and a summary of digital logic families. These topics are covered from a very basic point of view. This will allow the readers with some background in digital devices to see how they are utilized in designing digital systems.

1.4.1   Diodes

A diode is an electronic switch. It is a two-terminal device. Figure 1.1 shows the symbolic representation. The positive terminal (made with the *p*-type semiconductor material) is called the anode; the negative terminal (made with the *n*-type semiconductor material) is called a cathode. When a voltage, $V = 0.6$ volt is applied across the anode and the cathode, the switch closes and a current I flows from anode to the cathode.

1.4.2   Transistors

A bipolar junction transistor (BJT) or commonly called the transistor is also an electronic switch like the diode. Both electrons (*n*-channel) and holes (*p*-channel) are used for carrier flow; hence, the name "bipolar" is used. The BJT is used in transistor logic circuits that have several advantages over diode logic circuits. First of all, the transistor acts as a logic device called an inverter. Note that an inverter provides a LOW output for a HIGH input and a HIGH output for a LOW input. Secondly, the transistor is a current amplifier (buffer). Transistors can, therefore, be used to amplify these currents to control external devices such as a light emitting diode (LED) requiring high currents. Finally, transistor logic gates operate faster than diode gates.

There are two types of transistors, namely *npn* and *pnp*. The classification depends on the fabrication process. npn transistors are widely used in digital circuits. Figure 1.2 shows the symbolic representation of an *npn* transistor. The transistor is a three-terminal device. These are base, emitter, and collector.

The transistor is a current-controlled switch. This means that an adequate current at the base will close the switch allowing a current to flow from the collector to the emitter.

This current direction is identified on the *npn* transistor symbol in Figure 1.2(a) by a downward arrow on the emitter. Note that a base resistance is required to generate the base current.

The transistor has three modes of operation: cutoff, saturation, and active. In digital circuits, a transistor is used as a switch, which is either ON (closed) or OFF (open). When no base current flows, the emitter~collector switch is open and the transistor operates in the cutoff (OFF) mode. On the other hand, when a base current flows such that the voltage across the base and the emitter is at least 0.6V, the switch closes. If the base current is further increased, there will be a situation in which V_{CE} (voltage across the collector and the emitter) attains a constant value of approximately 0.2V. This is called the saturation (ON) mode of the transistor. The "active" mode is between the cutoff and saturation modes. In this mode, the base current (I_B) is amplified so that the collector current, IC = $\beta\, I_B$ where β is called the gain, and is in the range of 10 to 100 for typical transistors. Note that when the transistor reaches saturation, increasing I_B does not drop V_{CE} below V_{CE} (Sat.) of 0.2V. On the other hand, V_{CE} varies from 0.8V to 5V in the active mode. Therefore, the cutoff (OFF) and saturation (ON) modes of the transistor are used in designing digital circuits. The active mode of the transistor in which the transistor acts as a current amplifier (also called buffer) is used in digital output circuits.

Operation of the Transistor as an Inverter   Figure 1.3 shows how to use the transistor as an inverter. When $V_{IN} = 0$, the transistor is in cutoff (OFF), and the collector-emitter switch is open. This means that no current flows from $+V_{CC}$ to ground. V_{OUT} is equal to $+V_{CC}$. Thus, V_{OUT} is high.

On the other hand, when V_{IN} is HIGH, the emitter-collector switch is closed. A current flows from $+V_{CC}$ to ground. The transistor operates in saturation, and $V_{OUT} = V_{CE}$ (Sat) = 0.2V ≈ 0. Thus, V_{OUT} is basically connected to ground.

Therefore, for V_{IN} = LOW, V_{OUT} = HIGH, and for V_{IN} = HIGH, V_{OUT} = LOW. Hence, the *npn* transistor in Figure 1.3 acts as an inverter.

Note that V_{CC} is typically +5V DC. The input voltage levels are normally in the range of 0 to 0.8 volts for LOW and 2 volts to 5 volts for HIGH. The output voltage levels, on the other hand, are normally 0.2 volts for LOW and 3.6 volts for HIGH.

Light Emitting Diodes (LEDs) and Seven Segment Displays   LEDs are extensively used as outputs in digital systems as status indicators. An LED is typically driven by low voltage and low current. This makes the LED a very attractive device for use with digital systems. Table 1.1 provides the current and voltage requirements of red, yellow, and green LEDs.

Basically, an LED will be ON, generating light, when its cathode is sufficiently negative with respect to its anode. A digital system such as a microcomputer can therefore light an LED either by grounding the cathode (if the anode is tied to +5V) or by applying +5V to the anode (if the cathode is grounded) through an appropriate resistor value. A typical hardware interface between a microcomputer and an LED is depicted in Figure 1.4. A digital circuit using BJTs normally outputs 400 μA at a minimum voltage, V_M = 2.4 volts for a HIGH. The red LED requires 10 mA at 1.7 volts. A buffer (current amplifier) such as a transistor is required to turn the LED ON. Since the transistor is an inverter, a HIGH input to the transistor will turn the LED ON. We now design the interface; that is, the values of R_1, R_2, and the gain β for the transistor will be determined.

A HIGH at the output of a digital circuit will turn the transistor ON into active mode. This will allow a path of current to flow from the +5V source through R_2 and the LED to the ground. The appropriate value of R_2 needs to be calculated to satisfy the voltage and current requirements of the LED. Also, suppose that VBE = 0.6V when the transistor is in active mode. This means that R1 needs to be calculated with the specified values of V_M = 2.4V and I = 400 μA. The values of R_1, R_2, and β are calculated as follows:

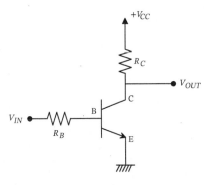

FIGURE 1.3   An inverter

TABLE 1.1   Current and Voltage Requirements of LEDs

LEDs	Red	Yellow	Green
Current	10 mA	10 mA	20 mA
Voltage	1.7V	2.2V	2.4V

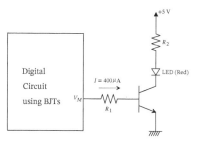

FIGURE 1.4   Digital circuit - LED interface

$$R_1 = \frac{V_M - V_{BE}}{400\,\mu A} = \frac{2.4 - 0.6}{400\,\mu A} = 4.5\ K\Omega$$

Assuming $V_{CE} \cong 0$,

$$R_2 = \frac{5 - 1.7 - V_{CE}}{10\ mA} = \frac{5 - 1.7}{10\ mA} = 330\ \Omega$$

$$\beta = \frac{I_C}{I_B} = \frac{10\ mA}{400\,\mu A} = \frac{10 \times 10^{-3}}{400 \times 10^{-6}} = 25$$

Therefore, the interface design is complete, and a transistor with a minimum β of 25, $R_1 = 4.5$ KΩ, and $R_2 = 330\ \Omega$ are required.

An inverting buffer chip such as the 74LS04 can be used in place of a transistor in Figure 1.4. A typical interface of a LED to a BJT-based digital circuit via an inverter is shown in Figure 1.5. Note that the transistor base resistance is inside the inverter. Therefore, R_1 is not required to be connected to the output of the digital circuit. The symbol $\multimap\!\!\!\triangleright\!\!\!\multimap$ is used to represent an inverter. Inverters will be discussed in more detail later. In Figure 1.5, when the digital circuit outputs a HIGH, the transistor switch inside the inverter closes. A current flows from the +5V source, through the 330-ohm resistor and the LED, into the ground inside the inverter. The LED is thus turned ON.

Note that if 5V is used to turn the LED ON and 0V to turn it OFF, the LED should be connected as shown in Figure 1.6. However, if 0 is used to turn the LED ON and 5V to turn it OFF, the LED should be connected as shown in Figure 1.7.

A seven-segment display can be used to display, for example, decimal numbers from 0 to 9. The name "seven segment" is based on the fact that there are seven LEDs — one in each segment of the display. Figure 1.8 shows a typical seven-segment display.

In Figure 1.8, each segment contains an LED. All decimal numbers from 0 to 9 can be displayed by turning the appropriate segment "ON" or "OFF". For example, a zero can be displayed by turning the LED in segment g "OFF" and turning the other six LEDs in segments a through f "ON." There are two types of seven segment displays. These are common cathode and common anode. Figure 1.9 shows these display configurations.

In a common cathode arrangement, the computer can send a HIGH to light a segment and a LOW to turn it off. In a common anode configuration, on the other hand, the computer sends a LOW to light a segment and a HIGH to turn it off. In both configurations, R = 330 ohms can be used.

Transistor Transistor Logic (TTL) and its Variations   The transistor transistor logic (TTL) family of chips evolved from diodes and transistors. This family used to be called DTL (diode transistor logic). The diodes were then replaced by transistors, and thus the name "TTL" evolved. The power supply voltage (V_{CC}) for TTL is +5V. The two logic levels are approximately 0 and 3.5V.

There are several variations of the TTL family. These are based on the saturation mode (saturated logic) and active mode (nonsaturated logic) operations of the transistor. In the saturation

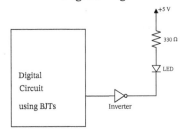

FIGURE 1.5　　Digital circuit - LED interface via an inverter

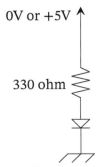

FIGURE 1.6　　An LED connection to be turned ON by 5V and turned OFF by 0V

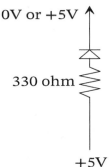

FIGURE 1.7　　An LED connection to be turned ON by 0V and turned OFF by 5V

mode, the transistor takes some time to come out of the saturation to switch to the cutoff mode. On the other hand, some TTL families define the logic levels in the active mode operation of the transistor and are called nonsaturated logic. Since the transistors do not go into saturation, these families do not have any saturation delay time for the switching operation. Therefore, the nonsaturated logic family is faster than saturated logic.

The saturated TTL family includes standard TTL (TTL), high-speed TTL (H-TTL), and low-power TTL (L-TTL). The nonsaturated TTL family includes Schottky TTL (S-TTL), low-power Schottky TTL (LS-TTL), advanced Schottky TTL (AS-TTL), and advanced low-power Schottky TTL (ALS-TTL). The development of LS-TTL made TTL, H-TTL, and L-TTL obsolete. Another technology, called emitter-coupled logic (ECL), utilizes nonsaturated logic. The ECL family provides the highest speed. ECL is used in digital systems requiring ultrahigh speed, such as supercomputers.

The important parameters of the digital logic families are fan-out, power dissipation, propagation delay, and noise margin. Fan-out is defined as the maximum number of inputs that can be connected to the output of a gate. It is expressed as a number. The output of a gate is normally connected to the inputs of other similar gates. Typical fan-out for TTL is 10. On the other hand, fan-outs for S-TTL, LS-TTL, and ECL, are 10, 20, and 25, respectively.

Power dissipation is the power (milliwatts) required to operate the gate. This power must be supplied by the power supply and is consumed by the gate. Typical power consumed by TTL is 10 mW. On the other hand, S-TTL, LS-TTL, and ECL absorb 22 mW, 2 mW, and 25 mW respectively.

Propagation delay is the time required for a signal to travel from input to output when the binary output changes its value. Typical propagation delay for TTL is 10 nanoseconds (ns). On the other

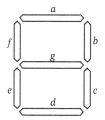

FIGURE 1.8   A seven-segment display

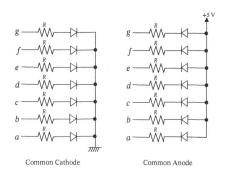

Common Cathode   Common Anode

FIGURE 1.9   Seven-segment display configurations

hand, S-TTL, LS-TTL, and ECL have propagation delays of 3 ns, 10 ns, and 2 ns, respectively.

Noise margin is defined as the maximum voltage due to noise that can be added to the input of a digital circuit without causing any undesirable change in the circuit output. Typical noise margin for TTL is 0.4V. Noise margins for S-TTL, LS-TTL, and ECL are 0.4V, 0.4V, and 0.2V, respectively.

TTL Outputs   There are three types of output configurations for TTL. These are open-collector output totem-pole output, and tristate (three-state) output.

The open-collector output means that the TTL output is a transistor with nothing connected to the collector. The collector voltage provides the output of the gate. For the open-collector output to work properly, a resistor (called the pullup resistor), with a value of typically 1K, should be connected between the open collector output and a +5V power supply.

If the outputs of several open-collector gates are tied together with an external resistor (typically 1K) to a +5V source, a logical AND function is performed at the connecting point. This is called wired-AND logic. Figure 1.10 shows two open-collector outputs (A and B) are connected together to a common output point C via a 1 KΩ resistor and a +5V source.

The common-output point C is HIGH only when both transistors are in cutoff (OFF) mode, providing A = HIGH and B = HIGH. If one or both of the two transistors is turned ON, making one (or both open-collector outputs) LOW, this will drive the common output C to LOW. Note that a LOW (Ground for example) signal when connected to a HIGH (+5V for example) signal generates a LOW. Thus, C is obtained by performing a logical AND operation of the open collector outputs A and B.

Let us briefly review the totem-pole output circuit shown in Figure 1.11. The circuit operates as follows:

When transistor Q_1 is ON, transistor Q_2 is OFF. When Q_1 is OFF, Q_2 is ON. This is how the totem-pole output is designed. The complete TTL gate connected to the bases of transistors Q_1 and Q_2 is not shown; only the output circuit is shown.

In the figure, Q_1 is turned ON when the logic gate circuit connected to its base sends a HIGH output. The switches in transistor Q_1 and diode D close while the switch in Q_2 is open. A current flows from the +5V source through R, Q_1, and D to the output. This current is called I_{source} or output high current, I_{OH}. This is typically represented by a negative sign in front of the current value in the TTL data

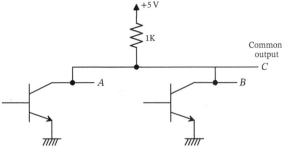

FIGURE 1.10   Two open-collector outputs A and B tied together

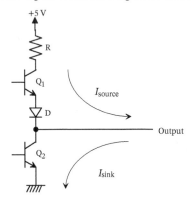

FIGURE 1.11   TTL Totem-pole output

sheet, a notation indicating that the chip is losing current. For a low output value of the logic gate, the switches in Q_1 and D are open and the switch in Q_2 closes. A current flows from the output through Q_2 to ground. This current is called I_{sink} or Output Low current, I_{OL}. This is represented by a positive sign in front of the current value in the TTL data sheet, indicating that current is being added to the chip. Either I_{source} or I_{sink} can be used to drive a typical output device such as an LED. Isource (I_{OH}) is normally much smaller than I_{sink} (IOL). I_{source} (I_{OH}) is typically –0.4 mA (or –400 μA) at a minimum voltage of 2.7V at the output. I_{source} is normally used to drive devices that require high currents. A current amplifier (buffer) such as a transistor or an inverting buffer chip such as the 74LS368 needs to be connected at the output if I_{source} is used to drive a device such as an LED requiring high current (10 mA to 20 mA). I_{sink} is normally 8 mA.

The totem-pole outputs must not be tied together. When two totem-pole outputs are connected together with the output of one gate HIGH and the output of the second gate LOW, the excessive amount of current drawn can produce enough heat to damage the transistors in the circuit.

Tristate is a special totem-pole output that allows connecting the outputs together like the open-collector outputs. When a totem-pole output TTL gate has this property, it is called a tristate (three state) output. A tristate has three output states:

1.   A LOW level state when the lower transistor in the totem-pole is ON and the upper transistor is OFF.

2.   A HIGH level when the upper transistor in the totem-pole is ON and the lower transistor is OFF.

3.   A third state when both output transistors in the totem-pole are OFF. This third state provides an open circuit or high-impedance state which allows a direct wire connection of many outputs to a common line called the bus.

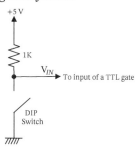

FIGURE 1.12   A typical circuit for connecting an input to a TTL gate

A Typical Switch Input Circuit for TTL   Figure 1.12 shows a switch circuit that can be used as a single bit into the input of a TTL gate. When the DIP switch is open, V_{IN} is HIGH. On the other hand, when the switch is closed, V_{IN} is low. V_{IN} can be used as an input bit to a TTL logic gate for performing laboratory experiments.

1.4.3   MOS Transistors

Metal-Oxide Semiconductor (MOS) transistors occupy less space in the circuit and consume much less power than bipolar junction transistors. Therefore, MOS transistors are used in highly integrated circuits. The MOS transistor is unipolar. This means that one type of carrier flow, either electrons (n-type) or holes (p-type) are used. The MOS transistor works as a voltage-controlled resistance. In digital circuits, a MOS transistor operates as a switch such that its resistance is either very high (OFF) or very low (ON). The MOS transistor is a three-terminal device: gate, source, and drain. There are two types of MOS transistors, namely, nMOS and pMOS.

Figure 1.13 shows the symbolic representation of an nMOS transistor. When $V_{GS} = 0$, the resistance between drain and source (RDS) is in the order of megaohms (Transistor OFF state). On the other hand, as V_{GS} is increased, RDS decreases to a few tens of ohms (Transistor ON state). Note that in a MOS transistor, there is no connection between the gate and the other two terminals (source and drain). The nMOS gate voltage (V_{GS}) increases or decreases the current flow from drain to source by changing RDS. Popular 8-bit microprocessors such as the Intel 8085 and the Motorola 6809 were designed using nMOS.

Figure 1.14 depicts the symbol for a pMOS transistor. The operation of the pMOS transistor is very similar to the nMOS transistor except that V_{GS} is typically zero or negative. The resistance from drain to source (RDS) becomes very high (OFF) for $V_{GS} = 0$. On the other hand, RDS decreases to a very low value (ON) if V_{GS} is decreased. pMOS was used in fabricating the first 4-bit microprocessors (Intel 4004/4040) and 8-bit microprocessor (Intel 8008). Basically, in a MOS transistor (nMOS or pMOS), V_{GS} creates an electric field that increases or decreases the current flow between source and drain. From the symbols of the MOS transistors, it can be seen that there is no connection between the gate and the other two terminals (source and drain). This symbolic representation is used in order to indicate that no current flows from the gate to the source, irrespective of the gate voltage.

Operation of the nMOS Transistor as an Inverter   Figure 1.15 shows an nMOS inverter. Furthermore, when V_{in} = LOW, the resistance between the drain and the source (R_{DS}) is very high, and no current flows from V_{CC} to the ground. V_{out} is, therefore, high. On the other hand, when V_{in} = high, R_{DS} is very low, a current flows from V_{CC} to the source, and V_{out} is LOW. Therefore, the circuit acts as an inverter.

Complementary MOS (CMOS)   CMOS dissipates low power and offers high circuit density compared to TTL. CMOS is fabricated by combining nMOS and pMOS transistors together. The nMOS transistor transfers logic 0 well and logic 1 inefficiently. The pMOS transistor, on the other hand, outputs logic 1 efficiently and logic 0 poorly. Therefore, connecting one pMOS and one nMOS transistor in parallel provides a single switch called *transmission gate* that offers efficient output drive capability for CMOS

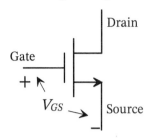

FIGURE 1.13   nMOS transistor symbol

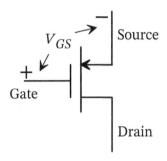

FIGURE 1.14   pMOS transistor symbol

logic gates. The transmission gate is controlled by an input logic level.

Although MOS devices are voltage-controlled devices, they can be visualized as switches. The nMOS transistor is a switch which turns ON when the gate voltage, V_{gs} = +5V; otherwise, the nMOS transistor is OFF (Logic 0). The PMOS transistor is also a switch which turns ON (Logic 1) when the gate voltage, V_{gs} = 0V; otherwise, the pMOS transistor is OFF (Logic 0). Figures 1.16 (a) and (b) show the new symbols for nMOS and pMOS illustrating the concept just described. The nMOS and pMOS transistors can be combined to obtain CMOS.

Figure 1.17 shows a typical CMOS inverter with the new symbols for nMOS and pMOS. The CMOS inverter is very similar to the TTL totem-pole output circuit. That is, when Q_1 is ON (low resistance), Q_2 is OFF (high resistance), and vice versa. When Vinput = LOW, Q_1 is ON and Q_2 is OFF. This makes V_{out} HIGH. On the other hand, when V_{in} = HIGH, Q_1 is OFF (high resistance) and Q_2 is ON (low resistance). This provides a low V_{out}. Thus, the circuit works as an inverter.

Figures 1.18 and 1.19 show the equivalent circuits with switches for nMOS and pMOS with V_{in} = 0V and V_{in} = +5V respectively. In Figure 1.18, note that for V_{in} = +5V, the pMOS transistor is OFF while the nMOS transistor is ON. Hence, V_{out} is 0. In Figure 1.19, on the other hand, for V_{in} = 0V, the nMOS transistor is OFF while the pMOS transistor is ON. Hence, V_{out} = +5V.

Digital circuits using CMOS consume less power than MOS and bipolar transistor circuits. In addition, CMOS provides high circuit density. That is, more circuits can be placed in a chip using CMOS. Finally, CMOS offers high noise immunity. In CMOS, unused inputs should not be left open. Because of the very high input resistance, a floating input may change back and forth between a LOW and a HIGH, creating system problems. All unused CMOS inputs should be tied to V_{cc}, ground, or another high or low signal source appropriate to the device's function. CMOS can operate over a large range of power supply voltages (3V to 15V). Two CMOS families, namely CD4000 and 54C/74C, were first introduced. CD 4000A is in the declining stage.

There are four members in the CMOS family which are very popular these days: the high-speed CMOS (HC), high-speed CMOS/TTL-input compatible (HCT), advanced CMOS (AC), and advanced CMOS/TTL-input compatible (ACT). The HCT chips have a specifically designed input circuit that is compatible with LS-TTL logic levels (2V for HIGH input and 0.8V for LOW input). LS-TTL outputs can directly drive HCT inputs while HCT outputs can directly drive HC inputs. Therefore, HCT buffers can be placed between LS-TTL and HC chips to make the LS-TTL outputs compatible with the HC inputs.

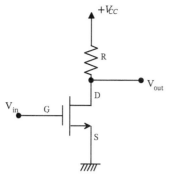

FIGURE 1.15 A typical nMOS inverter

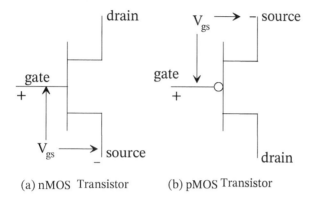

(a) nMOS Transistor (b) pMOS Transistor

FIGURE 1.16 NMOS and PMOS transistors

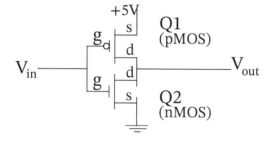

FIGURE 1.17 A CMOS inverter

Several characteristics of 74HC and 74HCT are compared with 74LS-TTL and nMOS technologies in Table 1.2. Note that in the table, HC and HCT have the same source (I_{OH}) and sink (I_{OL}) currents. This is because in a typical CMOS gate, the ON resistances of the pMOS and nMOS transistors are approximately the same.

The input characteristics of HC and HCT are compared in Table 1.3.

Table 1.3 shows that LS-TTL is not guaranteed to drive an HC input. The LS-TTL output HIGH is greater than or equal to 2.7V while an HC input needs at least 3.15V. Therefore, the HCT input requiring VIH of 2.0V can be driven by the LS-TTL output, providing at least 2.7V; 74HCT244 (unidirectional) and 74HCT245 (bidirectional) buffers can be used.

HCMOS Outputs Like TTL, the MOS logic offers three types of outputs. These are push-pull (totem-pole in TTL), open drain (open collector in TTL), and tristate outputs. For example, the 74HC00 contains four independent 2-input NAND gates and includes push-pull output. The 74HC03 also contains four independent 2-input NAND gates, but has open drain outputs. The 74HC03 requires a pull-up resistor for each gate. The 74HC125 contains four independent tri-state buffers in a single chip.

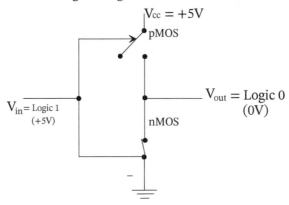

FIGURE 1.18   Representation of the CMOS inverter using switches with V_{in} = 5V and V_{out} = 0V

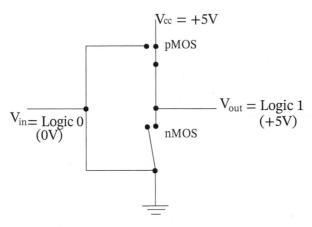

FIGURE 1.19   Representation of the CMOS inverter using switches with V_{in} = 0V and V_{out} = +5V

A Typical Switch Input Circuit for MOS Chips   Figure 1.20 shows a switch circuit that can be used as a single bit into the input of a MOS gate. When the DIP switch is open, V_{IN} is HIGH. On the other hand, when the switch is closed, V_{IN} is LOW. V_{IN} can be used as an input bit for performing laboratory experiments. Note that unlike TTL, a 1K resistor is connected between the switch and the input of the MOS gate. This provides for protection against static discharge. This 1-Kohm resistor is not required if the MOS chip contains internal circuitry providing protection against damage to inputs due to static discharge.

1.5   Integrated Circuits (ICs)

Device level design utilizes transistors to design circuits called gates, such as AND gates and OR gates. One or more gates are fabricated on a single silicon chip by an integrated circuit (IC) manufacturer in an IC package.

       An IC chip is packaged typically in a ceramic or plastic package. The commercially available ICs can be classified as small-scale integration (SSI), medium-scale integration (MSI), large-scale integration (LSI), and very large-scale integration (VLSI).

- A single SSI IC contains a maximum of approximately 10 gates. Typical logic functions such as AND, OR, and NOT are implemented in SSI IC chips. The MSI IC, on the other hand, includes from 11 to up to 100 gates in a single chip. The MSI chips normally perform specific functions such as add.

- The LSI IC contains more than 100 to approximately 1000 gates. Digital systems such as 8-bit microprocessors and memory chips are typical examples of LSI ICs.

TABLE 1.2   Comparison of output characteristics of LS-TTL, nMOS, HC, and HCT

	V_{OH}	I_{OH}	V_{OL}	I_{OL}
LS-TTL	2.7V	–400 μA	0.5V	8 mA
nMOS	2.4V	–400 μA	0.4V	2 mA
HC	3.7V	–4 mA	0.4V	4 mA
HCT	3.7V	–4 mA	0.4V	4 mA

TABLE 1.3   Comparison of input characteristics of HC and HCT

	V_{IH}	I_{IH}	V_{IL}	I_{IL}	Fanout
HC	3.15V	1μA	0.9V	1μA	10
HCT	2.0V	1μA	0.8V	1μA	10

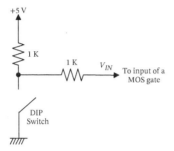

FIGURE 1.20   A typical switch for MOS input

- The VLSI IC includes more than 1000 gates. More commonly, the VLSI ICs are identified by the number of transistors (containing over 500,000 transistors) rather than the gate count in a single chip. Typical examples of VLSI IC chips include 32-bit microprocessors and one megabit memories. For example, the Intel Pentium is a VLSI IC containing 3.1 million transistors in a single chip.

An IC chip is usually inserted in a printed-circuit board (PCB) that is connected to other IC chips on the board via pins or electrical terminals. In laboratory experiments or prototype systems, the IC chips are typically placed on breadboards or wire-wrap boards and connected by wires. The breadboards normally have noise problems for frequencies over 4 MHz. Wire-wrap boards are used above 4 MHz. The number of pins in an IC chip varies from ten to several hundred, depending on the package type. Each IC chip must be powered and grounded via its power and ground pins. The VLSI chips such as the Pentium have several power and ground pins. This is done in order to reduce noise by distributing power in the circuitry inside the chip.

The SSI and MSI chips normally use an IC package called *dual in-line package* (DIP). The LSI and VLSI chips, on the other hand, are typically fabricated in surface-mount or pin grid array (PGA) packages. The DIP is widely used because of its low price and ease of installation into the circuit board.

SSI chips are identified as 5400-series (these are for military applications with stringent requirements on voltage and temperature and are expensive) or 7400 series (for commercial applications). Both series have identical pin assignments on chips with the same part numbers, although the first two numeric digits of the part name are different. Typical commercial SSI ICs can be identified as follows:

> 74S   Schottky TTL
> 74LS   Low-power Schottky TTL
> 74AS   Advanced Schottky TTL
> 74F   Fast TTL (Similar to 74AS; manufactured by Fairchild)
> 74ALS   Advanced low-power Schottky TTL

Note that two digits appended at the end of each of these IC identifications define the type of logic operation performed, the number of pins, and the total number of gates on the chip. For example, 74S00, 74LS00, 74AS00, 74F00, and 74ALS00 perform NAND operation. All of them have 14 pins and contain four independent NAND gates in a single chip.

The gates in the ECL family are identified by the part numbers 10XXX and 100XXX, where XXX indicates three digits. The 100XXX family is faster, requires low power supply, but it consumes more power than the 10XXX. Note that 10XXX and 100XXX are also known as 10K and 100K families.

The commercially available CMOS family is identified in the same manner as the TTL SSI ICs. For example, 74LS00 and 74HC00 (High-speed CMOS) are identical, with 14 pins and containing four independent NAND gates in a single chip. Note that 74HCXX gates have operating speeds similar to 74LS-TTL gates. For example, the 74HC00 contains four independent two-input NAND gates. Each NAND gate has a typical propagation delay of 10 ns and a fanout of 10 LS-TTL.

Unlike TTL inputs, CMOS inputs should never be held floating. The unused input pins must be connected to V_{CC}, ground, or an output. The TTL input contains an internal resistor that makes it HIGH when unused or floating. The CMOS input does not have any such resistor and therefore possesses high resistance. The unused CMOS inputs must be tied to V_{CC}, ground, or other gate outputs. In some CMOS chips, inputs have internal pull-up or pull-down resistors. These inputs, when unused, should be connected to V_{CC} or ground to make the inputs high or low.

The CMOS family has become popular compared to TTL due to better performance. Some major IC manufacturers such as National Semiconductor do not make 7400 series TTL anymore. Although some others, including Fairchild and Texas Instruments still offer the 7400 TTL series, the use of the SSI TTL family (74S, 74LS, 74AS, 74F, and 74ALS) is in the declining stage, and will be obsolete in the future. On the other hand, the use of CMOS-based chips such as 74HC has increased significantly because of their high performance. These chips will dominate the future market.

1.6   CAD (Computer-Aided Design)

Digital logic circuits were used in building the first computers. With the advent of VLSI technology, millions of transistors are contained in the same chip. Hence, it has become a difficult task to design these circuits without using computer-aided design tools.

CAD tools include programs that assist in developing the digital hardware. The CAD tools perform the design process automatically, and comes up with an optimized circuit which will satisfy design specifications. The designer is required to provide the precise description of the design in order to obtain the best possible circuit. In order to accomplish this, the designer must have a clear understanding of the theory of digital logic.

CAD tools along with Hardware Description Language (HDL) can be used to design digital logic circuits. FPGAs have become popular in recent years. These logic circuits can be implemented in FPGAs using CAD tools and HDL. These topics are covered in this book in a very simplified manner.

1.7   Evolution of Digital Logic, Microprocessors, and Microcontrollers

George Boole, an English mathematician, introduced the theory of digital logic called "Boolean Algebra" in 1847. The term "Boolean variable" is used to mean the two-valued binary digit 0 or 1. Devices such as transistors are used to represent the binary digits (bits). Many years after creation of Boolean logic, Claude Shannon of MIT, successfully implemented the theory of Boolean logic in electric circuits with relays in 1938. This provided the foundation for emergence of today's computer.

Dr. Maurice Karnaugh of Bell Laboratories, developed Karnaugh maps in 1953 to reduce cost of designing a digital circuit by minimizing the logic gates . Due to complexity of digital logic circuits since the 70s, designers needed software to design digital circuits. Hence, HDLs evolved.

Design using Programmable Logic Devices (PLDs) became popular during the late 1970s. Note that PLD chips are capable of being programmed by the user after they are manufactured. CPLD (Complex PLD) containing several PLDs in a single chip and Field Programmable Gate Array (FPGA) were introduced. Later, Data I/O Corporation introduced the first HDL called ABEL. With the popularity of VLSI design, the first modern HDL called Verilog (no acronym), based on C-language, was introduced by Gateway Design Automation in 1985. Cadence Design Systems later acquired the rights to Verilog - XL, the HDL simulator de facto standard of Verilog simulators. Verilog was then accepted as an IEEE number 1364 in 1995.

In 1987, U.S. Department of Defense developed the HDL called VHDL (Very High Speed Integrated Circuits). VHDL is based on Ada programming language. Note that VHDL was introduced in 1983, and after going several versions, was formally accepted as an IEEE standard number 1076 in 1987.

In the past, industries developed products for specific applications. It was difficult for the users to redesign these products according to their requirements. This led to the introduction of a flexible IC chip called the FPGA. An FPGA-based circuit board would mean that it can be programmed and re-configured according to the user's specification. Altera and Xilinx are two leading manufacturers of FPGA chips. Altera, founded in 1981, introduced the first EPROM-based reprogrammable logic device in 1984. Altera became a leading manufacturer of FPGA later on. Note that Intel acquired Altera in 2015.

CPLDs are less flexible. FPGAs, on the other hand, have the far more flexibility of interconnecting various digital blocks. CPLDs are typically used in smaller applications while FPGAs are used in larger applications. Both CPLDs and FPGAs may be used in a single application. In such a system, CPLDs usually perform "glue logic" functions including booting the FPGA and controlling the reset and boot sequence of the complete circuit board. Note that glue logic is a special form of digital circuitry that allows different types of logic circuits to work together by acting as an interface between them.

With the rapid growth of the FPGA applications primarily in telecommunications and networking, FPGAs were eventually used in consumer, automative, and industrial applications during the early 2000's. FPGAs are widely used for simulating a design. This means that designers can develop prototype hardware on FPGAs first, and then manufacture the final product on the ICs in a very short period of time.

Next, we discuss the evolution of microprocessors and microcontrollers.

Intel Corporation is generally acknowledged as the company that introduced the first microprocessor successfully into the marketplace. Its first microprocessor, the 4004, was introduced in 1971 and evolved from a development effort while making a calculator chip set. The 4004 microprocessor was the central component in the chip set, which was called the MCS-4. The other components in the set were a 4001 ROM, a 4002 RAM, and a 4003 shift register.

Shortly after the 4004 appeared in the commercial marketplace, three other general-purpose microprocessors were introduced: the Rockwell International 4-bit PPS-4, the Intel 8-bit 8008, and the National Semiconductor 16-bit IMP-16. Other companies, such as General Electric, RCA, and Viatron, also made contributions to the development of the microprocessor prior to 1971.

The microprocessors introduced between 1971 and 1972 were the first-generation systems designed using PMOS technology. In 1973, second-generation microprocessors such as the Motorola 6800 and the Intel 8080 (8-bit microprocessors) were introduced. The second-generation microprocessors were designed using NMOS technology. This technology resulted in a significant increase in instruction execution speed over PMOS and higher chip densities. Since then, microprocessors have been fabricated using a variety of technologies and designs. NMOS microprocessors such as the Intel 8085, the Zilog Z80, and the Motorola 6800/6809 were introduced based on second-generation microprocessors. A third generation HMOS microprocessor, introduced in 1978 is typically represented by the Intel 8086 and the Motorola 68000, which are 16-bit microprocessors.

During the 1980's, fourth-generation HCMOS and BICMOS (a combination of bipolar and HCMOS) 32-bit microprocessors evolved. Intel introduced the first commercial 32-bit microprocessor, the problematic Intel 432, which was eventually discontinued. Since 1985, more 32-bit microprocessors have been introduced. These include Motorola's 68020, 68030, 68040, 68060, PowerPC, Intel's 80386, 80486, the Intel Pentium family, Core Duo, and Core2 Duo microprocessors.

The performance offered by the 32-bit microprocessor is more comparable to that of superminicomputers such as Digital Equipment Corporation's VAX11/750 and VAX11/780. Intel and Motorola also introduced RISC microprocessors: the Intel 80960 and Motorola 88100/PowerPC, which had simplified instruction sets. Note that the purpose of RISC microprocessors is to maximize speed by reducing clock cycles per instruction. Almost all computations can be obtained from a simple instruction set. Note that, in order to enhance performance significantly, Intel Pentium Pro and other succeeding members of the Pentium family and Motorola 68060 are designed using a combination of RISC and CISC.

Single-chip microcomputers such as the Intel 8048 evolved during the 80's. Soon afterwards, based on the concept of single-chip microcomputers, Intel introduced the first 8-bit microcontroller---the Intel 8051. The 8051 contains a CPU, memory, I/O, A/D (Analog-to-Digital) and D/A (Digital-to-Analog) converters, timer, serial communication interface----- all in a single chip. The microcontrollers became popular during the 1980's.

Microcontrollers gained popularity over the last several years. These microcontrollers are small enough for many embedded applications, but also powerful enough to allow a lot of complexity and flexibility in the design process of an embedded system. Several billion 8-bit microcontrollers were sold during the last decade. Microchip Technology Inc., with its PIC18F microcontroller family is one of the leading manufacturer of popular microcontrollers.

Note that embedded microcontroller systems, also called embedded controllers, are designed to manage specific tasks. Once programmed, the embedded controllers can manage the functions of a wide variety of electronic products. In embedded applications, the microcontrollers are embedded in the host system, their presence and operation are basically hidden from the host system.

Typical embedded control applications include office automation products such as copiers, laser products, fax machines, and consumer electronics such as microwave ovens. Applications such as printers typically utilize a microcontroller. The microcontrollers are ideal for these types of applications. Note that the Personal Computer interfaced to the printer is the host, and the microcontroller is embedded (hidden) in the printer controller.

1.8   A Typical Application of a Digital System such as a Microcontroller

To put basic digital concepts such as binary numbers into perspective, it is important to explore a simple application.

As an example, consider a simple application using a digital system such as a microcontroller as shown in Figure 1.21. Suppose that it is necessary to maintain the temperature of a furnace to a desired level to maintain the quality of a product. Assume that the designer has decided to control this temperature by adjusting the fuel. This can be accomplished using a typical microcontroller such as the PIC18F along with the interfacing components as follows. Temperature is an analog (continuous) signal. It can be measured by a temperature-sensing (measuring) device such as a thermocouple. The thermocouple provides the measurement in millivolts (mV) equivalent to the temperature.

Since microcontrollers only understand binary numbers (0's and 1's), each analog mV signal must be converted to a binary number using the microcontroller's on-chip analog-to-digital (A/D) converter. Note that the PIC18F contains an on-chip A/D converter. The PIC18F does not include an on-chip digital-to-analog (D/A) converter. However, the D/A converter chip can be interfaced to the PIC18F externally.

First, the millivolt signal is amplified by a mV/V amplifier to make the signal compatible for A/D conversion. A microcontroller such as the PIC18F can be programmed to solve an equation with the furnace temperature as an input. This equation compares the temperature measured with the temperature desired which can be entered into the microcontroller using the keyboard. The output of this equation will provide the appropriate opening and closing of the fuel valve to maintain the appropriate temperature. Since this output is computed by the microcontroller, it is a binary number. This binary output must be converted into an analog current or voltage signal.

The D/A (digital-to-analog) converter chip inputs this binary number and converts it into an analog current (I). This signal is then input into the current/pneumatic (I/P) transducer for opening or closing the fuel input valve by air pressure to adjust the fuel to the furnace. The furnace temperature desired can thus be achieved. Note that a transducer converts one form of energy (electrical current in this case) to another form (air pressure in this example).

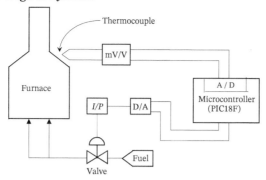

FIGURE 1.21   Furnace temperature control

2

NUMBER SYSTEMS, ARITHMETIC/LOGIC OPERATIONS, AND CODES

This chapter describes the basics of number systems, codes, arithmetic/logic operations, and error detection/correction. Note that adequate coverage of these topics is included in this chapter. This will provide sufficient background to understand the concepts described in the chapters that follow.

2.1   Number Systems

A computer, like all digital systems, utilizes two states to represent information. These two states are given the symbols 0 and 1. It is important to remember that these 0's and 1's are symbols for the two states and have no inherent numerical meanings of their own. These two digits are called binary digits (bits) and can be used to represent numbers of any magnitude.

Digital systems such as microcontrollers and microcomputers carry out all arithmetic and logic operations internally using binary numbers. Because binary numbers are long, a more compact form using some other number system is preferable to represent them. The computer user finds it convenient to work with this compact form. Hence, it is important to understand the various number systems used with computers. These are described in the following sections.

2.1.1   General Number Representation

In general, N can be written as a string of digits whose integer parts $(d_p\text{-}1, d_p\text{-}2, \ldots\ldots, d_1, d_0)$, and fractional parts $(d_{-1}\cdots d_{-q})$ are separated by the radix or decimal point ($\bullet$). In this format, the number N is represented as:

$$N = d_{p\text{-}1}\, d_{p\text{-}2} \cdots d_1\, d_0 \bullet d_{-1} \cdots d_{-q}$$

If a number has no fractional portion, then the number is called an integer number or an integer. Conversely, if the number has no integer portion, then the number is called a fractional number or a fraction. The number, N can also be represented in the following form:

$$N = d_{p\text{-}1} \times b^{p\text{-}1} + d_{p\text{-}2} \times b^{p\text{-}2} + \cdots + d_0 \times b^0 + d_{-1} \times b^{-1} + \cdots + d_{-q} \times b^{-q} \tag{2.1}$$

where b is the base or radix of the number system, the d's are the digits of the number system, p is the number of integer digits, and q is the number of fractional digits.

Decimal Number System   The decimal number system has a base or radix of 10 and has 10 allowable digits, 0 through 9. As an example, consider the number 125.532_{10}.

$$125.532_{10} = 1 \times 10^2 + 2 \times 10^1 + 5 \times 10^0 + 5 \times 10^{-1} + 3 \times 10^{-2} + 2 \times 10^{-3} \tag{2.2}$$

Comparing the right-hand side of Equation 2.2 with equation 2.1 yields $b = 10, p = 3, q = 3, d_2 = 1, d_1 = 2, d_0 = 5, d_{-1} = 5, d_{-2} = 3$, and $d_{-3} = 2$.

Digital Logic with an Introduction to Verilog and FPGA-Based Design. First Edition. M. Rafiquzzaman and Steven A. McNinch.
© 2019 John Wiley & Sons, Inc. Published 2019 by John Wiley & Sons, Inc.

TABLE 2.1   Octal digits along with the corresponding binary values

Octal digits	Binary values
0	000
1	001
2	010
3	011
4	100
5	101
6	110
7	111

Binary Number System   The binary number system has a base or radix of 2 and has two allowable digits, 0 and 1. From Equation 2.1, a 4-bit binary number 1110_2 can be interpreted as an integer decimal as follows:

$$1110_2 = 1 \times 2^3 + 1 \times 2^2 + 1 \times 2^1 + 0 \times 2^0 = 14_{10}$$

This conversion from binary to integer decimal can be obtained by inspecting the binary number as follows:

$$\overset{3}{2}\ \overset{2}{2}\ \overset{1}{2}\ \overset{0}{2} \longleftarrow \text{Weighting}$$
$$1\ 1\ 1\ 0$$

Bit 3 → Bit 0 or Least significant bit
or
Most significant bit — Bit 1
— Bit 2

Note that bits 0, 1, 2, and 3 have corresponding weighting values of 1, 2, 4, and 8. Because a binary number only contains 0's and 1's, adding the weighting values of only the bits of the binary number containing 1's will provide its decimal value. The decimal value of 1110_2 is 14_{10} (2 + 4 + 8), because bits 1, 2, and 3 have binary digit 1, whereas bit 0 contains a '0'.

Therefore, the decimal (integer) value of any binary number can be readily obtained by just adding the weighting values for the bit positions containing 1's. Furthermore, the value of the least significant bit (bit 0) determines whether the number is odd or even. For example, if the least significant bit is 1, the number is odd; on the other hand, if the least significant bit is 0, the number is even.

Next, consider converting a mixed binary number (containing both integer and fractional parts), 101.01_2 into decimal using equation 2.1 as follows:

$$101.01_2 = 1 \times 2^2 + 0 \times 2^1 + 1 \times 2^0 + 0 \times 2^{-1} + 1 \times 2^{-2}$$

The decimal or base 10 value of 101.01_2 can be found from the right-hand side of the above equation as $4 + 0 + 1 + 0 + \frac{1}{4} = 5.25_{10}$.

Octal Number System   The radix or base of the octal number system is 8. There are eight digits, 0 through 7, allowed in this number system. Table 2.1 shows the octal digits along with their corresponding binary values.

Consider the octal number 25.32_8, which can be interpreted as:

$$2 \times 8^1 + 5 \times 8^0 + 3 \times 8^{-1} + 2 \times 8^{-2}$$

The decimal value of this number is found by completing the summation as follows:

$$16 + 5 + 3 \times 1/8 + 2 \times 1/64 = 16 + 5 + 0.375 + 0.03125 = 21.40625_{10}$$

TABLE 2.2 Hexadecimal number system and their corresponding binary and decimal values

Decimal	Hexadecimal	Binary
0	0	0000
1	1	0001
2	2	0010
3	3	0011
4	4	0100
5	5	0101
6	6	0110
7	7	0111
8	8	1000
9	9	1001
10	A	1010
11	B	1011
12	C	1100
13	D	1101
14	E	1110
15	F	1111

Hexadecimal Number System The hexadecimal or base-16 number system has 16 individual digits. Each of these digits, as in all number systems, must be represented by a single unique symbol. The digits in the hexadecimal number system are 0 through 9 and the letters A through F. Letters were chosen to represent the hexadecimal digits greater than 9 because a single symbol is required for each digit. Table 2.2 lists the 16 digits of the hexadecimal number system and their corresponding binary and decimal values.

2.1.2 Converting Numbers from One Base to Another

Binary-to-Decimal Conversion and Vice Versa Consider converting 1100.01_2 to its decimal equivalent. As before,

$$1100.01_2 = 1 \times 2^3 + 1 \times 2^2 + 0 \times 2^1 + 0 \times 2^0 + 0 \times 2^{-1} + 1 \times 2^{-2}$$

$$= 8 + 4 + 0 + 0 + 0 + .25$$

$$= 12.25_{10}$$

Next, convert the decimal number 12.25_{10} back to its binary equivalent.

Note that continuous division by 2, keeping track of the remainders, provides a simple method of converting a decimal number to its binary equivalent. Hence, to convert decimal 12_{10} to its binary equivalent 1100_2, proceed as follows:

	quotient	+	remainder
$\dfrac{12}{2} =$	6	+	0
$\dfrac{6}{2} =$	3	+	0
$\dfrac{3}{2} =$	1	+	1
$\dfrac{1}{2} =$	0	+	1

$$1\ 1\ 0\ 0_{2}$$

Next, convert the fractional part 0.25_{10} to its binary equivalent. Note that continuous multiplication by 2 and keeping track of the integer parts will accomplish this as follows:

$$
\begin{array}{cc}
0.25 & 0.50 \\
\underline{\times 2} & \underline{\times 2} \\
\boxed{0}50 & \boxed{1}00 \\
\downarrow & \downarrow \\
0 & 1
\end{array}
$$

Thus $0.25_{10} = 0.01_2$. Therefore $12.25_{10} = 1100.01_2$.

Unfortunately, binary-to-decimal fractional conversions are not always exact. Suppose that it is desired to convert 0.3615 into its binary equivalent:

$$
\begin{array}{ccccc}
0.3615 & 0.7230 & 0.4460 & 0.8920 & 0.7840 \\
\underline{\times 2} & \underline{\times 2} & \underline{\times 2} & \underline{\times 2} & \underline{\times 2} \\
\boxed{0}7230 & \boxed{1}4460 & \boxed{0}8920 & \boxed{1}7840 & \boxed{1}5680 \\
\downarrow & \downarrow & \downarrow & \downarrow & \downarrow \\
0 & 1 & 0 & 1 & 1
\end{array}
$$

The answer is 0.01011... As a check, let us convert back:

$$0.01011_2 = 0 \times 2^{-1} + 1 \times 2^{-2} + 0 \times 2^{-3} + 1 \times 2^{-4} + 1 \times 2^{-5}$$

$$= 0 + 0.25 + 0 + 0.0625 + 0.03125$$

$$= 0.34375$$

The difference is $0.3615 - 0.34375 = 0.01775$. This difference is caused by the neglected remainder 0.5680. The neglected remainder (0.5680) multiplied by the smallest computed term (0.03125) gives the total error:

$$0.5680 \times 0.03125 = 0.01775$$

Note that the same procedure applies for converting a decimal integer number to other number systems such as octal or hexadecimal. Continuous division by the appropriate base (8 or 16) and keeping track of the remainders will convert a decimal integer to the selected number system. Also, continuous multiplication by the base (8 or 16), and keeping track of the integer parts will convert the fractional part of a decimal number to the selected number system.

Binary-to-Octal Conversion and Vice Versa   One can convert a number from binary to octal representation easily by taking the binary digits in groups of 3 bits to an octal digit. The octal digit is obtained by considering each group of 3 bits as a separate binary number capable of representing the octal digits 0 through 7. The radix point remains in its original position. The following example illustrates the procedure.

Suppose that it is desired to convert 1001.11_2 into octal form. First take the groups of 3 bits starting at the radix point. Where there are not enough leading or trailing bits to complete the triplet, 0's are appended. Now each group of 3 bits is converted to its corresponding octal digit.

$$\underbrace{001}_{1} \ \underbrace{001}_{1} \ . \ \underbrace{110_2}_{6} = 11.6_8$$

The conversion back to binary from octal is simply the reverse of the binary-to-octal process. For example, conversion from 11.6_8 to binary is accomplished by expanding each octal digit to its equivalent binary values as shown:

$$\underset{001}{1} \ \underset{001}{1} \ . \ \underset{110}{6}$$

Octal-to-Decimal Conversion and Vice Versa   Consider converting the octal number 230.16_8 into its decimal equivalent and vice versa. This can be accomplished as follows:

$$230.16_8 = 2 \times 8^2 + 3 \times 8^1 + 0 \times 8^0 + 1 \times 8^{-1} + 6 \times 8^{-2}$$

$$= 128 + 24 + 0 + 0.125 + 0.09375 = 152.21875_{10} = 152.22_{10} \text{ (approximately)}$$

Now to convert 152.22_{10} back to 230.16_8.

First, convert the integer part 152_{10} to octal as follows:

	quotient	+	remainder
$\dfrac{152}{8} =$	19	+	0
$\dfrac{19}{8} =$	2	+	3
$\dfrac{2}{8} =$	0	+	2

$$2 \quad 3 \quad 0$$

Thus, $152_{10} = 230_8$.

Next, convert the fractional part $.22_{10}$ as follows:

$$
\begin{array}{cc}
0.22 & 0.76 \\
\times 8 & \times 8 \\
\hline
1.76 & 6.08 \\
\uparrow & \uparrow \\
1 & 6
\end{array}
$$

Hence, $152.22_{10} = 230.16_8$.

Binary-to-Hexadecimal Conversion and Vice Versa   The conversions between hexadecimal and binary numbers are done in exactly the same manner as the conversions between octal and binary, except that groups of 4 are used. The following examples illustrate this:

$$1011011_2 = \underbrace{0101}_{5} \quad \underbrace{1011}_{B} = 5B_{16}$$

Note that the binary integer number is grouped in 4-bit units, starting from the least significant bit. Zeros are added with the most significant 4 bits if necessary. As with octal numbers, for fractional numbers this grouping into 4 bits is started from the radix point. Now consider converting $2AB_{16}$ into its binary equivalent as follows:

$$
\begin{array}{cccc}
2AB_{16} = & 2 & A & B \\
& \downarrow & \downarrow & \downarrow \\
& 0010 & 1010 & 1011
\end{array}
$$

$$= 001010101011_2$$

Hexadecimal-to-Decimal Conversion and Vice Versa   Consider converting the hexadecimal number $23A.2B_{16}$ into its decimal equivalent and vice versa. This can be accomplished as follows.

Convert $23A.2B_{16}$ into decimal as follows:

$$23A.2B_{16} = 2 \times 16^2 + 3 \times 16^1 + 10 \times 16^0 + 2 \times 16^{-1} + 11 \times 16^{-2}$$

$$= 512 + 48 + 10 + .125 + .043 = 570.17_{10} \text{ (approximately)}$$

Note that in the equation, the values 10 and 11 are substituted for A and B respectively. Now, convert 570.17_{10} to hexadecimal. First, convert 570_{10} into hexadecimal as follows:

	quotient	+	remainder
$\dfrac{570}{16} =$	35	+	A
$\dfrac{35}{16} =$	2	+	3
$\dfrac{2}{16} =$	0	+	2

$$2 \quad 3 \quad A$$

Thus, $570_{10} = 23A_{16}$.

Next, convert the fractional part $.17_{10}$ into hexadecimal as follows:

$$
\begin{array}{cc}
.17 & 0.72 \\
\times 16 & \times 16 \\
\hline
2.72 & 11.52 \\
\uparrow & \uparrow \\
2 & B
\end{array}
$$

Hence, $570.17_{10} = 23A.2B_{16}$ (approximately).

Example 2.1

Determine whether each of the following hexadecimal numbers is odd or even by first converting each of the hexadecimal numbers to binary, and then by inspecting the binary numbers. Finally, verify the results by converting to decimal:

(a) $2B_{16}$ (b) $A2_{16}$

Solution

One can determine whether a hexadecimal number is odd or even (without converting to decimal) by first converting it to binary and then inspecting the least significant bit (bit 0) of the number; the number is even if bit 0 is zero while the number is odd if bit 0 is one. This is verified as follows:

(a)
$$2B_{16} = \begin{array}{cccccccc} 128 & 64 & 32 & 16 & 8 & 4 & 2 & 1 \\ 0 & 0 & 1 & 0 & 1 & 0 & 1 & 1 \end{array}_2 \leftarrow \text{Weighting}$$

The number is odd, since the least significant bit is 1.

Decimal value $= 32 + 8 + 2 + 1 = 43_{10}$, which is odd.

(b)
$$A2_{16} = \begin{array}{cccccccc} 128 & 64 & 32 & 16 & 8 & 4 & 2 & 1 \\ 1 & 0 & 1 & 0 & 0 & 0 & 1 & 0 \end{array}_2 \leftarrow \text{Weighting}$$

The number is even, since the least significant bit is 0.

Decimal value $= 128 + 32 + 2 = 162_{10}$, which is even.

2.2   Unsigned and Signed Binary Numbers

An unsigned binary number has no arithmetic sign. Unsigned binary numbers are, therefore, always positive. Typical examples are your age or a memory address which are always positive numbers. An 8-bit unsigned binary integer represents all numbers from 00_{16} through FF_{16} (0_{10} through 255_{10}).

Signed binary numbers, on the other hand, include both positive and negative numbers. The techniques used to represent the signed integers are:

- Sign-magnitude approach

- One's complement approach

- Two's complement approach

Because the sign of a number can be either positive or negative, only one bit, referred to as the sign bit, is needed to represent the sign. The widely used sign convention is that if the sign bit is zero, the number is positive; otherwise it is negative. (The rationale behind this convention is that the quantity $(-1)^s$ is positive when s = 0 and is negative when s = 1). Also, in all three approaches, the most significant bit of the number is considered as the sign bit.

In sign-magnitude representation, the most significant bit of the given n-bit binary number holds the sign, and the remaining $n - 1$ bits directly give the magnitude of the negative number. For example, the sign-magnitude representation of +7 is 0111 and that of −4 is 1100. Table 2.3 represents 4-bit integers and their meanings in sign-magnitude form.

In Table 2.3, the sign-magnitude approach represents a signed number in a natural manner. With 4 bits, one can only represent numbers in the range $-7 \leq x \leq +7$ with 0 being positive. In general, if there are n bits, then one can cover all numbers in the range $\pm(2^{n-1} - 1)$. Note that with $n - 1$ bits, any value from 0 to $2^{n-1} - 1$ can be represented. However, this approach leads to confusion because there are two representations for the number zero (0000 means +0 while 1000 means −0). Hence, the sign-magnitude is not used by computers for representing negative binary numbers.

In one's complement approach, positive numbers have the same representation as the sign-magnitude representation. However, in this technique negative numbers are represented in a different manner. Before we proceed, let us define the term one's complement of a number. The one's complement of a number A, written as $\overline{A}$ (or A′) is obtained by taking bit-by-bit complement of A. In other words, each 0 in A is replaced with 1 and vice versa. For example, the one's complement of the number 0100_2 is 1011_2 and that of 1111_2 is 0000_2. In the ones complement approach, a negative number, −x, is the ones complement of its positive representation. For example, let us find the ones complement representation of 0100_2 ($+4_{10}$). The complement of 0100 is 1011, and this denotes the negative number -4_{10}. Table 2.4

TABLE 2.3	4-bit integers represented in sign-magnitude form
4-bit Integers	Interpretation using Sign Magnitude
0000	+0
0001	+1
0010	+2
0011	+3
0100	+4
0101	+5
0110	+6
0111	+7
1000	−0
1001	−1
1010	−2
1011	−3
1100	−4
1101	−5
1110	−6
1111	−7

summarizes 4-bit integers and their interpretations using one's complement numbers.

From Table 2.4, the ones complement approach does not handle negative numbers naturally. In other words, if the number is negative (when the sign bit is 1), its magnitude is not obvious from its one's complement. To determine its magnitude, one needs to take its ones complement. For example, consider the binary number 110110. Since the most significant bit is 1, the binary number 110110 is a negative number. Because the number is negative, its magnitude cannot be obtained by directly looking at 110110. Instead, one needs to take the one's complement of 110110 to obtain 001001. The value of 001001 as a sign-magnitude number is +9. On the other hand, 110110 represents −9 in ones complement form. Note that one's complement of a binary number is equivalent to negating the number.

Like the sign-magnitude representation, the ones complement approach does not increase the range of numbers covered by a fixed number of bit patterns. For example, four bits cover the range −7 to +7. The same range is obtained with sign-magnitude representation. Note that the confusion of two distinct representations for zero exists in the ones complement approach. Hence, ones complement is not used for representing negative binary numbers. Next, let us discuss the two's complement approach.

In this method, positive integers are represented in the same manner as they are in the sign-magnitude method. In other words, if the sign bit is zero, the number is positive and its magnitude can be directly obtained by looking at the remaining $n - 1$ bits just like the sign-magnitude approach.

However, a negative number $-x$ can be represented in two's complement form as follows:
- Represent $+x$ in sign magnitude form and call this result y.

- Take the one's complement of y to get $\bar{y}$ (or y').

- $\bar{y} + 1$ is the two's complement representation of $-x$.

Table 2.5 lists 4-bit integers along with their two's complement forms. From Table 2.5, it can be concluded that:
- Two's complement approach does not provide two representations for zero. Hence, computers use two's complement approach to represent signed numbers.

- Two's complement approach covers up to −8 in the negative side, and this is more than can be achieved with the other two methods. In general, with n bits, and using two's complement approach, one can cover all the numbers in the range $-(2^{n-1})$ to $+ (2^{n-1} - 1)$ with 0 being positive. For example, for 4-bit integers (Table 2.5), n = 4. Hence, 4-bit signed numbers using two's complement approach cover all numbers from 0 through + 7 and, -1 through -8 (right column of Table 2.5). Note that taking two's complement of a binary number is equivalent to negating the number.

For example, consider the 8-bit number 00000111_2 which is +7 in decimal. The two's complement of 00000111_2 can be obtained as follows: Ones complement of 00000111_2 is 11111000_2; two's complement

TABLE 2.4   4-bit integers represented in One's Complement Form

4-bit Integers	Interpretation using Ones Complement
0000	+0
0001	+1
0010	+2
0011	+3
0100	+4
0101	+5
0110	+6
0111	+7
1000	−7
1001	−6
1010	−5
1011	−4
1100	−3
1101	−2
1110	−1
1111	−0

TABLE 2.5 4-bit integers represented in Two's complement

4-bit Integers	Interpretation using Two's Complement
0000	0
0001	+1
0010	+2
0011	+3
0100	+4
0101	+5
0110	+6
0111	+7
1000	-8
1001	-7
1010	-6
1011	-5
1100	-4
1101	-3
1110	-2
1111	-1

can be obtained by adding one to the one's complement and the result will be 11111001_2. Note that 11111001_2 is a negative number since its most significant bit is 1. This can be converted to decimal after taking its two's complement, and then placing a negative sign in front of it. The result will be -7 in decimal. Thus, taking two's complement of a binary number is equivalent to negating the number.

Example 2.2

Represent the following decimal numbers in two's complement. Use 7 bits to represent the numbers.
(a)   +39
(b)   −43

Solution

(a)   Because the number +39 is positive, its two's complement representation is the same as its sign-magnitude representation as shown here:

$$y = 0\ \underbrace{1\ 0\ 0\ 1\ 1\ 1}_{39}$$

with bit positions labeled $2^5\ 2^4\ 2^3\ 2^2\ 2^1\ 2^0$ and the leading 0 marked as the sign bit (+).

(b)   In this case, the given number −43 is negative. The two's complement form of the number can be obtained as follows:

1.   Step 1: Represent +43 in sign magnitude form:

$$y = 0\ \underbrace{1\ 0\ 1\ 0\ 1\ 1}_{43}$$

with bit positions labeled $2^5\ 2^4\ 2^3\ 2^2\ 2^1\ 2^0$ and the leading 0 marked as the sign bit (+).

2.   Step 2: Take the one's complement of y:
$\bar{y} = 1\ 0\ 1\ 0\ 1\ 0\ 0$

3.   Step 3: Add one to $\bar{y}$ to get the final answer.

```
  1010100
+       1
  1010101
```

Hence, $-43 = 1010101_2$.

It should be pointed out that 11111111_2 is $+255_{10}$ when interpreted as an unsigned number (since there is no sign bit and each of the 8-bit number has a value). On the other hand, 11111111_2 is -1_{10} when interpreted as a signed number using two's complement. Since the most significant bit of the 8-bit number is 1, the number is negative. Hence, ones complement of 11111111_2 is 00000000_2 and two's complement can be obtained by adding one to obtain 00000001_2 (1_{10}). Since taking two's complement of a binary number is equivalent to negating the number, two's complement of 11111111_2 is -1_{10}.

Note that typical 16-bit microprocessors such as Motorola 68000 have separate unsigned and signed multiplication and division instructions as follows: MULU (Multiply two unsigned numbers), MULS (Multiply two signed numbers), DIVU (Divide two unsigned numbers), and DIVS (Divide two signed numbers). It is important for the programmer to clearly understand how to use these instructions.

For example, suppose that it is desired to compute $(X^2)/255$. Now, if X is a signed 8-bit number, the programmer should use MULS instruction to compute $X * X$ which is always unsigned (Square of a number is always positive), and then use DIVU to compute $(X^2)/255$ (16-bit by 8-bit unsigned divide) since 255_{10} is positive. But, if the programmer uses DIVS, then both $X * X$ and 255_{10}(FF_{16}) will be interpreted as signed numbers. FF_{16} will be interpreted as -1_{10}, and the result will be wrong. On the other hand, if X is an unsigned number, the programmer needs to use MULU and DIVU to compute $(X^2)/255$.

2.3   Codes

Codes are used extensively with computers to define alphanumeric characters and other information. Some of the codes used with computers are described in the following sections.

2.3.1   Binary-Coded-Decimal Code (8421 Code)

The 10 decimal digits 0 through 9 can be represented by their corresponding 4-bit binary numbers. The digits coded in this fashion are called binary-coded-decimal (BCD) digits in 8421 code, or BCD digits. Table 2.6 provides the bit encodings of the 10 decimal numbers.

The six possible remaining 4-bit codes as shown in Table 2.6 are not used and represent invalid BCD codes if they occur.

TABLE 2.6   BCD Bit encoding of the 10 decimal numbers

Decimal Numbers	BCD Bit encoding
0	0000
1	0001
2	0010
3	0011
4	0100
5	0101
6	0110
7	0111
8	1000
9	1001
10	1010
11	1011
12	1100
13	1101
14	1110
15	1111

Invalid BCD Code (for decimal numbers 10 through 15)

Consider obtaining the binary and BCD equivalents of the decimal number 35 as follows:

Note that decimal number 35 is represented as 00100011 in binary. In contrast, decimal number 35 is represented as 00110101 in BCD. It should be pointed out that it is very convenient to display binary outputs of digital systems in BCD. For example, digital systems such as an 8-bit adder performs add operation in binary, and provide addition result in binary. It is very inconvenient for the users to interpret the binary result. However, converting the binary result into BCD, and then displaying the result in BCD on two seven-segment displays (in this case) can easily be interpreted by the users.

2.3.2 Alphanumeric Codes

A computer must be capable of handling non -numeric information if it is to be very useful. In other words, a computer must be able to recognize codes that represent numbers, letters, and special characters. These codes are classified as alphanumeric or character codes. A complete and adequate set of necessary characters includes these:

- 26 lowercase letters
- 26 uppercase letters
- 10 numeric digits (0-9)
- about 25 special characters which include + / # x, and so on.

This totals 87 characters. To represent 87 characters with some type of binary code would require at least 7 bits. With 7 bits there are $2^7 = 128$ possible binary numbers; 87 of these combinations of 0 and 1 bits serves the code groups representing the 87 different characters.

The 8-bit byte has been universally accepted as the data unit for representing character codes. The two common alphanumeric codes are known as the *American Standard Code for Information Interchange* (*ASCII*) and the *Extended Binary-Coded Decimal Interchange Code* (*EBCDIC*). ASCII is typically used by computer keyboards. IBM used EBCDIC code. Although EBCDIC is an obsolete code, it will be used here for illustrative purposes. Eight bits are used to represent characters, although 7 bits suffice, because the eighth bit is frequently used to test for errors and is referred to as a *party bit*. It can be set to 1 or 0, so that the number of bits in the byte is always odd or even.

Table 2.7 shows a list of ASCII and EBCDIC codes. Some EBCDIC codes do not have corresponding ASCII codes. Note that decimal digits 0 through 9 are represented by 30_{16} through 39_{16} in ASCII. On the other hand, these decimal digits are represented by $F0_{16}$ through $F9_{16}$ in EBCDIC.

A computer program is usually written for code conversion when input/output devices of different codes are connected to the computer. For example, suppose it is desired to enter a number 5 into a computer via an ASCII keyboard and print this data on an EBCDIC printer. The ASCII keyboard will generate 35_{16} when the number 5 is pushed. The ASCII code 35_{16} for the decimal digit 5 enters into the computer and resides in the computer's memory. To print the 5 on the EBCDIC printer, a program must be written that will convert the ASCII code 35_{16} for 5 in its EBCDIC code $F5_{16}$. The output of this program is $F5_{16}$. This will be input to the EBCDIC printer. Because the printer only understands EBCDIC codes, it inputs the EBCDIC code $F5_{16}$ and prints the digit 5.

Let us now discuss packed and unpacked BCD codes in more detail. Note that the numbers 00_{16} through 09_{16} are called unpacked BCD numbers. Two unpacked BCD bytes are usually packed into a byte to form "packed BCD." For example, two unpacked BCD bytes such as 0205_{16} (16-bit number) can be combined as a packed BCD byte 25_{16}.

The concept of unpacked and packed BCD numbers is illustrated next. For example, in order to enter data 24 in decimal into a computer, the two keys (2 and 4) are pushed on the ASCII keyboard of the computer. This will generate 32 and 34 (32 and 34 are ASCII codes in hexadecimal for 2 and 4 respectively) inside the computer. A program can be written to convert these ASCII codes, 3234_{16} into unpacked BCD 0204_{16}, and then convert to packed BCD 24 or to binary inside the computer to perform the desired operation.

2.3.3 Excess-3 Code

The excess-3 representation of a decimal digit d can be obtained by adding 3 to its value. All decimal digits and their excess-3 representations are listed in Table 2.8.

TABLE 2.7   ASCII and EBCDIC Codes in Hex

Character	ASCII	EBCDIC	Character	ASCII	EBCDIC	Character	ASCII	EBCDIC	Character	ASCII	EBCDIC
@	40			60		blank	20	40	NUL	00	
A	41	C1	a	61	81	!	21	5A	SOH	01	
B	42	C2	b	62	82	"	22	7F	STX	02	
C	43	C3	c	63	83	#	23	7B	ETX	03	
D	44	C4	d	64	84	$	24	5B	EOT	04	37
E	45	C5	e	65	85	%	25	6C	ENQ	05	
F	46	C6	f	66	86	&	26	50	ACK	06	
G	47	C7	g	67	87	'	27	7D	BEL	07	
H	48	C8	h	68	88	(	28	4D	BS	08	16
I	49	C9	i	69	89	)	29	5D	HT	09	05
J	4A	D1	j	6A	91	*	2A	5C	LF	0A	25
K	4B	D2	k	6B	92	+	2B	4E	VT	0B	
L	4C	D3	l	6C	93	,	2C	6B	FF	0C	
M	4D	D4	m	6D	94	-	2D	60	CR	0D	15
N	4E	D5	n	6E	95	.	2E	4B	SO	0E	
O	4F	D6	o	6F	96	/	2F	61	SI	0F	
P	50	D7	p	70	97	0	30	F0	DLE	10	
Q	51	D8	q	71	98	1	31	F1	DC1	11	
R	52	D9	r	72	99	2	32	F2	DC2	12	
S	53	E2	s	73	A2	3	33	F3	DC3	13	
T	54	E3	t	74	A3	4	34	F4	DC4	14	
U	55	E4	u	75	A4	5	35	F5	NAK	15	
V	56	E5	v	76	A5	6	36	F6	SYN	16	
W	57	E6	w	77	A6	7	37	F7	ETB	17	
X	58	E7	x	78	A7	8	38	F8	CAN	18	
Y	59	E8	y	79	A8	9	39	F9	EM	19	
Z	5A	E9	z	7A	A9	:	3A		SUB	1A	
[	5B		{	7B		;	3B	5E	ESC	1B	
\	5C		|	7C	4F	<	3C	4C	FS	1C	
]	5D		}	7D		=	3D	7E	GS	1D	
^	5E		~	7E		>	3E	6E	RS	1E	
_	5F	6D	DEL	7F	07	?	3F	6F	US	1F	

TABLE 2.8   Excess-3 Representation of Decimal Digits

Decimal Digits	Excess-3 Representation
0	0011
1	0100
2	0101
3	0110
4	0111
5	1000
6	1001
7	1010
8	1011
9	1100

The excess-3 code is an unweighted code because its value is obtained by adding three to the corresponding binary value. The excess-3 code is self-complementing. For example, decimal digit 0 in excess-3 (0011) is ones complement of 9 in excess three (1100). Similarly, decimal digit 1 is ones complement of 8, and so on. This is why some older computers used excess-3 to obtain the one's complement of a decimal number by using a decimal to excess-3 conversion table stored in its memory. Conversion between excess-3 and decimal numbers is illustrated below:

Decimal number	1	9	8	3
	$\updownarrow$	$\updownarrow$	$\updownarrow$	$\updownarrow$
Excess-3 Representation	0100	1100	1011	0110

2.3.4 Gray Code

Sometimes codes can also be constructed using a property called reflected symmetry. One such code is known as Gray code. The Gray code is used in Karnaugh maps for simplifying combinational logic design. This topic is covered in Chapter 4. Before we proceed, we briefly explain the concept of reflected symmetry. Consider the two bits 0 and 1, and stack these two bits. The definition of Gray code implies that any two adjacent bit patterns differ only in one bit. Hence, one-bit Gray code is:

$$0$$
$$1$$

Now, in order to find two-bit Gray code, the following procedure is followed. Assume that there is a plane mirror in front of this stack and produce the reflected image of the stack as shown in the following:

$$0$$
$$1$$
$$\text{mirror} \leftarrow \overline{}$$
$$1$$
$$0$$

Appending a zero to all elements of the stack above the plane mirror and append a one to all elements of the stack that lies below the mirror will provide the following result:

$$
\begin{array}{l}
\text{Appended} \left\{ \begin{array}{cc} 0 & 0 \\ 0 & 1 \end{array} \right. \\
\text{zeros} \\
\\
\text{Appended} \left\{ \begin{array}{cc} 1 & 1 \\ 1 & 0 \end{array} \right. \\
\text{ones}
\end{array}
$$

Now, removal of the plane mirror will result in a stack of two-bit Gray Code as follows:

$$0\,0$$
$$0\,1$$
$$1\,1$$
$$1\,0$$

Here, any two adjacent bit patterns differ only in one bit. For example, the patterns 11 and 10 differ only in the least significant bit. Two-bit Gray code along with corresponding decimal and binary equivalents are provided in Figure 2.1.

Repeating the reflection operation on the stack of two-bit binary patterns, a three-bit Gray code can be obtained. Two adjacent binary numbers differ in only one bit. The result is shown in Figure 2.2. Applying the reflection process to the three-bit Gray code, four-bit Gray Code can be obtained. This is shown in Figure 2.3.

Decimal	Binary`	Gray code
0	00	00
1	01	01
2	10	11
3	11	10

FIGURE 2.1   Two-bit Gray code along with corresponding decimal and binary equivalents

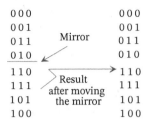

Decimal	Binary`	Gray code
0	000	000
1	001	001
2	010	011
3	011	010
4	100	110
5	101	111
6	110	101
7	111	100

FIGURE 2.2   Three-bit Gray code along with corresponding decimal and binary equivalents

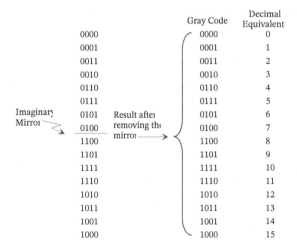

Decimal	Binary`	Gray code
0	0000	0000
1	0001	0001
2	0010	0011
3	0011	0010
4	0100	0110
5	0101	0111
6	0110	0101
7	0111	0100
8	1000	1100
9	1001	1101
10	1010	1111
11	1011	1110
12	1100	1010
13	1101	1011
14	1110	1001
15	1111	1000

FIGURE 2.3   Four-bit Gray code along with corresponding decimal and binary equivalents

The Gray code is useful in instrumentation systems to digitally represent the position of a mechanical shaft. In these applications, one bit change between characters is required. For example, suppose a shaft is divided into eight segments and each shaft is assigned a number. If binary numbers are used, an error may occur while changing segment 7 (0111_2) to segment 8 (1000_2). In this case, all 4 bits need to be changed. If the sensor representing the most significant bit takes longer to change, the result will be 0000_2, representing segment 0. This can be avoided by using Gray code, in which only one bit changes when going from one number to the next.

2.3.5 Unicode

Basically, Computers work with numbers. Note that letters and other characters are stored in computers as numbers; a number is assigned to each one of them.

Before invention of unicode, there were numerous encoding systems for assigning these numbers. It was not possible for a single encoding system to cover all the languages in the world. For example, a single encoding system was not able to assign all the letters, punctuation, and common technical symbols. Typical encoding systems can conflict with each other. For example, two different characters can be assigned with the same number in two different encoding systems. Also, different numbers can be assigned to the same character in two different encodings. These types of assignments of numbers can create problems for certain computers such as servers which need to support several different encodings. Hence, when data is transferred between different encodings or platforms, that data may be corrupted.

Unicode avoids this by assigning a unique number to each character regardless of the platform, the program, or the language. More information on Unicode can be obtained from the Web site www.unicode.org.

2.4 Fixed-Point and Floating-Point Representations

A number representation assuming a fixed location of the radix point is called *fixed-point representation*. The range of numbers that can be represented in fixed-point notation is severely limited. The following numbers are examples of fixed-point numbers:

$$0110.1100_2, \ 51.12_{10}, \ DE.2A_{16}$$

In typical scientific computations, the range of numbers is very large. Floating-point representation is used to handle such ranges. A floating-point number is represented as $N \times r^p$, where N is the mantissa or significand, r is the base or radix of the number system, and p is the exponent or power to which r is raised.

Some examples of numbers in floating-point notation and their fixed-point decimal equivalents are:

fixed-point numbers	floating-point representation
0.0167_{10}	0.167×10^{-1}
1101.101_2	0.1101101×2^4
$BE.2A9_{16}$	$0.BE2A9 \times 16^{-2}$

In converting from fixed-point to floating-point number representation, we normalize the resulting mantissas, that is, the digits of the fixed-point numbers are shifted so that the highest-order nonzero digit appears to the right of the decimal point, and consequently a 0 always appears to the left of the decimal point. This convention is normally adopted in floating-point number representation. Because all numbers will be assumed to be in normalized form, the binary point is not required to be represented in the computers.

Typical 32-bit microprocessors such as the Intel 80486/Pentium and the Motorola 68040 and PowerPC contain on-chip floating-point hardware. This means that these microprocessors can be programmed using instructions to perform operations such as addition, subtraction, multiplication, and division using floating-point numbers.

2.5   Arithmetic Operations

As mentioned before, computers can only add. Therefore, all other arithmetic operations are typically accomplished via addition. All numbers inside the computer are in binary form. These numbers are usually treated internally as integers, and any fractional arithmetic must be implemented by the programmer in the program. The arithmetic and logic unit (ALU) in the computer's CPU performs typical arithmetic and logic operations. The ALU performs functions such as addition, subtraction, magnitude comparison, ANDing, and ORing of two binary or packed BCD numbers. The procedures involved in executing these functions are discussed now to provide an understanding of the basic arithmetic operations performed in a typical microcontroller and microprocessor. The logic operations are covered in Chapter 3

2.5.1   Binary Arithmetic

Addition   The addition of two binary numbers is carried out in the same way as the addition of decimal numbers. However, only four possible combinations can occur when adding two binary digits (bits):

augend	+	addend	=	carry	sum	decimal value
0	+	0	=	0	0	0
1	+	0	=	0	1	1
0	+	1	=	0	1	1
1	+	1	=	1	0	2

The following are some examples of binary addition. The corresponding decimal additions are also included.

$$
\begin{array}{ll}
010 & (2) \\
+\ 011 & (3) \\
\hline
101 & (5)
\end{array}
\qquad\qquad
\begin{array}{ll}
111 \leftarrow \text{carry} \\
101.11 & (5.75) \\
+\ 011.10 & (3.50) \\
\hline
1\ \ 001.01 & (9.25)
\end{array}
$$

final carry

Addition is the most important arithmetic operation in microcontrollers and microprocessors because the operations of subtraction, multiplication, and division as they are performed in most digital computers use only addition as their basic operation.

Subtraction   As mentioned before, computers can usually only add binary numbers; they cannot directly subtract. Therefore, the operation of subtraction in microcontrollers and microprocessors is performed using addition with complement arithmetic.

In general, the b's complement of an m-digit number, M is defined as $b^m - M$ for $M \neq 0$ and 0 for $M = 0$. Note that for base 10, $b = 10$ and 10^m is a decimal number with a 1 followed by m 0's. For example, 10^4 is 10000; 1 followed by four 0's. On the other hand, $b = 2$ for binary and 2^m indicates 1 followed by m 0's. For example, 2^3 means 1000 in binary.

The $(b–1)$'s complement of an m-digit number, M is defined as $(b^m–1) – M$. Therefore, the b's complement of an m-digit number, M can be obtained by adding 1 to its $(b-1)$'s complement. Next, let us illustrate the concept of complement arithmetic by means of some examples. Consider a 4-digit decimal number, 5786. In this case, $b = 10$ for base 10 and $m = 4$ since there are four digits.

Now, let us obtain 10's complement of 5786 using $(10 – 1)$'s or 9's complement arithmetic as follows: 9's complement of 5786 $= (10^4 - 1) - 5786 = 9999 - 5786 = 4213$

Hence, 10's complement of 5786 = 9's complement of 5786 + 1 = 4213 + 1 = 4214.

Next, let us determine the 2's complement of a three-bit binary number, 010 via its one's complement. In this case, $b = 2$ for binary and $m = 3$ since there are three bits in the number.

The 2's complement of 010_2 $(+2_{10})$ can be obtained using its 1's complement as follows:

$$1\text{'s complement of } 010 = (2^3 – 1) – 010 = 111 – 010 = 101$$

$$2\text{'s complement of } 101 = 101 + 1 = 110$$

Now, let us find the decimal equivalent of 110_2. Since the most significant bit of 110 is 1, the two's complement of 110 must be taken. Hence, $110_2 = -2_{10}$. Therefore, two's complement of a number negates the number being complemented. This will be explained later in this section.

From the above procedure for finding the 1's complement of 010, it can be concluded that the 1's complement of a binary number can be obtained by subtracting each bit of the binary number from 1. This means that when subtracting a bit (0 or 1) from 1, one can have either $1 - 0 = 1$ or $1 - 1 = 0$; that is, the 1's complement of 0 is 1 and the 1's complement of 1 is 0. In general, the 1's complement of a binary number can be obtained by changing 0's to 1's and 1's to 0's.

The procedure for performing X-Y (both X and Y are in base 2) using 1's complement can be performed as follows:

1. Add X to 1's complement of Y.
2. Check the result in step 1 for a carry. If there is a carry, add 1 to the least significant bit to obtain the result. If there is no carry, take the 1's complement of the number obtained in step 1 and place a negative sign in front of the result.

For example, consider two 6-bit numbers (arbitrarily chosen), $X = 010011_2 = 19_{10}$ and $Y = 110001_2 = 49_{10}$. X-Y= 19 - 49 = -30 in decimal. The operation X-Y using 1's complement can be performed as follows:

$$X = 010011$$
$$\text{Add 1's complement of } Y = 001110$$
$$\overline{}$$
$$100001$$

Since there is no carry, Result = - (1's Complement of 100001) = $-011110_2 = -30_{10}$. Next consider, $X = 101100_2 = 44_{10}$ and $Y = 011000_2 = 24_{10}$. In decimal, X-Y = 44 -24 = 20.

Using 1's complement, X-Y can be obtained as follows: X = 101100
$$\text{Add 1's Complement of } Y = 100111$$
$$\overline{}$$
$$\text{Carry} \rightarrow 1\ 010011$$

Since there is a carry, Result = $010011 + 1 = +010100_2 = + 20_{10}$.

Next, let us describe the procedure of subtracting decimal numbers using addition. This process requires the use of the 10's complement form. The 10's complement of a number can be obtained by subtracting the number from 10.

Consider the decimal subtraction $7 - 4 = 3$. The 10's complement of 4 is $10 - 4 = 6$. The decimal subtraction can be performed using the 10's complement addition as follows:

$$\begin{array}{rr} \text{minuend} & 7 \\ \text{10's complement of subtrahend} & +6 \\ \hline & 13 \end{array}$$

ignore final carry of 1 to obtain
the subtraction result of 3.

When a larger number is subtracted from a smaller number, there is no carry to be discarded. Consider the decimal subtraction $4 - 7 = -3$. The 10's complement of 7 is $10 - 7 = 3$
Therefore,

$$\begin{array}{rr} \text{minuend} & 4 \\ \text{10's complement of subtrahend} & + 3 \\ \hline & 7 \end{array}$$

no final carry

When there is no final carry, the final answer is the negative of the 10's complement of 7. Therefore, the correct result of subtraction is $- (10- 7) = -3$.

The same procedures can be applied for performing binary subtraction. However, microcontrollers and microprocessors do not utilize the final carry to perform binary subtraction; instead, they add minuend with the two's complement of the subtrahend, and then determine the sign of the result by inspecting its most significant bit of the result. This is illustrated in the following by means of examples.

As mentioned before, the two's complement of a binary number is obtained by replacing each 0 with a 1 and each 1 with a 0 and, then adding 1 to the resulting number. The first step generates a one's complement or simply the complement of a binary number. For example, the one's complement of 10010101 is 01101010. Note that the one's complement of a binary number can be obtained by using inverters; for example, eight inverters are required for generating one's complement of an 8-bit number.

The two's complement of a binary number is formed by adding 1 to its one's complement of the number. For example, the two's complement of 10010101 is found as follows:

$$
\begin{array}{lr}
\text{binary number} & 10010101 \\
\text{1's complement} & 01101010 \\
\text{add 1} & \underline{+\,1} \\
\text{2's complement} & 01101011
\end{array}
$$

Now, using the two's complement, binary subtraction can be carried out.

Consider the following four-bit subtraction using the normal (pencil and paper) procedure:

$$
\begin{array}{lll}
\text{minuend} & 0101 & (5) \\
\text{subtrahend} & \underline{-0011} & (-3) \\
\text{result} & 0010_2 = 2_{10}
\end{array}
$$

Using the two's complement subtraction,

$$
\begin{array}{lr}
\text{minuend} & 0101 \\
\text{Add 2's complement of subtrahend} & 1101 \\
(0011) & \overline{10010} \\
\end{array}
$$

Final Carry = 1

The final answer is 0010 (decimal 2) by discarding the final carry as shown with decimal subtraction using 10's complement. However, microcontrollers and microprocessors determine the sign of the result by inspecting the most significant bit (sign bit) of the result. Since the sign bit (most significant bit) of the result, 0010 is 0, the result in decimal is +2.

Consider another example. Using pencil and paper (analytical) method:

$$
\begin{array}{lll}
\text{minuend} & 0101 & (5) \\
\text{subtrahend} & \underline{-0110} & (-6) \\
\text{result} & -0001 & (-1)
\end{array}
$$

Using the two's complement,

$$
\begin{array}{lr}
\text{minuend} & 0101 \\
\text{Add 2's complement of subtrahend} & \underline{1010} \\
\text{result} & 1111
\end{array}
$$

Sign bit

Since the sign bit (most significant bit) of 1111 is 1, the final answer is $-$(two's complement of 1111) $= -1_{10}$. Note that a negative sign is placed in front of the result since its two's complement is taken.

As mentioned before, computers including microcontrollers and microcomputers use two's complement of a binary number to represent its negative value, and obtain the sign of the result from the most significant bit. Hence, microcontrollers and microprocessors typically handle signed numbers by using the most significant bit of a number as the sign bit. If this bit is zero, the number is positive; if this bit is one, the number is negative. The sign bit of the result rather than the final carry is used in performing binary subtraction as follows.

For example, the number $+22_{10}$ can be represented using 8 bits as:

$+22_{10} = 0\ 0010110$ Two's complement of $+22_{10} = 11\ 101010$

↑   ↑

    sign bit (positive)   sign bit (negative)

Next, the concept of overflow will be explained. An error (indicated by overflow in a microcontroller or a microprocessor) may occur while performing two's complement arithmetic for signed numbers. The overflow arises from the representation of the sign flag by the most significant bit of a binary number in signed binary operation. The computer automatically sets an overflow bit to 1 if the result of an arithmetic operation is too big for the computer's maximum word size; otherwise it is reset to 0.

To clearly understand the concept of overflow, consider the following examples for 8-bit numbers. Let C_7 be the carry out of the most significant bit (sign bit) and C_6 be the carry out of the previous (bit 6) data bit (seventh bit). We will show by means of numerical examples that as long as C_7 and C_6 are the same, the result is always correct. If, however, C_7 and C_6 are different, the result is incorrect and sets the overflow bit to 1. Now consider the following cases.

Case 1: C_7 and C_6 are the same.

$$
\begin{array}{ll}
\quad\ 0\,0\,0\,0\,0\,1\,1\,0 & \quad 06_{16} \\
\underline{\quad\ 0\,0\,0\,1\,0\,1\,0\,0} & \underline{+14_{16}} \\
0\ \ 0\,0\,0\,1\,1\,0\,1\,0 & \quad 1A_{16}
\end{array}
$$

$C_7 = 0$ $C_6 = 0$

$$
\begin{array}{ll}
\quad\ 0\,1\,1\,0\,1\,0\,0\,0 & \quad 68_{16} \\
\underline{\quad\ 1\,1\,1\,1\,1\,0\,1\,0} & \underline{-06_{16}} \\
1\ \ 0\,1\,1\,0\,0\,0\,1\,0 & \quad 62_{16}
\end{array}
$$

$C_7 = 1$ $C_6 = 1$

Therefore when C_7 and C_6 are either 0 or both 1, a correct answer is obtained.

Case 2: C_7 and C_6 are different.

$$
\begin{array}{ll}
\quad\ 0\,1\,0\,1\,1\,0\,0\,1 & \quad 59_{16} \\
\underline{\quad\ 0\,1\,0\,0\,0\,1\,0\,1} & \underline{+45_{16}} \\
0\ \ 1\,0\,0\,1\,1\,1\,1\,0 & \quad -62_{16}\ ?
\end{array}
$$

$C_7 = 0$ $C_6 = 1$

$C_6 = 1$ and $C_7 = 0$ give an incorrect answer because the result shows that the addition of two positive numbers is negative.

$$
\begin{array}{ll}
\quad 1\,0\,1\,1\,0\,1\,1\,0 & 4A\,_{16} \\
\quad 1\,0\,0\,0\,0\,0\,0\,1 & 7F\,_{16} \\
\hline
1\quad 0\,0\,1\,1\,0\,1\,1\,1 & +37\,_{16}\ ?
\end{array}
$$

$C_7 \neq 1$ $\qquad$ $C_6 = 0$

$C_6 = 0$ and $C_7 = 1$ provide an incorrect answer because the result indicates that the addition of two negative numbers is positive. Hence, the overflow bit will be set to zero if the carries C_7 and C_6 are the same, that is, if both C_7 and C_6 are either 0 or 1. On the other hand, the overflow flag will be set to 1 if the carries C_7 and C_6 are different. The answer is incorrect when the overflow bit is set to 1. Thus, Overflow $= C_7 \oplus C_6$. In general, Overflow $= C_f \oplus C_p$.

Note that the symbol $\oplus$ represents exclusive-OR logic operation. Exclusive-OR means that when two inputs are the same (both one or both zero), the output is zero. On the other hand, if two inputs are different, the output is one. The overflow can be considered as the output while C_p (Previous Carry) and C_f (Final Carry) are the two inputs. The exclusive-OR operation is covered in Chapter 3.

While performing signed arithmetic using pencil and paper (analytically), one must consider the overflow bit to ensure that the result is correct. An overflow of one after a signed operation indicates that the result is too large to be accommodated in the number of bits assigned. One must increase the number of bits for the correct result.

Example 2.3

Perform the following signed operations and comment on the results. Assume two's complement numbers.

(a) $A = 1010_2$, $B = 0111_2$. Find $A - B$.
(b)   Perform $(-3_{10}) - (-2_{10})$ using two's complement and 4 bits.

Solution

(a)   The most significant bit of A is 1, so A is a negative number whereas B is a positive number.

$$
\begin{array}{lll}
A = & 1\,0\,1\,0 & (-6_{10}) \\
\text{Add 2's complement of } B = & +1\,0\,0\,1 & -(+7_{10}) \\
\hline
& 0\,0\,1\,1 = 3_{10} & -13_{10}
\end{array}
$$

$C_3 = 1$ $\qquad$ $C_2 = 0$

Because C3 and C2 are different, there is an overflow and the result is incorrect. Four bits are too small to hold the correct answer. If we increase the number of bits for A and B to 5, the correct result can be obtained as follows:

$$
A = -6 = 11010_2
$$
$$
B = +7 = 00111_2
$$

$$
\begin{array}{ll}
A = & 1\,1\,0\,1\,0_2 \\
\text{Add 2's complement of } B = & +1\,1\,0\,0\,1_2 \\
\hline
& 1\,0\,0\,1\,1_2
\end{array}
$$

$C_4 = 1$ $\qquad$ $C_3 = 1$

The result is correct because C_4 and C_3 are the same. The most significant bit of the result is 1. This means that the result is negative. Therefore, to express the result in base-10, one must take the two's complement and convert the binary number to a decimal and place a negative sign in front of it. Thus, two's complement of $10011_2 = -01101 = -13_{10}$.

(b)

$$-3_{10} = 2\text{'s complement of } +3_{10}$$

$$=1101_2$$

$$-2_{10} = 2\text{'s complement of } +2_{10}$$

$$=1110_2$$

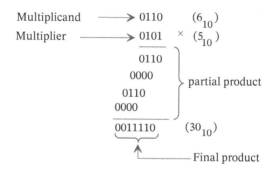

$$\text{Add 2's complement of } \begin{array}{r} -3_{10} = 1\ 1\ 0\ 1 \ _2 \\ -2_{10} = +0\ 0\ 1\ 0 \ _2 \\ \hline 1\ 1\ 1\ 1 \end{array} \qquad \begin{array}{r} (-3_{10}) \\ -(-2_{10}) \\ \hline -1_{10} \end{array}$$

$$C_3 = 0 \longleftarrow \qquad C_2 = 0$$

C_2 and C_3 are the same, so the result is correct. The most significant bit of the result is 1. This means that the result is negative. To find the result in decimal, one must take two's complement of the result and place a negative sign in front of it.
Two's complement of $1111_2 = -1_{10}$.

Unsigned Multiplication   Multiplication of two binary numbers can be carried out in the same way as is done with the decimal numbers using pencil and paper. Consider the following example:

$$
\begin{array}{ll}
\text{Multiplicand} \longrightarrow 0110 & (6_{10}) \\
\text{Multiplier} \longrightarrow 0101 \quad \times & (5_{10}) \\
\hline
\left.\begin{array}{l} 0110 \\ 0000 \\ 0110 \\ 0000 \end{array}\right\} & \text{partial product} \\
\hline
0011110 & (30_{10}) \\
\end{array}
$$

Final product

Several multiplication algorithms are available. Multiplication of two unsigned numbers can be accomplished via repeated addition. For example, to multiply 4_{10} by 3_{10}, the number 4_{10} can be added twice to itself to obtain the result, 12_{10}.

Signed Multiplication   Signed multiplication can be performed using various algorithms. A simple algorithm follows. Assume that M (multiplicand) and Q (multiplier) are in two's-complement form. Also that M_n and Q_n are the most significant bits (sign bits) of the multiplicand (M) and the multiplier (Q) respectively; hence, the sign bit of the product is determined as $M_n \oplus Q_n$, where M_n and Q_n are the most significant bits (sign bits) of the multiplicand (M) and the multiplier (Q) respectively. To perform signed multiplication, proceed as follows:
1. If $M_n = 1$, compute the two's complement of M.
2. If $Q_n = 1$, compute the two's complement of Q.
3. Multiply the n − 1 bits of the multiplier and the multiplicand using unsigned multiplication.
4. The sign of the result, $S_n = M_n \oplus Q_n$.
5. If $S_n = 1$, compute the two's-complement of the result obtained in step 3.

Next, consider a numerical example. Assume that M and Q are two's-complement numbers. Suppose that $M = 1100_2$ and $Q = 0111_2$. Because $M_n = 1$, take the two's-complement of $M = 0100_2$; because $Q_n = 0$, do not change Q. Multiply 0111_2 and 0100_2 using the unsigned multiplication (repeated addition) method discussed before. The product is 00011100_2 ($+28_{10}$). The sign of the product $S_n = M_n \oplus Q_n = 1 \oplus 0 = 1$. Hence, take the two's-complement of the product 00011100_2 to obtain 11100100_2, which is the final answer: -28_{10}.

Unsigned Division   Division between unsigned numbers can be accomplished via repeated subtraction. For example, consider dividing 7_{10} by 3_{10} as follows:

Dividend	Divisor	Subtraction Result	Counter
7_{10}	3_{10}	$7 - 3 = 4$	1
		$4 - 3 = 1$	$1 + 1 = 2$

Quotient = Counter value = 2
Remainder = subtraction result = 1

In the above, Counter is cleared to 0 initially, and one is added to the Counter whenever the subtraction result is greater than the divisor. The result is obtained as soon as the subtraction result is smaller than the divisor.

Signed Division   Signed division can be performed using various algorithms. A simple algorithm follows. Assume that DV (Dividend) and DR (Divisor) are in two's-complement form. If DV and DR are negative numbers, take their 2's complement; else, keep DV and DR the same. For the first case, perform unsigned division using repeated subtraction of the magnitudes without the sign bits. The sign bit of the quotient is determined by $DV_n \oplus DR_n$, where DV_n and DR_n are the most significant bits (sign bits) of the dividend (DV) and the divisor (DR) respectively. To perform signed division, proceed as follows:

Step 1: If $DV_n = 1$, compute the twos complement of DV; else keep DV unchanged.

Step 2: If $DR_n = 1$, compute the twos complement of DR; else keep DR unchanged.

Step 3: Divide the $n - 1$ bits of the dividend by the divisor using unsigned division algorithm (repeated subtraction).

Step 4: The sign of the Quotient, Qn = DVn $\oplus$ DRn. The sign of the remainder is the same as the sign of the dividend unless the remainder is zero. The following numerical examples illustrate this: The general equation for division can be used for signed division. Note that the general equation for division is dividend = quotient * divisor + remainder. For example, consider dividend = -9, divisor = 2. Three possible solutions are shown below:
    (a) $-9 = -4 * 2 - 1$, Quotient = -4, Remainder = -1.
    (b) $-9 = -5 * 2 + 1$, Quotient = -5, Remainder = $+1$.
    (c) $-9 = -6 * 2 + 3$, Quotient = -6, Remainder = $+3$.
However, the correct answer is shown in (a), in which, the Quotient = -4 and the remainder = -1.   Hence, for signed division, the sign of the remainder is the same as the sign of the dividend, unless the remainder is zero.

Step 5: If $Q_n = 1$, compute the two's-complement of the quotient obtained in step 3, else keep the quotient unchanged.

The above algorithm will be verified using numerical examples provided in the following:

Case 1: Signed division with zero remainder

Note that in decimal, ($+6$) / (-2) will provide a quotient of (-3) and remainder of 0. Next, perform the above division using 4-bit numbers as follows.

Dividend = $+6 = 0110_2$ Divisor = $-2 = $ Two's complement of 2 = 1110_2

Since, the sign bit of Dividend is 0, do not change dividend. Because the sign bit of divisor is 1, take 2's complement of 1110 which is 0010. Now, divide 0110 by 0010 using repeated subtraction as follows:

DIVIDEND	DIVISOR	SUBTRACTION RESULT USING 2'S COMPLEMENT	COUNTER (Initial Value = 0000)
0110	0010	0110-0010=0100	0001
		0100-0010=0010	0010
		0010-0010=0000	0011

Result of unsigned division: Quotient = Counter value = 0011_2,

Remainder = Subtraction result = 0000_2

Result of signed division 6 (0110) divided by -2 (1110):

Sign of the quotient = (Sign of dividend) $\oplus$ (Sign of divisor) = $0 \oplus 1 = 1$

Hence, Quotient = 2's complement of $0011_2 = 1101_2 = -3_{10}$, Remainder = 0000_2

Next a few numerical division examples will be provided using decimal numbers with zero remainder:

(i) Assume both dividend and divisor are positive

Dividend = +6 Divisor = +2

Result: Quotient = +3 Remainder = 0

(ii) Assume dividend is negative and divisor is positive.

Dividend = -6 Divisor = +2

Result: Quotient = -3 Remainder = 0

(iii) Assume dividend is positive and divisor is negative.

Dividend = +6 Divisor = -2

Result: Quotient = -3 Remainder = 0

(iv) Assume both dividend and divisor are negative.

Dividend = -6 Divisor = -2

Result: Quotient = +3 Remainder = 0

Next a few numerical examples will be provided to show that the sign of the remainder is the same as the sign of the dividend unless the remainder is 0. This can be verified by the following numerical examples using decimal numbers:

Case 2: When the remainder is non-zero

Since, Dividend = Quotient x Divisor + Remainder

Hence, Remainder = Dividend - Quotient x Divisor.

(i) Assume both dividend and divisor are positive.

Dividend = +5 Divisor = +2

Result: Quotient = +2 Remainder can be obtained from the equation, Remainder = Dividend - Quotient x Divisor. Hence, Remainder = +5 - (+2 x +2) = +1.

(ii) Assume dividend is negative and divisor is positive.

Dividend = -5 Divisor = +2

Result: Quotient = -2 Remainder can be obtained from the equation, Remainder = Dividend - Quotient x Divisor. Hence, Remainder = -5 - (-2 x +2) = - 1.

(iii) Assume dividend is positive and divisor is negative.

Dividend = +5 Divisor = -2

Result: Quotient = -2 Remainder can be obtained from the equation, Remainder = Dividend - Quotient x Divisor. Hence, Remainder = +5 - (-2 x -2) = + 1.

(iv) Assume both dividend and divisor are negative.

Dividend = -5 Divisor = -2

Result: Quotient = +2 Remainder can be obtained from the equation, Remainder = Dividend - Quotient x Divisor. Hence, Remainder = -5 - (+2 x -2) = - 1.

From above, the sign of the remainder is the same as the sign of the dividend unless the remainder is zero.

2.5.2   BCD Arithmetic

Many computers have instructions to perform arithmetic operations using packed BCD numbers. Next, we consider some examples of packed BCD addition and subtraction.

BCD Addition   The two cases that may occur while adding two packed BCD numbers are considered next. Consider adding packed BCD numbers 25 and 33:

$$
\begin{array}{rll}
25 & 0010 & 0101 \\
+33 & 0011 & 0011 \\
\hline
58 & 0101 & 1000 \\
\end{array}
$$

In this example, none of the sums of the pairs of decimal digits exceeded 9; therefore, no decimal carries were produced. For these reasons, the BCD addition process is straightforward and is actually the same as binary addition.

Now, consider the addition of 8 and 4 in BCD:

$$
\begin{array}{rll}
8 & 0000 & 1000 \\
+4 & 0000 & 0100 \\
\hline
12 & 0000 & 1100 \quad \leftarrow \text{invalid code group for BCD} \\
\end{array}
$$

The sum 1100 does not exist in BCD code. It is one of the six forbidden or invalid 4-bit code groups. This has occurred because the sum of two digits exceeds 9. Whenever this occurs, the sum has to be corrected by the addition of 6 (0110) to skip over the six invalid code groups.

For example,

8	0000	1000
+4	0000	0100
12	0000	1100 invalid sum
	+0000	0110 add 6 for correction
	0001	0010 BCD for 12
	1	2

As another example, add packed BCD numbers 56 and 81:

56	0101	0110 BCD for 56
+81	1000	0001 BCD for 81
137	1101	0111 invalid sum in 2nd digit
	+0110	add 6 for correction
0001	0011	0111 $\leftarrow$ correct answer 137
1	3	7

Therefore, it can be concluded that addition of two BCD digits is correct if the binary sum is less than or equal to 1001_2 (9 in decimal). A binary sum greater than 1001_2 results into an invalid BCD sum; adding 0110_2 to an invalid BCD sum provides the correct sum with an output carry of 1. Furthermore, addition of two BCD digits (each digit having a maximum value of 9) along with carry will provide a sum not exceeding 19 in decimal (10011_2). Hence, a correction is necessary for the following:

i) If the binary sum is greater than or equal to decimal 16 (this will generate a carry of one).
ii) If the binary sum is 1010_2 through 1111_2.

For example, consider adding packed BCD numbers 97 and 39:

```
                      111 ←Intermediate Carries
   97       1001          0111    BCD for 97
  +39       0011          1001    BCD for 39
  136       1101          0000    invalid sum
          +0110         +0110    add 6 for correction
 0001      0011          0110    ← correct answer 136
 ‿‿‿       ‿‿‿           ‿‿‿
   1          3             6
```

BCD Subtraction   Subtraction of packed BCD numbers can be accomplished in a number of different ways. One method is to add the 10's complement of the subtrahend to the minuend using packed BCD addition rules, as described earlier.

One means of finding the 10's complement of a d-digit packed BCD number N is to take the two's complement of each digit individually, producing a number N_1. Then, ignoring any carries, add the d-digit factor M to N_1, where the least significant digit of M is 1010 and all remaining digits of M are 1001.

As an example, consider subtracting 26_{10} from 84_{10} using BCD subtraction. This can be accomplished as follows:

26_{10}	$\underset{2}{\underbrace{0010}}$	$\underset{6}{\underbrace{0110}}$

Now, the 10's complement of 26_{10} can be found according to the rules by individually determining the two's complement of 2 and 6, adding the 10's complement factor, and discarding any carries. The two's complement of 2 is 1110, and the twos complement of 6 is 1010.

Therefore,

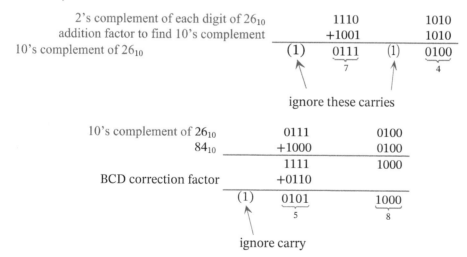

```
2's complement of each digit of 26₁₀              1110        1010
   addition factor to find 10's complement       +1001        1010
10's complement of 26₁₀                      (1)  0111   (1)  0100
                                                  ‿‿‿          ‿‿‿
                                                   7            4
                                        ignore these carries

10's complement of 26₁₀              0111        0100
               84₁₀                 +1000        0100
                                     1111        1000
BCD correction factor               +0110
                              (1)    0101        1000
                                     ‿‿‿         ‿‿‿
                                      5           8
                             ignore carry
```

Therefore, the final answer is 58_{10}.

2.5.3   Multiword Binary Addition and Subtraction

In many cases, the word length of a particular computer may not be large enough to represent the desired magnitude of a number. Suppose, for example, that numbers in the range from 0 to 65,535 are to be used in an 8-bit microcontroller in binary addition and subtraction operations using the two's complement number representation. This can be accomplished by storing the 16-bit numbers each in two 8-bit memory locations. Addition or subtraction of the two 16-bit numbers is implemented by adding or subtracting the lower 8 bits of each number, storing the result in 8-bit memory location or register, and then adding the two high-order parts of the number with any carry or borrow generated from the first addition or subtraction. The latter partial sum or difference will be the high-order portion of the result. Therefore, the two 8-bit operations together comprise the 16-bit result.

Here are some examples of 16-bit addition and subtraction.

16-Bit Addition:

Consider $4B7A_{16} + 2E2D_{16} = 79A7_{16}$. The details are as follows:

	upper half of the 16-bit number	lower half of the 16-bit number
	0 1 0 0 1 0 1 1	0 1 1 1 1 0 1 0
	+ 0 0 1 0 1 1 1 0	0 0 1 0 1 1 0 1
intermediate carries	0 0 0 1 1 1 0 0	1 1 1 1 0 0 0
	0 1 1 1 1 0 0 1	1 0 1 0 0 1 1 1
	high byte of the answer	low byte of the answer

The low-order 8-bit addition can be computed by using the microprocessor's ADD instruction and the high-order 8-bit sum can be obtained by using the ADC (ADD with carry) instruction in the program.

16-Bit Subtraction:

Consider $23A6_{16} - 124A_{16} = 115C_{16}$.

	high byte 23	low byte A6	
	0 0 1 0 0 0 1 1	1 0 1 0 0 1 1 0	
1's complement of $124A_{16}$	1 1 1 0 1 1 0 1	1 0 1 1 0 1 0 1	
		1	add 1 to find 2's complement of $124A_{16}$
ignore this carry	1 0 0 0 1 0 0 0 1	0 1 0 1 1 1 0 0	
	1 1	5 C	

The low-order 8-bit subtraction can be obtained by using SUB instruction of the microcontroller, and the high-order 8-bit subtraction can be obtained by using SBB (SUBTRACT with borrow) instruction in the program.

2.5.4 Binary Multiplication and Division by Shift Operations

A binary number can be shifted one bit to the left or one bit to the right. This is a basic shift operation. There are two types of shift operations. They are logical shift and arithmetic shift. The logical shift operation performs multiplication or division operation for unsigned numbers while the arithmetic shift operation performs multiplication or division operation for signed numbers.

For example, in a logical right shift operation, a bit shifted out from the least significant bit will be stored in an internal one-bit memory such as a flip-flop called the carry flag in a microcontroller or a microprocessor. The vacant position (Most Significant Bit) will be filled with a '0'. Figure 2.4 shows the result after logically shifting the decimal number $(24)_{10}$ once to the right.

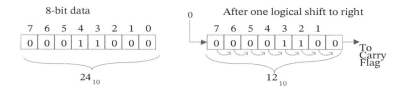

FIGURE 2.4   Logical right shift

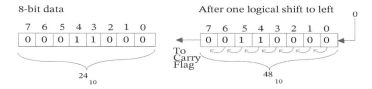

FIGURE 2.5   Logical left shift

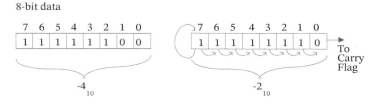

FIGURE 2.6   Arithmetic right shift

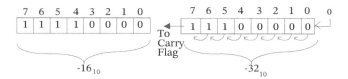

FIGURE 2.7 Arithmetic left shift

Logical shift once to the right is equivalent to dividing an unsigned number (24_{10}) by 2^1 in this case as long as a '1' is not shifted out from the least significant bit. If ones are shifted out, then the remainder will be discarded.

Also, the least significant bit shifted into the carry flag of a microcontroller or a microprocessor will determine whether the original number before shifting is odd or even. The number is even if the carry flag is 0; the number is odd if the carry flag is 1. A program in a microcontroller or a microprocessor can be written to verify this.

Similarly, in a logical left shift operation, on the other hand, a bit shifted out from the most significant bit will be stored in the carry flag in a microcontroller or a microprocessor. The vacant position (Least Significant Bit) will be filled with a '0'. For example, Figure 2.5 shows the result after a logical right shift of the number 24_{10}.

A logical shift once to the left is equivalent to multiplying an unsigned number (24_{10}) in this case by 2^1 as long as a '1' is not shifted out from the most significant bit. Logical left shift can also be used to determine the sign of a signed number. For example, the most significant bit shifted into the carry flag of a microcontroller or a microprocessor will determine whether the original number before shifting is positive or negative. The number is positive if this bit is 0; the number is negative if the carry flag is 1. A program in a microcontroller or a microprocessor can be written to verify this. A logical left or right shift of an unsigned number by 'n' positions implies multiplication or division of the number by 2^n respectively, provided that a 1 is not shifted out during the operation.

In the case of true arithmetic left or right shift operations, the sign bit of the number to be shifted must be retained. However, in microcontrollers and microprocessors, this is true for the right shift operation and not true for the left shift operation. For example, if a register is shifted right arithmetically, the most significant bit (MSB) of the register is retained; this will ensure that the sign of the number will remain unchanged. This is illustrated in Figure 2.6. Note that arithmetic right shift once is equivalent to dividing a signed number (-4_{10}) by 2^1 in this case as long as a '1' is not shifted out from the least significant bit.

There is no difference between arithmetic and logical left shift operations. This means that, in an arithmetic left shift operation, a bit shifted out from the most significant bit will be stored in the carry flag in a microcontroller or a microprocessor. The vacant position (Least Significant Bit) will be filled with a 0. For example, if we have the number -16_{10}, then after a logical right shift, the result shown in Figure 2.7 occurs.

The arithmetic shift left operation can be used to multiply a signed number by 2^n after 'n' shifts as long as the sign bit of the number does not change during or after shifting. If the most significant bit changes from 0 to 1 or vice versa, during or after shifting in an arithmetic left shift, the result will be incorrect and the microcontroller or microprocessor will set the overflow flag (flip-flop) to 1. This will mean that the signed multiplication by 2^n will be incorrect if the overflow flag is '1' after shifting. Note that the overflow flags due to arithmetic shift left and signed arithmetic operation covered earlier are interpreted in a different way.

Arithmetic left shift like logical left shift can also be used to determine the sign of a signed number. For example, the most significant bit shifted into the carry flag of a microcontroller or a microprocessor will determine whether the original number before shifting is positive or negative. The number is positive if this bit is 0; the number is negative if the carry flag is 1. A program in a microcontroller or a microprocessor can be written to verify this.

Note that execution times of multiplication and division instructions compared to shift instructions of typical microcontrollers and microprocessors are very slow. This implies that multiplication and division in real-time applications such as DSP (Digital Signal Processing) are performed using shift instructions. For example, the average or a mean value (M) of a signal is defined as:

$M = (x_0 + x_1 + ... + x_n)/N$ where x_0, x_1, ..., x_n are the samples of the signal and N is the total number of samples. The designer has the option of choosing the total number of samples, N based on a theory called "Nyquist rate"; obviously, coverage of this theory is beyond the scope of this book. The designer can select N as powers of 2 such as $128_{10}(2^7)$, $256_{10}(2^8)$, and so on. Suppose that N=256. Hence, the mean value, M is computed by logically shifting the sum eight times to right. Note that in many cases, the sum is a large number, and the remainder can be discarded.

2.6   Error Correction and Detection

In digital systems, it is possible that the transmitted information is not received correctly. Note that a computer is a digital system in which information transfer can take place in many ways. For example, data may be moved from a CPU register to another device or vice versa. When the transmitted data is not received correctly at the receiving end, an error occurs. One possible cause for such errors is noise problems during transmission. To avoid these problems, error detection and correction may be necessary. In a digital system, an error occurs when a 0 is changed to a 1 and vice versa. Correction of this error means replacement of a 1 with 0 and vice versa. The reliability of digital data depends on the methods employed for error detection and correction.

The simplest way to detect the presence of an error is by adding a single bit, called the "parity" bit, to the message bits and then transmitting the message along with the parity bit. The parity bit is usually computed in two ways: even parity and odd parity. In the even parity method, the parity bit is added in such a way that after its inclusion, the number of 1's in the message together with the parity bit is an even number. On the other hand, in an odd parity scheme, the parity bit is added in such a way that the number of 1's in the message and the parity bit is an odd number. For example, suppose a message to be transmitted is 0110. If even parity is used by the transmitting computer, the transmitted data along with the parity will be 00110. On the other hand, if odd parity is used, the data to be transmitted will be 10110. The parity computation can be implemented in hardware by using exclusive-OR gates (to be discussed in Chapter 3). Usually for a given message, the parity bit is generated using either an even or odd parity scheme by the transmitting computer. The message is then transmitted along with the parity bit. At the receiving end, the parity is checked by the receiving computer. If there is a discrepancy, the data received will obviously be incorrect. For example, suppose that the message bits are 1101. The even parity bit for this message is 1. The transmitted data will be:

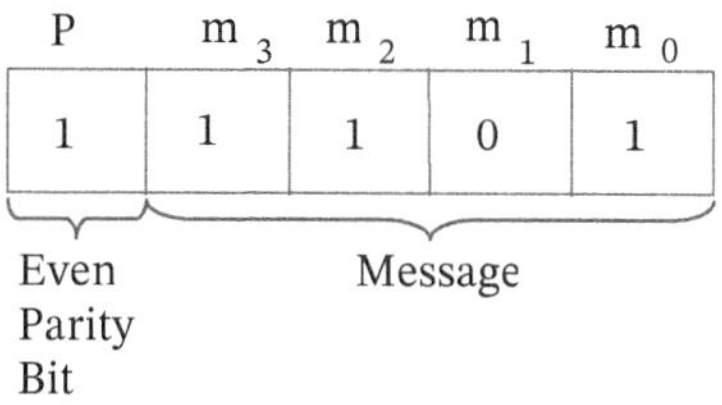

P	m_3	m_2	m_1	m_0
1	1	1	0	1

Even
Parity   Message
Bit

Suppose that an error occurs in the least significant bit; that is m0 is changed from 1 to 0 during transmission. The received data will be:

1	1	1	0	0

The receiving computer performs parity check on this data by counting the number of ones and finds it to be an odd number, three. Therefore, an error is detected.

With a single parity bit, an error due to a single bit change can be detected. Errors due to two-bit changes during transmission will go undetected. In such situations, multiple parity bits are used. One such technique is the "Hamming code," which uses three parity bits for a 4-bit message. The extended Hamming code with additional parity bits is popular in computer memory systems where it is known as SECDED *(Single Error Correction Double Error Detection)*. The SECDED code uses 8-bit data plus five parity bits.

QUESTIONS AND PROBLEMS

2.1 Convert the following unsigned binary numbers into their decimal equivalents:
    (a) 01110101_2
    (b) 1101.101_2
    (c) 1000.111_2

2.2 Convert the following numbers into binary:
    (a) 152_{10}
    (b) 343_{10}

2.3 Convert the following numbers into octal:
    (a) 1843_{10}
    (b) 1766_{10}

2.4 Convert the following numbers into hexadecimal:
    (a) 1987_{10}
    (b) 3072_{10}

2.5 Convert the following binary numbers into octal and hexadecimal numbers:
    (a) 1101011100101
    (b) 11000011100110000011

2.6 Using 8 bits, represent the integers -48 and 52 in:
    (a) sign magnitude form
    (b) one's complement form
    (c) two's complement form

2.7 Identify the following unsigned binary numbers as odd or even without converting them to decimal: 11001100_2; 00100100_2; 01111001_2.

2.8 Convert 532.372_{10} into its binary equivalent.

2.9 Convert the following hex numbers to binary: $15FD_{16}$; $26EA_{16}$.

2.10 Provide the BCD bit encoding for the following decimal numbers:
    (a) 11264
    (b) 8192

2.11 Represent the following numbers in excess-3:
    (a) 678
    (b) 32874
    (c) 61440

2.12 What is the excess-3 equivalent of octal 1543?

2.13 Represent the following binary numbers in BCD:
    (a) 0001 1001 0101 0001
    (b) 0110 0001 0100 0100 0000

2.14 Express the following binary numbers into excess-3:
    (a) 0101 1001 0111
    (b) 0110 1001 0000

2.15 Perform the following unsigned binary addition. Include the answer in decimal.

$$\begin{array}{r} 1011.01 \\ +\ 0110.011 \\ \hline \end{array}$$

2.16 Perform the indicated arithmetic operations in binary. Assume that the numbers are in decimal and represented using 8 bits. Express results in decimal. Use two's complement approach for carrying out all subtractions.

(a) 14
+17

(c) 32
−14

(b) 34
+28

(d) 34
−42

2.17 Using twos complement, perform the following subtraction: $3AFA_{16} - 2F1E_{16}$. Include answer in hex.

2.18 Using 9's and 10's complement arithmetic, perform the following arithmetic operations:
(a) $254_{10} - 132_{10}$
(b) $783_{10} - 807_{10}$

2.19 Perform the following arithmetic operations in binary using 6 bits. Assume all numbers are signed decimal. Use two's complement arithmetic. Indicate if there is any overflow.

(a) 14
+ 8

(b) 7
+(−7)

(c) 27
+(−19)

(d) (−24)
+(−19)

(e) 19
−(−12)

(f) (−17)
−(−16)

2.20 Perform the following unsigned multiplication in binary using a minimum number of bits required for each decimal number using pencil and paper method:

$$12 \times 52$$

2.21 Perform the following unsigned division in binary using a minimum number of bits required for each decimal number:

$$3 \overline{)14}$$

2.22 Obtain the bit encoding of the following decimal numbers and then perform the indicated arithmetic operations using BCD:

(a) 54
+48

(b) 782
+219

(c) 82
−58

2.23 Obtain the bit encoding of the following decimal numbers and then perform addition using BCD: $999 + 999$

2.24 Find the odd parity bit for the following binary message to be transmitted: 10110000.

2.25 Repeat Problem 2.20 using repeated addition.

2.26 Repeat Problem 2.21 using repeated subtraction.

2.27 Assume 2 two's-complement signed numbers, $M = 11111101_2$ and $Q = 1111100_2$. Perform signed multiplication using the algorithm described in Section 2.5.1.

2.28 Using the signed division algorithm described in section 2.5.1, find the quotient and remainder of (-25)/3.

2.29   Assume an 8-bit number, 0001100_2. Find the result after:

   (a)   logically shifting the number twice to the left. Will the number be multiplied by 4 correctly if the number is considered unsigned?

   (b)   arithmetically shifting the number two times to the right. Will the number be correctly divided by 8 if the number is considered signed?

2.30   If a transmitting computer sends an 8-bit binary message 11000111 using an even parity bit. Write the 9-bit data with the parity bit in the most significant bit. If the receiving computer receives the 9-bit data as 110000111, is the 8-bit message received correctly? Comment.

2.31   Perform the following binary addition operation; assume that the numbers are in two's complement form. Express result in decimal. Determine sign and overflow flags.

$$(0000\ 1111) + (1111\ 1100)$$

3

DIGITAL LOGIC GATES, BOOLEAN ALGEBRA, AND SIMPLIFICATION

Digital circuits contain hardware elements called "gates" that perform logic operations on binary numbers. Devices such as transistors can be used to perform the logic operations. Boolean algebra is a mathematical system that provides the basis for these logic operations. George Boole, an English mathematician, introduced this theory of digital logic. The term *Boolean Variable* is used to mean the two-valued binary digit 0 or 1.

This chapter describes fundamentals of digital logic gates, basic logic operations, Boolean algebra, and minimization of Boolean functions using identities. Finally, topics such as Concensus theorem, glitches in combinational circuits, obtaining complement of a Boolean function, and XOR/XNOR operations are also included.

3.1 Basic Logic Operations

Boolean algebra uses three basic logic operations namely, NOT, OR, and AND. These operations are described next.

3.1.1 NOT Operation

The NOT operation inverts or provides the ones complement of a binary digit. This operation takes a single input and generates one output. The NOT operation of a binary digit provides the following result:

$$NOT\ 0 = 1$$
$$NOT\ 1 = 0$$

Therefore, NOT of a Boolean variable A, written as $\overline{A}$ (or A') is 1 if and only if A is 0. Similarly, $\overline{A}$ is 0 if and only if A is 1. This definition may also be specified in the form of a truth table:

Input	Output
A	$\overline{A}$
0	1
1	0

The truth table contains the inputs and outputs of a digital logic circuit. Note that the truth table is used to verify the correct operation of the digital circuit. The symbolic representation of an electronic circuit that implements a NOT operation is shown in Figure 3.1. The NOT gate is also referred to as an "inverter" because it inverts the voltage levels. As discussed in Chapter 1, a transistor acts as an inverter. A 0-volt at the input generates a 5-volt output; a 5-volt input provides a 0-volt output.

Bipolar or MOS transistors are used for implementing the logic gates. 74HC chips use CMOS while 74LS chips use TTL. For example, 74HC04 uses CMOS and 74LS04 uses TTL. Both are commercially available 14-pin inverter chips. Each contains six independent inverters in the same chip as shown in Figure 3.2.

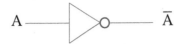

FIGURE 3.1   Symbol for a NOT gate

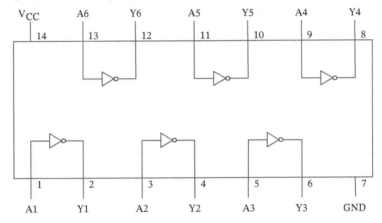

FIGURE 3.2   Pin diagram for the 74HC04 or 74LS04

Computers normally include a NOT instruction to perform the ones complement of a binary number on a bit-by-bit (bitwise) basis. An 8-bit computer can perform NOT operation on an 8-bit binary number. For example, the computer can execute a NOT instruction on an 8-bit binary number 01101111 to provide the result 10010000. The computer utilizes an internal electronic circuit consisting of eight inverters to invert the 8-bit data in parallel.

3.1.2   OR operation

The OR operation for two variables A and B generates a result of 1 if A or B, or both are 1. However, if both A and B are zero, then the result is 0.

A plus sign + (logical sum) or ∨ symbol is normally used to represent OR. The OR operation between two binary digits is

$$0 + 0 = 0$$
$$0 + 1 = 1$$
$$1 + 0 = 1$$
$$1 + 1 = 1$$

The truth table for the OR operation is:

Inputs		
A	B	$Output = A + B$
0	0	0
0	1	1
1	0	1
1	1	1

Figure 3.3 shows the symbolic representation of an OR gate.

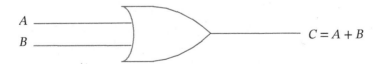

FIGURE 3.3   Symbol for an OR gate

The 74HC32 (or 74LS32) is a commercially available quad two-input 14-pin OR gate chip. This chip contains four two-input/1-output independent OR gates as shown in Figure 3.4.

To understand the logic OR operation, consider Figure 3.5. V is a voltage source, A and B are switches, and L is an electrical lamp. L will be turned ON if either switch A or B, or both, are closed; otherwise, the lamp will be OFF. Hence, $L = A + B$. Computers normally contain an OR instruction to perform the OR operation between two binary numbers. For example, the computer can execute an OR instruction to OR $3A_{16}$ with 21_{16} on a bit-by-bit (bitwise) basis:

$$
\begin{aligned}
3A_{16} &= 0011\ 1010 \\
21_{16} &= 0010\ 0001 \\
\hline
&\ \ \underbrace{0011}_{3}\ \underbrace{1011}_{B}{}_{16}
\end{aligned}
$$

The computer typically utilizes eight two-input OR gates to accomplish this.

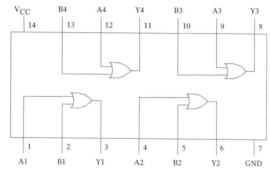

FIGURE 3.4   Pin diagram for 74HC32 or 74LS32

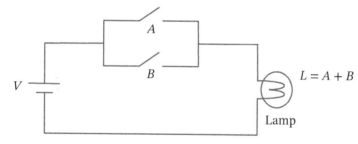

FIGURE 3.5   An example of the OR operation

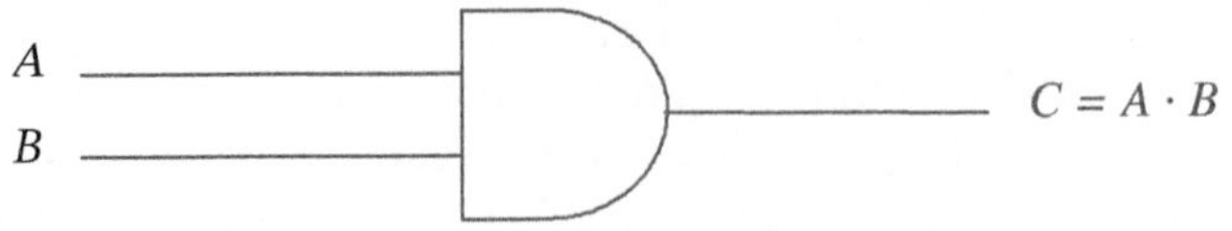

$$A$$
$$B$$
$$C = A \cdot B$$

FIGURE 3.6   AND gate symbol

3.1.3   AND operation

The AND operation for two variables A and B generates a result of 1 if both A and B are 1. However, if either A or B, or both are zero, then the result is 0.

The dot $\cdot$ and $\wedge$ symbol are both used to represent the AND operation. The AND operation between two binary digits is:

$$0 \cdot 0 = 0$$

$$0 \cdot 1 = 0$$

$$1 \cdot 0 = 0$$

$$1 \cdot 1 = 1$$

The truth table for the AND operation is

Inputs		
A	B	$Output = A \cdot B = AB$
0	0	0
0	1	0
1	0	0
1	1	1

Figure 3.6 shows the symbolic representation of an AND gate.

The 74HC08 (or 74LS08) is a commercially available quad two-input 14-pin AND gate chip. This chip contains four two-input/one-output independent AND gates as shown in Figure 3.7. To illustrate the logic AND operation, consider Figure 3.8. The lamp L will be on when both switches A and B are closed; otherwise, the lamp L will be turned OFF. Hence,

$$L = A \cdot B$$

Computers normally have an instruction to perform the AND operation between two binary numbers. For example, the computer can execute an AND instruction to perform ANDing 31_{16} with $A1_{16}$ on a bit-by-bit basis (bit-wise) as follows:

$$
\begin{aligned}
31_{16} &= 0011\ 0001 \\
A1_{16} &= 1010\ 0001 \\
\hline
&\quad\ 0010\ 0001 \\
&\qquad\ 2 \qquad\ 1_{16}
\end{aligned}
$$

The computer utilizes eight two-input AND gates to accomplish this.

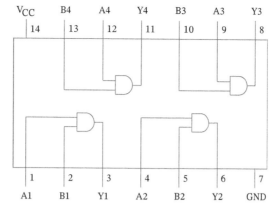

FIGURE 3.7   Pin Diagram for 74HC08 or 74LS08

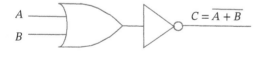

FIGURE 3.8   An example of the AND operation

3.2   Other Logic Operations

The four other important logic operations are NOR, NAND, Exclusive-OR (XOR) and Exclusive-NOR (XNOR).

3.2.1   NOR operation

Inverted OR is called NOR. This means that the NOR output is produced by inverting the output of an OR operation. Figure 3.9 shows a NOR gate along with its truth table. Figure 3.10 shows the symbolic representation of a NOR gate. In the figure, the small circle at the output of the NOR gate is called the inversion bubble. The 74HC02 (or 74LS02) is a commercially available quad two-input 14-pin NOR gate chip. This chip contains four two-input/1-output independent NOR gates as shown in Figure 3.11.

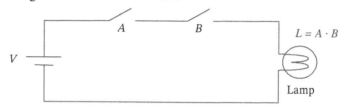

NOR gate Truth Table		
A	B	$C = \overline{A + B}$
0	0	1
0	1	0
1	0	0
1	1	0

FIGURE 3.9   A NOR gate with its truth table

FIGURE 3.10   NOR gate symbol

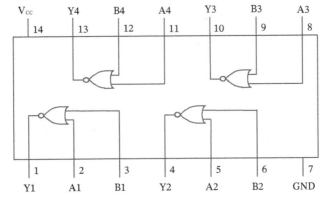

FIGURE 3.11   Pin diagram for 74HC02 or 74LS02

3.2.2   NAND operation

Inverted AND is called NAND. This means that the NAND output is generated by inverting the output of an AND operation. Figure 3.12 shows a NAND gate and its truth table. Figure 3.13 shows the symbolic representation of a NAND gate.

The 74HC00 (or 74LS00) is a commercially available quad two-input/1-output 14-pin NAND gate chip. This chip contains four two-input/1-output independent NAND gates as shown in Figure 3.14.

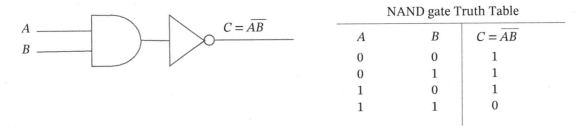

NAND gate Truth Table		
A	B	$C = \overline{AB}$
0	0	1
0	1	1
1	0	1
1	1	0

FIGURE 3.12   NAND gate and its truth table

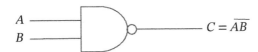

FIGURE 3.13   NAND gate symbol

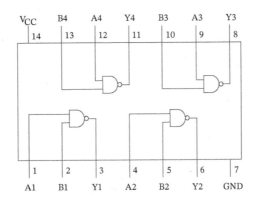

FIGURE 3.14   Pin diagram for 74HC00 or 74LS00

3.2.3 Exclusive-OR operation (XOR)

The Exclusive-OR operation (XOR) generates an output of 1 if the inputs are different and 0 if the inputs are the same. The $\oplus$ or $\forall$ symbol is used to represent the XOR operation. The XOR operation between two binary digits is:

$$0 \oplus 0 = 0$$

$$0 \oplus 1 = 1$$

$$1 \oplus 0 = 1$$

$$1 \oplus 1 = 0$$

Most computers have an instruction to perform the bit-by-bit (bit-wise) XOR operation. Consider XORing $3A_{16}$ with 21_{16}:

$$3A_{16} = 0011 \ 1010$$
$$21_{16} = 0010 \ 0001$$
$$\overline{\quad\quad\quad\quad\quad}$$
$$\underbrace{0001}_{1} \ \underbrace{1011}_{B_{16}}$$

Note that XORing a number with another binary number of the same length with all 1's will generate the ones complement of the original number. For example, consider XORing 31_{16} with FF_{16}:

$$
\begin{array}{lcc}
& 31_{16} & 0011 \ 0001 \\
\text{1's complement of } 31_{16} & & 1100 \ 1110 \\
& & \underbrace{1100}_{C} \ \underbrace{1110}_{E_{16}}
\end{array}
$$

$$
\begin{array}{lcc}
31_{16} \oplus FF_{16} & & 0011 \ 0001 \\
& & 1111 \ 1111 \\
& & \overline{\quad\quad\quad\quad} \\
& & \underbrace{1100}_{C} \ \underbrace{1110}_{E_{16}}
\end{array}
$$

The truth table for Exclusive-OR operation is

Inputs		Output
A	*B*	$C = A \oplus B$
0	0	0
0	1	1
1	0	1
1	1	0

The equation for output (C) in terms of the inputs (A,B) can be obtained by inspecting the truth table. From the truth table, $C = 1$ for:

$$\bar{A} \ (A = 0) \text{ AND } B \ (B = 1)$$

OR

$$A \ (A = 1) \text{ AND } \bar{B} \ (B = 0).$$

Therefore,

$$C = A \oplus B = \bar{A} B + A \bar{B}$$

Figure 3.15 shows the AOI (AND-OR-INVERT) implementation of an XOR gate using AND, OR, and NOT gates. Figure 3.16 (a) shows the symbolic representation of the Exclusive-OR gate while Figure 3.16(b) shows the truth table.

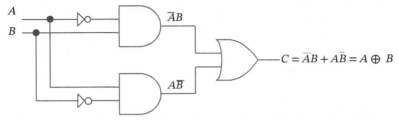

FIGURE 3.15   AND-OR-INVERTER (AOI) Implementation of the Exclusive-OR gate

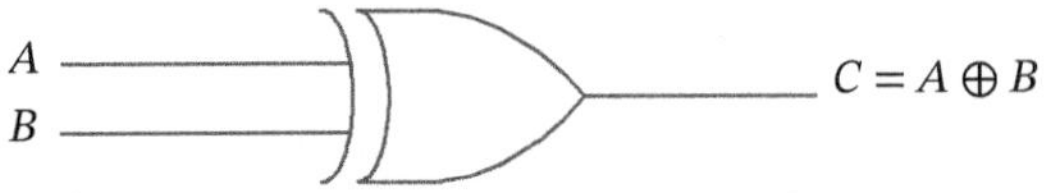

A ————\
B ———— $C = A \oplus B$

(a)   XOR symbol

Inputs		Output
A	B	$C = A \oplus B$
0	0	0
0	1	1
1	0	1
1	1	0

(b)   Truth table for XOR

FIGURE 3.16   XOR gate and its truth table

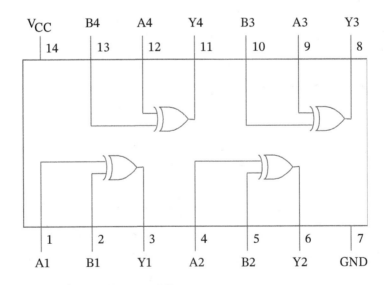

FIGURE 3.17   Pin diagram for 74HC86 or 74LS86

The 74HC86 (or 74LS86) is a commercially available quad 2-input 14-pin Exclusive-OR gate chip. This chip contains four 2-input/1-output independent exclusive-OR gates as shown in Figure 3.17.

3.2.4   Exclusive-NOR Operation (XNOR)

Inverted Exclusive-OR is called Exclusive-NOR. This means that the XNOR output is generated by inverting the output of an XOR operation.

Figure 3.18 shows the AOI (AND-OR-INVERT) implementation of an XNOR gate using AND, OR, and NOT gates. Figures 3.19 (a) and (b) show its symbolic representation along with the truth table. The XNOR operation is represented by the symbol $\odot$. Therefore $C = \overline{A \oplus B} = A \odot B$. The XNOR operation is also called *equivalence*. From the truth table, output C is 1 if both A and B are 0's or both A and B are 1's; otherwise, C is 0. That is, $C = 1$, for $\overline{A}$ $(A = 0)$ AND $\overline{B}$ $(B = 0)$ OR A $(A = 1)$ AND B $(B = 1)$. Hence, $C = A \odot B = \overline{A}\,\overline{B} + AB$.

The 74HC266 (or 74LS266) is a quad 2-input/1-output 14-pin Exclusive-NOR gate chip. This chip contains four 2-input/1-output independent Exclusive-NOR gates shown in Figure 3.20.

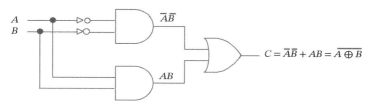

FIGURE 3.18   AND-OR-INVERTER (AOI) Implementation of the Exclusive-OR gate

(a) XNOR Symbol

Inputs		Output
A	*B*	$C = \overline{A \oplus B}$
0	0	1
0	1	0
1	0	0
1	1	1

(b) XNOR Truth Table

FIGURE 3.19   Exclusive-NOR symbol along with its truth table

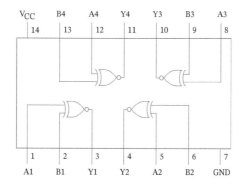

FIGURE 3.20   Pin Diagram for 74HC266 or 74LS266

Note that the symbol C is chosen arbitrarily in all the above logic operations to represent the output of each logic gate. Also, note that all logic gates (except NOT) can have at least two inputs with only one output. The NOT gate, on the other hand, has one input and one output.

3.3   Positive and Negative Logic

The inputs and outputs of logic gates are represented by either logic 1 or logic 0. There are two ways of assigning voltage levels to the logic levels, positive logic and negative logic. The positive logic convention assigns a HIGH (H) voltage for logic 1 and LOW (L) voltage for logic 0. On the other hand, in the negative logic convention, a logic 1 = LOW (L) voltage and logic 0 = HIGH (H) voltage.

The IC data sheets typically define these levels in terms of voltage levels rather than logic levels. The designer decides on whether to use positive or negative logic. As an example, consider a gate with the following truth table:

A	B	f
L	L	H
L	H	H
H	L	H
H	H	L

Using positive logic, (H = 1 and L = 0) the following table is obtained:

A	B	f
0	0	1
0	1	1
1	0	1
1	1	0

This is the truth table for a NAND gate. However, negative logic, (H = 0 and L = 1) provides the following table:

A	B	f
1	1	0
1	0	0
0	1	0
0	0	1

This is the truth table for a NOR gate. Note that converting from positive to negative logic and vice versa for logic gates basically provides the dual (discussed later in this chapter) of a function. This means that changing 0's to 1's and 1's to 0's for both inputs and outputs of a logic gate, the logic gate is converted from a NOR gate to a NAND gate as shown in the example. In this book, the positive logic convention will be used.

Note that positive logic and active high logic are equivalent (HIGH = 1, LOW = 0). On the other hand, negative logic and active low logic are equivalent (HIGH = 0, LOW = 1). A signal is "active high" if it performs the required function when HIGH (H = 1). An "active low" signal, on the other hand, performs the required function when LOW (L = 0). A signal is said to be asserted when it is active. A signal is disasserted when it is not at its active level.

Active levels may be associated with inputs and outputs of logic gates. For example, an AND gate performs a logical AND operation on two active HIGH inputs and provides an active HIGH output. This also means that if both the inputs of the AND gate are asserted, the output is asserted.

3.4   Boolean Algebra

Boolean algebra provides basis for logic operations using binary variables. Alphabetic characters are used to represent the binary variables. A binary variable can have either true or complement value. For example, the binary variable A can be either A and/or $\overline{A}$ in a Boolean function.

A Boolean function is an operation expressing logical operations between binary variables. The Boolean function can have a value of 0 or 1. As an example of a Boolean function, consider the following:

$$f(A, B, C) = \overline{A}\,\overline{B} + C$$

Here, the Boolean function f is 1 if both $\overline{A}$ and $\overline{B}$ are 1 or C is 1; otherwise, C is 0. Note that $\overline{A}$ means that if $A = 1$, then $\overline{A} = 0$. Thus, when $B = 1$, then $\overline{B} = 0$. It can, therefore, be concluded that f is one when $A = 0$ and $B = 0$ or $C = 1$.

A truth table can be used to represent a Boolean function. As mentioned before, the truth table lists inputs and outputs. Furthermore, the truth table provides the value of the Boolean function (f) as 1 or 0 for each combination of the input binary variables (A,B,C). Table 3.1 provides the truth table for the Boolean function $f(A,B,C) = \overline{A}\,\overline{B} + C$. Table 3.1 contains three input variables (A,B,C) and one output variable (f).

Note that the priorities of the basic operators for evaluating Boolean expressions are as follows:

1. Parentheses
2. NOT
3. AND
4. OR

This means that for evaluating a Boolean expression, the parentheses will have the highest priority while the OR operation will have the lowest priority. For example, consider the truth table of Table 3.1. In order to compute f of the first line (top row) of Table 3.1, the input values are $A = 0$, $B = 0$, and $C = 0$. The equation for f is $f = \overline{A}\,\overline{B} + C$. Since there are no parentheses, the NOT operation will have the highest priority followed by AND, and then OR. Hence, $f = \overline{0}.\overline{0} + 0 = 1.1 + 0 = 1 + 0 = 1$. Similarly, the values for output, f for other input values can be obtained.

As mentioned in sections 3.2.3 and 3.2.4, output, f can be obtained from the truth table as $f = \overline{A}\,\overline{B}\,C + \overline{A}\,BC + \overline{A}B\overline{C} + A\overline{B}C + ABC$. However, the function, f can be simplified as $f = \overline{A}\,\overline{B} + C$ using the Boolean identities to be discussed in the next section. This simplified form of output, f can be implemented using fewer gates resulting in lower implementation cost. Note that the original equation for f obtained from the truth table and the simplified form for f are equivalent since they have the same truth table of Table 3.1.

Next, the Boolean function, f can be represented in the form of a logic diagram or schematic. Figure 3.21 shows the logic diagram or schematic for $f = \overline{A}\,\overline{B} + C$. The Boolean expression, $f = \overline{A}\,\overline{B} + C$ contains two terms $\overline{A}\,\overline{B}$ and C, which are inputs to logic gates. Each term may include a single or multiple variables, called"literals," that may or may not be complemented. For example, $f = \overline{A}\,\overline{B} + C$ contains three literals, $\overline{A}$, $\overline{B}$ and C. Note that a variable and its complement are both called literals. For two variables, the literals are A, B, $\overline{A}$, and $\overline{B}$.

TABLE 3.1   Truth Table for $f = \overline{A}\,\overline{B} + C$

A	B	C	f
0	0	0	1
0	0	1	1
0	1	0	0
0	1	1	1
1	0	0	0
1	0	1	1
1	1	0	0
1	1	1	1

FIGURE 3.21   Logic diagram for $f = \overline{A}\,\overline{B} + C$

3.4.1   Boolean Identities

Here is list of Boolean identities that are useful in simplifing Boolean expressions:

1.   a) $A + 0 = A$ b) $A \cdot 1 = A$
2.   a) $A + 1 = 1$ b) $A \cdot 0 = 0$
3.   a) $A + A = A$ b) $A \cdot A = A$
4.   a) $A + \overline{A} = 1$ b) $A \cdot \overline{A} = 0$
5.   a) $\overline{\overline{A}} = A$
6.   Commutative Law:
      a) $A + B = B + A$ b) $A \cdot B = B \cdot A$
7.   Associative Law:
      a) $A + (B + C) = (A + B) + C$ b) $A \cdot (B \cdot C) = (A \cdot B) \cdot C$
8.   Distributive Law:
      a) $A \cdot (B + C) = A \cdot B + A \cdot C$ b) $A + B \cdot C = (A + B) \cdot (A + C)$
9.   DeMorgan's Theorem:
      a) $\overline{A + B + C \cdots} = \overline{A} \cdot \overline{B} \cdot \overline{C} \cdots$ b) $\overline{A \cdot B \cdot C \cdots} = \overline{A} + \overline{B} + \overline{C} \cdots$

In the list, each identity identified by b) on the right is the dual of the corresponding identity a) on the left. Note that the dual of a Boolean expression is obtained by changing 1's to 0's and 0's to 1's if they appear in the equation, and AND to OR and OR to AND on both sides of the equal sign.

For example, consider identity 4. Expression 4a is the dual of Expression 4b because going from left to right, the OR in 4a is replaced by AND in 4b and then, 1 in 4a is replaced by 0 in 4b. Thus, 4a is dual of 4b and vice versa. This implies that if an expression is true, then its dual is also true. As another example, consider $1 + 1 = 1$, which is a true Boolean statement, its dual $0.0 = 0$ is also a true statement.

Next, in order to verify some of the identities, consider the following examples:

i)   Identity 2a) $A + 1 = 1$. For $A = 0, A + 1 = 0 + 1 = 1$. For $A = 1, A + 1 = 1 + 1 = 1$
ii)   Identity 4b) $A \cdot \overline{A} = 0$. If $A = 1$, then $\overline{A} = 0$. Hence, $A \cdot \overline{A} = 1 \cdot 0 = 0$
iii) Identity 8b) $A + B \cdot C = (A + B) \cdot (A + C)$ is very useful in manipulating Boolean expressions. This identity can be verified by means of a truth table as follows:

A	B	C	$B \cdot C$	$A + B$	$A + C$	$A + B \cdot C$	$(A+B) \cdot (A+C)$
0	0	0	0	0	0	0	0
0	0	1	0	0	1	0	0
0	1	0	0	1	0	0	0
0	1	1	1	1	1	1	1
1	0	0	0	1	1	1	1
1	0	1	0	1	1	1	1
1	1	0	0	1	1	1	1
1	1	1	1	1	1	1	1

iv) Identities 9a) and 9b) (DeMorgan's Theorem) are useful in determining one's complement of a Boolean expression. DeMorgan's theorem can be verified by means of a truth table as follows:

A	B	$\bar{A}$	$\bar{B}$	$\bar{A}\cdot\bar{B}$	$A+B$	$\overline{A+B}$	$A\cdot B$	$\overline{A\cdot B}$	$\bar{A}+\bar{B}$
0	0	1	1	1	0	1	0	1	1
0	1	1	0	0	1	0	0	1	1
1	0	0	1	0	1	0	0	1	1
1	1	0	0	0	1	0	1	0	0

De Morgan's Theorem can be expressed in a general form for n variables as follows:
$$\overline{A + B + C + D + \cdots} = \bar{A}\cdot\bar{B}\cdot\bar{C}\cdot\bar{D}\cdots$$
$$\overline{A\cdot B\cdot C\cdot D\cdots} = \bar{A} + \bar{B} + \bar{C} + \bar{D} + \cdots$$

The logic gates except for the inverter can have more than two inputs if the logic operation performed by the gate is commutative and associative (Identities 6a and 7a). For example, the OR operation has these two properties as follows: A + B = B + A (Commutative) and A + (B + C) = (A +B) + C = A + B + C (Associative). This can be verified using a truth table. Thus, the OR gate can have more than two inputs. Also, this means that the OR gate inputs can be interchanged. Figure 3.22(a) shows implementation of $f = A + B + C$ using two two-input OR gates. However, implementation of the single three-input OR gate of Figure 3.22(b) requires fewer transistors and less time delay . In contrast, implementation of the three-input OR gate with two two-input OR gates (Figure 3.22(a)) requires more transistors and more time delays. Hence, designers typically implement multiple-input OR gates using a single OR gate (Figure 3.22(b)). The same rule applies to multiple-input AND gates.

Similarly, using the identities 6b and 7b, it can be shown that the AND gate can also have more than two inputs. Note that the NOR and NAND operations, on the other hand, are commutative, but not associative. Therefore, it is not possible to have NOR and NAND gates with more than two inputs. However, NOR and NAND gates with more than two inputs can be obtained by using inverted OR and inverted AND respectively. The Exclusive-OR and Exclusive-NOR operations are both commutative and associative. Thus, these gates can have more than two inputs. However, Exclusive-OR and Exclusive-NOR gates with more than two inputs are uncommon from the hardware point of view.

3.4.2   Simplification Using Boolean Identities
Although there are no defined set of rules for minimizing a Boolean expression, appropriate identities can be used to accomplish this. Consider the Boolean function
$$f = ABCD + \bar{A}BCD + \overline{BC}$$

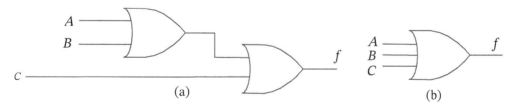

(a)   (b)

FIGURE 3.22   Obtaining a three input OR gate (a) using two two-input OR gates
(b) using a Three-input OR gate

This equation can be implemented using logic gates as shown in Figure 3.23(a). The expression can be simplified by using identities as follows:

$$f = BCD\,(A + \overline{A}) + \overline{BC} \qquad \text{By identity 4a)}$$

$$= BCD \cdot 1 + \overline{BC} \qquad \text{By identity 1b)}$$

$$= BCD + \overline{BC}$$

Assume $BC = E$, then $\overline{BC} = \overline{E}$ and,

$$f = ED + \overline{E}$$

$$= (E + \overline{E})\,(\overline{E} + D) \qquad \text{By identity 8b)}$$

$$= \overline{E} + D \qquad \text{By identity 4a)}$$

Substituting $\overline{E} = \overline{BC}, f = \overline{BC} + D.$

The simplified form is implemented using logic gates in Figure 3.23(b). The logic diagram in Figure 3.23(b) requires only one NAND gate and an OR gate. This implementation is inexpensive compared to the circuit of Figure 3.23(a). Both logic circuits perform the same function. The truth table of Table 3.2 can be used to show that the outputs produced by both circuits are equivalent.

TABLE 3.2 Truth table for f

A	B	C	D	$f = ABCD + \bar{A}BCD + \overline{BC}$	$f = \overline{BC} + D$
0	0	0	0	1	1
0	0	0	1	1	1
0	0	1	0	1	1
0	0	1	1	1	1
0	1	0	0	1	1
0	1	0	1	1	1
0	1	1	0	0	0
0	1	1	1	1	1
1	0	0	0	1	1
1	0	0	1	1	1
1	0	1	0	1	1
1	0	1	1	1	1
1	1	0	0	1	1
1	1	0	1	1	1
1	1	1	0	0	0
1	1	1	1	1	1

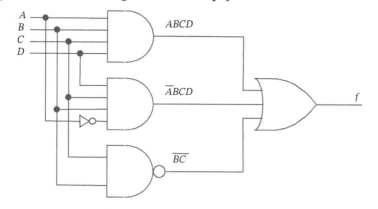

(a) Implementation of $f = ABCD + \bar{A}BCD + \overline{BC}$

(b) Implementation of the simplified function $f = \overline{BC} + D$

FIGURE 3.23   Implementation of Boolean function using logic gates

Example 3.1

Simplify the following functions using Boolean identities:

(i) $f(x, y, z) = \bar{x} + \bar{y} + \overline{xy} + \overline{xy}z$

(ii) $f = \overline{ab}cd + \bar{a}cd + \bar{b}cd + (1 \oplus ab)\, cd$

(iii) $F(X, Y, Z) = XY + X\bar{Z} + XZ$

(iv) $F(A, B, C) = A\,\overline{BC} + AB + \bar{A}\,C$

(v) $F(x, y) = x + \overline{xy} + x + \bar{y}$

(vi) $f(A, B) = A(B \oplus 1)(\bar{A} + B)$

(vii) $F = B(A + B) + A\bar{B} + \bar{B}$

(viii) $F = (x + y + z)(\overline{xy} + \bar{y}z)$

(ix) $f = xy + xy\bar{z} + \bar{x}\,\bar{y}$

(x) $F = \bar{A}BC + ABC + B\bar{C}$

Solution

(i) $f(x, y, z) = \bar{x} + \bar{y} + \overline{xy} + \overline{xy}z = \overline{xy} + \overline{xy} + \overline{xy}z = \overline{xy}(1 + z) = \overline{xy}$

(ii) $f = \bar{a}bcd + \bar{a}cd + \bar{b}cd + (1 \oplus ab)\,cd = \bar{a}bcd + cd(\bar{a} + \bar{b}) + \overline{ab}cd$
        $\quad = \bar{a}bcd + \overline{ab}cd + \overline{ab}cd = \overline{ab}cd$

Note: $1 \oplus ab = \bar{1}.(ab) + 1.\overline{(ab)} = 0 + \overline{(ab)} = \overline{(ab)}$

(iii) $F(X,Y,Z) = XY + X\bar{Z} + XZ = X(Y + \bar{Z} + Z) = X(Y + 1) = X.\,1 = X$

(iv) $F(A,B,C) = A\overline{BC} + AB + \bar{A}\,\bar{C} = A(\bar{B} + \bar{C}) + AB + \bar{A}\,\bar{C} = A\bar{B} + A\,\bar{C} + AB + \bar{A}\,\bar{C}$
        $\quad = A(B + \bar{B}) + \bar{C}(A + \bar{A}) = A + \bar{C}$

(v) $f(x, y) = x + \overline{xy} + x + \bar{y} = x + \overline{xy} + \bar{y} = (x + \bar{x})(x + y) + \bar{y} = x + y + \bar{y} = x + 1 = 1$

(vi) $f(A, B) = A(B \oplus 1)(\bar{A} + B) = A\bar{B}(\bar{A} + B) = A\bar{B}\bar{A} + A\bar{B}B = 0$

(vii) $F = B(A + B) + A\bar{B} + \bar{B} = AB + BB + A\bar{B} + \bar{B} = AB + B + A\bar{B} + \bar{B} = 1 + AB + A\bar{B} = 1$

(viii) $f = (x + y + z)(\overline{xy} + \overline{yz}) = \overline{xy}x + \overline{xy}y + \overline{xy}z + \overline{yz}x + \overline{yz}y + \overline{yz}z$
        $\quad = xy + xyz + yzx + yz = xy(1 + z) + yz(x + 1) = xy + yz$

(ix) $f = xy + xy\bar{z} + \bar{x}\,\bar{y} = xy(1 + \bar{z}) + \bar{x}\,\bar{y} = xy + \bar{x}\,\bar{y} = x \odot y$

(x) $F = \bar{A}BC + ABC + B\bar{C} = BC(\bar{A} + A) + B\bar{C} = B(C + \bar{C}) = B.1 = B$

Example 3.2

(i)   Show that $f(a, b) = \overline{(a + \bar{b})(\bar{a} + b)}$ can be implemented using a single logic gate.

(ii)   Show that $f(A, B, C, D) = \overline{(\bar{A} + \bar{B})(\bar{C} + \bar{D})}$ can be implemented using two AND and one OR gates.

(iii)   Express $f(X, Y) = (X + \bar{X}Y)(X + Y)$ using a single two-input gate.

(iv)   Express $f(A, B, C)$ given $\bar{f}(A, B, C) = (\bar{A} + \bar{B} + \bar{C}) + \overline{ABC}$ using two two-input logic gates.

Solution

(i)   Show that $f(a, b) = \overline{(a + \bar{b})(\bar{a} + b)}$ can be implemented using a single logic gate.

Solution: Using DeMorgan's theorem, $f = \overline{(a + \bar{b})(\bar{a} + b)}$
$$= \overline{(a + \bar{b})} + \overline{(\bar{a} + b)} = (\bar{a} \cdot b) + (a \cdot \bar{b}) = \bar{a}\,b + a\,\bar{b} = a \oplus b$$

(ii)   Show that $f(A, B, C, D) = \overline{(\bar{A} + \bar{B})(\bar{C} + \bar{D})}$ can be implemented using two AND and one OR gates.

Solution: $f(A, B, C, D) = \overline{(\overline{AB})(\overline{CD})}$ using DeMorgan's theorem. Again using De Morgan's theorem,

$\quad f = AB + CD.$

(iii)   Express $f(X, Y) = (X + \bar{X}Y)(X + Y)$ using a single two-input OR gate.

Solution: $f(X,Y) = (X + \bar{X})(X + Y)(X + Y)$ using distributive law. Hence, $f = X + Y.$

(iv)   Express $f(A, B, C)$ given $\bar{f}(A, B, C) = (\bar{A} + \bar{B} + \bar{C}) + \overline{ABC}$ using two two-input logic gates.

Solution: Using DeMorgan's theorem, $f(A, B, C) = \bar{\bar{f}} = \overline{(\bar{A} + \bar{B} + \bar{C}) + \overline{ABC}}$
$$= (ABC) \cdot (ABC) = ABC$$

Example 3.3

Simplify each of the following Boolean expressions as much as possible using identities:

(i) $f(x,y,z) = \overline{y}z + x\overline{y}z + \overline{x}\,\overline{y}z$

(ii) $F(A, B) = (A + \overline{AB})(\,\overline{A+B})(\overline{A})$

(iii) $f(x,y,z) = x\overline{z} + z + \overline{y}z$

(iv) $F(A, B) = (A + \overline{B})(A + B)(\overline{AB})$

(v) $F(A, B, C) = \overline{B}C + \overline{A}\,\overline{B}C + B\overline{C}$

(vi) $F(A, B, C) = ((A + \overline{B}) + (A + \overline{B})C)(\overline{A}\,\overline{B}\,\overline{C})$

Solution

(i) $f(x, y, z) = \overline{y}z + x\overline{y}z + \overline{x}\,\overline{y}z$

Solution: $f(x, y, z) = \overline{y}z(1 + x + \overline{x}) = \overline{y}z.(1) = \overline{y}z$

(ii) $F(A, B) = (A + \overline{AB})(A + B)(\overline{A})$

Solution: $F(A, B) = (A + \overline{A})(A + B)(\overline{A+B})(\overline{A}) = (A + B)(\overline{A}) = A\overline{A} + \overline{A}B = \overline{A}B$

(iii) $f(x, y, z) = x\overline{z} + z + \overline{y}z$

Solution: $f(x, y, z) = x\overline{z} + z(1 + \overline{y}) = x\overline{z} + z = z + x\overline{z} = (z + x)(z + \overline{z}) = x + z$

(iv) $F(A, B) = (A + \overline{B})(A + B)(\overline{AB})$

Solution: $F(A, B) = (AA + A\overline{B} + AB + B\overline{B})(\overline{A} + \overline{B}) = (A + A(\overline{B} + B) + 0)(\overline{A} + \overline{B})$
$\qquad\qquad = A(\overline{A} + \overline{B}) = A\overline{A} + A\overline{B} = A\overline{B}$

(v) $F(A, B, C) = \overline{B}C + \overline{A}\,\overline{B}C + B\overline{C}$

Solution: $F(A, B, C) = \overline{B}C(1 + \overline{A}) + B\overline{C} = \overline{B}C + B\overline{C} = B \oplus C$

(vi) $F(A, B, C) = ((A + \overline{B}) + (A + \overline{B})C)(\overline{A}\,\overline{B}\,\overline{C})$

Solution: Let $D = A + \overline{B}$. Hence $F(A, B, C) = (D + DC)(\overline{A}\,\overline{B}\,\overline{C}) = D(1 + C)(\overline{A}\,\overline{B}\,\overline{C}) = D(\overline{A}\,\overline{B}\,\overline{C})$
Therefore, $F(A, B, C) = (A + \overline{B})(\overline{A}\,\overline{B}\,\overline{C}) = A(\overline{A}\,\overline{B}\,\overline{C}) + \overline{B}(\overline{A}\,\overline{B}\,\overline{C}) = 0 + (\overline{A}\,\overline{B}\,\overline{C}) = \overline{A}\,\overline{B}\,\overline{C}$

3.4.3   Consensus Theorem

The Consensus Theorem is expressed as $AB + \overline{A}C + BC = AB + \overline{A}C$.

The theorem states that the AND term BC can be eliminated from the expression if one of the literals such as B is ANDed with the true value of another literal (A) and the other term C is ANDed with its complement $(\overline{A})$. This theorem can sometimes be applied to simplify Boolean equations. The Consensus theorem can be proved as follows:

$$AB + \overline{A}C + BC = AB + \overline{A}C + BC(A + \overline{A})$$

$$= AB + \overline{A}C + ABC + \overline{A}BC$$

$$= AB + ABC + \overline{A}C + \overline{A}BC$$

$$= AB(1 + C) + \overline{A}C(1 + B)$$

$$= AB + \overline{A}C$$

The dual of the Consensus Theorem can be expressed as

$$(A + B)(\overline{A} + C)(B + C) = (A + B)(\overline{A} + C)$$

To illustrate how a Boolean expression can be manipulated by applying the Consensus Theorem, consider the following:

$$f = (B + \bar{D})(\bar{B} + C)$$

$$= B\bar{B} + BC + \bar{B}\bar{D} + C\bar{D}$$

$$= BC + \bar{B}\bar{D} + C\bar{D} \text{, since } B\bar{B} = 0$$

Because C is ANDed with B, and $\bar{D}$ is ANDed with its complement $\bar{B}$, by using the Consensus theorem, $C\bar{D}$ can be eliminated. Thus, $f = BC + \bar{B}\,\bar{D}$.

3.4.4   Getting Rid of Glitches or Hazards in Combinational Circuits

The Consensus Theorem can be used in logic circuits for avoiding undesirable behavior. To illustrate this, consider the logic circuits in Figure 3.24. In Figure 3.24(a), the output is one (i) if B and C are 1 and $A = 0$ or (ii) if B and C are 1 and $A = 1$.

Suppose that in Figure 3.24 (a), $B = 1$, $C = 1$, and $A = 0$. Assume that the propagation delay time of each gate is 10 ns (nanoseconds). The circuit output f will be 1 after 30 ns (3 gate delays). Now, if input A changes from 0 to 1, the outputs of NOT gate 1 and AND gate 2 will be 0 and 1 respectively after 10 ns. This will make output $f = 1$ after 20 ns. The output of AND gate 3 will be low after 20 ns, which will not affect the output of f.

Now, assume that B and C stay at 1 while A changes from 1 to 0. The outputs of NOT gate 1 and AND gate 2 will be 1 and 0 respectively after 10 ns. Because the output of AND gate 3 is 0 from the previous case, this will change the output of OR gate 4 to 0 for a brief period of time. After 10 ns, the output of AND gate 3 changes to 1, making the output of f HIGH (desired value). Note that, for $B = 1$, $C = 1$, and $A = 0$, the output f should have stayed at 1 from the equation $f = AB + \bar{A}C$. However, f changed to zero for a short period of time. This change is called a "glitch" or "hazard" and occurs from the gate delays in a circuit. Glitches can cause circuit malfunction and should be eliminated. Application of the Consensus theorem gets rid of the glitch. By adding the redundant term BC, the modified logic circuit for f is obtained. Figure 3.24(b) shows the logic circuit. Now, consider the case in which the glitch occurs in Figure 3.24(a) when B and C stay at 1 while A changes from 1 to 0. For the circuit in Figure 3.24(b) the glitch will disappear, because $BC = 1$ throughout any changes in values of A and $\bar{A}$. Thus, minimization of logic gates might not always be desirable; rather, a circuit without any hazards would be the main objective of the designer.

There are two types of hazards: static and dynamic. Static hazard occurs when a signal should remain at one value, but instead it oscillates a few times before settling back to its original value. Dynamic hazard occurs, when a signal should make a clean transition to a new logic value, but instead it oscillates between the two logic values before making the transition to its final value. Both types of hazards occur because of races in the various paths of a circuit. A race is a situation in which signals traveling through two or more paths compete with each other to affect a common signal. It is, therefore, possible for the final signal value to be determined by the winner of the race. One way to eliminate races is by applying the Consensus theorem as illustrated in the preceding example.

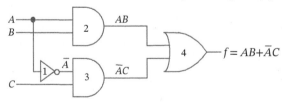

(a) Logic circuit for $f = AB + \bar{A}C$

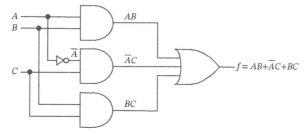

(b) Logic circuit for $f = AB + \overline{A}C + BC$

FIGURE 3.24   Logic circuit for the Consensus Theorem

3.4.5   Complement of a Boolean Function

The complement of a function f can be obtained algebraically by applying DeMorgan's Theorem. It follows from this theorem that the complement of a function can also be derived by taking the dual of the function and complementing each literal.

Example 3.4

Find the complement of the function $f = \overline{C}(AB + \overline{A}\,\overline{B}D + \overline{A}B\overline{D})$

i) Using DeMorgan's Theorem ii) By taking the dual and complementing each literal

Solution

i) Using DeMorgan's Theorem as many times as required, the complement of the function can be obtained:

$$\overline{f} = \overline{\overline{C}\left(AB + \overline{A}\,\overline{B}D + \overline{A}B\overline{D}\right)}$$

$$= \overline{\overline{C}} + \overline{\left(AB + \overline{A}\,\overline{B}D + \overline{A}B\overline{D}\right)}$$

$$= C + \left(\overline{AB} \cdot \overline{\overline{A}\,\overline{B}D} \cdot \overline{\overline{A}B\overline{D}}\right)$$

$$= C + (\overline{A} + \overline{B})(A + B + \overline{D})(A + \overline{B} + D)$$

ii) By taking the dual and complementing each literal, we have:

The dual of f: $\overline{C} + (A + B)(\overline{A} + \overline{B} + D)\,(\overline{A} + B + \overline{D})$

Complementing each literal: $C + (\overline{A} + \overline{B})(A + B + D)(A + \overline{B} + D) = \overline{f}$

3.5   XOR / XNOR Implementations

As mentioned before, the Exclusive-OR operation between two variables A and B can be expressed as:

$$A \oplus B = A\overline{B} + \overline{A}B$$

The Exclusive-NOR or equivalence operation between A and B can be expressed as:

$$A \odot B = \overline{A \oplus B} = AB + \overline{A}\,\overline{B}$$

The following identities are applicable to the Exclusive-OR operation:

i) $A \oplus 0 = A \cdot 1 + \overline{A} \cdot 0 = A$

ii) $A \oplus 1 = A \cdot 0 + \overline{A} \cdot 1 = \overline{A}$

iii) $A \oplus A = A \cdot \overline{A} + \overline{A} \cdot A = 0$

iv) $A \oplus \overline{A} = A \cdot A + \overline{A} \cdot \overline{A} = A + \overline{A} = 1$

Finally, Exclusive-OR is commutative and associative:

$$A \oplus B = B \oplus A$$
$$(A \oplus B) \oplus C = A \oplus (B \oplus C)$$
$$= A \oplus B \oplus C$$

The Exclusive-NOR operation among three or more variables is called an "even function" because the Exclusive-NOR operation among three or more variables includes product terms in which each term contains an even number of 1's. For example, consider Exclusive-NORing three variables as follows:

$$f = \overline{A \oplus B \oplus C} = \overline{(A\overline{B} + \overline{A}B) \oplus C}$$

Let $D = A\overline{B} + \overline{A}B$. Then $\overline{D} = \overline{A\overline{B}} + \overline{\overline{A}B} = AB + \overline{A}\,\overline{B}$.

Hence, $f = \overline{D \oplus C}$

$$= DC + \overline{D}\,\overline{C}$$

$$= (A\overline{B} + \overline{A}B)C + (AB + \overline{A}\,\overline{B})\overline{C}$$

Hence, $f = A\overline{B}C + \overline{A}BC + AB\overline{C} + \overline{A}\,\overline{B}\,\overline{C}$.

Note that in this equation, $f = 1$ when one or more product terms in the equation are 1. However, by inspection, the binary equivalents of the right-hand side of the equation are 101, 011, 110, and 000. That is, the function is expressed as the logical sum (OR) of product terms containing even numbers of ones. Therefore, the function is called an even function. Similarly, it can be shown that Exclusive-OR operation among three or more variables is an odd function.

Exclusive-OR or Exclusive-NOR operation can be used for error detection and correction using parity during data transmission. Note that parity can be classified as either odd or even. The parity is defined by the number of 1's contained in a string of data bits. When the data contains an odd number of 1's, the data is said to have "odd parity"; on the other hand, the data has "even parity" when the number of 1's is even. To illustrate how parity is used as an error check bit during data transmission, consider Figure 3.25.

Suppose that Computer X is required to transmit a 3-bit message to Computer Y. To ensure that data is transmitted properly, an extra bit called the parity bit can be added by the transmitting Computer X before sending the data. In other words, Computer X generates the parity bit depending on whether odd or even parity is used during the transmission. Suppose that odd parity is used. Table 3.3 shows the truth table for the odd parity bit for the three-bit message.

Here $P = 1$ when the three-bit message ABC contains an even number of 1's. Thus, inclusion of the parity bit will ensure that the three-bit message contains an even number of 1's before transmission. $P = 1$ when the message contains an even number of 1's. Therefore, P is an even function. Thus,

$$P = \overline{A \oplus B \oplus C}$$

FIGURE 3.25   Parity generation and checking

TABLE 3.3   Truth table for three-bit message with odd parity

Message			Odd Parity Bit
A	B	C	P
0	0	0	1
0	0	1	0
0	1	0	0
0	1	1	1
1	0	0	0
1	0	1	1
1	1	0	1
1	1	1	0

The transmitting Computer X generates this parity bit. Computer X then transmits 4-bit information (a three-bit message along with the parity bit) to Computer Y. Computer Y receives this 4-bit information and checks to see whether each 4-bit data item contains an odd number of 1's (odd parity). If the parity is odd, Computer Y accepts the 3-bit message; otherwise the computer sends the 4-bit information back to Computer X for retransmission. Note that Computer Y checks the parity of the transmitted data using the equation:

$$E = \overline{P \oplus A \oplus B \oplus C}$$

Here the error $E = 1$ if the four bits have an even number of ones (even parity). That is, at least one of the four bits is changed during transmission. On the other hand, the error bit, $E = 0$ if the 4-bit data has an odd number of ones. Figure 3.26 shows the implementation of the parity bit, $P = \overline{A \oplus B \oplus C}$, and the error bit, $E = \overline{P \oplus A \oplus B \oplus C}$.

Example 3.5

Simplify the following Boolean functions:
(a) $F(A, B) = (A\,\overline{B} \oplus (A\overline{B} \oplus (B \oplus B)))$

(b) $F(A, B) = \overline{(\overline{A} + \overline{B})} + (A \oplus A \oplus AB)$

Solution

(a) $F(A, B) = (A\,\overline{B} \oplus (A\,\overline{B} \oplus (B \oplus B)))$
            $= A\,\overline{B} \oplus (A\,\overline{B} \oplus (0))$
            $= A\,\overline{B} \oplus (A\,\overline{B})$
            $= 0$

(b) $F(A, B) = \overline{(\overline{A}+\overline{B})} + (A \oplus (A \oplus AB))$
            $= (AB) + (0 \oplus AB)$
            $= AB + AB$
            $= 1$

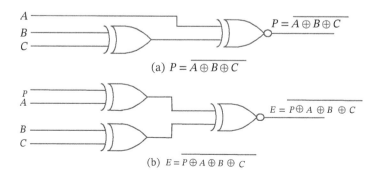

(a) $P = \overline{A \oplus B \oplus C}$

(b) $E = \overline{P \oplus A \oplus B \oplus C}$

FIGURE 3.26   Implementation of parity generation and checking using XOR / XNOR gates

QUESTIONS AND PROBLEMS

3.1 Perform the following operations. Include your answers in hexadecimal. $A6_{16}$ OR 31_{16}; $F7A_{16}$ AND $D80_{16}$; $36_{16} \oplus 2A_{16}$

3.2 Given $A = 1001_2$, $B = 1101_2$, find: A OR B; $B \wedge A$; $\overline{A}$; $A \oplus A$.

3.3 Perform the following operation: $A7_{16} \oplus FF_{16}$
What is the relationship of the result to $A7_{16}$?

3.4 Draw a logic diagram to implement $F = ABCDE$ using only 3-input AND gates.

3.5 Draw a logic diagram using two-input AND and OR gates to implement the following function $F = P(P + Q)(P + Q + R)(P + Q + R + S)$ without any simplification; then analyze the logic circuit to verify that $F = P$.

3.6 Prove the following identities algebraically and by means of truth tables:

(a) $(A + B)\overline{(A + B)} = 0$
(b) $A + \overline{A}B = A + B$
(c) $XY + \overline{X}\,\overline{Y} + X\overline{Y} + \overline{X}Y = 1$
(d) $\overline{(A + \overline{A}B)} = \overline{A}\,\overline{B}$
(e) $(\overline{X} + Y)(X + \overline{Y}) = \overline{X \oplus Y}$
(f) $\overline{B}C + ABC + A\overline{C} = C \oplus (AB)$

3.7 Simplify each of the following Boolean expressions as much as possible using identities:

(a) $XY + (1 \oplus X) + X\overline{Z} + X\overline{Y} + XZ$
(b) $AB\overline{C} + AB\overline{C}D + AB\overline{D}$
(c) $BC + ABC\overline{D} + \overline{A}BCD + ABCD$
(d) $(\overline{X} + \overline{Y})\,\overline{(XY)} + ZXY + X\overline{Z}Y$
(e) $(A + \overline{B})(A + B)(\overline{AB})$
(f) $xz + xyz + xy$
(g) $yz + x\overline{y}z + xz + y$
(h) $(A + \overline{A}B)(A + B) + \overline{B}$

3.8 Using DeMorgan's theorem, draw logic diagrams for $F = AB\overline{C} + \overline{A}\overline{B} + BC$

(a) Using only AND gates and inverters.
(b) Using only OR gates and inverters.

You may use two-input and three-input AND and OR gates for (a) and (b).

3.9 It is desired to compare two 4-bit numbers for equality. If the two numbers are equal, the circuit will generate an output of 1. Draw a logic circuit using a minimum number of gates of your choice.

3.10 Draw a logic diagram for a two-input (A,B) Exclusive-OR operation using only four two-input (A,B) NAND gates. Assume that complemented inputs $\overline{A}$ and $\overline{B}$ are not available.

3.11 Simplify each of the following expressions as much as possible:

(a) $F(X,Y) = (X \oplus \overline{Y}) + (X \oplus (X \oplus XY))$

3.12 Show analytically that $0 \oplus (1 \oplus B) + B = 1$

3.13 Show that the Boolean function, $f = A \oplus B \oplus AB$ between two variables, A and B, can be implemented using a single two-input gate.

3.14 Simplify f, given $f = (0 \oplus x) \oplus (1 \oplus x)$

3.15 From Figure P3.15, find output, F in simplified form.

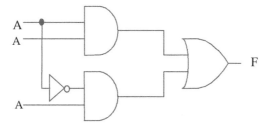

FIGURE P3.15

3.16 Design a parity generation circuit for a 5-bit data (4-bit message with an even parity bit) to be transmitted by computer X. The receiving computer Y will generate an error bit, $E = 1$, if the 5-bit data received has an odd parity; otherwise, $E = 0$. Draw logic diagrams for both parity generation and checking using XOR gates.

3.17 Determine by inspection whether the function, F in each of the following is odd or even, and comment on the result:

(a) $\overline{F} = A \oplus B \oplus C$

(b) $F = A \oplus B \oplus C$

4
MINTERMS, MAXTERMS, AND KARNAUGH MAP

This chapter describes standard representations of a Boolean function using minterms and maxterms, and simplification using Karnaugh maps. An overview of simplification of a Boolean function using Quine-McCluskey method is also provided. Finally, digital circuit implementation using NAND-only and NOR-only gates are included.

4.1   Standard Representations

The standard representations of a Boolean function typically contain either logical product (AND) terms called"minterms" or logical sum (OR) terms called "maxterms." Expressing a Boolean function using literals may lead to errors. However, it is very convenient to express a Boolean function in terms of minterms or maxterms. Furthermore, these standard representations make the minimization procedures easier. The standard representations are also called "Canonical forms."

There are four terms associated with two variables, A and B. These terms are: $\bar{A}\bar{B}$, $\bar{A}B$, $A\bar{B}$, and AB. Each of these four terms is called a minterm. Hence, a minterm is a product (AND) term of all variables in which each variable can be either complemented or uncomplemented. Similarly, there are eight minterms for three variables, A, B, and C. These minterms are $\bar{A}\,\bar{B}\,\bar{C}$, $\bar{A}\,\bar{B}\,C$, $\bar{A}\,B\,\bar{C}$, $\bar{A}\,B\,C$, $A\,\bar{B}\,\bar{C}$, $A\,\bar{B}\,C$, $A\,B\,\bar{C}$, and $A\,B\,C$. These product terms represent numeric values from 0 through 7. In general, there are 2^n minterms for n variables.

A minterm is represented by the symbol m_j, where the subscript j is the decimal equivalent of the binary number of the minterm. For example, the decimal equivalents (j) of the binary numbers represented by the four minterms of two variables, A and B, are $0\,(\bar{A}\,\bar{B})$, $1(\bar{A}\,B)$, $2(A\,\bar{B})$, and $3(A\,B)$. Table 4.1 shows the symbolic representations of the four minterms of two variables are m_0, m_1, m_2, and m_3. In general, the n minterms of p variables ($n = 2^p$) are: m_0, m_1, m_2, ... m_{n-1}.

It has been shown that a Boolean function can be defined by a truth table. A Boolean function can also be expressed in terms of minterms. For example, consider the truth table of Table 4.2. One can determine the function f by logically summing (ORing) the product terms for which f is 1. Therefore, $f(A,B) = \bar{A}\,\bar{B} + A\bar{B} + AB$.

TABLE 4.1   Minterms of two variables A, B

A	B	Minterm	Symbol
0	0	$\bar{A}\bar{B}$	m_0
0	1	$\bar{A}B$	m_1
1	0	$A\bar{B}$	m_2
1	1	AB	m_3

TABLE 4.2   Truth table for expressing f in minterm form

A	B	f
0	0	1
0	1	0
1	0	1
1	1	1

TABLE 4.3   Maxterms of two variables A, B

A	B	Maxterm	Symbol
0	0	$A + B$	M_0
0	1	$A + \bar{B}$	M_1
1	0	$\bar{A} + B$	M_2
1	1	$\bar{A} + \bar{B}$	M_3

This is called the *sum-of-Products* (SOP) expression. A logic diagram of a *sum-of-products* expression contains several AND gates followed by a single OR gate. In terms of minterms, $f(A,B)$ can be expressed as:

$$f(A, B) = \Sigma m(0, 2, 3)$$

The symbol Σ denotes the logical sum (OR) of the minterms.

A maxterm, on the other hand, is obtained by complementing each variable, and then ORing them. Hence, the four maxterms of two variables are $A + B$, $A + \bar{B}$, $\bar{A} + B$, and $\bar{A} + \bar{B}$. Each maxterm is represented by the symbol M_j, where subscript j is the decimal equivalent of the binary number of the maxterm. The symbolic representations of the four maxterms of two variables are M_0, M_1, M_2, and M_3 as shown in Table 4.3.

In the Table 4.3, consider maxterm M_2 as an example. Since $A = 1$ and $B = 0$, the maxterm M_2 is found as $\bar{A} + B$ by taking the logical sum (OR) of complement of A (since $A = 1$) and true value of B (since $B = 0$). In general, there are n maxterms (M_0, M_1, ... , M_{n-1}) for p variables, where $n = 2^p$.

The relationship between minterm and maxterm can be established by using DeMorgan's theorem. Consider, for example, minterm m_1 and maxterm M_1 for two variables:

$$m_1 = \bar{A}B, \qquad M_1 = A + \bar{B}$$

Taking the complement of m_1,
$$\overline{m_1} = \overline{\bar{A}B}$$
$$= \bar{\bar{A}} + \bar{B} \text{ by DeMorgan's Theorem}$$
$$= A + \bar{B}$$
$$= M_1$$

Therefore, $\overline{m_1} = M_1$, or $m_1 = \overline{M_1}$. This implies that $m_j = \overline{M_j}$ or $\overline{m_j} = M_j$. That is, a minterm is the complement of its corresponding maxterm and vice versa.

In order to represent a Boolean function in terms of maxterms, consider the truth table of Table 4.4.

Taking the logical sum of minterms of $\bar{f}(A, B)$,

$$\bar{f}(A, B) = \bar{A}B + A\bar{B} + AB$$

$$= m_1 + m_2 + m_3$$

$$= \Sigma m(1, 2, 3)$$

By taking complement of $\bar{f}(A, B)$,

$$f(A, B) = \bar{\bar{f}}(A, B) = \overline{m_1 + m_2 + m_3} = \overline{m_1} \cdot \overline{m_2} \cdot \overline{m_3}$$

$$= M_1 M_2 M_3 \text{ (since } M_j = \overline{m_j})$$

$$= (A + \bar{B})(\bar{A} + B)(\bar{A} + \bar{B})$$

TABLE 4.4   Truth table for expressing f in maxterm form

A	B	$f(A,B)$	$\bar{f}(A,B)$
0	0	1	0
0	1	0	1
1	0	0	1
1	1	0	1

TABLE 4.5   Truth table for $f(A, B, C) = A + B\bar{C}$

A	B	C	$f = A + B\bar{C}$
0	0	0	0
0	0	1	0
0	1	0	1
0	1	1	0
1	0	0	1
1	0	1	1
1	1	0	1
1	1	1	1

This is called the *product-of-sums* (POS) expression. The logic diagram of a *product-of-sums* expression contains several OR gates followed by a single AND gate. Hence, $f(A,B) = \Pi M(1,2,3)$ where the symbol Π (capital Pi) represents the logical product (AND) of maxterms M_1, M_2, and M_3 in this case. Note that one can express a Boolean function in terms of maxterms by inspecting a truth table and then logically ANDing the maxterms for which the Boolean function has a value of 0.

A Boolean function that is not expressed in terms of sums of minterms or product of maxterms can be represented by a truth table. The function can then be expressed in terms of minterms or maxterms. For example, consider $f(A, B, C) = A + B\bar{C}$. The function $f(A, B, C)$ is not in a sum of minterms or product of maxterms form, since each term does not include all three literals of A, B, and C.

Table 4.5 shows the truth table for $f(A, B, C)$.

From the truth table, the sum of minterm form ($f = 1$) is:
$$f(A, B, C) = \Sigma m(2, 4, 5, 6, 7) = \bar{A}B\bar{C} + A\bar{B}\bar{C} + A\bar{B}C + AB\bar{C} + ABC$$

From the truth table, the product of maxterm form ($f = 0$) is:
$$f(A, B, C) = \Pi M(0, 1, 3) = (A + B + C)(A + B + \bar{C})(A + \bar{B} + \bar{C})$$

Note that $\bar{f}(A, B, C) = \Sigma m(0, 1, 3)$, is obtained by the logical sum of minterms for $f(A, B, C) = 0$. Also, note that a function containing all minterms is 1. This means that in the above truth table, if $f(A, B, C) = 1$ for all eight combinations of A, B, and C, then $f(A, B, C) = \Sigma m(0, 1, 2, 3, 4, 5, 6, 7) = 1$.

As mentioned before, the logic diagram of a sum of minterm form contains several AND gates and a single OR gate. This is illustrated by the logic diagram for $f = \Sigma m(2, 4, 5, 6, 7) = \bar{A}B\bar{C} + A\bar{B}\bar{C} + A\bar{B}C + AB\bar{C} + ABC$ as shown in Figure 4.1.

Similarly, the logic diagram of a product of maxterm expression form contains several OR gates and a single AND gate. This is illustrated by the logic diagram for $f = \Pi M(0, 1, 3) = (A + B + C)(A + B + \bar{C})(A + \bar{B} + \bar{C})$ as shown in Figure 4.2. Note that it is assumed in Figures 4.1 and 4.2 that both true and complemented inputs are available.

Finally, consider converting $f(A,B,C) = (A + B + C)(A + B + \bar{C})(A + \bar{B} + \bar{C})$ into maxterm form using DeMorgan's theorem as follows:
$$f = \bar{\bar{f}}$$

Hence, $f(A, B, C) = \overline{\overline{(A + B + C)(A + B + \bar{C})(A + \bar{B} + \bar{C})}}$.

Next, using DeMorgan's theorem and then converting to maxterm form as follows:

$$f(A, B, C) = \overline{\overline{(A + B + C)} + \overline{(A + B + \bar{C})} + \overline{(A + \bar{B} + \bar{C})}}$$

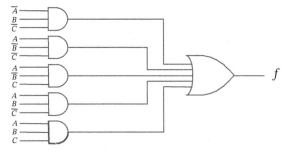

FIGURE 4.1   Logic diagram of a sum of minterms

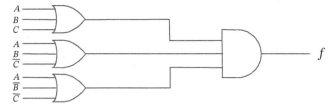

FIGURE 4.2   Logic diagram of a product of maxterms

$$= \overline{\overline{\overline{A}\,\overline{B}\,\overline{C} + \overline{A}\,\overline{B}C + \overline{A}BC}}$$

$$= \overline{\overline{m_0 + m_1 + m_3}}$$

$$= \overline{m_0} \cdot \overline{m_1} \cdot \overline{m_3}$$

$$= M_0 \cdot M_1 \cdot M_3$$

$$= \Pi M(0, 1, 3)$$

Example 4.1

Using the following truth table, express the Boolean function f in terms of sum-of-products (minterms) and product-of-sums (maxterms):

A	B	C	f
0	0	0	0
0	0	1	1
0	1	0	1
0	1	1	1
1	0	0	0
1	0	1	0
1	1	0	1
1	1	1	0

Solution

From the truth table, $f = 1$ for minterms m_1, m_2, m_3, and m_6. Therefore, the Boolean function f can be expressed by taking the logical sum (OR) of these minterms as follows:

$$f = \Sigma m(1, 2, 3, 6) = \overline{A}\,\overline{B}C + \overline{A}B\overline{C} + \overline{A}BC + AB\overline{C}$$

Now, let us express f in terms of maxterms. By inspecting the truth table, $f = 0$ for maxterms M_0, M_4, M_5, and M_7. Therefore, the function f can be obtained by logically ANDing these maxterms as follows:

$$f = \Pi M(0, 4, 5, 7) = (A + B + C)(\overline{A} + B + C)(\overline{A} + B + \overline{C})(\overline{A} + \overline{B} + \overline{C})$$

4.2   Karnaugh Maps

A Karnaugh map, or simply a K-map, is a diagram showing the graphical form of a truth table. Since there is no specific set of rules for minimizing a Boolean function using identities, it is difficult to know whether the minimum expression is obtained. The K-map provides a systematic procedure for simplifying Boolean functions of typically up to five variables. It is difficult to obtain K-maps analytically for more than five variables. However, a computer program using a tabular method such as the Quine-McCluskey algorithm can be used to minimize Boolean functions with more than five variables. Note that the theory behind K-map is based on Gray code and the identity, $A + \overline{A} = 1$.

The K-map is a diagram containing squares with each square representing one of the minterms of the Boolean function. For example, the K-map of two variables (A, B) contains four squares. The four minterms $\overline{A}\,\overline{B}$, $\overline{A}B$, $A\overline{B}$, and AB are represented by each square. Similarly, there are 8 squares for three variables, 16 squares for four variables, and 32 squares for five variables. Since any Boolean function can be expressed in terms of minterms, the K-map can be used to visually represent a Boolean function.

The K-map is drawn in such a way that there is only a one-bit change from one square to the next (Gray code). Squares can be combined in groups of 2^n where $n = 0, 1, 2, 3, 4, 5$, and the Boolean function can be minimized by following certain rules. This minimum expression will reduce the total number of gates for implementation. Thus, the cost of building the logic circuit is reduced.

4.2.1   Two-Variable K-map

Figure 4.3 shows the K-map for two variables.

Since there are four minterms with two variables, four squares are required to represent them. This is depicted in the map of Figure 4.3(a). Each square represents a minterm. Figure 4.3(b) shows the K-map for two variables. Since each variable $(A$ or $B)$ has a value of 0 or 1 in the K-map of Figure 4.3(b), the 0 and 1 shown on the left of the map corresponds to 'A' while the 0 and 1 on the top are assigned to the variable 'B'. The squares containing minterms with one variable change are called "adjacent" squares. A square is adjacent to another square placed horizontally or vertically next to it. For example, consider the minterms m_0 and m_1. Since $m_0 = \overline{A}\,\overline{B}$ and $m_1 = \overline{A}B$, there is a one variable change ($\overline{B}$ in m_0 and B in m_1, $\overline{A}$ is the same in both squares). Therefore, m_0 and m_1 are adjacent squares. Similarly, other adjacent squares in the map include m_0 and m_2, or m_1 and m_3. m_0 ($\overline{A}\,\overline{B}$) and m_3 (AB) are not adjacent squares since both variables change from 0's to 1's. The adjacent squares can be combined to eliminate one of the variables. This is based on the Boolean identities $A + \overline{A} = 1$ or $B + \overline{B} = 1$.

The adjacent squares can also be identified by considering the map as a book. By closing the book at the middle vertical line, m_0 and m_2 will respectively be placed on m_1 and m_3. Thus, m_0 and m_1 are adjacent; squares m_2 and m_3 are also adjacent. Similarly, by closing the map at the middle horizontal line, m_0 will fall on m_2 while m_1 will be placed on m_3. Thus, m_0 and m_2 or m_1 and m_3 are adjacent squares.

Now, let us consider a Boolean function, $F = \Sigma m(0, 1)$. Figure 4.4 shows that the function F containing two minterms m_0 and m_1 are identified by placing 1's in the corresponding squares of

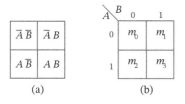

(a)   (b)

FIGURE 4.3   Two-variable K-map

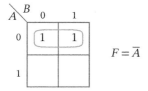

$F = \overline{A}$

FIGURE 4.4   K-Map for $F = \Sigma m(0, 1)$

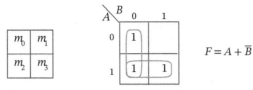

$$F = A + \overline{B}$$

FIGURE 4.5   K-Map for F = Σm(0, 2, 3)

The adjacent squares can also be identified by considering the map as a book. By closing the book at the middle vertical line, m_0 and m_2 will respectively be placed on m_1 and m_3. Thus, m_0 and m_1 are adjacent; squares m_2 and m_3 are also adjacent. Similarly, by closing the map at the middle horizontal line, m_0 will fall on m_2 while m_1 will be placed on m_3. Thus, m_0 and m_2 or m_1 and m_3 are adjacent squares.

Now, let us consider a Boolean function, $F = \Sigma m(0, 1)$. Figure 4.4 shows that the function F containing two minterms m_0 and m_1 are identified by placing 1's in the corresponding squares of the map. In order to minimize the function F, the two squares can be combined as shown since they are adjacent. The map is then inspected for common variables looking at the squares vertically and horizontally. Since $A = 0$ is common to both squares, $F = \overline{A}$. This can be proven analytically by using Boolean identities as follows:

$$F = m(0, 1) = \overline{A}\,\overline{B} + \overline{A}B$$

$$= \overline{A}(\overline{B} + B) = \overline{A} \text{ (since } \overline{B} + B = 1)$$

In a two-variable K-map, adjacent squares can be combined in groups of two or four.

Next, consider $F = \Sigma m(0, 2, 3)$. The K-map is shown in Figure 4.5. 1's are placed in the squares defined by the minterms m_0, m_2, and m_3. By combining the adjacent squares m_0 with m_2 and m_2 with m_3, the common terms can be determined to simplify the function F. For example, by inspecting m_0 and m_2 vertically and horizontally, the term $\overline{B}$ is the common term. On the other hand, by looking at m_2 and m_3 horizontally and vertically, variable A is the common term. The minimized form of the function F can be obtained by logically ORing these common terms. Therefore,

$$F = A + \overline{B}.$$

Note that the function $F = 1$ for $F = \Sigma m(0, 1, 2, 3)$ in which all squares (minterms) in the K-map are 1's.

4.2.2   Three-Variable K-map

Figure 4.6 shows the K-map for three variables. Figure 4.6(a) shows a map with three literals in each square. There are eight minterms $(m_0, m_1, \ldots, m_7)$ for three variables. Figure 4.6(b) shows these minterms — one for each square in the K-map.

Like the two-variable K-map, a square in a three-variable K-map is adjacent to the squares placed horizontally or vertically next to it. Consider the minterms m_1, m_2, m_3 and m_7. For example, m_3 is adjacent to m_1, m_2, and m_7; m_1 is adjacent to m_3; m_2 is adjacent to m_3; and m_7 is adjacent to m_3. But, m_7 is adjacent neither to m_1 nor to m_2; m_1 is not adjacent to m_2 and vice versa.

Like the two-variable map, the K-map can be considered as a book. The adjacent squares can also be determined by closing the book at the middle horizontal and vertical lines. For example, closing the book at the middle horizontal line, the adjacent pair of squares are m_0 and m_4, m_1 and m_5, m_3 and m_7, m_2 and m_6. On the other hand, closing the book at the middle vertical line, the adjacent pair of squares are m_0 and m_2, m_1 and m_3, m_4 and m_6, m_5 and m_7.

For a three variable K-map, adjacent squares can be combined in powers of 2: 1 (2^0), 2 (2^1), 4

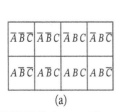

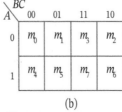

(a)   (b)

FIGURE 4.6   Three-variable K-map

m_0	m_1	m_3	m_2
m_4	m_5	m_7	m_6

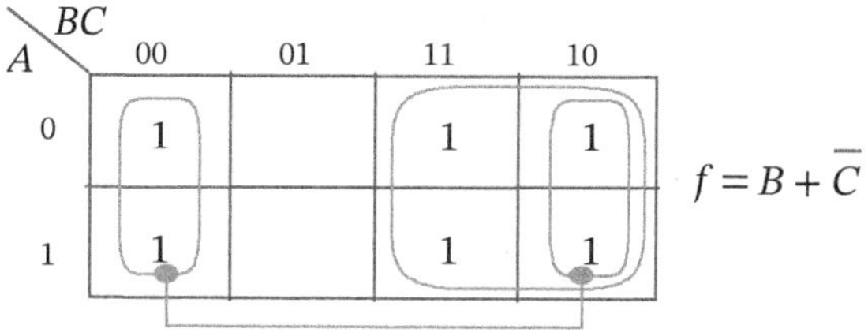

$f = B + \overline{C}$

FIGURE 4.7   K-map for $f(A, B, C) = \Sigma m(0, 2, 3, 4, 6, 7)$

(2^2) and 8 (2^3). The Boolean function is one when all eight squares are 1's. It is desirable to combine as many squares as possible. Note that grouping 2^p adjacent squares n-variable in a K-map will provide a product term of (n-p) literals. This means that, for a three-variable K-map, grouping two (2^1) adjacent squares will provide a product term of two literals and combining four (2^2) adjacent squares will provide a product term of one literal. The following examples illustrate this.

Example 4.2

Simplify the Boolean function using a K-map.

$$f(A, B, C) = \Sigma m(0, 2, 3, 4, 6, 7)$$

Solution

Figure 4.7 shows the K-map along with the grouping of adjacent squares. First, a 1 is placed in the K-map for each minterm that represents the function. Next, the adjacent squares are identified by squares next to each other. Therefore, m_2, m_3, m_6, and m_7 can be combined as a group of adjacent squares. The common term for this grouping is B. Note that combining four (2^2) squares provides the result with only one literal, B. Next, by folding the K-map at the middle vertical line, adjacent squares m_0, m_2, m_4, and m_6 can be identified. Combining them together will provide the single common term $\overline{C}$. Therefore,
$$f = B + \overline{C}.$$

This result can be verified analytically by using the identities as follows:

$$
\begin{aligned}
f &= \Sigma m(0, 2, 3, 4, 6, 7) \\
&= \overline{A}\,\overline{B}\,\overline{C} + \overline{A}B\overline{C} + \overline{A}BC + A\overline{B}\,\overline{C} + AB\overline{C} + ABC \\
&= \overline{B}\,\overline{C}(A + \overline{A}) + B\overline{C}(\overline{A} + A) + BC(\overline{A} + A) \\
&= \overline{B}\,\overline{C} + B\overline{C} + BC \\
&= \overline{C}(\overline{B} + B) + BC \\
&= \overline{C} + BC \\
&= (B + \overline{C})(C + \overline{C}) = B + \overline{C} \text{ (using the Distributive Law)}
\end{aligned}
$$

Example 4.3

Simplify the Boolean function using a K-map.
$$f(A, B, C) = \Sigma m(0, 1, 2, 6)$$

Solution

Figure 4.8 shows the K-map along with the grouping of adjacent squares.

From the K-map, grouping adjacent squares and logically ORing common product terms,

$$f = \overline{A}\,\overline{B} + B\overline{C}.$$

Example 4.4

(a) Simplify the Boolean function using a K-map.

$$F(A, B, C) = \overline{A}\,\overline{B}\,\overline{C} + A\overline{B}\,\overline{C} + B\overline{C}$$

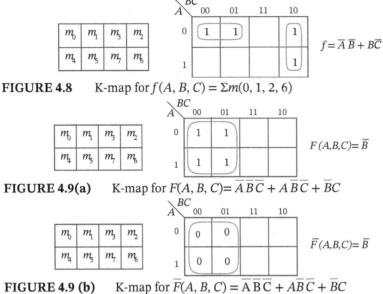

FIGURE 4.8 K-map for $f(A, B, C) = \Sigma m(0, 1, 2, 6)$

FIGURE 4.9(a) K-map for $F(A, B, C) = \overline{A}\,\overline{B}\,\overline{C} + A\overline{B}\,\overline{C} + \overline{B}C$

FIGURE 4.9 (b) K-map for $\overline{F}(A, B, C) = \overline{A}\,\overline{B}\,\overline{C} + A\overline{B}\,\overline{C} + \overline{B}C$

(b) Simplify the Boolean function for $F(A, B, C)$ given $\overline{F}(A, B, C) = \Sigma m(0, 1,\; 4, 5)$ using a K-map.

Solution

(a) The function contains three variables, A, B, and C, and is not expressed in minterm form. The first step is to express the function in terms of minterms as follows:

$$F(A, B, C) = \overline{A}\,B\overline{C} + A\overline{B}\,\overline{C} + \overline{B}C(A + \overline{A})$$

$$= \overline{A}\,\overline{B}\,\overline{C} + A\overline{B}\,\overline{C} + A\overline{B}C + \overline{A}\,\overline{B}C$$

$$= \Sigma m(0,1,4,5)$$

Figure 4.9(a) shows the K-map. Note that the four (2^2) adjacent squares are grouped to provide a single literal $\overline{B}$ by eliminating the other literals. Therefore, $F(A, B, C) = \overline{B}$. Although $F(A, B, C)$ is not expressed in minterm form, one can usually identify the squares with 1's in the K-map for the function $F(A, B, C) = \overline{A}\,\overline{B}\,\overline{C} + A\overline{B}\,\overline{C} + \overline{B}C$ by inspection. This will avoid the lengthy process of converting such functions into minterm form.

(b) Figure 4.9 (b) shows the K-map along with the grouping of adjacent squares.

From the K-map, $\overline{F}(A, B, C) = \overline{B}$. Hence, $F(A, B, C) = B$.

4.2.3 Four-Variable K-map

A four-variable K-map, depicted in Figure 4.10, contains 16 squares because there are 16 minterms. Figure 4.10(a) includes four literals in each square. Figure 4.10(b) lists each minterm in its respective square. As before, a square is adjacent to the squares placed horizontally or vertically next to it. For example, m_7 is adjacent to m_3, m_5, m_6, and m_{15}. Also, by closing the K-map at the middle vertical line, the adjacent pairs of squares are m_3 and m_1, m_2 and m_0, m_4 and m_6, m_{12} and m_{14}, m_8 and m_{10}, and so on. On the other hand, closing it at the middle horizontal line will provide the following adjacent squares: m_0 and m_8, m_1 and m_9, m_3 and m_{11}, m_2 and m_{10}, and so on.

For a four-variable K-map, adjacent squares can be grouped in powers of 2: 1 (2^0), 2 (2^1), 4 (2^2), 8 (2^3), and 16 (2^4). The Boolean function is one when all 16 minterms are 1. Combining two adjacent squares will provide a product term of three literals; four adjacent squares will provide a product term of two literals; eight adjacent squares will yield a product term of one literal.

CD AB	00	01	11	10
00	$\bar{A}\bar{B}\bar{C}\bar{D}$	$\bar{A}\bar{B}\bar{C}D$	$\bar{A}\bar{B}CD$	$\bar{A}\bar{B}C\bar{D}$
01	$\bar{A}B\bar{C}\bar{D}$	$\bar{A}B\bar{C}D$	$\bar{A}BCD$	$\bar{A}BC\bar{D}$
11	$AB\bar{C}\bar{D}$	$AB\bar{C}D$	$ABCD$	$ABC\bar{D}$
10	$A\bar{B}\bar{C}\bar{D}$	$A\bar{B}\bar{C}D$	$A\bar{B}CD$	$A\bar{B}C\bar{D}$

(a)

CD AB	00	01	11	10
00	m_0	m_1	m_3	m_2
01	m_4	m_5	m_7	m_6
11	m_{12}	m_{13}	m_{15}	m_{14}
10	m_8	m_9	m_{11}	m_{10}

(b)

FIGURE 4.10 Four-variable K-map

Example 4.5

(a) Simplify the Boolean function using a K-map.

$$f(A, B, C, D) = \Sigma m(0, 1, 2, 3, 8, 9, 10, 11, 12, 13, 14, 15)$$

(b) Simplify the Boolean function for $f(A, B, C, D)$ using a K-map given:

$$\bar{f}(A, B, C, D) = \Sigma m(0, 1, 2, 3, 8, 9, 10, 11, 12, 13, 14, 15).$$

Solution

(a)　　　Figure 4.11(a) shows the K-map. The 8 adjacent squares combined in the bottom two rows yield the common product term of one literal, A. Because the top row is adjacent to the bottom row, combining the minterms in these two rows will provide a common product term of a single literal, $\bar{B}$. Therefore, by ORing these two terms, the minimized form of the function, $f = A + \bar{B}$ is obtained.

　　　　Grouping 0's, $\bar{f}(A, B, C, D) = \bar{A}B$, Using DeMorgan's theorem, $f(A, B, C, D) = A + \bar{B}$

(b)　　　Figure 4.11(b) shows the K-map. Since the equation for $\bar{f}(A, B, C, D)$ is given, the specified minterms are marked as 0's in the K-map. After grouping, $\bar{f}(A, B, C, D) = A + \bar{B}$ is obtained. Hence,

$$f(A, B, C, D) = \bar{\bar{f}}(A, B, C, D) = \overline{A + \bar{B}}. \text{ Using DeMorgan's theorem, } f(A, B, C, D) = \bar{A}B.$$

Next, grouping 1's, $f(A, B, C, D) = \bar{A}B$.

Example 4.6

Simplify the Boolean function $F(A, B, C, D) = \Sigma m(0, 2, 4, 5, 6, 8, 10)$ using a K-map.

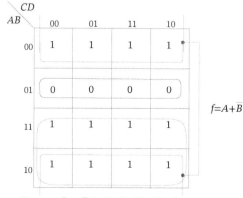

$f = A + \bar{B}$

FIGURE 4.11(a)　　　K-map for $f(A, B, C, D) = \Sigma m(0, 1, 2, 3, 8, 9, 10, 11, 12, 13, 14, 15)$

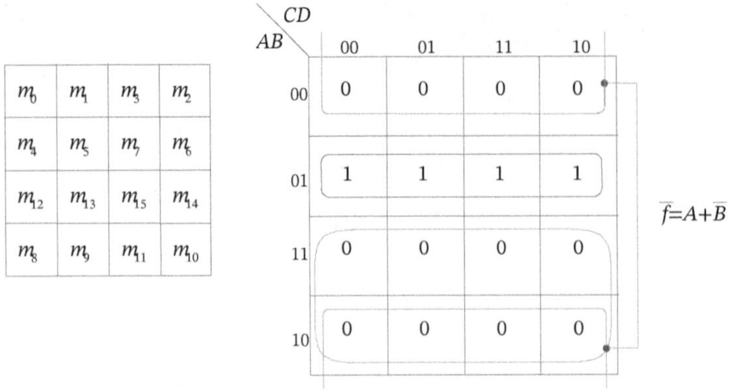

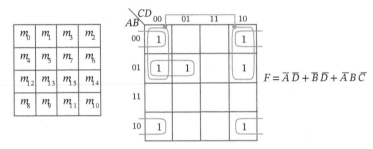

FIGURE 4.11(b)   K-map for $\bar{f}(A, B, C, D)=\Sigma m(0, 1, 2, 3, 8, 9, 10, 11, 12, 13, 14, 15)$

FIGURE 4.12   K-map for $F(A, B, C, D) = \Sigma m(0, 2, 4, 5, 6, 8, 10)$

Solution

Figure 4.12 shows the K-map. The common product term obtained by grouping the adjacent squares m_0, m_2, m_4, and m_6 will contain $\bar{A}\,\bar{D}$. The common product term obtained by grouping the adjacent squares m_0, m_2, m_8, and m_{10} will be $\bar{B}\,\bar{D}$. Combining the adjacent squares m_4 and m_5 will provide the common term $\bar{A}B\bar{C}$. ORing these common product terms will yield the minimum function, $F(A, B, C, D)= \bar{A}\,\bar{D}+ \bar{B}\,\bar{D} + \bar{A}B\bar{C}$.

Example 4.7

Simplify the Boolean Function, $F=\bar{A}\,\bar{B}\,\bar{C}+ \bar{A}B\bar{C} + \bar{A}B\bar{D} + \bar{A}\,\bar{B}CD$ using a K-map.

Solution

Figure 4.13 shows the K-map. In the figure, the function F can be expressed in terms of minterms as follows:

$$F = \bar{A}\,\bar{B}\,\bar{C}(D + \bar{D})+ \bar{A}B\bar{C}(D + \bar{D})+ \bar{A}B\bar{D}(C + \bar{C})+ \bar{A}\,\bar{B}CD$$

$$= \bar{A}\,\bar{B}\,\bar{C}D + \bar{A}\,\bar{B}\,\bar{C}\,\bar{D} + \bar{A}B\bar{C}D + \bar{A}B\bar{C}\bar{D} + \bar{A}B\bar{D}C + \bar{A}B\bar{D}\bar{C} + \bar{A}\,\bar{B}CD$$

$$= m_1 + m_0 + m_5 + m_4 + m_6 + m_4 + m_2$$

$$= m_1 + m_0 + m_5 + m_4 + m_6 + m_2$$

because $m_4 + m_4 = m_4$

FIGURE 4.13 K-map for $F = \overline{A}\,\overline{B}C + \overline{A}B\overline{C} + \overline{A}B\overline{D} + \overline{A}BC\overline{D}$

Rearranging the terms: $F = m_0 + m_1 + m_2 + m_4 + m_5 + m_6$. Therefore, $F = \Sigma m(0, 1, 2, 4, 5, 6)$. These minterms are marked as 1 in the K-map. The adjacent squares are grouped as shown. The minimum form of the function, $F = \overline{A}\,\overline{C} + \overline{A}\,\overline{D}$.

4.2.4 Prime Implicants

A prime implicant is the product term obtained as a result of grouping the maximum number of allowable adjacent squares in a K-map. The prime implicant is called "essential" if it is the only term covering the minterms. A prime implicant is called "nonessential" if another prime implicant covers the same minterms. The simplified expression for a function can be determined using the K-map as follows: i) Determine all the essential prime implicants. ii) Express the minimum form of the function by logically ORing the essential prime implicants obtained in i) along with other prime implicants that may be required to cover any remaining minterms not covered by the essential prime implicants.

Example 4.8

Find the prime implicants from the K-map of Figure 4.14 and then determine the simplified expression for the function.

Solution

The essential prime implicants are AB and $\overline{A}\,\overline{B}$ because minterms m_0 and m_1 can only be covered by the term $\overline{A}\,\overline{B}$ and minterms m_6 and m_7 can only be covered by the term AB.

The terms AC and $\overline{B}C$ are nonessential prime implicants because minterm m_5 can be combined with either m_1 or m_7. The term AC can be obtained by combining m_5 with m_7, whereas the term $\overline{B}C$ is obtained by combining m_5 with m_1. The function can be expressed in two simplified forms as follows:

$$f = \overline{A}\,\overline{B} + AB + AC$$

or

$$f = \overline{A}\,\overline{B} + AB + \overline{B}C$$

Example 4.9

Find the essential prime implicants from the K-map of Figure 4.15 and then find the simplified expression for the function.

Solution

The prime implicants can be obtained as follows:
By combining minterms m_5, m_7, m_{13}, and m_{15}, the prime implicant BD is obtained.
By combining minterms m_8, m_{10}, m_{12}, and m_{14}, the prime implicant $A\overline{D}$ is obtained.
By combining minterms m_{12}, m_{13}, m_{14}, and m_{15}, the prime implicant AB is obtained.

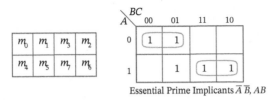

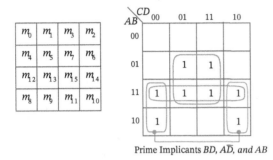

FIGURE 4.14   K-map for Example 4.8

Prime Implicants BD, $A\overline{D}$, and AB

FIGURE 4.15   K-map for Example 4.9

The terms BD and $A\overline{D}$ are essential prime implicants, whereas AB is a nonessential prime implicant because minterms m_5 and m_7 can only be covered by the term BD and minterms m_8 and m_{10} can only be covered by the term $A\overline{D}$. However, minterms m_{12}, m_{13}, m_{14}, and m_{15} can be covered by these two prime implicants (BD and $A\overline{D}$). Therefore, the term AB is not an essential prime implicant. Because all minterms are covered by the essential prime implicants, BD and $A\overline{D}$, the term AB is not required to simplify the function. Therefore,

$$f = BD + A\overline{D}$$

Example 4.10

Find the prime implicants and then simplify the function using a K-map.

$$f = \Sigma m(2, 4, 5, 8, 9, 13)$$

Solution

Figure 4.16 shows the K-map. The essential prime implicants are $\overline{A}\,\overline{B}C\overline{D}$, $\overline{A}B\overline{C}$, and $A\overline{B}\,\overline{C}$ because minterms m_4 and m_5 can only be covered by the term $\overline{A}B\overline{C}$, minterms m_8 and m_9 can only be covered by the term $A\overline{B}\,\overline{C}$, and minterm m_2 can only be covered by the term $\overline{A}\,\overline{B}C\overline{D}$.

Minterm m_{13} can be combined with either m_5 or m_9. Combining m_{13} with m_5 will yield the term $B\overline{C}D$; combining m_{13} with m_9 will provide the term $A\overline{C}D$. Therefore, minterm m_{13} can be covered by either $B\overline{C}D$ or $A\overline{C}D$. Therefore, $B\overline{C}D$ and $A\overline{C}D$ are nonessential prime implicants. Hence, the function has two simplified forms:

$$f = \overline{A}\,\overline{B}C\overline{D} + \overline{A}B\overline{C} + A\overline{B}\,\overline{C} + B\overline{C}D$$

or

$$f = \overline{A}\,\overline{B}C\overline{D} + \overline{A}B\overline{C} + A\overline{B}\,\overline{C} + A\overline{C}D$$

m_0	m_1	m_3	m_2
m_4	m_5	m_7	m_6
m_{12}	m_{13}	m_{15}	m_{14}
m_8	m_9	m_{11}	m_{10}

AB\\CD	00	01	11	10
00				1
01	1	1		
11		1		
10	1	1		

FIGURE 4.16   K-map for $f = \Sigma m(2, 4, 5, 8, 9, 13)$

4.2.5   Expressing a Boolean function in Product-of-sums (POS) form using a K-map

So far, the simplified Boolean functions derived from the K-map were expressed in sum-of-products (SOP) form. This section will describe the procedure for obtaining the simplified Boolean function in product-of-sums (POS) form.

Also, the minterms of a function, f in the K-map are represented by 1's. This means that the empty squares in the K-map can be identified as 0's. Hence, combining the appropriate adjacent squares for 0's will provide the simplified expression of the complement of the function ($\bar{f}$). By taking the complement of f and then using DeMorgan's theorem, the simplified expression for the function, f can be obtained. The following example illustrates this.

Example 4.11

(a)   Simplify the Boolean function, $f(A, B, C, D) = \Sigma m(0, 1, 4, 5, 6, 7, 8, 9, 14, 15)$
in product-of-sums (POS) form using a K-map.

(b)   Simplify the Boolean function
$f(A, B, C, D) = (\bar{A} + B + C + D)(A + B + \bar{C} + D)(A + B + C + D)(\bar{A} + B + \bar{C} + D)$
in product-of-sums (POS) form using a K-map.

Solution

(a)   Figure 4.17(a) shows the K-map. Combining the 0's, a simplified expression for the complement of the function can be obtained as follows:

$$\bar{f}(A, B, C, D) = \bar{B}C + AB\bar{C}$$

By DeMorgan's theorem,
$$f(A, B, C, D) = \bar{\bar{f}}(A, B, C, D) = \overline{(\bar{B}C + AB\bar{C})} = \overline{(\bar{B}C)} \cdot \overline{(AB\bar{C})} = (B + \bar{C}) \cdot (\bar{A} + \bar{B} + C)$$

(b)   The example in (a) illustrates the procedure for obtaining a simplified expression for $\bar{f}$ in product-of-sums (POS) form using a K-map from f expressed in minterm form. The procedure is similar for simplifying a function expressed in product-of-sums (maxterms) form.

To represent a function expressed in product-of-sums in the K-map, the complement of the function must first be obtained. The squares will then be identified as 1's for the minterms of the complement of the function. For example, consider the following function expressed in maxterm form:

$$f(A, B, C, D) = (\bar{A} + B + C + D)(A + B + \bar{C} + D)(A + B + C + D)(\bar{A} + B + \bar{C} + D) = \Pi m(0, 2, 8, 10)$$

From Section 4.1, the function, $\bar{f}(A, B, C, D)$ can be obtained as follows:

$$\bar{f}(A, B, C, D) = \Sigma m(0, 2, 8, 10)$$

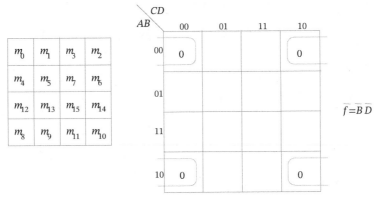

FIGURE 4.17 (a)   K-map for $f(A, B, C, D) = \Sigma m(0, 1, 4, 5, 6, 7, 8, 9, 14, 15)$

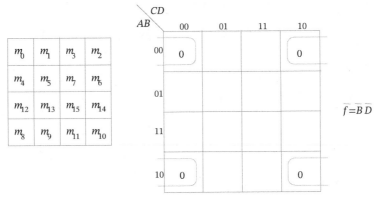

$$f = \bar{B}\,\bar{D}$$

FIGURE 4.17 (b)   K-map for $\bar{f}(A, B. C, D) = \Sigma m(0, 2, 8, 10)$

Placing 0's in the K-map for m_0, m_2, m_8, and m_{10}, and then grouping adjacent 0's will provide the simplified expression for $\bar{f}$. This is shown in Figure 4.17(b). Finally, the product-of-sums (POS) form of the function, f, can be obtained by complementing the function, $\bar{f}$ and then applying DeMorgan's theorem. From K-map of Figure 4.16(b), $\bar{f}(A, B, C, D) = \bar{B}\bar{D}$

Hence, $f(A, B, C, D) = \bar{\bar{f}}(A, B, C, D) = \overline{\bar{B}\,\bar{D}} = B + D$

4.2.6 Don't Care Conditions

So far, the squares of a K-map are marked with 1's for the minterms of a function. The other squares are assumed to be 0's. This is not always true, because there may be situations in which the function is not defined for all combinations of the variables. Such functions having undefined outputs for certain combinations of literals are called "incompletely specified functions." One does not normally care about the value of the output for undefined minterms. Therefore, the undefined minterms of a function are called "don't care conditions." Simply put, the don't care conditions are situations in which one or more literals in a minterm can never happen, resulting in nonoccurrence of the minterm.

As an example, BCD numbers include ten digits (0 through 9) and are defined by four bits (0000_2 through 1001_2). However, one can represent binary numbers from 0000_2 through 1111_2 using four bits. This means that the binary combinations 1010_2 through 1111_2 (10_{10} through 15_{10}) can never occur in BCD. Therefore, these six combinations (1010_2 through 1111_2) are don't care conditions in BCD. The functions for these six combinations of the four literals are unspecified. The don't care condition is represented by the symbol X. This means that the symbol X will be placed inside a square in the K-map for which the function is unspecified. The don't care minterms can be used to simplify a function. The function can be minimized by assigning 1's or 0's for X's in the K-map while determining adjacent squares. These assigned values of X's can then be grouped with 1's or 0's in the K-map, depending on the combination that provides the minimum expression. Note that a don't care condition may not be required if it does not help in minimizing the function.

To help in understanding the concept of don't care conditions, the circuit of Figure 4.18 is provided. In the figure, suppose that the digital circuit is required to turn the LED ON when the BCD

inputs (W, X, Y, Z) are 0000_2 through 0110_2 and turn the LED OFF when the BCD inputs (W, X, Y, Z) are 0111_2 through 1001_2. However, when the inputs (W,X,Y,Z) are invalid inputs 1010_2 through 1111_2, it is not specified in the problem whether the output LED will be turned ON or OFF. Hence, the outputs are undefined for inputs 1010_2 through 1111_2, and we do not care whether the output LED is ON or OFF. In such a situation, we say that the output LED (L) are the don't care conditions (X) for invalid inputs (1010_2 through 1111_2) for W, X, Y, and Z. The truth table for this problem is provided in Table 4.6. From the truth table, $L = \Sigma m(0,1,2,3,4,5,6)$. L can be minimized using a K-map shown in Figure 4.19 in which the X's (don't care conditions) can be used as 1's as needed to simplify the equation for L as
$L = \overline{W}\,\overline{Y} + \overline{W}\,\overline{X} + Y\overline{Z}$

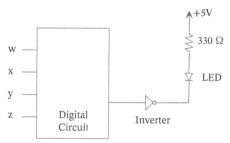

FIGURE 4.18   Figure illustrating the concept of Don't care conditions

TABLE 4.6   Truth table for Figure 4.17 with don't care conditions for 1010_2 through 1111_2

INPUTS	LED Output
WXYZ	L
0000	1
0001	1
0010	1
0011	1
0100	1
0101	1
0110	1
0111	0
1000	0
1001	0
1010	X
1011	X
1100	X
1101	X
1110	X
1111	X

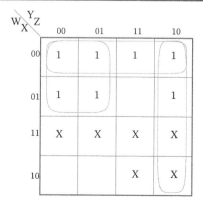

FIGURE 4.19   K-map for the digital circuit of truth table of Table 4.6 with invalid BCD inputs

TABLE 4.7   Truth table for Figure 4.17 with no don't care conditions Inputs

Inputs	Output
WXYZ	L
0000	1
0001	1
0010	1
0011	1
0100	1
0101	1
0110	1
0111	1
1000	1
1001	1
1010	0
1011	0
1100	0
1101	0
1110	0
1111	0

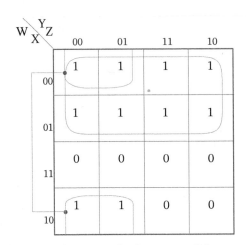

FIGURE 4.20   K-map for Table 4.7 without any don't care condition

Note that don't care conditions are used as needed for simplification. One must first group 1's along with don't care conditions (if needed) to minimize the equation. If 1's can be grouped without don't care conditions, then don't care conditions are not needed for simplification. The same rule applies while grouping 0's.

Now, suppose we re-define the problem of Figure 4.18 as follows: Turn the LED ON for valid BCD inputs (WXYZ = 0000_2 through 1001_2) and turn the LED OFF for invalid BCD inputs (WXYZ = 1010_2 through 1111_2). In this case, there are no don't care conditions since LED outputs for invalid BCD inputs are not undefined; they are defined as 0's.

The LED outputs for the valid BCD inputs in the truth table will be 1's while the LED outputs for the invalid BCD inputs in the truth table will be 0's. Table 4.7 shows the truth table. As before, from the truth table,

$L = \Sigma m(0, 1, 2, 3, 4, 5, 6, 7, 8, 9)$.

Figure 4.20 shows the K-map. The minimum equation for L (LED output) can be obtained in terms of the inputs (W,X,Y,Z) from the K-map as: $L = \overline{W} + \overline{X}\,\overline{Y}$.

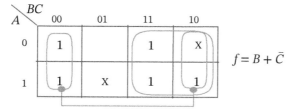

BC
A
00
01
11
10
0
1
1
X
1
1
X
1
1
1
f = B + C̄

FIGURE 4.21 K-map for $f(A, B, C) = \Sigma m(0, 3, 4, 6, 7)$ with don't care conditions, $d(A, B, C) = \Sigma m(2, 5)$

Example 4.12

Simplify the Boolean function

$$f(A, B, C) = \Sigma m(0, 3, 4, 6, 7)$$

using a K-map with the don't care conditions, $d(A, B, C) = \Sigma m(2, 5)$.

Solution

Figure 4.21 shows the K-map. To find the minimum equation for $f(A, B, C)$, one must always group the adjacent squares with 1's first, and use the don't care condition (s) only if needed to find the most minimum solution. One must not use the don't care condition(s) if not needed to simplify. In this example, the don't care minterm, m_2 is used to obtain the minimum equation for $f(A, B, C)$, while the don't care minterm, m_5 is not required. Hence, $f(A, B, C) = B + \bar{C}$.

Example 4.13

Simplify the function $f(A, B, C, D) = \Sigma m(0, 2, 5, 8, 10, 12)$ using a K-map. Assume that the minterms m_1, m_4, m_6, m_7, and m_{15} can never occur.

Solution

The don't care conditions are

$$d(A, B, C, D) = \Sigma m(1, 4, 6, 7, 15)$$

Figure 4.22 shows the K-map. By assigning X = 1 and combining 1's as shown, f can be expressed in sum-of-products form as follows:

$$f = \bar{C}\bar{D} + \bar{A}B + \bar{B}\bar{D}$$

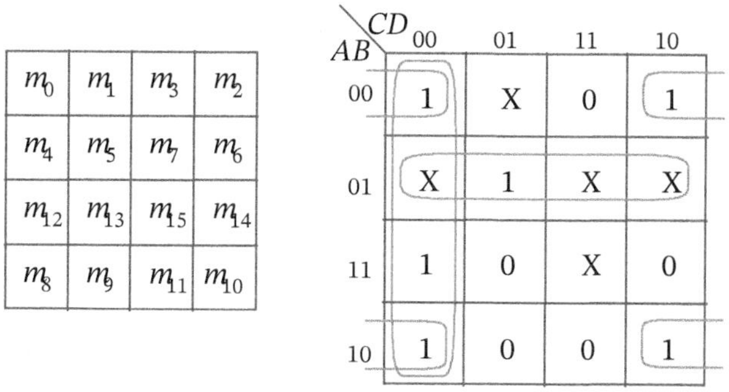

m0 m1 m3 m2
m4 m5 m7 m6
m12 m13 m15 m14
m8 m9 m11 m10
CD
AB
00
01
11
10
00
1
X
0
1
01
X
1
X
X
11
1
0
X
0
10
1
0
0
1

FIGURE 4.22 K-map for Example 4.13 by grouping 1's and don't care conditions

AB \ CD	00	01	11	10
00	1	X	0	1
01	X	1	X	X
11	1	0	X	0
10	1	0	0	1

FIGURE 4.23 K-map for Example 4.14 by grouping 0's and don't care conditions

Example 4.14

Repeat Example 4.13 by grouping 0's.

Solution

In example 4.13, *f*(*A*, *B*. *C*, *D*) is determined by grouping 1's along with X's.

Note that, by assigning X = 0 and combining 0's as shown in Figure 4.23, *f* can be obtained as a product-of-sums form. Thus,

$$\bar{f} = CD + AD + BC$$

$$f = \bar{\bar{f}} = \overline{CD + AD + BC}$$

$$= (\overline{CD})(\overline{AD})(\overline{BC})$$

$$= (\bar{C} + \bar{D})(\bar{A} + \bar{D})(\bar{B} + \bar{C})$$

4.2.7 Five-Variable K-map

Figure 4.24 shows a five-variable K-map. The five-variable K-map contains 32 squares. It contains two four-variable maps for *BCDE* with *A* = 0 in one of the two maps and *A* = 1 in the other. The value of a minterm in each map can be determined by the decimal value of the five literals.

For example, minterm m_{14} from Figure 4.24(a) can be expressed in terms of the five literals as $\bar{A}BCD\bar{E}$. On the other hand, minterm m_{26} can be expressed in terms of the five literals from Figure 4.24(b) as $AB\bar{C}D\bar{E}$.

When simplifying a function, each K-map can first be considered as an individual four-variable map with *A* = 0 or *A* = 1. Combining of adjacent squares will be identical to typical four-variable maps. Next, the adjacent squares between the two K-maps can be determined by placing the map in Figure 4.24(a) on top of the map in Figure 4.24(b). Two squares are adjacent when a square in Figure 4.24(a) falls on the square in Figure4.24(b) and vice versa. For example, minterm m_0 is adjacent to minterm m_{16}, minterm m_1 is adjacent to minterm m_{17}, and so on.

A = 0

BC \ DE	00	01	11	10
00	m_0	m_1	m_3	m_2
01	m_4	m_5	m_7	m_6
11	m_{12}	m_{13}	m_{15}	m_{14}
10	m_8	m_9	m_{11}	m_{10}

(a)

A = 1

BC \ DE	00	01	11	10
00	m_{16}	m_{17}	m_{19}	m_{18}
01	m_{20}	m_{21}	m_{23}	m_{22}
11	m_{28}	m_{29}	m_{31}	m_{30}
10	m_{24}	m_{25}	m_{27}	m_{26}

(b)

FIGURE 4.24 Five-Variable K-map

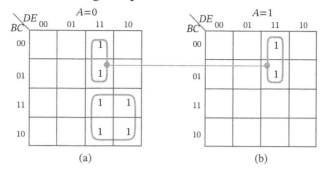

FIGURE 4.25   K-map for Example 4.15

Example 4.15

Simplify the function using a K-map.

$$f(A, B, C, D, E) = \Sigma m(3, 7, 10, 11, 14, 15, 19, 23)$$

Solution

Figure 4.25 shows the K-map.

$$f = \overline{A}BD + \overline{B}DE$$

To find the adjacent squares, the K-maps are first considered individually. From Figure 4.25(a), combining minterms m_{10}, m_{11}, m_{14}, and m_{15} will yield the product term $\overline{A}BD$.

Minterms m_{19} and m_{23} are in the K-map of Figure 4.25(b). However, they are adjacent to minterms m_{3} and m_{7} in Figure 4.25(a). Combining m_{3}, m_{7}, m_{19}, and m_{23} together, the product term $\overline{B}DE$ can be obtained. Literals A or $\overline{A}$ are not included here because adjacent squares belong to both $A = 0$ and $A = 1$.

Therefore, the minimum form of f is

$$f = \overline{A}BD + \overline{B}DE$$

4.3   Quine–McCluskey Method

When the number of variables in a K-map is more than five, it becomes impractical to use K-maps in order to minimize a function. A tabular method known as Quine–McCluskey can be used. A computer program is usually written for the Quine–McCluskey method. One uses this program to simplify a function with more than five variables.

Like the K-map, the Quine–McCluskey method first finds all prime implicants of the function. A minimum number of prime implicants is then selected that defines the function. In order to understand the Quine–McCluskey method, an example will be provided using tables and manual check-off procedures. Although a computer program, rather than manual approach, is normally used by logic designers, a simple manual example is presented here so that the method can be easily understood. The Quine–McCluskey method first tabulates the minterms that define the function. The following example illustrates how a Boolean function is minimized using the Quine–McCluskey method.

Example 4.16

In Example 4.6, $F(A, B, C, D) = \Sigma m(0, 2, 4, 5, 6, 8, 10)$ is simplified using a K-map. The minimum form is $F = \overline{A}\overline{D} + \overline{B}\overline{D} + \overline{A}B\overline{C}$. Verify this result using the Quine–McCluskey method.

Solution

First, arrange the binary representation of the minterms as shown in Table 4.8.

TABLE 4.8   Simplifying $F = \Sigma m(0, 2, 4, 5, 6, 8, 10)$ using the Quine–McCluskey Method

Minterm	(i) A	B	C	D			(ii) A	B	C	D			(iii) A	B	C	D
0	0	0	0	0	✓	0,2	0	0	–	0	✓	0,2,4,6	0	–	–	0
2	0	0	1	0	✓	0,4	0	–	0	0	✓	0,2,8,10	–	0	–	0
4	0	1	0	0	✓	0,8	–	0	0	0	✓	0,4,2,6	0	–	–	0
8	1	0	0	0	✓	2,6	0	–	1	0	✓	0,8,2,10	–	0	–	0
5	0	1	0	1	✓	2,10	–	0	1	0	✓					
6	0	1	1	0	✓	4,5	0	1	0	–						
10	1	0	1	0	✓	4,6	0	1	–	0	✓					
						8,10	1	0	–	0	✓					

In the table, the minterms are grouped according to the number of 1's contained in their binary representations. For example, consider column (i). Because minterms m_2, m_4, and m_8 contain one 1, they are grouped together. On the other hand, minterms m_5, m_6, and m_{10} contain two 1's, so they are grouped together.

Next, consider column (ii). Any two minterms that vary by one bit in column (i) are grouped together in column (ii). Starting from the top row, proceeding to the bottom row, and comparing the binary representation of each minterm in column (i), pairs of minterms having only a one-variable change are grouped together in column (ii) with the variable bit replaced by the symbol –. For example, comparing $m_0 = 0000$ with $m_2 = 0010$, there is a one-variable change in bit position 1. This is shown in column (ii) by placing – in bit position 1 with the other three bits unchanged. Therefore, the top row of column (ii) contains 00-0. The procedure is repeated until all minterms are compared from top to bottom for one unmatched bit and are represented by replacing this bit position with – and other bits unchanged. A √ is placed on the right-hand side to indicate that this minterm is compared with all others and its pair with one bit change is found. If a minterm does not have another minterm with one bit change, no check mark is placed on its right. This means that the prime implicant will contain four literals and will be included in the simplified from of the function F. In column (i), for each minterm, which has a corresponding pair with one bit change is identified. These pairs are listed in column (ii).

Finally, consider column (iii). Each minterm pair in column (ii) is compared to the next, starting from the top, to find another pair with one bit change; for example m_0, $m_2 = 00$–0 and m_4, $m_6 = 01$–0. For this case, bit position 2 does not match. This bit position is replaced by – in the top row of column (iii). Therefore, in column (iii), the top row groups these four minterms 0, 2, 4, 6 with $ABCD$ as 0 -- 0. Similarly, all other pairs in column (ii) are compared from top to bottom for one bit change and are listed accordingly in column (iii) if an unmatched bit is found. A check mark is placed in the right of column (ii) if an unmatched bit is found between two pairs. Note that minterms 4 and 5 do not have any other pair in the list of column (ii) having one unmatched bit. Therefore, this pair is not checked on the right and must be included in the simplified form of F as a prime implicant containing three variables. The two rows of column (iii) (0, 2, 4, 6 and 0, 4, 2, 6) are the same and contain 0 -- 0. Therefore, this term should be considered once. Similarly, the groups 0, 2, 8, 10 and 0, 8, 2, 10 containing -0-0 should be considered once. In column (iii), there are no more groups that exist with one unmatched bit.

The comparison process stops. The prime implicants will be the unchecked terms $\overline{A}B\overline{C}$ (from column (ii)) along with, $\overline{A}\,\overline{D}$ and $\overline{B}\,\overline{D}$ (from column (iii)). Thus, the simplified form for F is

$$F = \overline{A}\,\overline{D} + \overline{B}\,\overline{D} + \overline{A}B\overline{C}.$$

This agrees with the result of Example 4.6.

4.4   Implementation of Digital Circuits with NAND, and NOR Gates

This section covers implementation of logic circuits using NAND and NOR gates. The NAND and NOR gates are called "universal gates" because any digital circuit can be implemented with them. These gates are, therefore, more commonly used than AND and OR gates.

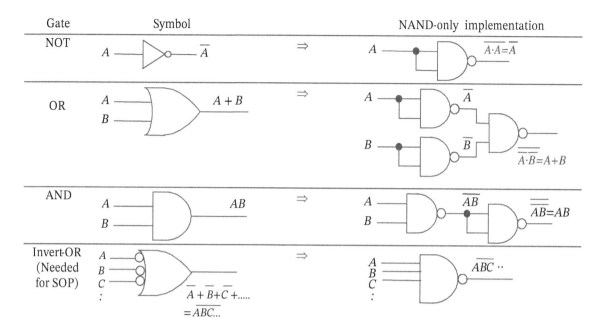

FIGURE 4.26   Logic equivalents using NAND gates

4.4.1   NAND Gate Implementation

Any logic operation can be implemented using NAND gates. Figure 4.26 shows how NOT, AND, OR, and Invert-OR operations can be implemented with NAND gates. Note that Invert-OR operation is required for sum-of-products (SOP) implementation. This will be shown later in this section.

A Boolean function can be implemented using NAND gates by first obtaining the simplified expression of the function in terms of AND-OR-NOT logic operations. The function can then be converted to NAND-only logic. A function expressed in sum-of-products (SOP) form can be readily implemented using only NAND gates.

Example 4.17

Draw the schematic for the simplified function $F = \overline{XY + XZ}$ using only NAND gates.

Solution

First implement the function using AND, OR, and NOT gates as follows:

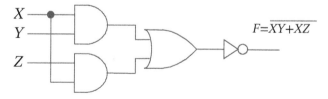

Now convert the AND, OR, and NOT gates to NAND gates as follows:

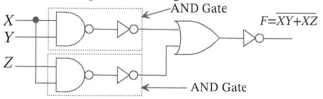

The NOT gates can be represented as bubbles at the inputs of the OR gate as follows:

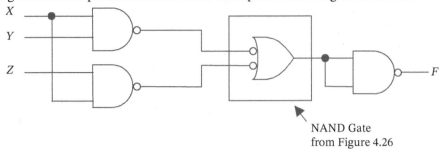

NAND Gate
from Figure 4.26

Therefore, the function $F = \overline{XY + XZ}$ can be implemented using only NAND gates as follows:

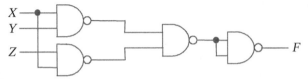

This is a three-level implementation since three gate delays are required to obtain the output F. This circuit may not be cost effective. But it may be convenient to build the circuit with only NAND gates without any other logic gates.

Example 4.18

Simplify the following Boolean function using a K-map, and then draw a schematic using only NAND gates:

$$f(A, B, C, D) = m(0, 4, 8, 11, 12, 15)$$

Solution

In order to draw a schematic using only NAND gates, we must express $f(A, B, C, D) =$ in SOP form by grouping adjacent 1's in the K-map as shown in Figure 4.27. From the K-map,

$$f(A, B, C, D) = \overline{C}\,\overline{D} + ACD$$

Figure 4.28 shows the logic diagram for AOI (AND-OR-INVERT) implementation which uses AND, OR, and NOT gates.

   Note that the logic circuit has four gate delays. Figure 4.29 shows the various steps for converting the AOI schematic of Figure 4.28 to a logic diagram with NAND gates. In Figure 4.29(a), each AND gate of Figure 4.28 is represented by an AND gate with two inverters at the output. For example, consider AND gate 1 of Figure 4.28. The AND gate and an inverter are used to form the NAND gate shown in the top row of Figure 4.29(b) with an inverter (indicated by a bubble at the OR gate input). AND gate 3 is represented in the same way as AND gate 1 in Figure 4.29(b).

   Finally, in Figure 4.29(c), the OR gate with the bubbles at the input in Figure 4.29(b) is replaced by a NAND gate. Thus, the NAND gate implementation in Figure 4.29(c) is obtained.

4.4.2   NOR Gate Implementation

As with NAND gates, any logic operation can be implemented using NOR gates. Figure 4.30 shows how NOT, AND, OR, and Invert-AND operations can be implemented with NOR gates. Note that Invert-AND operation is required for product-of-sums (POS) implementation. This will be shown later in this section.

m_0	m_1	m_3	m_2
m_4	m_5	m_7	m_6
m_{12}	m_{13}	m_{15}	m_{14}
m_8	m_9	m_{11}	m_{10}

AB \ CD	00	01	11	10
00	1			
01	1			
11	1		1	
10	1		1	

FIGURE 4.27 K-map for Example 4.18

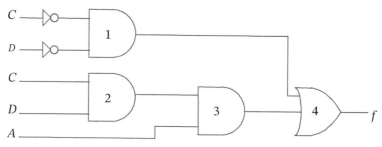

FIGURE 4.28 Logic diagram for AOI (AND-OR-INVERT) implementation of $f = \overline{C}\,\overline{D} + ACD$

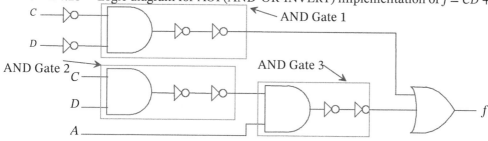

FIGURE 4.29 (a)

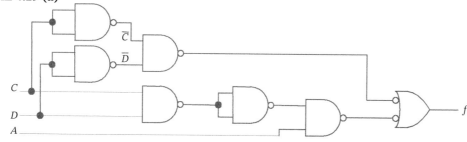

FIGURE 4.29 (b)

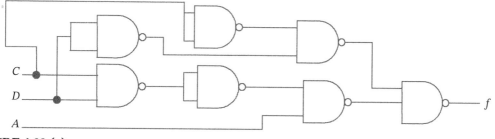

FIGURE 4.29 (c)

FIGURE 4.29 Steps for NAND gate implementation of Figure 4.28

Gate	Symbol		NOR-only Implementation

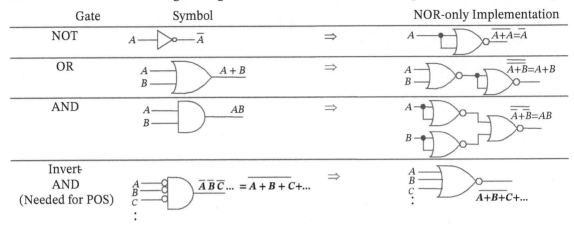

Invert AND (Needed for POS)		

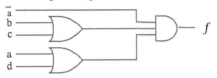

FIGURE 4.30   Logic equivalents using NOR gates

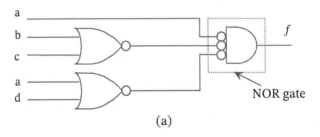

FIGURE 4.31   AND-OR implementation of Example 4.19(a)

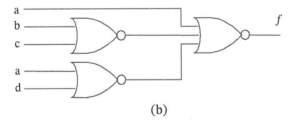

(a)

(b)

FIGURE 4.32   NOR implementation of Example 4.19

A Boolean function can be implemented using NOR gates by first obtaining the simplified expression of the function in terms of AND-OR-INVERT logic operations. The function can then be converted to NOR-only logic. A function expressed in product-of-sums (POS) form can be readily implemented using only NOR gates.

Example 4.19

Implement the following function using NOR gates:

$$f = \bar{a}(b + c)(a + d)$$

Solution

Figure 4.31 shows the AND-OR implementation of the logic equation. Figure 4.32 shows the NOR implementation.

Example 4.20

Simplify the Boolean function $\bar{f}(A, B, C, D) = \Sigma m(3, 9, 11, 13, 14)$ using a K-map. Assume that the don't care conditions are $d(A, B, C, D) = \Sigma m(1, 4, 6, 7, 15)$. Draw a schematic for $f(A,B,C,D)$ using only NOR gates.

Solution

In order to draw a schematic using only NOR gates, we must express $\bar{f}(A, B, C, D) = \Sigma m(3, 9, 11, 13, 14)$ in POS form by grouping adjacent 0's in the K-map.

Figure 4.33 shows the K-map. By assigning X = 0 and combining adjacent 0's as shown, $\bar{f}(A, B, C, D)$ can be expressed in product-of-sums (POS) form as follows: $\bar{f} = CD + AD + BC$

Hence,

$$f = \bar{\bar{f}} = \overline{CD + AD + BC}$$

$$= (\overline{CD})(\overline{AD})(\overline{BC})$$

$$= (\overline{C} + \overline{D})(\overline{A} + \overline{D})(\overline{B} + \overline{C})$$

Figure 4.34(a) shows the logic diagram for AOI (AND-OR-INVERT) implementation which uses AND, OR and NOT gates. Figure 4.34(b) and 4.34(c) show the various steps for converting the AOI schematic of Figure4.34(a) to a logic diagram with NOR gates.

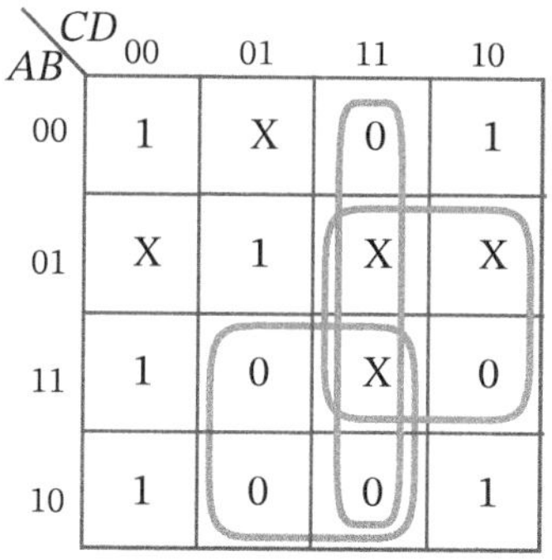

CD \ AB	00	01	11	10
00	1	X	0	1
01	X	1	X	X
11	1	0	X	0
10	1	0	0	1

Figure 4.33   K-map for Example 4.20

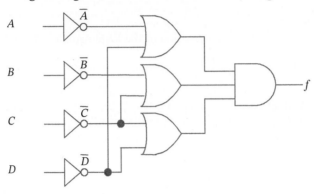

FIGURE 4.34 (a)

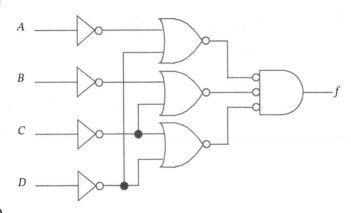

FIGURE 4.34 (b)

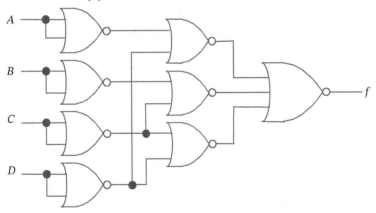

FIGURE 4.34 (c)

FIGURE 4.34   Figure for Example 4.20

QUESTIONS AND PROBLEMS

4.1   Using truth tables, express each one of the following functions and their complements in terms of sum of minterms and product of maxterms.
   (a) $F = ABC + \overline{A}BD + \overline{A}\,\overline{B}C + ACD$
   (b) $F = (W + X + Y)(W\overline{X} + Y)$

4.2   Express each of the following expressions in terms of minterms and maxterms.
   (a) $F = \overline{B}C + \overline{A}B + B(A + C)$
   (b) $F = (A + \overline{B} + C)(\overline{A} + B)$

4.3   Minimize each of the following functions using a K-map.
   (a) $F(A, B, C) = \Sigma m(0, 1, 4, 5)$
   (b) $F(A, B, C) = \Sigma m(0, 1, 2, 3, 6)$
   (c) $F(W, X, Y, Z) = \Sigma m(0, 2, 4, 6)$

4.4   Minimize each of the following expressions for F using a K-map.
   (a) $F(A, B, C) = \overline{B}\,\overline{C} + ABC + AB\overline{C}$
   (b) $F(A, B, C) = \overline{A}B\overline{C} + BC$
   (c) $F(A, B, C) = \overline{A}\,\overline{C} + A(\overline{B}\,\overline{C} + B\overline{C})$

4.5   Simplify each of the following functions for F using a K-map.
   (a) $F(W, X, Y, Z) = \Sigma m(0, 1, 4, 5, 8, 9)$
   (b) $F(A, B, C, D) = \Sigma m(0, 2, 8, 10, 12, 14)$

4.6   Simplify each of the following functions for F using a K-map.
   (a) $F(W, X, Y, Z) = \Sigma m(2, 3, 6, 7, 8, 9, 12, 13)$
   (b) $F(W, X, Y, Z) = \Sigma m(1, 3, 5, 7, 9, 11, 13, 15)$

4.7   Simplify each of the following functions for F using a K-map.
   (a) $\overline{F}(A, B, C, D) = \Sigma m(2, 4, 5, 6, 7, 10, 14)$
   (b) $F(W, X, Y, Z) = \Sigma m(0, 2, 4, 6, 8, 10, 12, 14)$

4.8   Minimize each of the following expressions for $\overline{F}$ using a K-map in sums-of-product form.
   (a) $F(W, X, Y, Z) = \overline{W}XYZ + WYZ$
   (b) $F = \overline{A}\,\overline{B}\,\overline{C}D + \overline{A}CD + ABCD$
   (c) $F = (\overline{A} + \overline{B} + C + D)(\overline{A} + B + C + \overline{D})(A + \overline{B} + C + \overline{D})$

4.9   Find essential prime implicants and then minimize each of the following functions for F using a K-map.
   (a) $F(A, B, C, D) = \Sigma m(3, 4, 5, 7, 11, 12, 15)$
   (b) $F(W, X, Y, Z) = \Sigma m(2, 3, 6, 7, 8, 9, 12, 13, 15)$

4.10   Minimize each of the following functions for f using a K-map and don't care conditions, d.
   (a) $f(A, B, C) = \Sigma m(1, 2, 4, 7)$
          $d(A, B, C) = \Sigma m(5, 6)$
   (b) $f(X, Y, Z) = \Sigma m(2, 6)$
          $d(X, Y, Z) = \Sigma m(0, 1, 3, 4, 5, 7)$

4.11   Minimize each of the following functions for f using a K-map and don't care conditions, d.
   (a) $f(A, B, C, D) = \Sigma m(0, 2, 3, 11)$
          $d(A, B, C, D) = \Sigma m(1, 8, 9, 10)$
   (b) $f(A, B, C, D) = \Sigma m(4, 5, 10, 11)$
          $d(A, B, C, D) = \Sigma m(12, 13, 14, 15)$

4.12 Minimize each of the following functions for F using a K-map and don't care conditions, d.
   (a) $F(A, B, C, D) = \Pi M(1, 3, 5, 6, 8, 9, 10, 14, 15)$, Don't Cares, $d(A, B, C, D) = \Sigma m(0, 4)$
   (b) $F(A, B, C, D) = \Sigma m(0, 1, 4, 5, 12, 13)$, Don't Cares, $d(A, B, C, D) = \Sigma m(2, 6, 14)$

4.13 Minimize each of the following functions for F using a K-map and don't care conditions, d.
   (a) $F(A, B, C, D) = \Sigma m(3, 7, 8, 9, 12, 15)$, Don't Cares, $d(A, B, C, D) = \Sigma m(0, 1)$
   (b) $F(W, X, Y, Z) = \Sigma m(4, 6, 8, 12)$, Don't Cares, $d(W, X, Y, Z) = \Sigma m(11, 14)$

WX\YZ	00	01	11	10
00	X	X	X	X
01	X	X	X	X
11	X	X	X	X
10	0	X	X	X

FIGURE P4.14

4.14 Find the output F for the K-map given in Figure P4.14.

4.15 Minimize the following expression using the Quine–McCluskey method. Verify the results using a
K-map. Draw logic diagrams using NAND gates.
$$F(A, B, C, D) = \Sigma m(0, 1, 4, 5, 8, 12)$$

4.16 Minimize the following expression using a K-map:
$$F = AB + \overline{A}\,\overline{B}C\overline{D} + C\overline{D} + \overline{A}\,\overline{B}CD$$
draw a schematic using:
   (a) NAND gates.
   (b) NOR gates.

4.17 Minimize the following function $F(A, B, C, D) = \Sigma m(6, 7, 8, 9)$ assuming that the condition $AB = 11_2$ will never occur. Draw schematics using:
   (a) NAND-only gates
   (b) NOR-only gates

4.18 Simplify each of the following functions for F using a K-map. Draw a logic diagram for each using NAND-only and NOR-only gates.
   (a) $F(W, X, Y, Z) = \Sigma m(0, 2, 4, 8, 12)$
   (b) $F(W, X, Y, Z) = \Sigma m(0, 2, 4, 7, 11, 12, 13)$

4.19 Minimize each of the following functions for F using a K-map and don't care conditions, d.
   (a) $\overline{F}(A, B, C, D) = \Sigma m(0, 1, 4, 5, 12, 13)$, Don't Cares, $d(A, B, C, D) = \Sigma m(2, 6, 14)$
   (b) $F(W, X, Y, Z) = \Sigma m(4, 6, 8, 12)$, Don't Cares, $d(W, X, Y, Z) = \Sigma m(11, 14)$

4.20 Minimize each of the following functions for F using a K-map and don't care conditions, d.
   (a) $F(A, B, C, D) = \Pi M(1, 3, 5, 6, 8, 9, 10, 14, 15)$, Don't Cares, $d(A, B, C, D) = \Sigma m(0, 4)$
   (b) $F(A, B, C, D) = \Sigma m(0, 1, 4, 5, 12, 13)$, Don't Cares, $d(A, B, C, D) = \Sigma m(2, 6, 14)$

4.21 Minimize each of the following functions for F using a K-map and don't care conditions, d.
   (a) $\overline{F}(A, B, C, D) = \Sigma m(3, 7, 8, 9, 12, 15)$, Don't Cares, $d(A, B, C, D) = \Sigma m(2, 6, 14)$
   (b) $F(W, X, Y, Z) = \Sigma m(4, 6, 8, 12)$, Don't Cares, $d(W, X, Y, Z) = \Sigma m(11, 14)$

4.22 Minimize each of the following functions for F using a K-map and don't care conditions, d.
   (a) $F(A, B, C, D) = \Pi M(1, 3, 5, 6, 8, 9, 10, 14, 15)$, Don't Cares, $d(A, B, C, D) = \Sigma m(0, 4)$
   (b) $F(A, B, C, D) = \Sigma m(0, 1, 4, 5, 12, 13)$, Don't Cares, $d(A, B, C, D) = \Sigma m(2, 6, 14)$

4.23 Minimize each of the following functions for F using a K-map and don't care conditions, d.
   (a) $F(A, B, C, D) = \Sigma m(3, 7, 8, 9, 12, 15)$, Don't Cares, $d(A, B, C, D) = \Sigma m(2, 6, 14)$
   (b) $F(W, X, Y, Z) = \Sigma m(4, 6, 8, 12)$, Don't Cares, $d(W, X, Y, Z) = \Sigma m(11, 14)$

5

ANALYSIS AND DESIGN OF COMBINATIONAL CIRCUITS USING GATES

This chapter describes analysis and design of combinational circuits using logic gates. Design procedure is standardized into three steps. This will make it easier to design combinational circuits using a structured procedure.

5.1   Basic Concepts

Digital logic circuits can be classified into two types: combinational and sequential. As mentioned before, combinational circuits have no memory while sequential circuits contain memory. Sequential circuits will be covered later in this book.

In this chapter, analysis and design of typical combinational circuits will be described. A combinational circuit is designed using logic gates in which application of inputs will generate the outputs at any time. An example of a combinational circuit is an adder, which produces the result of addition as output upon application of the two numbers to be added as inputs.

5.2   Analysis of a Combinational Logic Circuit

Analyzing a combinational circuit means that the circuit is given, the output equation(s) in terms of the input(s) and the truth table need to be determined. Hence, the combinational logic circuit can be analyzed by (i) first, identifying the number of inputs and outputs, (ii) expressing the outputs in terms of the inputs, and (iii) determining the truth table for the logic diagram.

As an example, consider the combinational circuit in Figure 5.1. There are three inputs (X, Y, and Z) and two outputs (Z_1 and Z_2) in the circuit.

Let us now express the outputs F_1 and F_2 in terms of the inputs. The output F_1 of the AND gate #1 is $F_1 = XY$. The output F_2 of NOR gate #2 is $F_2 = \overline{X + Y}$. The output of the XOR gate #3 is $F_3 = X \oplus F_1$.

Because one of the inputs of the XOR gate #4 is 1, its output is inverted. Therefore,

$$Z_1 = \overline{F_2} = X + Y$$

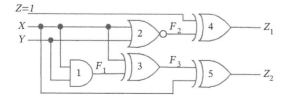

FIGURE 5.1   Analysis of a combinational logic circuit

Digital Logic with an Introduction to Verilog and FPGA-Based Design. First Edition. M. Rafiquzzaman and Steven A. McNinch.

Finally,

$$Z_2 = X \oplus F_3 = X \oplus (X \oplus XY)$$

Therefore,

$$Z_2 = X \oplus (X \cdot \overline{XY} + \overline{X} \cdot XY)$$

$$= X \oplus (X(\overline{X} + \overline{Y}))$$

$$= X \oplus (X\overline{Y})$$

$$= X(\overline{X\overline{Y}}) + \overline{X}(X\overline{Y})$$

$$= X(\overline{X} + Y)$$

$$= XY$$

Another way of determining Z_2 is provided below:

$$Z_2 = X \oplus F_3 = X \oplus (X \oplus XY) = X \oplus X \oplus XY = 0 \oplus (XY) = XY$$

The truth table shown in Table 5.1 can be obtained by using the logic equations for Z_1 and Z_2.

5.3   Design of Combinational Circuits Using Logic Gates

Design of a combinational circuit is basically a reverse process of analyzing the circuit. Note that the term "design" means that a designer needs to come up with a logic circuit following certain criteria such as minimum cost and highest speed. In this book, logic circuits are designed based on minimum cost. That is why minimization techniques are used to reduce the number of logic gates in a circuit. This will provide lower implementation cost. In summary, a combinational circuit can be designed using three steps as follows:

Step 1   *Truth Table:* If the truth table is given, go to step 2; else, determine the inputs and outputs from problem definition and then obtain the truth table.

TABLE 5.1   Truth table for Figure 5.1 with Input, $Z = 1$

Inputs		Outputs	
X	Y	Z_1	Z_2
0	0	0	0
0	1	1	0
1	0	1	0
1	1	1	1

TABLE 5.2   Truth table for F

A	B	C	F
0	0	0	0
0	0	1	1
0	1	0	1
0	1	1	1
1	0	0	1
1	0	1	1
1	1	0	1
1	1	1	0

Step 2 *Minimization:* Minimize the number of inputs (literals) in order to express the outputs. This reduces the number of gates and thus, the implementation cost. In order to accomplish this, first use K-map(s). Note that the number of K-maps is determined by the number of outputs. If the output(s) cannot be simplified using K-map(s), then obtain output equation(s) from the truth table directly, and then simplify using Boolean identities. Simplification is also sometimes possible using the K-map(s), first and then using Boolean identities.

Step 3 *Logic diagram or schematic:* Draw the logic diagram or schematic using logic gates. Note that since the terms "Logic diagram" and "Schematic" mean the same thing, they will be used interchangeably throughout this book. In order to illustrate the design procedure, the following examples are provided.

Example 5.1

Design a combinational circuit using logic gates with three inputs (A, B, and C) and one output, F. The output F is one if A, B, and C are not equal ($A \neq B \neq C$); otherwise $F = 0$.

Solution

The three steps for designing the circuit are provided below:

Step 1: *Truth Table:* Since the truth table is not given, the number of inputs and outputs are determined. There are three inputs (A, B, and C) and one output, F. The truth table is then obtained from problem definition and is shown in Table 5.2

Step 2: *Minimization:* Output, F in the truth table of Table 5.2 is simplified using a K-map (Figure 5.2(a)). The output equation is obtained as $F = A\overline{B} + \overline{A}C + B\overline{C}$.

Step 3: *Logic diagram or Schematic:* Using equations of Step 2, the schematic is drawn as shown in Figure 5.2 (b).

Example 5.2

Design a combinational circuit using logic gates that will accept three inputs (w, x, y) and generate one output as follows:

If w = 0, then z = x + y. On the other hand, if w = 1, then z = x ⊕ y.

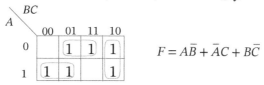

$$F = A\overline{B} + \overline{A}C + B\overline{C}$$

(a) K-map for F

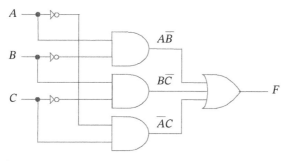

(b) Logic Diagram for the output, F

FIGURE 5.2 K-map and schematic for F

TABLE 5.3   Truth table for z

Inputs			Output
w	x	y	z
0	0	0	0
0	0	1	1
0	1	0	1
0	1	1	1
1	0	0	0
1	0	1	1
1	1	0	1
1	1	1	0

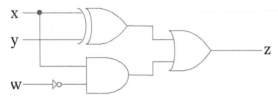

$z = \bar{x}y + x\bar{y} + \bar{w}x$
$= (x \oplus y) + \bar{w}x$

(a) K-map for z

(b) Schematic for z

FIGURE 5.3   K-map and schematic for z

Solution

The three steps for designing the circuit are provided below:

Step 1: *Truth Table:* Since the truth table is not given, the number of inputs and outputs are determined. There are three inputs (w, x and y) and one output (z). The truth table is then obtained from problem definition and is shown in Table 5.3.

Step 2: *Minimization:* Output, z in the truth table of Table 5.3 is simplified using a K-map (Figure 5.3(a)). The output equation is obtained as $z = \bar{x}y + x\bar{y} + \bar{w}x$ which can further be simplified as $z = (x \oplus y) + \bar{w}x$.

Step 3: *Logic diagram or Schematic:* Using equations of Step 2, the schematic is drawn as shown in Figure 5.3 (b).

Example 5.3

Design a combinational circuit using logic gates that will accept two inputs (x, y) and generate two outputs (z1, z2) as follows:
$z1 = x \oplus xy$ and $z2 = x + \overline{x + y}$

Solution

The three steps for designing the circuit are provided below:

Step 1: *Truth Table:* Since the truth table is not given, the number of inputs and outputs are determined. There are two inputs (x and y) and two outputs (z1 and z2). The truth table is then obtained from problem definition and is shown in Table 5.4.

TABLE 5.4   Truth table for z1 and z2

Inputs		Outputs	
x	y	z1	z2
0	0	0	1
0	1	0	0
1	0	1	1
1	1	0	1

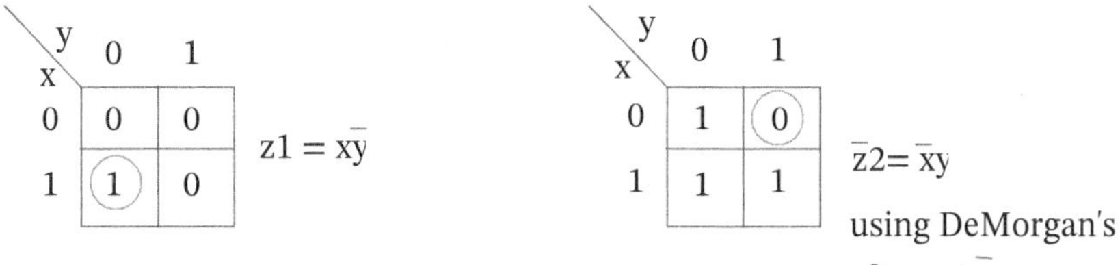

(a) K-maps for z1 and z2

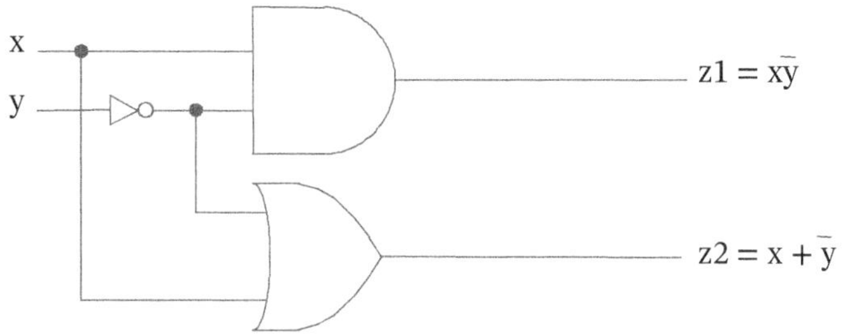

$z1 = x\bar{y}$

$\overline{z2} = \bar{x}y$

using DeMorgan's

$z2 = x + \bar{y}$

(b) Schematic for z1 and z2

$z1 = x\bar{y}$

$z2 = x + \bar{y}$

FIGURE 5.4   K-maps and schematic for z1 and z2

Step 2: *Minimization:* Outputs z1 and z2 in the truth table of Table 5.4 are simplified using K-maps (Figure 5.4(a)). The output equations are obtained as $z1 = x\bar{y}$ and $z2 = x + \bar{y}$.

Step 3: *Logic diagram or Schematic:* Using equations of Step 2, the schematic is drawn as shown in Figure 5.4 (b).

Example 5.4

Design a combinational circuit using logic gates that will accept two input bits (a, b) and generate output bits such that output bits = a plus b plus 2.

Solution

The three steps for designing the circuit are provided below:

Step 1: *Truth Table:* Since the truth table is not given, the number of inputs and outputs are determined from problem definition. There are two inputs (a, b) and three outputs (f2, f1, f0). The truth table is then obtained from problem definition and is shown in Table 5.5. Since inputs $a = 1$ and $b = 1$ will generate binary output 100, three output bits (f2, f1, f0) are needed in the truth table.

Step 2: *Minimization:* Outputs, (f2, f1, f0) in the truth table of Table 5.5 are simplified using K-maps (Figure 5.5(a)). The output equations are obtained as: $f2 = ab$, $f1 = \overline{ab}$, $f0 = a \oplus b$.

Step 3: *Logic diagram or Schematic:* Using equations of Step 2, the schematic is drawn as shown in Figure 5.5 (b).

TABLE 5.5   Truth table for Example 5.5

Inputs		Outputs		
a	b	f2	f1	f0
0	0	0	1	0
0	1	0	1	1
1	0	0	1	1
1	1	1	0	0

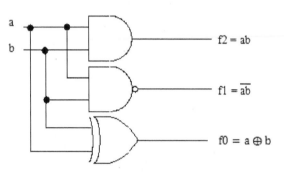

(a) K-maps for f2, f1, and f0

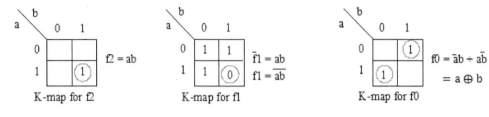

(b) Schematic for Example 5.4

FIGURE 5.5   K-maps and schematic for Example 5.4

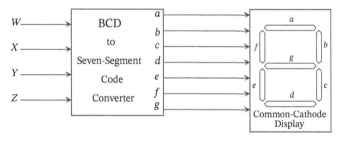

FIGURE 5.6   BCD to seven-segment code converter with a common-cathode display

TABLE 5.6   Truth Table for Converting Decimal Digits (since common-cathode, a 1 will turn a segment ON and a 0 will turn it OFF)

Decimal Digit to be Displayed	BCD Input Bits				Seven-Segment Output Bits						
	W	X	Y	Z	a	b	c	d	e	f	g
2	0	0	1	0	1	1	0	1	1	0	1
4	0	1	0	0	0	1	1	0	0	1	1
9	1	0	0	1	1	1	1	0	0	1	1

5.4   Multiple-Output Combinational Circuits

A combinational circuit may have more than one output. In such a situation, each output must be expressed as a function of the inputs. A digital circuit called the "code converter" is an example of multiple-output circuits. A code converter transforms information from one binary code to another. As an example, consider the BCD to seven-segment code converter shown in Figure 5.6. The code converter in the figure can be designed to translate a BCD input digit (W, X, Y, and Z) to its corresponding seven-segment code for displaying the decimal digit. Note that seven-segment displays (both common cathode display and common anode display) are covered in Chapter 1.

The inputs W, X, Y, and Z can be entered into the code converter via four switches as was discussed in Chapter 1. A combinational circuit can be designed for the code converter that will translate each digit entered using four bits into appropriate seven output bits (one bit for each segment) of the display.

In this case, the code converter has four inputs and seven outputs. This code converter is commonly known as a "BCD to seven-segment decoder." With four bits (W, X, Y, and Z), there are sixteen combinations (0000_2 through 1111_2) of 0's and 1's. BCD allows only 10 (0000_2 through 1001_2) of these 16 combinations, so the invalid numbers (1010_2 through 1111_2) will never occur for BCD and can be considered as don't cares in K-maps because it does not matter what the seven outputs (a through g) are for these invalid combinations.

The 7447 (TTL) is a commercially available BCD to seven-segment decoder/driver chip. It is designed for driving a common-anode display. A LOW output will light a segment while a HIGH output will turn it OFF. For normal operation, the LT (Lamp test) and BI/RBO (Blanking Input / Ripple Blanking Input) must be open or connected to HIGH. The 7448 chip, on the other hand, is designed for driving a common-cathode display. To illustrate the design of a BCD to seven-segment decoder, the following examples are provided.

Example 5.5

Design a code converter using logic gates for displaying the decimal digits 2, 4, and 9 using the diagram shown in Figure 5.6. Also, the code converter will turn the seven-segment display OFF for all valid decimal digits (0, 1, 3, 5, 6, 7, 8) which are not to be displayed.

Solution

First, it is obvious that the BCD to seven-segment decoder has four inputs and seven outputs. Three design steps are provided in the following.

Step 1:   *Truth Table:* Table 5.6 shows the truth table.

Step 2:   *Minimization:* Figures 5.7 (a) through (d) shows the K-maps. Note that seven-segment output bits (a through g) with the same column values will need one K-map. For example, b and g with column values 111 will have the same K-map, c and f with column values 011 will have the same K-map, and finally, d and e with column values 100 will have the same K-map.

Step 3:   *Schematic:* Figure 5.7 (e) shows the schematic.
Note: For the valid BCD digits that are not displayed (0, 1, 3, 5, 6, 7, 8) in this example, the combinational circuit for the code converter will generate 0's for the seven output bits (a through g) to turn them OFF. However, these seven bits will be don't-cares in the K-map for the invalid BCD digits 10 through 15.

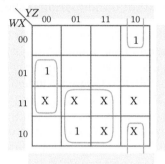

(a) K-map for a: $a = WZ + \bar{X}Y\bar{Z}$

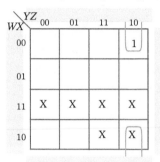

(b) K-map for b, g: $b, g = X\bar{Y}\bar{Z} + WZ + \bar{X}Y\bar{Z}$

(c) K-map for c, f: $c, f = X\bar{Y}\bar{Z} + WZ$

(d) K-map for d, e: $d, e = \bar{X}Y\bar{Z}$

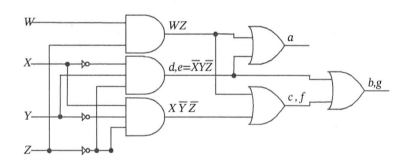

(e) Schematic

FIGURE 5.7   K-maps and schematic for BCD to seven-segment code converter for decimal digits 2, 4, and 9

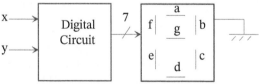

FIGURE 5.8   Figure for Example 5.6

Example 5.6

Design a digital circuit using logic gates that will input two bits (x,y) and display the square of the input bits on a seven-segment display as shown in Figure 5.8.

TABLE 5.7 Truth Table for Example 5.6

Inputs		Outputs						
x	y	a	b	c	d	e	f	g
0	0	1	1	1	1	1	1	0
0	1	0	0	0	0	1	1	0
1	0	0	1	1	0	0	1	1
1	1	1	1	1	0	0	1	1

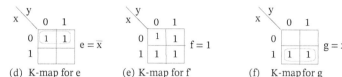

(a) K-map for a   (b) K-map for b, c   (c) K-map for d

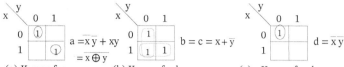

(d) K-map for e   (e) K-map for f   (f) K-map for g

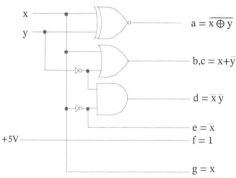

(g) Schematic for Example 5.6

FIGURE 5.9 K-maps and schematic for Example 5.6

Solution

Step 1: *Truth Table:* Table 5.7 shows the truth table. Note that the squared outputs for two-bit input (x, y) are 0000_2, 0001_2, 0100_2, and 1001_2. Since seven bits (a-g) are required to display these outputs on a seven- segment display, the digital circuit will have two inputs and seven outputs. Also, since the common line for the seven-segment display of Figure 5.8 is grounded, a common-cathode seven-segment display is used. This means that a '1' will turn a segment ON and a '0' will turn it OFF.

Step 2: *Minimization:* Figures 5.9 (a) through (f) show the K-maps. Note that seven-segment output bits (a through g) with the same column values will need one K-map. Hence, b and c with column values 1011 will have the same K-map

Step 3: *Schematic:* Figure 5.9 (g) shows the schematic.

Example 5.7

Design a digital circuit that will convert the BCD codes for the decimal digits (0 through 9) to their Gray codes.

Solution

Because both Gray code and BCD code are represented by four bits for each decimal digit, there are four inputs and four outputs. Note that 4-bit binary combination will provide 16 (2^4) combinations of 0's and 1's. Because only ten of these combinations (0000 through 1001) are allowed in BCD, the invalid combinations 1010 through 1111 can never occur in BCD. Therefore, these six binary inputs are considered as don't cares. This means that it does not matter what binary values are assumed by $f_3 f_2 f_1 f_0$ for $WXYZ = 1010$ through 1111.

Step 1: *Truth Table:* Table 5.8 shows the truth table.

Step 2: *Minimization:* Figures 5.10 (a) through (d) shows the K-maps.

Step 3: *Schematic:* Figure 5.10 (e) shows the schematic

TABLE 5.8   Truth table for Example 5.7

Decimal Digit	Input BCD Code				Output Gray Code			
	W	X	Y	Z	f_3	f_2	f_1	f_0
0	0	0	0	0	0	0	0	0
1	0	0	0	1	0	0	0	1
2	0	0	1	0	0	0	1	1
3	0	0	1	1	0	0	1	0
4	0	1	0	0	0	1	1	0
5	0	1	0	1	0	1	1	1
6	0	1	1	0	0	1	0	1
7	0	1	1	1	0	1	0	0
8	1	0	0	0	1	1	0	0
9	1	0	0	1	1	1	0	1

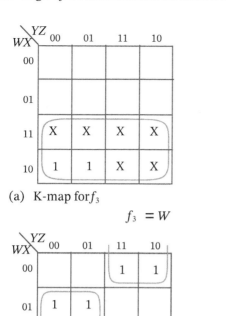

(a) K-map for f_3

$$f_3 = W$$

(b) K-map for f_2

$$f_2 = W + X$$

(c) K-map for f_1

(d) K-map for f_0

$$f_1 = X\bar{Y} + \bar{X}Y$$
$$= X \oplus Y$$

$$f_0 = \bar{Y}Z + Y\bar{Z}$$
$$= Y \oplus Z$$

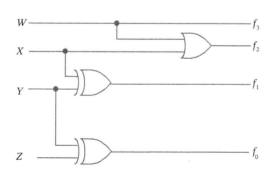

(e) Schematic for Example 5.7

FIGURE 5.10   K-maps and schematic for Example 5.8

QUESTIONS AND PROBLEMS

5.1   Find function F for the schematic shown in Figure P5.1.

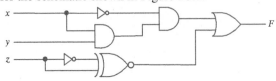

FIGURE P5.1

5.2   Consider Figure P5.2. Express the functions F_1 and F_2 in terms of the inputs A, B, and C. What is the relationship between F_1 and F_2?

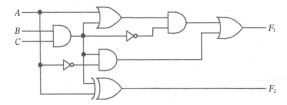

FIGURE P5.2

5.3   Analyze the schematic of Figure P5.3.

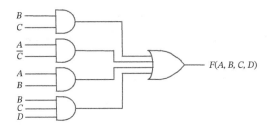

FIGURE P5.3

          (a)   Derive the Boolean expression for $F(A, B, C, D)$ in terms of the inputs
          (b)   Derive the truth table.

5.4   Determine the function F of the schematic of figure P5.4 and, then analyze the function using Boolean identities. Show that F can be represented by a single logic gate with A and B as inputs.

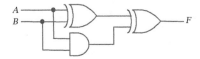

FIGURE P5.4

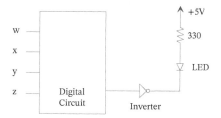

FIGURE P5.5

5.5 Suppose that the digital circuit shown in Figure P5.5 is required to turn an LED ON when the BCD inputs (W, X, Y, Z) are 0000_2 through 1000_2 and turn the LED OFF when the BCD inputs (W, X, Y, Z) are invalid inputs 1010_2 through 1111_2. Draw a schematic using logic gates. Show all steps clearly.

5.6 Design a combinational circuit that accepts a two-bit unsigned number, A and B such that the output, F = A plus B. Note that AB = 11_2 will never occur. Draw a schematic using logic gates. Show all steps clearly.

5.7 Design a combinational circuit with three inputs (A, B, C) and one output (F). The output is 1 when $A + C = 0$ or $AC = 1$; otherwise the output is 0. Draw a schematic using logic gates. Show

5.8 Design a combinational circuit that accepts a 3-bit unsigned number and generates an output binary number equal to the input number plus 1. Draw a schematic using logic gates. Show all steps clearly.

5.9 Design a combinational circuit with five input bits generating a 4-bit output that is the ones complement of four of the five input bits. Draw a logic diagram. Do not use NOT, NAND, or NOR gates.

5.10 Design a combinational circuit that converts a 4-bit BCD input to its nines complement output. Draw a logic diagram. Draw a schematic using logic gates. Show all steps clearly.

5.11 Design a combinational circuit using logic gates that will input a BCD digit (w, x, y, z), and output to LEDs (LED1 and LED2). If the BCD number is even, then the circuit will turn the LED1 ON and LED2 OFF. On the other hand, if the BCD number is odd, the circuit will turn an LED1 OFF and LED2 ON. Show all steps clearly.

5.12 Design a BCD to seven-segment decoder that will accept a decimal digit in BCD and generate the appropriate outputs for the segments to display a decimal digit (0–9). Use a common-anode display. Turn the seven-segment OFF for non-BCD digits. Draw a logic circuit. What will happen if a common cathode display is used? Comment on the interface between the decoder and the display.

5.13 Design a combinational circuit for a BCD to seven-segment code converter that will input a BCD number and output it on a seven segment common-anode display. The code converter will only display the number 8. The converter will turn the display OFF for all other valid BCD digits except digit 9 which will never occur. Draw a schematic using gates. Show all steps clearly.

5.14 Design a combinational circuit using gates for inputting a BCD digit (w, x, y, z) and outputting it to a seven-segment common-anode display. The code converter will only display the valid decimal numbers resulting from incrementing the input BCD digit. The converter will turn the display OFF for all invalid BCD digits. Draw a schematic using gates. Show all steps clearly.

5.15   Design a combinational circuit using gates for inputting a BCD digit (w, x, y, z) and outputting it to a seven-segment common-cathode display. The code converter will only display the decimal numbers 1 or 5. Show all steps clearly.

6

DESIGN OF TYPICAL COMBINATIONAL LOGIC COMPONENTS

This chapter contains design of typical combinational logic components. Topics such as design of comparators, decoders, encoders, multiplexers, demultiplexers, binary adder/subtractor, and BCD adder are included.

6.1 Design of Typical Combinational Logic Components

This following section describe design of typical combinational components using logic gates. Hence, three design steps of Chapter 5 will be used. Topics include design of comparators, decoders, encoders, multiplexers, demultiplexers, adders, and subtractors. These digital components are implemented in MSI chips. Note that MSI (Medium-Scale Integration) is defined in Chapter 1.

6.2 Comparators

The digital comparator is a widely used combinational circuit. Figure 6.1 shows a two-bit digital comparator, which provides the result of comparing two two-bit unsigned numbers. The comparison table is shown in Table 6.1.

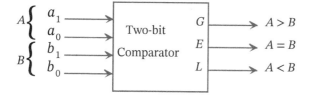

FIGURE 6.1 Block diagram of a two-bit comparator

TABLE 6.1 Comparison table for two unsigned numbers

Input Comparison	Outputs		
	G	E	L
$A > B$	1	0	0
$A < B$	0	0	1
$A = B$	0	1	0

TABLE 6.2   Truth table for the two-bit comparator

Inputs				Outputs		
a_1	a_0	b_1	b_0	G	E	L
0	0	0	0	0	1	0
0	0	0	1	0	0	1
0	0	1	0	0	0	1
0	0	1	1	0	0	1
0	1	0	0	1	0	0
0	1	0	1	0	1	0
0	1	1	0	0	0	1
0	1	1	1	0	0	1
1	0	0	0	1	0	0
1	0	0	1	1	0	0
1	0	1	0	0	1	0
1	0	1	1	0	0	1
1	1	0	0	1	0	0
1	1	0	1	1	0	0
1	1	1	0	1	0	0
1	1	1	1	0	1	0

The design steps for the two-bit comparator are provided below.

Step 1 *Truth Table:*   Table 6.2 provides the truth table for the two-bit comparator.

Step 2 *Minimization:* Figure 6.2 (a) shows the K-maps.

Step 3 *Schematic:*   Figure 6.2 (b) shows the schematic.

K-map for G:

$$G = a_1\bar{b}_1 + a_0\bar{b}_1\,\bar{b}_0 + a_1 a_0 \bar{b}_0$$

K-map for E:

a_1a_0 \ b_1b_0	00	01	11	10
00	1			
01		1		
11			1	
10				1

$$E = \overline{a_1}\,\overline{a_0}\,\overline{b_1}\,\overline{b_0} + \overline{a_1}\,a_0\,\overline{b_1}\,b_0 + a_1\,a_0\,b_1\,b_0 + a_1\,\overline{a_0}\,b_1\,\overline{b_0}$$

$$= \overline{a_1}\,\overline{b_1}\,(\overline{a_0}\,\overline{b_0} + a_0 b_0) + a_1 b_1 (a_0 b_0 + \overline{a_0}\,\overline{b_0})$$

$$= (a_0 b_0 + \overline{a_0}\overline{b_0})(a_1 b_1 + \overline{a_1}\overline{b_1})$$

$$= (a_0 \odot b_0)(a_1 \odot b_1)$$

K-map for L:

a_1a_0 \ b_1b_0	00	01	11	10
00		1	1	1
01			1	1
11				
10			1	

Note that the symbol $\odot$ means XNOR or equivalence operation.

$$L = \overline{a_1}b_1 + \overline{a_0}b_1 b_0 + \overline{a_1}\,\overline{a_0}b_0$$

(a) K-maps for the two-bit comparator

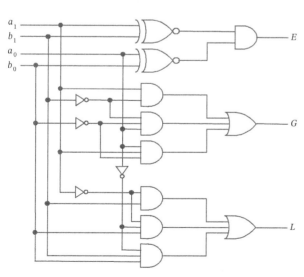

(b) Logic diagram of the two -bit comparator

FIGURE 6.2   Design of the two-bit comparator

6.3   Decoders

An n-bit binary number provides 2^n minterms or maxterms. For example, a two-bit binary number will generate $4 (2^2)$ minterms or maxterms. A decoder is a combinational circuit, when enabled, selects one of 2^n minterms or maxterms at the output based on 'n' input combinations. However, a decoder sometimes may have less than 2^n outputs. For example, the BCD to seven-segment decoder has four inputs and seven outputs rather than $16 (2^4)$ outputs. Note that a decoder may have a HIGH enable (for example, E), or a LOW enable (for example, $\bar{E}$) or multiple enables based on the design. Decoders are typically used for microcomputer memory systems for selecting different banks of memory and thus, providing larger memory sizes.

Next, the block diagram of a typical 2-to-4 decoder generating minterms is shown in Figure 6.3(a). This decoder generates a minterm when enabled by a HIGH. Table 6.3(a) provides the truth table. In the truth table, the symbol X is the don't care condition, which can be 0 or 1. Also, $E = 0$ disables the decoder. On the other hand, the decoder is enabled when $E = 1$. For example, when $E = 1$, $x_1 = 0$, $x_0 = 0$, and the output d_0 is one while the other outputs d_1, d_2, and d_3 are 0's, and we say that the decoder has generated the minterm m_0.

Next, the block diagram of a 2-to-4 decoder generating maxterms is shown in Figure 6.3(b). This decoder generates a maxterm when enabled by a HIGH. Table 6.3(b) provides the truth table. In the truth table, the symbol X is the don't care condition, which can be 0 or 1. Also, $E = 0$ disables the decoder. On the other hand, the decoder is enabled when $E = 1$. For example, when $E = 1$, $x_1 = 1$, $x_0 = 1$, then the output $\bar{d}3$ is 0 while the other outputs $\bar{d}0$, $\bar{d}1$, and $\bar{d}2$ are 1's, and we say that the decoder has generated the maxterm $m3$.

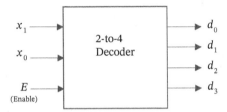

(a) 2-to-4 decoder generating minterms

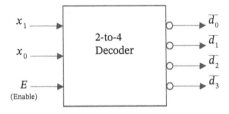

(b) 2-to-4 decoder generating maxterms

FIGURE 6.3   Block diagram of the 2-to-4 decoder

TABLE 6.3 (a)   Truth table of the 2-to-4 Decoder generating minterms for Figure 6.3(a)

	Inputs			Outputs		
E	x_1	x_0	d_0	d_1	d_2	d_3
0	X	X	0	0	0	0
1	0	0	1	0	0	0
1	0	1	0	1	0	0
1	1	0	0	0	1	0
1	1	1	0	0	0	1

TABLE 6.3 (b)   Truth table of the 2-to-4 Decoder generating maxterms for Figure 6.3(b)

Inputs			Outputs			
E	x_1	x_0	$\overline{d_0}$	$\overline{d_1}$	$\overline{d_2}$	$\overline{d_3}$
0	X	X	1	1	1	1
1	0	0	0	1	1	1
1	0	1	1	0	1	1
1	1	0	1	1	0	1
1	1	1	1	1	1	0

Next, the design of the decoder of Figure 6.3(a) will be provided. The three design steps are as follows:

Step 1: *Truth Table:* Table 6.3(a) provides the truth table for the 2-to-4 decoder.

Step 2: *Minimization:* By placing the minterms from the truth table on K-maps, minimization is not possible. Hence, output equations are obtained directly from the truth table. The equations are:
$d_0 = E\overline{x_1}\,\overline{x_0}, d_1 = E\overline{x_1}x_0, d_2 = Ex_1\overline{x_0}$ and $d_3 = Ex_1x_0$

Step 3: *Schematic:* Figure 6.4 shows the schematic.

In general, for n inputs, the n-to-2^n decoder, when enabled, selects one of 2^n minterms or maxterms at the output based on the input combinations. The decoder actually provides binary to decimal conversion operation. Large decoders can be designed using small decoders as the building blocks. For example, a 4-to-16 decoder can be designed using five 2-to-4 decoders as shown in Figure 6.5, and the truth table for the 4-to-16 decoder is provided in Table 6.4.

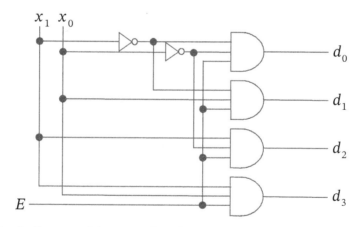

FIGURE 6.4   Logic diagram of the 2-to-4 decoder

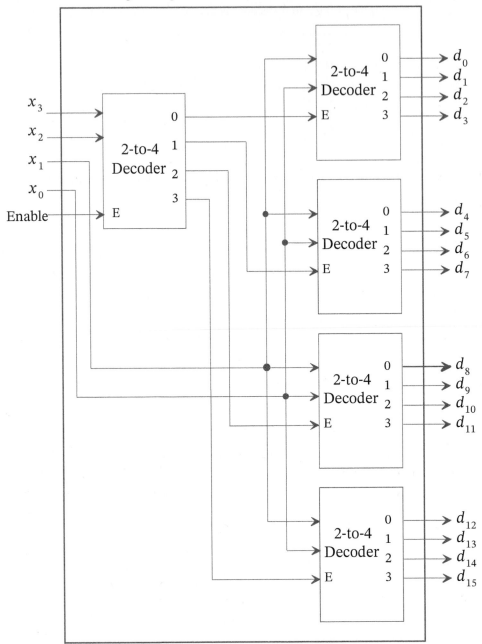

FIGURE 6.5   Implementation of a 4-to-16 decoder using 2-to-4 decoders

TABLE 6.4 Truth table of the 4-to-16 decoder generating minterms for Figure 6.5

INPUTS					OUTPUTS															
E	x_3	x_2	x_1	x_0	d_0	d_1	d_2	d_3	d_4	d_5	d_6	d_7	d_8	d_9	d_{10}	d_{11}	d_{12}	d_{13}	d_{14}	d_{15}
0	X	X	X	X	0	0	0	0	0	0	0	0	0	0	0	0	0	0	0	0
1	0	0	0	0	1	0	0	0	0	0	0	0	0	0	0	0	0	0	0	0
1	0	0	0	1	0	1	0	0	0	0	0	0	0	0	0	0	0	0	0	0
1	0	0	1	0	0	0	1	0	0	0	0	0	0	0	0	0	0	0	0	0
1	0	0	1	1	0	0	0	1	0	0	0	0	0	0	0	0	0	0	0	0
1	0	1	0	0	0	0	0	0	1	0	0	0	0	0	0	0	0	0	0	0
1	0	1	0	1	0	0	0	0	0	1	0	0	0	0	0	0	0	0	0	0
1	0	1	1	0	0	0	0	0	0	0	1	0	0	0	0	0	0	0	0	0
1	0	1	1	1	0	0	0	0	0	0	0	1	0	0	0	0	0	0	0	0
1	1	0	0	0	0	0	0	0	0	0	0	0	1	0	0	0	0	0	0	0
1	1	0	0	1	0	0	0	0	0	0	0	0	0	1	0	0	0	0	0	0
1	1	0	1	0	0	0	0	0	0	0	0	0	0	0	1	0	0	0	0	0
1	1	0	1	1	0	0	0	0	0	0	0	0	0	0	0	1	0	0	0	0
1	1	1	0	0	0	0	0	0	0	0	0	0	0	0	0	0	1	0	0	0
1	1	1	0	1	0	0	0	0	0	0	0	0	0	0	0	0	0	1	0	0
1	1	1	1	0	0	0	0	0	0	0	0	0	0	0	0	0	0	0	1	0
1	1	1	1	1	0	0	0	0	0	0	0	0	0	0	0	0	0	0	0	1

Commercially available decoders are normally built using NAND gates rather than AND gates because it is less expensive to produce the selected decoder output in its complement form. Also, most commercial decoders contain one or more enable inputs to control the circuit operation. An example of the commercial decoder is the 74HC138 or the 74LS138. This is a 3-to-8 decoder with three enable lines, G_1, $\overline{G_{2A}}$, and $\overline{G_{2B}}$. When $G_1 = H$, $\overline{G_{2A}} = L$ and $\overline{G_{2B}} = L$, the decoder is enabled. The decoder has three inputs: C (Most Significant Bit), B (Next), and A (Least Significant Bit), and eight outputs $\overline{Y_0}$, $\overline{Y_1}$, ..., $\overline{Y_7}$. With $CBA = 001$ and the decoder enabled, the selected output line (line 1) goes to LOW while the other output lines stay HIGH. Hence, the 74138 is a 3-to-8 decoder generating maxterms.

Decoders, along with logic gate(s), can be used to implement Boolean function(s). In order to accomplish this, the Boolean function(s) must be expressed in minterms or maxterms form. Examples 6.1 and 6.2 illustrate this.

Example 6.1

Draw a schematic to implement $F(W, X) = W$ using:

(a) a 2-to-4 decoder and a minimum number of logic gates. Assume that the decoder outputs a HIGH on the selected line when enabled by a LOW.

(b) a 2-to-4 decoder and a minimum number of logic gates. Assume that the decoder outputs a LOW on the selected line when enabled by a HIGH.

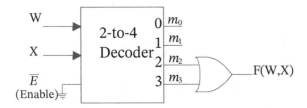

(a) Schematic for Example 6.1(a)

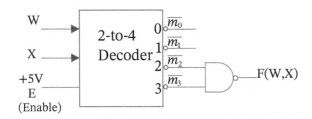

(b) Schematic for Example 6.1(b)

FIGURE 6.6   Schematics for Example 6.1

Solution

(a)   In order to implement this, the Boolean function F(W, X) must be expressed in minterm form. Hence,

$$F(W, X) = W(X + \overline{X}) = WX + W\overline{X} = m_3 + m_2$$

Hence, $F(W,X) = \Sigma m(2, 3)$

Figure 6.6(a) shows the schematic.

(b)   For this case, the Boolean function F(W, X) must be expressed in maxterm form. Hence,

$$F(W, X) = \overline{\overline{F}(W, X)} = \overline{\overline{m_2 + m_3}} = \overline{\overline{m_2} \cdot \overline{m_3}}$$

Figure 6.6(b) shows the schematic.

Example 6.2

A combinational circuit is specified by the following equations:

$$F_0(X, Y, Z) = \overline{X}YZ + XZ, \quad F_1(X, Y, Z) = Y(X + \overline{Z}), \quad F_2(X, Y, Z) = XY + \overline{X}YZ$$

Draw a schematic using a 3-to-8 decoder and external gates. Assume that the decoder outputs a HIGH on the selected line.

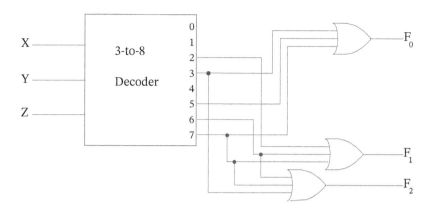

FIGURE 6.7 Solution for Example 6.2

Solution

In order implement the equations for F_0, F_1, and F_2 using a decoder, these equations must first be expressed in minterm form as follows:

$$F_0(X, Y, Z) = \overline{X}YZ + XZ(Y + \overline{Y}) = \overline{X}YZ + XYZ + X\overline{Y}Z = \Sigma m(3, 5, 7)$$

$$F_1(X, Y, Z) = Y(X + \overline{Z}) = XY + Y\overline{Z} = XY(Z + \overline{Z}) + Y\overline{Z}(X + \overline{X}) = XYZ + XY\overline{Z} + XY\overline{Z} + \overline{X}Y\overline{Z}$$

$$= \Sigma m(2, 6, 7)$$

$$F_2 = X Y + \overline{X} Y Z = XY(Z + \overline{Z}) + \overline{X} Y Z = XYZ + XY\overline{Z} + \overline{X} Y Z = \Sigma m(3, 6, 7)$$

Figure 6.7 shows the schematic.

Example 6.3

Design a combinational circuit using a decoder and logic gates to implement the functions depicted in Figure 6.8. In the figure, if $C = 0$, then $Z_1 = B$, and $Z_2 = A + B$. On the other hand, if $C = 1$, then $Z_1 = A + B$, and $Z_2 = AB$. Assume that the decoder output is HIGH when enabled by $E = 1$.

Solution

The truth table is shown in Table 6.5.
From the truth table,

$$Z_1 = \Sigma m(2, 3, 5, 6, 7)$$
$$Z_2 = \Sigma m(1, 2, 3, 7)$$

The logic diagram is shown in Figure 6.9.

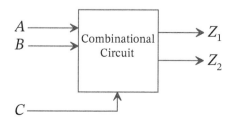

FIGURE 6.8 Figure for Example 6.3

TABLE 6.5   Truth table for Example 6.3

Inputs			Outputs	
C	B	A	Z_1	Z_2
0	0	0	0	0
0	0	1	0	1
0	1	0	1	1
0	1	1	1	1
1	0	0	0	0
1	0	1	1	0
1	1	0	1	0
1	1	1	1	1

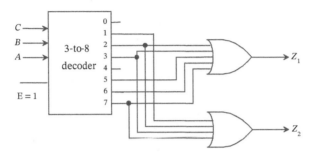

FIGURE 6.9   Implementation of Example 6.3 using a decoder and OR gates

6.4   Encoders

An encoder is a combinational circuit that performs the reverse operation of a decoder. An encoder has a maximum of 2^n inputs and n outputs. Figure 6.10 shows the block diagram of a 4-to-2 encoder. Table 6.6 provides the truth table of the 4-to-2 encoder.

From the truth table, it can be concluded that an encoder actually performs decimal-to-binary conversion. In the encoder defined by Table 6.6, it is assumed that only one of the four inputs can be HIGH at any time. If more than one input is 1 at the same time, an undefined output is generated. For example, if d_1 and d_2 are 1 at the same time, both x_0 and x_1 are 1.

TABLE 6.6   Truth table of the 4-to-2 encoder

Inputs				Outputs	
d_0	d_1	d_2	d_3	x_1	x_0
1	0	0	0	0	0
0	1	0	0	0	1
0	0	1	0	1	0
0	0	0	1	1	1

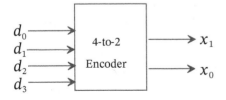

FIGURE 6.10   Block diagram of a 4-to-2 encoder

TABLE 6.7   Truth table of the 4-to-2 priority encoder

	Inputs			Outputs	
d_0	d_1	d_2	d_3	x_1	x_0
1	0	0	0	0	0
X	1	0	0	0	1
X	X	1	0	1	0
X	X	X	1	1	1

X means don't care

This represents decimal 3 rather than 1 or 2. Therefore, in an encoder in which more than one input can be active simultaneously, a priority scheme must be implemented in the inputs to ensure that only one input will be encoded at the output.

A 4-to-2 priority encoder will be designed next. Suppose that it is assumed that inputs with higher subscripts have higher priorities. This means that d_3 has the highest priority and d_0 has the lowest priority. Therefore, if d_0 and d_1 become one simultaneously, the output will be 01 for d_1. Three design steps are provided below:

Step 1: *Truth Table:*   Table 6.7 shows the truth table of the 4-to-2 priority encoder.

Step 2: *Minimization:*   Figures 6.11(a) and (b) show the K-maps. Note that $d_3 d_2 d_1 d_0 = X$ (don't care) in the K-map since this input combination does not occur in Table 6.7.

Step 3: *Schematic:*   Figure 6.11(c) shows the schematic.

<table>
<tr><td colspan="5">

$d_2 d_3$
$d_0 d_1$ \ 00 01 11 10

	00	01	11	10
00	X	1	1	0
01	1	1	1	0
11	1	1	1	0
10	0	1	1	0

</td></tr>
</table>

$d_2 d_3$
$d_0 d_1$ \ 00 01 11 10

	00	01	11	10
00	X	1	1	1
01	0	1	1	1
11	0	1	1	1
10	0	1	1	1

(a) K-map for $\overline{x_0}$ (b) K-map for $\overline{x_1}$

$$\overline{x_0} = \overline{d_1}\,\overline{d_3} + d_2\overline{d_3}$$

$$x_0 = (d_1 + d_3)(\overline{d_2} + d_3)$$

$$\overline{x_1} = \overline{d_2}\,\overline{d_3}$$

$$x_1 = d_2 + d_3$$

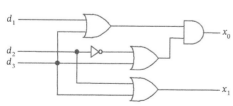

(c) Logic diagram

FIGURE 6.11   K-maps and logic diagram of a 4-to-2 priority encoder

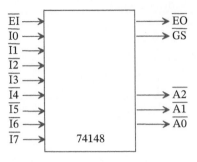

(a) 74148 Functional block diagram

INPUTS									OUTPUTS				
$\overline{EI}$	$\overline{I0}$	$\overline{I1}$	$\overline{I2}$	$\overline{I3}$	$\overline{I4}$	$\overline{I5}$	$\overline{I6}$	$\overline{I7}$	$\overline{A2}$	$\overline{A1}$	$\overline{A0}$	$\overline{GS}$	$\overline{EO}$
1	X	X	X	X	X	X	X	X	1	1	1	1	1
0	1	1	1	1	1	1	1	1	1	1	1	1	0
0	X	X	X	X	X	X	X	0	0	0	0	0	1
0	X	X	X	X	X	X	0	1	0	0	1	0	1
0	X	X	X	X	X	0	1	1	0	1	0	0	1
0	X	X	X	X	0	1	1	1	0	1	1	0	1
0	X	X	X	0	1	1	1	1	1	0	0	0	1
0	X	X	0	1	1	1	1	1	1	0	1	0	1
0	X	0	1	1	1	1	1	1	1	1	0	0	1
0	0	1	1	1	1	1	1	1	1	1	1	0	1

(b) 74148 Truth table [X can be 0 or 1]

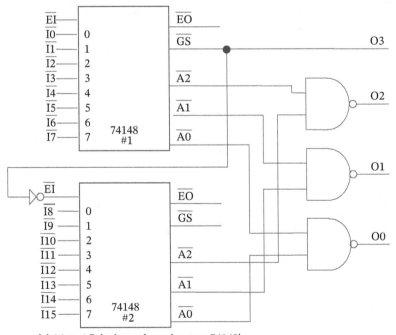

(c) 16-to-4 Priority ender using two 74148's

FIGURE 6.12   74148 Block diagram, Truth table, and expansion

Note that chips are limited by the number of pins. Priority encoders can sometimes be used to expand the number of input pins for handling more input signals. For example, the Motorola/Freescale/NXP 68000 16-bit 64-pin microprocessor provides three interrupt input pins. Using a 74148 (8-to-3 priority encoder) chip, the interrupt capability of the 68000 can be expanded to provide eight interrupt inputs rather than three.

The 74148 is a commercially available 8-to-3 priority encoder. Figure 6.12(a) shows the 74148 functional block diagram along the truth table in Figure 6.12(b). The operation of the 74148 shown in Figure 6.12(a) will now be explained. Suppose that $E1 = 0$ and $\overline{I0} = 0$ and $\overline{I1}$ through $\overline{I7}$ are 1's, then from the truth table of 6.12(b), $\overline{GS} = 0$, $\overline{EO} = 1$, $\overline{A2}\,\overline{A1}\,\overline{A0} = 111$. Note that the 74148 generates active low outputs.

Figure 6.12(c) shows the schematic of a 16-to-4 priority encoder obtained by connecting two 74148's along with three NAND gates. The configuration generates active high outputs.

For example, consider Figure 6.12(c). Suppose $\overline{I0}$ through $\overline{I7}$ of the 74148#1 are 1's and $\overline{EI}$ of the 74148#1 is connected to ground, outputs are 1's. Note that the output $\overline{GS}$ of the 74148#1 is inverted and connected to $\overline{EI}$ of the 74148#2. Hence, the priority encoder 74148#2 will be enabled. If $\overline{I15}$ (line 7) of the 74148#2 is 0 and $\overline{I8}$ through $\overline{I14}$ of the 74148#2 are 1's, then the outputs $\overline{A2}$, $\overline{A1}$, $\overline{A0}$ of the 74148#2 will be 000 (inverted 111). As mentioned before, the 74148 produces active low outputs. Hence, in Figure 6.12(c), $\overline{A2}$, $\overline{A1}$, $\overline{A0}$ of the 74148#2 are 000 while $\overline{A2}$, $\overline{A1}$, $\overline{A0}$ of the 74148#1 are 111. Since $\overline{A2}$, $\overline{A1}$, $\overline{A0}$ of the 74148#2 are NANDed with $\overline{A2}$, $\overline{A1}$, $\overline{A0}$ of the 74148#1, outputs O2, O1, O0 will be 111. Also, O3 = active HIGH when $\overline{I15} = 0$ at the output of the 16-to-4 encoder.

6.5   Multiplexers

A multiplexer (abbreviated as MUX) is a combinational circuit that selects one of n input lines and provides it on the output. Thus, the multiplexer has several inputs and only one output. One or more select lines identify or address one of several inputs and provide it on the output line. Multiplexers are typically used in designing a large amount of memory for a microcontroller or a microcomputer. This will reduce the amount of wiring necessary to connect this large memory to other parts of the microcontroller or microcomputer. Mux's are also used in FPGA.

Figures 6.13 (a) and 6.13 (b) show the block diagram and its symbol of a 2-to-1 multiplexer. The two inputs can be selected by one select line, S. When $S = 0$, input line 0 (d_0) will be presented at the output. On the other hand, when $S = 1$, input line 1 (d_1) will be produced at the output.

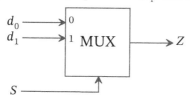

(a)   2-to-1 multiplexer block diagram

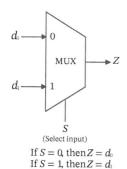

If $S = 0$, then $Z = d_0$
If $S = 1$, then $Z = d_1$

(b)   2-to-1 multiplexer symbol

FIGURE 6.13   2-to-1 multiplexer

The 2-to-1 MUX of Figure 6.13(a) is designed next. Three design steps are provided below:

Step 1: *Truth Table:*   Table 6.8 shows the truth table of the 2-to-1 multiplexer.

Step 2: *Minimization*:   Figure 6.14(a) shows the K-map. From the K-map, $Z = \bar{S}d_0 + Sd_1$

Step 3: *Schematic*:   Figure 6.14(b) shows the schematic.

In general, a multiplexer with n select lines can select one of 2^n data inputs. Hence, multiplexers are sometimes referred to as "data selectors."

A large multiplexer can be implemented using a small multiplexer as the building block. For example, consider the block diagram and the truth table of a 4-to-1 multiplexer shown in Figure 6.15 and Table 6.9 respectively. The four-input multiplexer can be implemented using three 2-to-1 multiplexers as shown in Figure 6.16.

In Figure 6.16, the select line S_0 is applied as input to the multiplexers MUX 0 and MUX 1. This means that $Z_0 = d_0$ or d_1 and $Z_1 = d_2$ or d_3, depending on whether $S_0 = 0$ or 1. The select line S_1 is given as input to the multiplexer MUX 2. This implies that $Z = Z_0$ if $S_1 = 0$; otherwise $Z = Z_1$. In this arrangement if $S_1S_0 = 11$, then $Z = d_3$ because $S_0 = 1$ implies that $Z_0 = d_1$ and $Z_1 = d_3$ because $S_1 = 1$, the MUX 2 selects

TABLE 6.8   Truth table of the 2-to-1 Multiplexer

S	d_0	d_1	Z
0	0	0	0
0	0	1	0
0	1	0	1
0	1	1	1
1	0	0	0
1	0	1	1
1	1	0	0
1	1	1	1

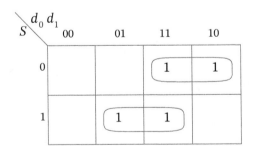

FIGURE 6.14(a)   K-map for the 2-to-1 MUX

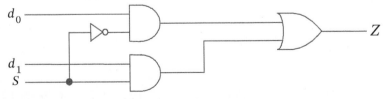

FIGURE 6.14(b)   Logic diagram of the 2-to-1 MUX

the data input Z_1, and thus $Z = d_3$. The other entries of the truth table of Table 6.9 can be verified in a similar manner.

Multiplexers can be used to implement Boolean equations. For example, consider realizing $f(x,y,z) = x\bar{z} + yz$ using a 4-to-1 multiplexer. First, the Boolean equation for $f(x,y,z)$ is expressed in minterm form as follows: $f(x,y,z) = x\bar{z}(y + \bar{y}) + yz(x + \bar{x}) = xy\bar{z} + x\bar{y}\,\bar{z} + xyz + \bar{x}yz$. The next step is to use two of the three variables (x,y,z) as select inputs. Suppose y and z are arbitrarily chosen as select inputs. The four combinations $(\bar{y}\bar{z}, \bar{y}z, y\bar{z}, yz)$ of the select inputs, y and z are then required to be factored out of minterm form for $f(x,y,z)$ to determine the inputs to the 4-to-1 multiplexer as follows: $f(x,y,z) = \bar{y}\,\bar{z}(x) + \bar{y}z(0) + y\bar{z}(x) + yz(x + \bar{x}) = \bar{y}\,\bar{z}(x) + \bar{y}z(0) + y\bar{z}(x) + yz(1)$. Hence, the above equation for $f(x,y,z)$ can be implemented using the 4-to-1 multiplexer of Figure 6.15 as follows: $S_1 = y$, $S_0 = z$, $d_0 = x$, $d_1 = 0$, $d_2 = x$, $d_3 = 1$, and $Z = f(x,y,z)$. Figure 6.17 shows the implementation.

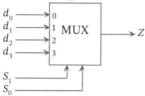

FIGURE 6.15   Block-diagram representation of a four-input multiplexer

TABLE 6.9   Truth table of 4-to-1 multiplexer

S_1	S_0	Z
0	0	d_0
0	1	d_1
1	0	d_2
1	1	d_3

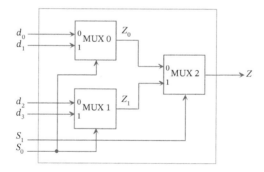

FIGURE 6.16   Implementation of a four-input multiplexer using only two-input multiplexers

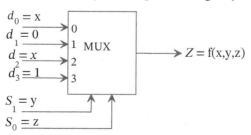

FIGURE 6.17   Implementation of a Boolean equation using a 4-to-1 multiplexer

Next, consider implementing $f(a,b,c) = \Sigma m(0, 2. 3. 7)$ using the 4-to-1 multiplexer of Figure 6.15. The first step is to obtain a table as follows:

```
a  b  c  f
0  0  0  1
0  0  1  0        f = c̄
-------------
0  1  0  1
0  1  1  1        f = 1
------------ -
1  0  0  0
1  0  1  0        f = 0
-------------
1  1  0  0
1  1  1  1        f = c
```

Next, select 'a' and 'b' as select inputs. Note that in each pair of the table, 'f' can be 0 or 1 or c or c̄. For example, when $ab = 00$, output $f = \bar{c}$ because $f = 1$ when $c = 0$, and $f = 0$ when $c = 1$.

Hence, the 4-to-1 multiplexer of Figure 6.15 can be connected as follows: $S_1 = a$, $S_0 = b$, $d_0 = \bar{c}$, $d_1 = 1$, $d_2 = 0$, $d_3 = c$. Note that the inputs to the multiplexer are selected from the table.

Example 6.4

Draw a schematic to implement a combinational circuit that will select one of two inputs $(x_1 x_0)$, and then perform the following functions based upon a select input, 's' depicted in Figure 6.18. Connect x_1 and x_0 to appropriate levels such that: when $s = 0$, then two-bit output $(y_1 y_0) = 11_2$; on the other hand, when $s = 1$, then the two-bit output $(y_1 y_0) = 00_2$. Use a minimum number of multiplexers. Do not use any logic gates.

Solution

Figure 6.19 shows the schematic.

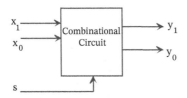

FIGURE 6.18   Figure for Example 6.4

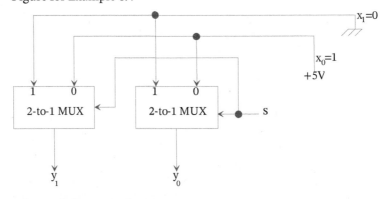

FIGURE 6.19   Schematic for Example 6.4

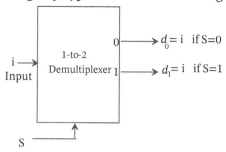

(a) 1-to-2 demultiplexer

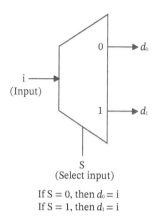

If S = 0, then d_0 = i
If S = 1, then d_1 = i

(b) 1-to-2 demultiplexer symbol

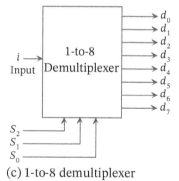

(c) 1-to-8 demultiplexer

FIGURE 6.20   Demultiplexer

6.6   Demultiplexers

The demultiplexer (abbreviated as demux) is a combinational circuit that performs the reverse operation of a multiplexer. The demultiplexer has only one input and several outputs. The input is transferred to one of the output lines selected by the combination of 0's and 1's of the select inputs; the output lines which are not selected will be 0's. This means that the select inputs determine one of the output lines to be selected; data input from the input line is then transferred to the selected output line. A demultiplexer with 2^n outputs has n select lines, which are used to send the selected input line to the output.

Demultiplexers are used to connect a single source to multiple destinations. For example, a specific output bit (such as bit 0) of an ALU (Arithmetic Logic Unit) can be fed as an input to a demultiplexer, and the output (line 0 selected by the demux selection bits) of the Demultiplexer can then be connected to bit 0 of each of the multiple registers. Thus, the output (bit 0) of the ALU can be transferred to bit 0 of the multiple registers. Hence, for an 8-bit ALU, outputs of eight 1-to-8 demultiplexers can be connected to bits 0 through 7 (line 0 output of the demux to bit 0 of each of the multiple registers, line 1 output of the demux to bit 1 of each of the multiple registers and so on) of the multiple 8-bit registers. Hence, the 8-bit output of the ALU can be transferred to several registers. Demultiplexers can also be used for serial to parallel data conversion.

Figure 6.20(a) and Figure 6.20(b), respectively, depict the block diagrams of a 1-to-2 demultiplexer and its symbol. When S = 0, then d_0 = i and when S = 1, then d_1 = i. Figure 6.20(c), on the other hand, shows the block diagram of a 1-to-8 demultiplexer. Suppose that $i = 1$ and $S_2S_1S_0 = 010$; output line d_2 will be selected and a 1 will be outputted on d_2.

The 1-to-2 demultiplexer of Figure 6.20(a) is designed next. Three design steps are provided below:

Step 1: *Truth Table:* Table: 6.10 shows the truth table of the 1-to-2 demultiplexer. Note that the output is 'i' when selected and '0' when not selected.

Step 2: *Minimization:* Output equations cannot be minimized using K-maps. Hence, output equations are obtained directly from the truth table as follows:
$d_1 = iS \quad d_0 = i\bar{S}$

Step 3: *Schematic:* Figure 6.21 shows the logic diagram of the 1-to 2 demultiplexer.

TABLE 6.10   Truth table of the 1-to-2 demultiplexer

	Inputs		Outputs	
S	i	d_1	d_0	
0	0	0	0	
0	1	0	1	
1	0	0	0	
1	1	1	0	

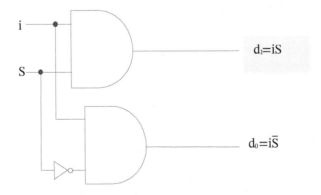

FIGURE 6.21   1-to-2 demultiplexer schematic

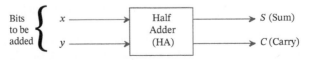

FIGURE 6.22   Block diagram of the half adder

6.7 Binary Adder/Subtractor and BCD Adder

When two bits x and y are added, a sum and a carry are generated. A combinational circuit that adds two bits is called a "half adder." Figure 6.22 shows a block diagram of the half adder. The half adder is designed next. Three design steps are provided below:

Step 1: *Truth Table:* Table 6.11 shows the truth table of the half adder.

Step 2: *Minimization:* Output equations cannot be minimized using K-maps. Hence, output equations are obtained directly from the truth table as follows:
$$S = \bar{x}y + x\bar{y} = x \oplus y, \quad C = xy$$

Step 3: *Schematic:* Figure 6.23 shows the logic diagram of the half adder.

Next, consider addition of two 4-bit numbers as follows:

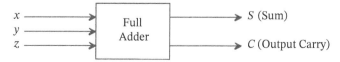

This addition of two bits will generate a sum and a carry. The carry may be 0 or 1. Also, there will be no previous carry while adding the least significant bits (bit 0) of the two numbers. This means that two bits need to be added for bit 0 of the two numbers. On the other hand, addition of three bits (two bits of the two numbers and a previous carry, which may be 0 or 1) is required for all the subsequent bits. A combinational circuit that adds three bits, generating a sum and a carry (which may be 0 or 1), is called a "full adder."

Figure 6.24 shows the block diagram of a full adder. The full adder adds three bits, x, y, and z, and generates a sum bit and a carry bit.

TABLE 6.11 Truth table of the half adder

Inputs		Outputs		Decimal Value
x	y	C	S	
0	0	0	0	0
0	1	0	1	1
1	0	0	1	1
1	1	1	0	2

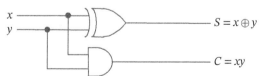

FIGURE 6.23 Logic diagram of the half adder

$$x \longrightarrow \boxed{\text{Full Adder}} \longrightarrow S \text{ (Sum)}$$
$$y, z \longrightarrow \longrightarrow C \text{ (Output Carry)}$$

FIGURE 6.24 Block diagram of a full adder

The full adder is designed next. Three design steps are provided below.

Step 1: *Truth Table:* Table 6.12 shows the truth table of the full adder.

Step 2: *Minimization:* The sum, S cannot be minimized using a K-map. Hence, the equation for the sum, S is obtained directly from the truth table and then simplified using Boolean identities as follows:

From the truth table, $S = \bar{x}\bar{y}z + \bar{x}y\bar{z} + x\bar{y}\bar{z} + xyz = (\bar{x}y + x\bar{y})\bar{z} + (xy + \bar{x}\bar{y})z$

Let $w = \bar{x}y + x\bar{y}$ then $\bar{w} = xy + \bar{x}\bar{y}$. Hence, $S = w\bar{z} + \bar{w}z = w \oplus z = x \oplus y \oplus z$

Also, from the truth table, $C = \bar{x}yz + x\bar{y}z + xy\bar{z} + xyz = (\bar{x}y + x\bar{y})z + xy(z + \bar{z}) = wz + xy$

where, $w = (\bar{x}y + x\bar{y}) = x \oplus y$. Hence, $C = (x \oplus y)z + xy$

Another form of Carry can be written as follows:

$C = \bar{x}yz + x\bar{y}z + xy\bar{z} + xyz = \bar{x}yz + x\bar{y}z + xy\bar{z} + xyz + xyz + xyz$ (Adding redundant terms xyz)

$= yz(\bar{x} + x) + xz(\bar{y} + y) + xy(\bar{z} + z) = yz + xz + xy$

This form of C can also be obtained using the K-map of figure 6.25(a) as follows:
$C = yz + xz + xy$

Step 3: *Schematic:* Figure 6.25(b) shows the schematic of the full adder.

TABLE 6.12   Truth table of the full adder

Inputs			Outputs		Decimal Value
x	y	z	C	S	
0	0	0	0	0	0
0	0	1	0	1	1
0	1	0	0	1	1
0	1	1	1	0	2
1	0	0	0	1	1
1	0	1	1	0	2
1	1	0	1	0	2
1	1	1	1	1	3

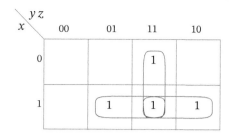

(a) K-map for C of the full adder

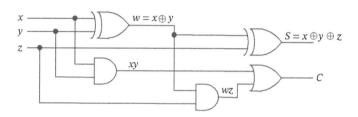

(b) Schematic of the full adder

FIGURE 6.25 K-map for C and the schematic of the full adder

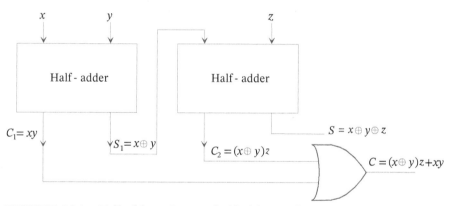

FIGURE 6.26 Full adder using two half adders and an OR gate

Note that the names "half adder" and "full adder" are based on the fact that two half adders are required to obtain a full adder. This can be obtained as follows. One of the two half adders with inputs, x and y will generate the sum, $S_1 = x \oplus y$ and the carry, $C_1 = xy$. The sum (S_1) output can be connected to one of the inputs of the second half adder with z as the other input. Thus, the sum output (S) and the carry output (C_2) of the second half adder will be $S = x \oplus y \oplus z$ and $C_2 = (x \oplus y)z$. The carry outputs of the two half adders can be logically ORed to provide the carry (C) of the full adder as $C = (x \oplus y)z + xy$. Therefore, two half adders and a two-input OR gate can be used to obtain a full adder. Figure 6.26 depicts this.

A 4-bit binary adder (also called "Ripple Carry Adder") for adding two 4-bit numbers $x_3x_2x_1x_0$ and $y_3y_2y_1y_0$ can be implemented using one half adder and three full adders as shown in Figure 6.27. A full adder adds two bits if one of its inputs is grounded. This means that the half adder in Figure 6.27 can be replaced by a full adder with its input C in grounded. Figure 6.28 shows implementation of a 4-bit binary adder using four full adders.

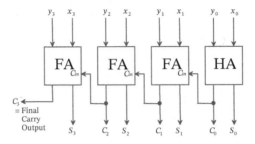

FIGURE 6.27   4-bit binary adder using one half adder and three full adders

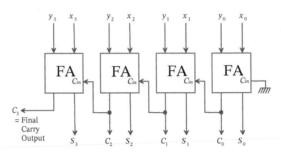

FIGURE 6.28   Four-bit binary adder using full adders

Next, design of a BCD adder for adding two single BCD digits will be provided. From Chapter 2, addition of two BCD digits is correct if the binary sum is less than or equal to 1001_2 (9 in decimal). A binary sum greater than 1001_2 results into an invalid BCD sum; adding 0110_2 to an invalid BCD sum provides the correct sum with an output carry of 1. Furthermore, addition of two BCD digits (each digit having a maximum value of 9) along with carry will provide a sum not exceeding 19 in decimal (10011_2). A BCD adder can be designed by implementing required corrections in the result for decimal numbers from 10 through 19 (1010_2 through 10011_2). Therefore, a correction is necessary for the following:

(a) if the binary sum is greater than or equal to decimal 16 (This will generate a carry of one).

(b) if the binary sum is 1010_2 through 1111_2

For example, consider adding packed BCD numbers 99 and 38:

99	1001	1001	BCD for 99
+38	0011	1000	BCD for 38
137	1101	0001	invalid sum
	+0110	+0110	add 6 for correction
0001	0011	0111	
1	3	7	← correct answer 137

This means that a circuit can be designed to indicate that BCD correction (addition of 0110 to the sum) is necessary after binary addition of two single BCD digits. The circuit will generate:

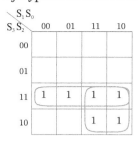

FIGURE 6.29 K-map for C_{11}

(a) an output (C_{11}) of '1' if the binary sum is $S_3 S_2 S_1 S_0 = 1010_2$ through 1111_2.

or

(b) a carry (C_0) of 1 if the binary sum produces a carry ; this means that the binary sum is greater than or equal to decimal 16.

For case (a), using the K-map of Figure 6.29,

$C_{11} = S_1 S_3 + S_2 S_3$
Hence, $C_{11} = S_1 S_3 + S_2 S_3 = S_3 (S_1 + S_2)$.

Combining cases (a) and (b), the output of the circuit, $C_1 = C_0 + S_3 (S_1 + S_2)$. This is implemented in the Figure 6.30, where A and B are two BCD digits, and SUM is the BCD result.

Note that C_1 is the output of the logic circuit which can be 0 or 1 based on the inputs C_0 or C_{11} of the circuit. When $C_1 = 0$, zeros are added to $S_3 S_2 S_1 S_0$. This situation occurs when $S_3 S_2 S_1 S_0$ is less than or equal to 1001_2. However, when $C_1 = 1$, the binary number 0110 is added to $S_3 S_2 S_1 S_0$ using the second 4-bit adder. This situation occurs when $S_3 S_2 S_2 S1$ is 1010_2 through 1111_2 or if a carry is generated. The carry output from the second 4-bit adder can be discarded. Note that BCD parallel adder for adding n BCD digits can be obtained using n BCD adders by connecting the output carry (C_0) of each low BCD adder to C_{in} of the next BCD adder.

Next, half-subtractor and full-subtractor will be discussed. Similar to half adder and full adder, there are half-subtractor and full-subtractor. Using half-subtractors and full-subtractors, subtraction operation can be implemented with logic circuits in a direct manner. A half-subtractor is a combinational circuit that subtracts two bits generating a result (R) bit and a borrow (B) bit. The truth table for the half-subtractor is provided in Table 6.13. The borrow (B) is 0 if x is greater than or equal to y; B = 1 if x is less than y. From the truth table, $R = \bar{x}y + x\bar{y} = x \oplus y$ and $B = \bar{x}y$.

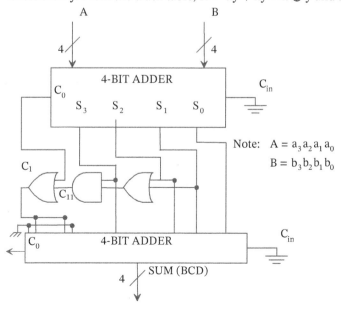

FIGURE 6.30 BCD Adder

TABLE 6.13   Truth table for the half-subtractor

x (minuend)	y (subtrahend)	B (borrow)	R (result)
0	0	0	0
0	1	1	1
1	0	0	1
1	1	0	0

TABLE 6.14   Truth table for the full-subtractor

x	y	z	B (borrow)	R (result)
0	0	0	0	0
0	0	1	1	1
0	1	0	1	1
0	1	1	1	0
1	0	0	0	1
1	0	1	0	0
1	1	0	0	0
1	1	1	1	1

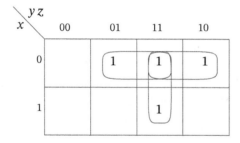

FIGURE 6.31   K-map for B

A full-subtractor is a combinational circuit that performs the operation among three bits x - y - z generating a result bit (R) and a borrow bit (B). The truth table for the full-subtractor is provided in Table 6.14.

The truth table for R (Table 6.14) is the same as the truth table for S of the full adder (Table 6.12). Hence, $R = x \oplus y \oplus z$. Also, using the K-map of Figure 6.31, $B = \bar{x}\, y + \bar{x}\, z + yz$. It is advantageous to implement addition and subtraction with full adders since both operations can be obtained using a single logic circuit.

Because any Boolean function can be expressed in terms of minterms or maxterms, a decoder can be used to implement the function or its complement. Since the 74138 generates a LOW (maxterm) on the selected output line, the complement of a Boolean function can be obtained by logically ANDing the appropriate minterms. For example, consider the truth table of the full adder listed in Table 6.12. The inverted sum and the inverted carry can be expressed in terms of minterms as follows:

$$\bar{S} = \Sigma m(0, 3, 5, 6)$$
$$\bar{C} = \Sigma m(0, 1, 2, 4)$$

Hence, using DeMorgan's theorem $S = \overline{m_0} \cdot \overline{m_3} \cdot \overline{m_5} \cdot \overline{m_6}$ and $C = \overline{m_0} \cdot \overline{m_1} \cdot \overline{m_2} \cdot \overline{m_3} \cdot \overline{m_4}$.

Fifure 6.32 shows the implementation of full adder using a 74138 decoder (c = x, b = y, a = z) and two 4-input AND gates. Note that the 74138 in the Manufacturer's data sheet uses the symbols c, b, a as three inputs to the decoder with 'c' as the most significant bit and 'a' as the least significant bit.

Next, consider implementing the full adder using a minimum number of 4-to-1 multiplexers. After grouping Table 6.12 of the full adder in pairs, the modified table of Table 6.15 is obtained. Since the full adder has two outputs (C, S), two 4-to-1 multiplexers are needed. The schematic is shown in Figure 6.33.

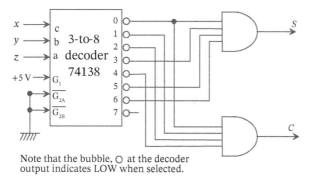

Note that the bubble, ○ at the decoder output indicates LOW when selected.

FIGURE 6.32   Implementation of a full adder using a 74138 decoder and two 4-input AND gates

TABLE 6.15   Table for implementing a full adder using multiplexers

Inputs			Outputs		
x	y	z	C	S	
0	0	0	0	0	$C = 0, S = z$
0	0	1	0	1	
0	1	0	0	1	$C = z, S = \bar{z}$
0	1	1	1	0	
1	0	0	0	1	$C = z, S = \bar{z}$
1	0	1	1	0	
1	1	0	1	0	$C = 1, S = z$
1	1	1	1	1	

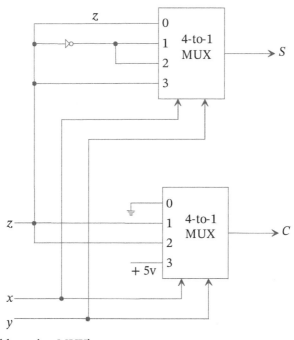

FIGURE 6.33   Full adder using MUX's

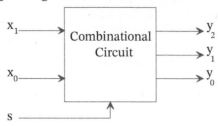

FIGURE 6.34   Figure for Example 6.5

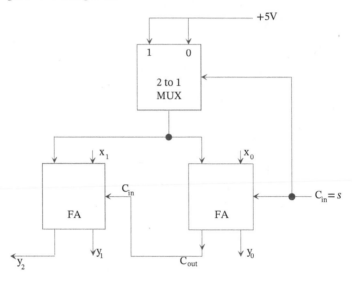

FIGURE 6.35   Schematic for Example 6.5

Example 6.5

Draw a schematic to implement a combinational circuit that will input a two-bit unsigned number (x_1x_0), and then perform the following functions based upon a select input, s, as depicted in the figure 6.34. Connect x_1, x_0 to appropriate logic levels such that if $s = 0$, then the three-bit output $(y_2y_1y_0) = x_1x_0$ + 3. On the other hand, if $s = 1$, then the three-bit output $(y_2y_1y_0) = x_1x_0 + 4$. Use a minimum number of full adders and multiplexers.

Do not use any logic gates.

Solution

Since the combinational circuit needs to perform two functions, one 2-to-1 mux is needed. Also, for two-bit arithmetic operations by the combinational circuit, two full adders are needed. Hence, by manipulating the inputs of the mux, the schematic shown in Figure 6.35 will accomplish this.

Example 6.6

Design combinational circuits using full adders and multiplexers as building blocks to implement (a) a 4-bit adder/subtractor; add when $S = 0$ and subtract when $S = 1$ and (b) multiply a 4-bit unsigned number by 2 when $S = 0$ and transfer zero to output when $S = 1$.

Solution

(a) The subtraction $x - y$ of two binary numbers can be performed using two's complement arithmetic. As discussed before, $x - y = x + $ (one's complement of y) + 1.

A 4-bit adder/subtractor is shown in Figure 6.36(a).

The adder/subtractor in Figure 6.36(a) utilizes four MUX's. Each MUX has one select line (S) and is capable of selecting one of two lines, y_n or $\overline{y}_n$.

The 4-bit adder/subtractor of Figure 6.36(a) either adds two 4-bit numbers and performs $(x_3x_2x_1x_0)$ ADD $(y_3y_2y_1y_0)$ when $S = 0$ or performs the subtraction operation $(x_3x_2x_1x_0)$ MINUS $(y_3y_2y_1y_0)$ for $S = 1$. The select bit S can be implemented by a switch. When $S = 0$, each MUX outputs the true value of y_n ($n = 0$ through 3) to the corresponding inputs of the full adder FA_n ($n = 0$ through 3). Because $S = 0$ (C_{in} for $FA_0 = 0$), the four full adders perform the desired 4-bit addition. When $S = 1$ (C_{in} for $FA_0 = 1$), each MUX generates the one's complement of y_n at the corresponding inputs of the full adder FA_n. Because $S = C_{in} = 1$, the four full adders provide the following operation: $(x_3x_2x_1x_0)$ - $(y_3y_2y_1y_0)$ = $(x_3x_2x_1x_0) + (\overline{y}_3\overline{y}_2\overline{y}_1\overline{y}_0) + 1$.

(b) Assume 4-bit output $S_3 S_2 S_1 S_0$. Figure 6.36 (b) shows the implementation.

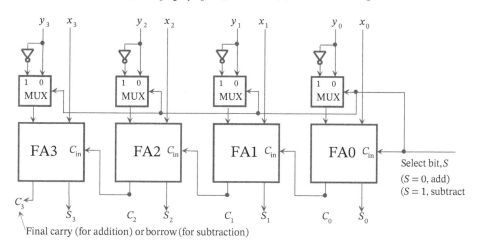

FIGURE 6.36 (a) Solution for Example 6.6 (a)

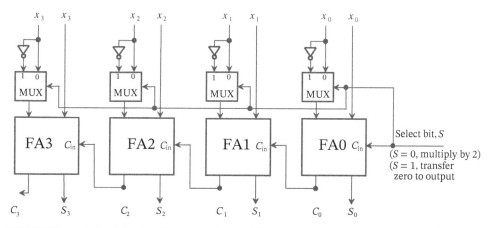

FIGURE 6.36 (b) Solution for Example 6.6 (b)

QUESTIONS AND PROBLEMS

6.1 Design a comparator for comparing two two-bit signed numbers.

6.2 Draw the block diagram of a 74138 decoder.

6.3 A combinational circuit is specified by the following equations:

$$F_0(A, B, C) = \overline{A}\,\overline{B}\,\overline{C} + A\overline{B}C + A\overline{B}\,\overline{C} \qquad F_2(A, B, C) = \overline{A}\,\overline{B}\,\overline{C} + A\,B\,C$$

$$F_1(A, B, C) = A\overline{B}\,\overline{C} + AB\overline{C} \qquad F_3(A, B, C) = \overline{A}\,B\,C + \overline{A}\,B\,\overline{C} + A\,B\,\overline{C}$$

Draw a logic diagram using a decoder and external gates. Assume that the decoder outputs a HIGH on the selected line.

6.4 Draw a logic diagram using a 74138 decoder and a minimum number of external gates to implement the following:

$$F_0\,(A, B, C) = \Sigma m(1, 3, 4), \qquad F_2\,(A, B, C) = \Sigma m(0, 1, 3, 5, 6),$$

$$F_1(A, B, C) = \Sigma m(0, 2, 4, 7), \qquad F_3\,(A, B, C) = \Sigma m(2, 6)$$

6.5 Obtain a 4 × 16 decoder using a minimum number of 74138 and logic gates.

6.6 Design a combinational circuit using a minimum number of 74138s (3 × 8 decoders) to generate the minterms m_1, m_5, and m_9 based on four switch inputs S_3, S_2, S_1, S_0. Then display the selected minterm number (1 or 5 or 9) on a seven-segment display by generating a 4-bit input (W, X, Y, Z) for a BCD to seven-segment code converter. Ignore the display for all other minterms. Note that these four inputs (W, X, Y, Z) can be obtained from the selected output line (1 or 5 or 9) of the decoders that is generated by the four input switches ($S3, S2, S1, S0$). Use a minimum number of logic gates. Determine the truth table, and then draw a block diagram of your implementation using the building blocks shown in Figure P6.6.

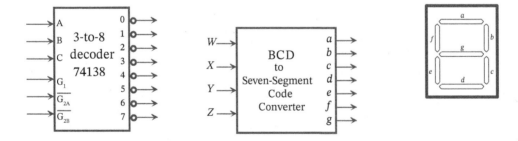

FIGURE P6.6

6.7 Implement each of the following using an 8-to-1 multiplexer:
(a) $F(A, B, C, D) = ABC + \overline{A}BD + \overline{A}\,\overline{B}\,\overline{C} + ACD$
(b) $F(W, X, Y, Z) = \Sigma m(2, 3, 6, 7, 8, 9, 12, 13, 15)$

6.8 Design a 1 x 4 demultiplexer with two select inputs.

6.9   Find d0, d1 for the schematic shown in Figure P6.9. Assume demultiplexer output is 1 when not selected.

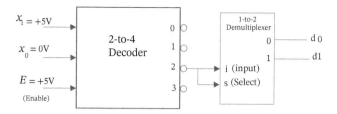

FIGURE P6.9

6.10   Obtain a combinational circuit that adds two 4-bit signed numbers and generates an output of 1 if the 4-bit result is zero; the output is 0 if the 4-bit result is nonzero. Draw a logic circuit using the block diagram of a 4-bit binary adder as the building block and a minimum number of logic gates.

6.11   Obtain a combinational circuit using a minimum number of full adders to decrement a 6-bit signed number by 2. Assume 6-bit result. Draw a logic diagram using the block diagram of a full adder as the building block.

6.12   Obtain a combinational circuit using full adders to multiply a 4-bit unsigned number by 2. Draw a logic diagram using the block diagram of a full adder as the building block.

6.13   Draw a schematic of a full adder using a 74138 and a minimum number of external gates. Use minterms of the full adder.

6.14   Determine the truth table for a hexadecimal-to-binary priority encoder with line 0 having the highest priority and line 15 with the lowest.

6.15   Implement a digital circuit to increment (for $C_{in} = 1$) or decrement (for $C_{in} = 0$) a 4-bit signed number by 1 generating outputs in twos complement form. Note that C_{in} is the input carry to the full adder for the least significant bit. Draw a schematic:
(a) Using only a minimum number of full adders and multiplexers.
(b) Using only a minimum number of full adders and inverters. Do not use any multiplexers.

6.16   Using a minimum number of full adders and multiplexers design an incrementer/decrementer circuit as follows: If $S = 0$, output $y = x + 1$; otherwise, $y = x - 1$. Assume x and y are 4-bit signed numbers and the result is 4 bits wide.

6.17   Design a combinational circuit using a minimum number of full adders, and logic gates with one BCD to seven-segment display, and which will perform A plus B or A minus B (A and B are signed numbers), depending on a mode select input, M. If $M = 0$, addition is carried out; if $M = 1$, subtraction is carried out. Assume $A = A_4 A_3 A_2 A_1 A_0$ and $B = B_4 B_3 B_2 B_1 B_0$ (Two 5-bit numbers). The circuit will be able to carry out the subtraction even if A < B. Use an LED to indicate the sign of the result (LED ON for negative result and LED OFF for positive result). The result of the operation should always appear in BCD form on the single seven-segment display. Assume that the result will be in the range of 0 through +9 in decimal and -1 through -9 in decimal. For example, if five-bit addition or subtraction provides a result of 10111 in binary, the circuit will take the two's complement of the number, and will display minus (Sign LED ON) 9 on the single seven-segment display. The Overflow bit (V) should be indicated by another LED (LED ON for V = 1 and LED OFF for V = 0). Do not use any multiplexers.

7

COMBINATIONAL SHIFTER, FAST ADDERS, ARRAY MULTIPLIERS, ALU, & PLDs

This chapter describes design of combinational shifter, fast adders, array multipliers, and ALU. Topics such as ROM, PLD, CPLD, and FPGA are also included.

7.1   Combinational Shifter

A high-speed shifter can be designed using combinational circuit component such as a multiplexer. The block diagram, internal organization, and truth table of a typical combinational shifter are shown in Figure 7.1. From the truth table, the following equations can be obtained:

$$y_3 = \overline{s_1}\,\overline{s_0}i_3 + \overline{s_1}s_0i_2 + s_1\overline{s_0}i_1 + s_1s_0i_0$$

$$y_2 = \overline{s_1}\,\overline{s_0}i_2 + \overline{s_1}s_0i_1 + s_1\overline{s_0}i_0 + s_1s_0i_{-1}$$

$$y_1 = \overline{s_1}\,\overline{s_0}i_1 + \overline{s_1}s_0i_0 + s_1\overline{s_0}i_{-1} + s_1s_0i_{-2}$$

$$y_0 = \overline{s_1}\,\overline{s_0}i_0 + \overline{s_1}s_0i_{-1} + s_1\overline{s_0}i_{-2} + s_1s_0i_{-3}$$

The 4×4 shifter of Figure 7.1(a) through 7.1(c) can be expanded to obtain a system capable of rotating 16-bit data to the left by 0, 1, 2, or 3 positions, which is shown in Figure 7.2. Table 7.1 shows the truth table.

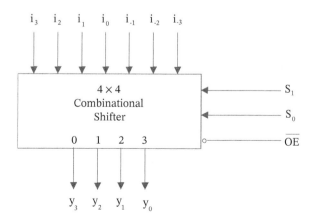

(a)   Block diagram

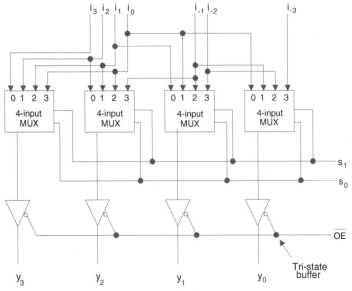

(b)   Internal schematic

	Shift Count		Output				Comment
$\overline{OE}$	s_1	s_0	y_3	y_2	y_1	y_0	
1	X	X	Z	Z	Z	Z	Outputs are tristated
0	0	0	i_3	i_2	i_1	i_0	Pass (no shift)
0	0	1	i_2	i_1	i_0	i_{-1}	Left Shift once
0	1	0	i_1	i_0	i_{-1}	i_{-2}	Left shift twice
0	1	1	i_0	i_{-1}	i_{-2}	i_{-3}	Left shift three times

(c)   Truth table (X is don't care in the above)

FIGURE 7.1 4×4 combinational shifter

This design can be extended to obtain a more powerful shifter called the *barrel shifter*. The shift is a cycle rotation, which means that the input binary information is shifted in one direction; the most significant bit is moved to the least significant position.   This shifter is capable of rotating the given 16-bit data to the left by n positions, where $0 \leq n \geq 15$. The barrel shifter is an on-chip component for typical 32-bit microprocessors such as the Pentium.

7.2   Central Processing Unit (CPU)

As mentioned before, the CPU contains three elements: registers, ALU (Arithmetic Logic Unit), and control unit. Since programs contain instructions and data, the register section of the CPU contains four basic registers to hold instructions, data, and their corresponding addresses. These registers are: Instruction Register (IR), Program Counter (PC), Memory Address Register (MAR), and General Purpose Register (GPR).

The Instruction Register (IR) stores instructions. The contents of the instruction register are always translated by the CPU as an instruction. After reading (fetching) an instruction code from memory, the CPU stores it in the instruction register. The instruction is decoded (translated) internally by the CPU, which then performs the operation required. The program counter contains the address of the instruction. The program counter normally contains the address of the next instruction to be executed. The Memory Address Register (MAR) contains the address of data. The CPU uses the address, which is stored in the memory address register, as a direct pointer to a memory address. The contents of

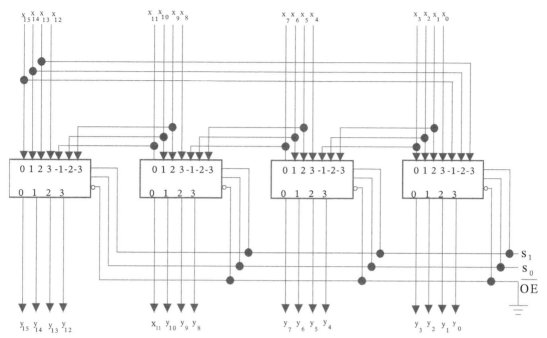

FIGURE 7.2   Logic diagram combinational shifter capable of rotating 16-bit data to the left by 0, 1, 2, or 3 positions

TABLE 7.1   Truth table for the combinational shifter capable of rotating 16-bit data to the left by 0, 1, 2, or 3 positions

Shift Count		Output																
s_1	s_0	y_{15}	y_{14}	y_{13}	y_{12}	y_{11}	y_{10}	y_9	y_8	y_7	y_6	y_5	y_4	y_3	y_2	y_1	y_0
0	0	x_{15}	x_{14}	x_{13}	x_{12}	x_{11}	x_{10}	x_9	x_8	x_7	x_6	x_5	x_4	x_3	x_2	x_1	x_0
0	1	x_{14}	x_{13}	x_{12}	x_{11}	x_{10}	x_9	x_8	x_7	x_6	x_5	x_4	x_3	x_2	x_1	x_0	x_{15}
1	0	x_{13}	x_{12}	x_{11}	x_{10}	x_9	x_8	x_7	x_6	x_5	x_4	x_3	x_2	x_1	x_0	x_{15}	x_{14}
1	1	x_{12}	x_{11}	x_{10}	x_9	x_8	x_7	x_6	x_5	x_4	x_3	x_2	x_1	x_0	x_{15}	x_{14}	x_{13}

the address is the actual data that is being transferred. The General Purpose Register (GPR) stores data. The CPU typically has instructions to shift the contents of the GPR one bit to the right or left. The CPU can execute an instruction to retrieve the contents of this register when needed.

A basic ALU performs arithmetic and logic operations. The Control unit, on the other hand, translates instructions and generates appropriate signals to execute an instruction. Note that the design of the control of the control unit is beyond the scope of this book. To execute a program, a conventional CPU repeats the following three steps for completing each instruction:

1.   *Fetch*   The CPU fetches (instruction read) the instruction from the memory (external to the CPU) into the instruction register.

2.   *Decode*   The CPU decodes or translates the instruction using the control unit. The control unit inputs the contents of the instruction register, and then decodes (translates) the instruction to determine the instruction type.

3.   *Execute* The CPU executes the instruction using the control unit. To accomplish the task, the control unit generates a number of enable signals required by the instruction.

For example, suppose that it is desired to add the contents of two general purpose registers, X and Y, and store the result in another general purpose register, Z. To accomplish this, the conventional CPU performs the following steps:

1. The CPU fetches the instruction into the instruction register.

2. The control unit (CU) decodes the contents of the instruction register.

3. The CU executes the instruction by generating enable signals for the register and ALU sections to perform the following:

    a.   Transfer the contents of registers X and Y from the register section into the ALU.

    b.   Commands the ALU to ADD.

    c.   Transfer the result from the ALU into register Z of the register section.

7.3   Arithmetic Logic Unit (ALU)

Functionally, an ALU can be divided up into two segments: the arithmetic unit and the logic unit. The arithmetic unit performs typical arithmetic operations such as addition, subtraction, and increment or decrement by 1. Usually, data may be signed or unsigned integers. In some cases, however, an arithmetic unit must handle 4-bit binary-coded decimal (BCD) numbers and floating-point numbers. Therefore, this unit must include the circuitry necessary to manipulate these data types. As the name implies, the logic unit contains hardware elements that perform typical logic operations such as NOT, AND, and OR. In this section, typical arithmetic operations performed by an ALU will be covered first. Design of a simple ALU will then be described.

Fast Adders   As mentioned before, addition is the basic arithmetic operation performed by an ALU. Other operations such as subtraction and multiplication can be obtained via addition. Thus, the time required to add two numbers plays an important role in determining the speed of the ALU. The basic concepts of half adder, full adder, and binary adder are already discussed in Chapter 6. The following equations for the full adder are obtained (Section 6.1.6) assuming $x_i = x$, $y_i = y$, $c_i = z$, and $C_{i+1} = C$, in the equations for the Sum (S_i) and the carry (C_{i+1}) of Table 6.12:

$$\text{Sum:} \quad S_i = \bar{x}_i\,\bar{y}_i c_i + \bar{x}_i y_i \bar{c}_i + x_i \bar{y}_i \bar{c}_i + x_i y_i c_i = x_i \oplus y_i \oplus c_i$$

$$\text{Carry: } C_{i+1} = y_i c_i + x_i c_i + x_i y_i$$

The logic diagrams for implementing these equations are shown in Figure 7.3.

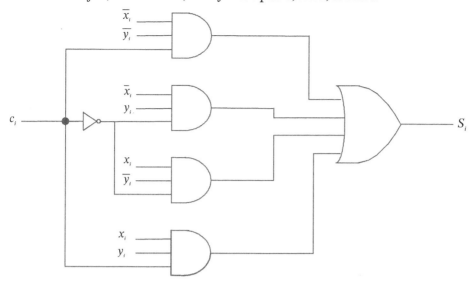

(a)   Full adder

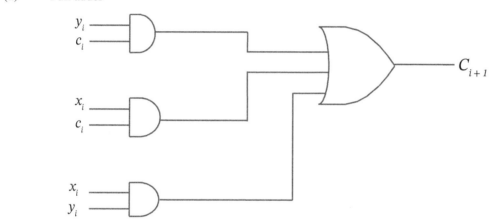

(b)   Carry

FIGURE 7.3   Logic circuit of the full adder

As has been made apparent by Figure 7.3, for generating C_{i+1} from C_i, two gate delays are required. To generate S_i from C_i, three gate delays are required because c_i must be inverted to obtain $\overline{c_i}$. Note that no inverters are required to get $\overline{x_i}$ or $\overline{y_i}$ from x_i or y_i respectively, because the numbers to be added are usually stored in a register that is a collection of flip-flops. The flip-flop generates both normal and complemented outputs. For the purpose of discussion, assume that the gate delay is Δ time units, and the actual value of Δ is decided by the technology. For example, if transistor translator logic (TTL) circuits are used, the value of Δ will be 10 ns.

By cascading n full adders, an n-bit binary adder capable of handling two n-bit data (X and Y) can be designed. The implementation of a 4-bit ripple carry or binary adder is shown in Figure 7.4. When two unsigned integers are added, the input carry, c_0, is always zero. The 4-bit adder is also called a "carry propagate adder" (CPA), because the carry is propagated serially through each full adder. This hardware can be cascaded to obtain a 16-bit CPA, as shown in Figure 7.5; $c_0 = 0$ or 1 for multiprecision operation.

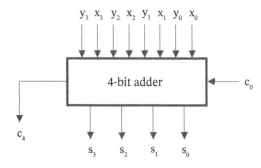

(a)   Block diagram of a 4-bit ripple carry adder

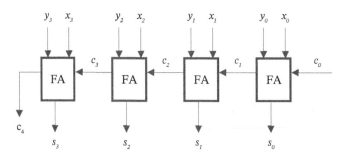

(b)   Four 4-bit full adders are cascaded to implement a 4-bit ripple carry adder

FIGURE 7.4   Implementation of a 4-bit Ripple-Carry Adder

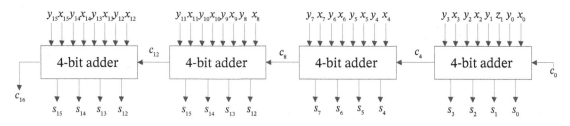

FIGURE 7.5   Implementation of a 16-bit adder using 4-bit adders as building block (16-bit CPA)

Although the design of an n-bit CPA is straightforward, the carry propagation time limits the speed of operation. For example, in the 16-bit CPA (Figure 7.5), the addition operation is completed only when the sum bits s_0 through s_{15} are available.

To generate s_{15}, c_{15} must be available. The generation of c_{15} depends on the availability of c_{14}, which must wait for c_{13} to become available, and so on. In the worst case, the carry process propagates through 15 full adders. Therefore, the worst-case add-time of the 16-bit CPA can be estimated as follows:

Time taken for carry to propagate through 15 full adders (the delay involved in the path from c_0 to c_{15})	$= 15 * 2\,\Delta$
Time taken to generate s_{15} from c_{15}	$= 3\,\Delta$
Total	$= 33\,\Delta$

If $\Delta = 10$ ns, then the worst-case add-time of a 16-bit CPA is 330 ns. This delay is prohibitive for high-speed systems, in which the expected add-time is typically less than 100 ns, which makes it necessary to devise a new technique to increase the speed of operation by a factor of 3. One such technique is known as the "carry look-ahead." In this approach, the extra hardware is used to generate each carry (c_i, for $i > 0$) directly from c_0.

To be more practical, consider the design of a 4-bit carry look-ahead adder (CLA). Let us see how this may be used to obtain a 16-bit adder that operates at a speed higher than the 16-bit CPA. Recall that, in a full adder for adding X_i, Y_i, and C_i, the output carry C_{i+1} is related to its carry input C_i, as follows:

$$C_i = X_iY_i + X_iC_i + Y_iC_i$$

The result can be rewritten as,

$$C_{i+1} = G_i + P_iC_i$$

where

$$G_i = X_iY_i \text{ and } P_i = X_i + Y_i$$

The function G_i is called the carry-generate function, because a carry is generated when $X_i = Y_i = 1$. If X_i or Y_i is a 1, then the input carry C_i is propagated to the next stage. For this reason, the function P_i is often referred to as the "carry-propagate" function. Using G_i and P_i, C_1, C_2, C_3, and C_4 can be expressed as follows:

$$C_1 = G_0 + P_0C_0$$
$$C_2 = G_1 + P_1C_1$$
$$C_3 = G_2 + P_2C_2$$
$$C_4 = G_3 + P_3C_3$$

All high-order carries can be generated in terms of C_0 as follows

$$C_1 = G_0 + P_0C_0$$
$$C_2 = G_1 + P_1(G_0 + P_0C_0) = G_1 + P_1G_0 + P_1P_0C_0$$
$$C_3 = G_2 + P_2C_2 = G_2 + P_2(G_1 + P_1G_0 + P_1P_0C_0)$$
$$= G_2 + P_2G_1 + P_2P_1G_0 + P_2P_1P_0C_0$$
$$C_4 = G_3 + P_3C_3 = G_3 + P_3(G_2 + P_2G_1 + P_2P_1G_0 + P_2P_1P_0C_0)$$
$$= G_3 + P_3G_2 + P_3P_2G_1 + P_3P_2P_1G_0 + P_3P_2P_1P_0C_0$$

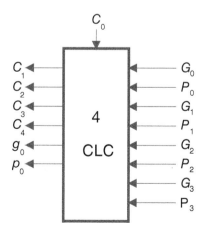

FIGURE 7.6   A four-stage carry look-ahead circuit (4 - CLC)

Therefore, C_1, C_2, C_3, and C_4 can generated directly from C_0. For this reason, these equations are called "carry look-ahead equations," and the hardware that implements these equations is called a "4-stage look-ahead circuit" (4-CLC). The block diagram of such circuit is shown in Figure 7.6. Note that *g0 and p0* shown in the figure are defined as follows:

$$g_0 = G_3 + P_3 G_2 + P_3 P_2 G_1 + P_3 P_2 P_1 G_0$$

$$p_0 = P_3 P_2 P_1 P_0$$

The following are some important points about this system:

- A 4-CLC can be implemented as a two-level AND-OR logic circuit (The first level consists of AND gates, whereas the second level includes OR gates).

- The outputs g_0 and p_0 are useful to obtain a higher-order look-ahead system.

To construct a 4-bit CLA, assume the existence of the basic adder cell shown in Figure 7.7. Using this basic cell and 4-CLC, the design of a 4-bit CLA can be completed as shown in Figure 7.8. Using this cell as a building block, a 16-bit adder can be designed as shown in Figure 7.9. The worst-case add-time of this adder can be calculated as follows:

		Delay
For P_i, G_i generation from X_i, Y_i $(0 \le i \le 15)$	...	Δ
To generate C_4 from C_0	...	2Δ
To generate C_8 from C_4	...	2Δ
To generate C_{12} from C_8	...	2Δ
To generate C_{15} from C_{12}	...	2Δ
To generate S_{15} from C_{15}	...	3Δ
Total delay	...	12Δ

A graphical illustration of this calculation can be shown as follows:

$$\text{Data available} \xrightarrow{\Delta} G_i P_i \xrightarrow{2\Delta} C_4 \xrightarrow{2\Delta} C_8 \xrightarrow{2\Delta} C_{12} \xrightarrow{2\Delta} C_{15} \xrightarrow{3\Delta} S_{15}$$

From this calculation, it is apparent that the new 16-bit adder is faster than the 16-bit CPA by a factor of 3 approximately. In fact, this system can be made faster by employing another 4-bit CLC and eliminating the carry propagation between the 4-bit CLA blocks. For this purpose, the g_i and p_i outputs generated by the 4-bit CLA are used. This design task is left as an exercise to the reader.

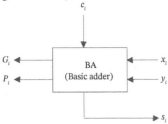

FIGURE 7.7　　Basic CLA cell

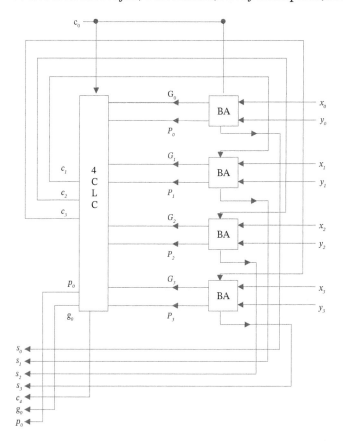

FIGURE 7.8 A 4-bit CLA

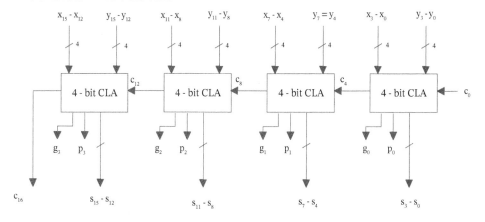

FIGURE 7.9 Design of a 16-bit adder using 4-bit CLAs

If there is a need to add more than three data, a technique known as "carry-save addition" is used. To see its effectiveness, consider the following example:

$$
\begin{array}{r}
44 \\
28 \\
32 \\
\underline{79} \\
\underline{63} \leftarrow \text{Sum vector} \\
\underline{12} \leftarrow \text{Carry vector} \\
\underline{183} \leftarrow \text{Final answer}
\end{array}
$$

In this example, four decimal numbers are added. First, the unit digits are added, producing a sum of 3 and a carry digit of 2. Similarly, the tens digits are added, producing a sum digit of 6 and a carry digit of 1. Because there is no carry propagation from the unit digit to the tenth digit, these summations can be carried out in parallel to produce a sum vector of 63 and a carry vector of 12. When all data are added, the sum and the shifted carry vector are added in the conventional manner, which produces the final answer. Note that the carry is propagated only in the last step, which generates the final answer no matter how many operands are added. The concept is also referred to as "addition by deferred carry assimilation."

Array Multipliers   Two unsigned integers can be multiplied using repeated addition as mentioned in Chapter 2. Also, they can be multiplied in the same way as two decimal numbers are multiplied by paper and pencil method. Consider the multiplication of two unsigned integers, where the multiplier $Q = 15$ and the multiplicand is $M = 14$, as illustrated:

$$M \to 1110 - Multiplicand\ (14_{10})$$
$$Q \to 1111 - Multiplier\ (15_{10})$$

```
          1110
          1110   ◄──────┐
          1110   ◄──────┤}  Partial Products
          1110   ◄──────┘
        11010010 ◄────────── Final Product, P
```

In the paper and pencil algorithm, shifted versions of multiplicands are added. This procedure can be implemented by using combinational circuit elements such as AND gates and full adders. Generally, a 4-bit unsigned multiplier Q and a 4-bit unsigned multiplicand M can be written as M: m_3 m_2 m_1 m_0 and Q: $q_3 q_2 q_1 q_0$. The process of generating the partial products and the final product can also be generalized as shown in Figure 7.10. Each cross-product term ($m_i q_j$) in this figure can be generated using an AND gate. This requires 16 AND gates to generate all cross-product terms that are summed by the full adder of Figure 7.11(a) as the basic block.

			m_3	m_2	m_1	m_0	
			q_3	q_2	q_1	q_0	
			m_3q_0	m_2q_0	m_1q_0	m_0q_0	◄──── Partial product PR$_0$
		m_3q_1	m_2q_1	m_1q_1	m_0q_1		◄──── Partial product PR$_1$
	m_3q_2	m_2q_2	m_1q_2	m_0q_2			◄──── Partial product PR$_2$
m_3q_3	m_2q_3	m_1q_3	m_0q_3				◄──── Partial product PR$_3$
p_7	p_6	p_5	p_4	p_3	p_2	p_1	p_0

FIGURE 7.10   Generalized version of them multiplication of two 4-bit numbers

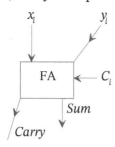

(a) Basic cell

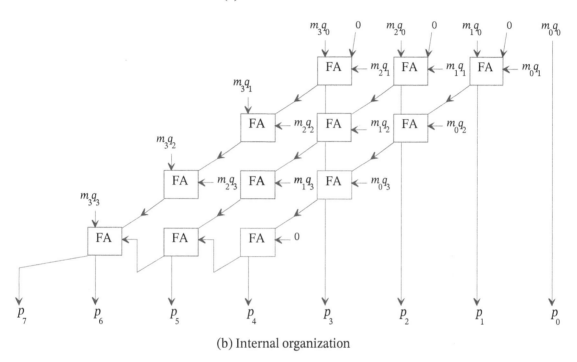

(b) Internal organization

FIGURE 7.11   4 ×4 array multiplier

Consider the generation of p_2 in Figure 7.11. From Figure 7.10, p_2 is the sum of m_2q_0, m_1q_1 and m_0q_2. The sum of these three elements is obtained by using two full adders. (See column for p_2 in Figure 7.10). The top full adder in this column generates the sum $m_2q_0 + m_1q_1$. This sum is then added to m_0q_2 by the bottom full adder along with any carry from the previous full adder for p_1.

The time required to complete the multiplication can be estimated by considering the longest carry propagation path comprising of the rightmost diagonal (which includes the full adder for p_1 and the bottom full adders for p_2 and p_3), and the last row (which includes the full adder for p_6 and the bottom full adders for p_4 and p_5). The time taken to multiply two *n*-bit numbers can be expressed as follows:

$$T(n) = \Delta \text{ AND gate} + (n - 1)\Delta \text{ carry propagation} + (n - 1)\Delta \text{ carry propagation}$$

In this equation, all cross-product terms m_iq_i can be generated simultaneously by an array of AND gates. Therefore, only one AND gate delay is included in the equation. Also, the rightmost diagonal and the bottom row contain (n - 1) full adders each for the n × n multiplier.
Assuming that:

$$\Delta \text{ AND gate} = \Delta \text{ carry propagation} = \text{Two gate delays} = 2\Delta$$

The preceding expression can be simplified as follows:

$$T(n) = 2\Delta + (2n - 2) * 2\Delta = (4n - 2)\Delta$$

The array multiplier that has been considered so far is known as Braun's multiplier. The hardware is often called a nonadditive multiplier (NM), since it does not include any additive inputs. An additive multiplier (AM) includes an extra input, R; it computes products of the form $P = M * Q + R$. This type of multiplier is useful in computing the sum of products of the form $\Sigma XiYi$.

ALU Design   In this section, the design of a simple 4-bit ALU using typical combinational elements such as gates, multiplexers, and a 4-bit binary adder is discussed. First, an arithmetic unit and a logic unit are designed separately; then, they are combined to obtain an ALU. For the first step, a two-function arithmetic unit, as shown in Figure 7.12 is designed. The key element of this system is the 4-bit binary adder. The multiplexers select one of the inputs (Y or $\overline{Y}$) of the binary adder. For example, if $s_0 = 0$, then $B = Y$; otherwise, $B = \overline{Y}$. Because the selection input (s_0) also controls the input carry (c_{in}), the following results are obtained:

$$if\ s_0 = 0$$
$$F = X + Y$$
$$else$$
$$F = X + \overline{Y} + 1$$
$$F = X\ minus\ Y$$

This arithmetic unit generates addition and subtraction operations. For the second step, let us design a two-function logic unit as shown in Figure 7.13. From the figure, it can be seen that when $s_0 = 0$, the output $G = X\ AND\ Y$; otherwise, the output $G = X \oplus Y$. Note that from these two Boolean operations, other equations such as NOT and OR can be derived by the following Boolean identities:

$$1 \oplus x = \overline{x} \quad and \quad x\ OR\ y = x \oplus y \oplus xy$$

Therefore, NOT and OR operations can be obtained by using additional circuits in Figure 7.13. The outputs generated by the arithmetic and logic units can be combined by using a set of multipleexers, as shown in Figure 7.14. From the figure, when the select line $s_1 = 1$, the multiplexers select outputs generated by the logic unit; otherwise, the outputs of the arithmetic unit are selected.

More commonly, the select line s_1 is referred to as the *mode input* because it selects the desired mode of operation (arithmetic or logic). A complete block diagram of this ALU is shown in Figure 7.15. The truth table illustrating the operation of this ALU is shown in Table 7.2. This table shows that this ALU is capable of performing two arithmetic and two logic operations on 4-bit data X and Y.

Note that the size of the ALU defines the size of a microcontroller or a microprocessor. For example, Microchip PIC18F is an 8-bit microcontroller since it contains an 8-bit ALU. Intel Pentium microprocessor, on the other hand, is a 32-bit microprocessor since its ALU is 32-bit.

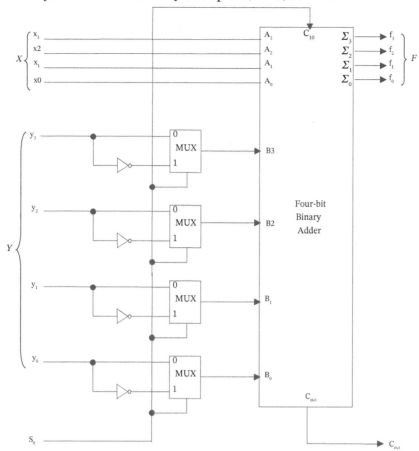

FIGURE 7.12   Organization of an arithmetic unit

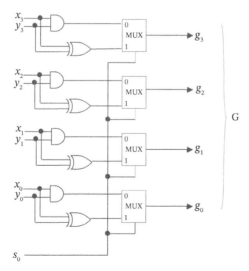

FIGURE 7.13   Organization of a 4-bit two-function logic unit

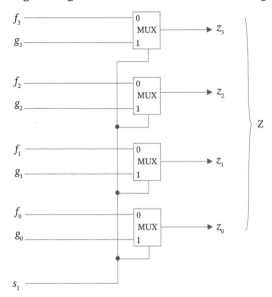

FIGURE 7.14   Combining the outputs generated by the arithmetic and logic units

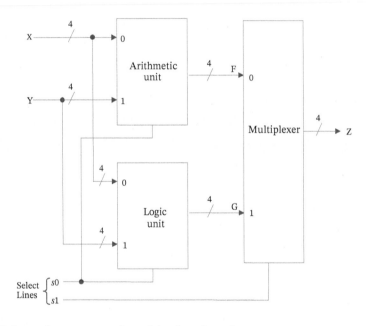

FIGURE 7.15   Schematic representation of the four functions

TABLE 7.2   Truth table selecting the operations of the ALU of Figure 7.15

Select Lines		Output Z	Comment
S_1	S_0		
0	0	X plus Y	Addition
0	1	X plus $\overline{Y}$ plus 1	2's Complement subtraction
1	0	X AND Y	Boolean AND
1	1	$X \oplus Y$	Exclusive-OR

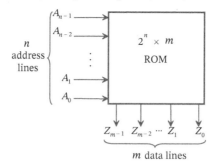

FIGURE 7.16   Block-diagram representation of a ROM

7.4   Read-Only Memories (ROMs)

Read-only memory, commonly called "ROM," is a nonvolatile memory (meaning that it retains information in case power is switched off) that provides read-only access to the stored data. A block-diagram representation of a ROM is shown in Figure 7.16. The total capacity of this ROM is $2^n \times m$ bits. Whenever an n-bit address is placed on the address line, the m-bit information stored in this address will appear on the data lines. The m-bit output generated by the ROM is also called a "word."

For example, a 1k × 8 -bit (1024 × 8) ROM chip contains 10 address pins ($2^{10} = 1024 = 1$k) and 8 data pins. Therefore, $n = 10$ and $m = 8$. On the other hand, an 8k × 8 -bit (8192 × 8) ROM chip includes 13 address pins ($2^{13} = 8192 = 8$k) and 8 data pins. Thus, $n = 13$ and $m = 8$.

A ROM is an LSI (Large Scale Integration) chip that is normally designed using an array of MOS transistors. A ROM is a combinational circuit. Internally, a ROM contains a decoder and OR gates; this is illustrated in Figure 7.17. Although diodes are not used for fabricating ROMs, a diode-based ROM is shown in Figure 7.18 for simplicity, and just for illustrative purposes.

A typical three-input diode OR gate is shown in Figure 7.18. Resistor R pulls the output down to a LOW level as long as all the inputs are LOW. However, if one or more inputs are connected to a high voltage source (3 to 5 volts), the output is pulled HIGH to within one diode drop of the input. Thus, the circuit operates as an OR gate. To illustrate the operation of a ROM, consider the 2 × 4-bit ROM of Figure 7.19. In this system , when $A_1 A_0 = 00$, the decoder output line 0 will be HIGH. This causes the diodes D_{00} and D_{01} to conduct, and thus the output $Z = Z_3 Z_2 Z_1 Z_0 = 0011$. Similarly, when $A_1 A_0 = 01$, the decoder output line 1 goes high, diode D_{10} conducts, and the output will be $Z = Z_3 Z_2 Z_1 Z_0 = 0100$.

Table 7.3 shows the truth table. Figure 7.20 shows the subcategories of ROMs. ROMs are designed using MOS technology.

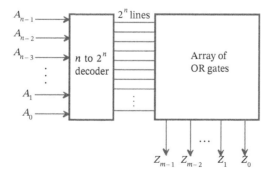

FIGURE 7.17   Internal structure of a ROM

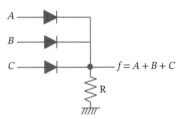

FIGURE 7.18   Diode-OR gate

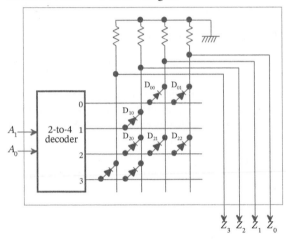

FIGURE 7.19   Hardware organization of a Typical 2×4 ROM

TABLE 7.3   Truth table implemented by the ROM of Figure 7.19

A_1	A_0	Z_3	Z_2	Z_1	Z_0
0	0	0	0	1	1
0	1	0	1	0	0
1	0	0	1	1	1
1	1	1	1	0	0

ROM

Mask ROM   PROM   EPROM
                                 and
                        (EEPROM or E^2PROM)

FIGURE 7.20   Subcategories of ROMs

A mask ROM must be programmed before it can be used. This involves placing the switching devices such as MOS transistors at the appropriate intersection points of the row and column lines. Hence, in a mask ROM, the contents of the ROM are programmed by the manufacturer at the time of its production. This means that this approach is well suited for producing a standard circuit such as a bar-code generator. Because these types of ROMs are mass produced, their costs are also very low. However, a mask ROM cannot be reconfigured by a user. That is, a user cannot alter its contents.

Occasionally, a user may wish to develop a specific ROM-based circuit as required by the application. In this case, a ROM that allows a user to initialize its contents is required. A ROM with such a flexibility is known as a PROM (programmable ROM). In this device, the manufacturer places a switching element along with a fusible link at each intersection. This implies that all ROM cells are initialized with a 1. If a user desires to store a zero in a particular cell, the fuse is blown at that point. This activity is called "programming," and it may be accomplished by passing electrical impulses. It should be pointed out that, in such a ROM, a user can program the ROM only once. That is, it is not possible to reprogram a PROM once the fuse is blown. Note that PROMs are obsolete.

When a new product is developed, it may be necessary for the designer to modify the contents of the ROM. A ROM with this capability is referred to as an EPROM (erasable programmable ROM). Usually, the contents of this memory are erased by exposing the ROM chip to ultraviolet light. Typical erase times vary between 10 and 30 minutes. After erasure, the ROM may be reprogrammed using an EPROM programmer. The 2764 chip is a typical example of an EPROM. It is a 28-pin 8k × 8 chip contained in a dual in-line package (DIP). It has 13 address input pins and 8 data output pins. Note that the 2764 needs 13 (2^{13} = 8192) pins to address 8192 (8k) locations.

The growth in IC technology allowed the production of another type of ROM whose contents may be erased using electrical impulses. These memory devices are customarily referred to as "electrically erasable PROMs" (EEPROMs or E^2PROMs). The main advantage of an EEPROM is that its contents can be changed without removing the chip from the circuit board.

7.5   Programmable Logic Devices (PLDs)

A programmable logic device (PLD) is a generic name for an IC (Integrated Circuit) chip capable of being programmed by the user after it is manufactured. It is programmed by blowing fuses. The theory behind PLD is based on the concept of SOP (Sum-Of-Products). Since a Boolean function can be expressed in SOP form, a PLD chip contains an array of AND gates and OR gates. There are two types of PLDs. They are identified by the location of the fuses used for programming on the AND-OR array as shown in Figure 7.21.

The PROM was discussed in the last section. A PROM contains a decoder (number of fixed AND gates) and programmable OR gates. PLDs evolved from PROMs. There are advantages of using PLDs over PROMs which will be discussed later in this section.

The PLA (Programmable Logic Array) was developed before PAL. The PLA includes several AND and OR gates, both of which are programmable. The PAL (Programmable Array Logic), on the other hand, includes programmable AND gates and fixed OR gates. The PLA is very flexible in the sense that the necessary AND terms can be logically ORed to provide the desired Boolean functions. The internal structure of a typical PLA is shown in Figure 7.22. The AND array of this system generates the required product terms, and the OR array is used to OR the product terms generated by the array. As in the case of the ROM, these gate arrays can be realized using MOS transistors. Some PLAs provide inverted outputs by XORing each output with one. Finally, product terms can be shared in PLAs.

In order to illustrate a PLA, a special AND gate or OR gate symbol with multiple inputs shown in Figure 7.23 will be utilized in the following examples.

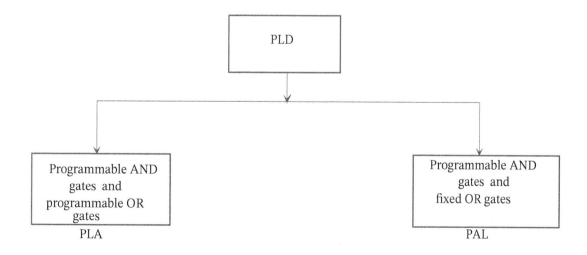

FIGURE 7.21   Types of PLD

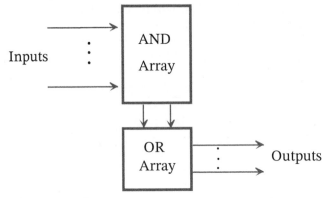

FIGURE 7.22   Internal structure of a PLA

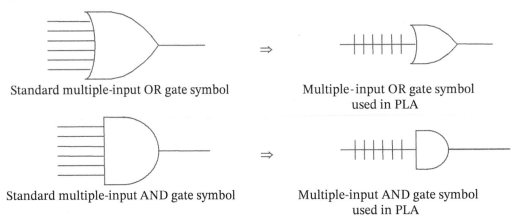

Standard multiple-input OR gate symbol

Multiple-input OR gate symbol used in PLA

Standard multiple-input AND gate symbol

Multiple-input AND gate symbol used in PLA

FIGURE 7.23   Multiple input AND and OR gate symbols for PLA

Next, consider implementing the following equations using a PLA:

$$Z_0 = \overline{A}\,\overline{B} + BC$$
$$Z_1 = \overline{A}\,B + AC$$
$$Z_2 = A\,\overline{C} + BC$$

Figure 7.24 shows the PLA with programmable links after programming. The schematic in Figure 7.24 is represented in Figure 7.25 in which the programmable links are replaced by dot symbols. Note that each AND gate shown in Figure 7.25 is with a single horizontal input line. A dot on the horizontal line indicates that an input connection to an AND gate is created by programming (shown by a programmable link in Figure 7.24). The dots at the OR gate input connections are created in a similar manner.

This PLA has three inputs, A, B, and C. The AND generates from product terms $\overline{A}\,\overline{B}$, $\overline{A}\,\overline{C}$, BC, and AC. These product terms are logically summed up in the OR array, and the outputs Z_0, Z_1, and Z_2 are generated. The use of PLAs is very cost-effective when the number of inputs in a combinational circuit realized by a ROM is very high and all input combinations are not used. For example, consider the following multiple output functions:

$W = AE + BC$
$X = CD + FE$
$Y = FG + HI$

To implement these Boolean functions in a ROM, a 512×3 array is needed because there are nine inputs (A through F) ($2^9 = 512$) and three outputs (W, X, Y), but the same functions can be realized in a PLA using six product terms, nine inputs, and three outputs, as shown in Figure 7.26. Therefore, a considerable savings in hardware can be achieved with PLAs.

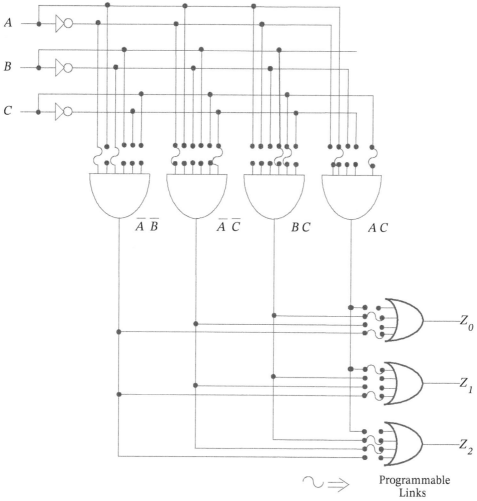

FIGURE 7.24 PLA with programmable links

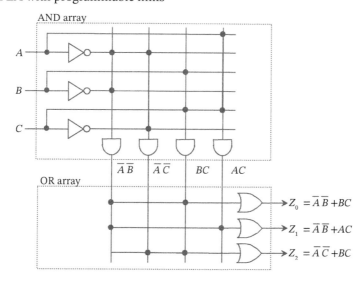

FIGURE 7.25 A PLA with three inputs, four product terms, and three outputs

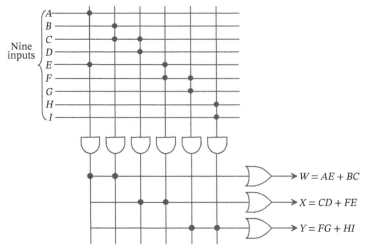

Nine inputs $\begin{cases} A \\ B \\ C \\ D \\ E \\ F \\ G \\ H \\ I \end{cases}$

$W = AE + BC$

$X = CD + FE$

$Y = FG + HI$

FIGURE 7.26   A PLA with nine inputs, six product terms, and three outputs

Example 7.1

Implement the following equations using PLAs:

$$Z_1(C,B,A) = \sum m(2, 3, 5, 6, 7)$$

$$= \overline{C}B\overline{A} + \overline{C}BA + C\overline{B}A + CB\overline{A} + CBA$$

$$Z_2(C,B,A) = \sum m(1, 2, 3, 7)$$

$$= \overline{C}\,\overline{B}A + \overline{C}B\overline{A} + \overline{C}BA + CBA$$

Solution

Figure 7.27 shows the PLA implementation.

7.6   Commercially Available Field Programmable Devices (FPDs)

Both mask programmable and field programmable PLAs are available. Mask programmable PLAs are similar to mask ROMs in the sense that they are programmed during fabrication. Field programmable PLAs (FPLAs) on the other hand, can be programmed by the user with a computer-aided design (CAD) program to select a minimum number of product terms to express the Boolean functions.

There are three types of commercially available Field Programmable Devices (FPDs). These are Simple PLD (SPLD), Complex PLD (CPLD), and Field Programmable Gate Array (FPGA). SPLDs can handle tens to hundreds of gates, and cannot be used for larger digital-design applications. Therefore, CPLD (complex PLD) chips are designed by the manufacturers such as Altera and Xlinix to accomplish this. CPLDs can handle thousands of gates. Both SPLD and CPLD are nonvolatile; they retain programs in case power is switched off. The FPGA can handle millions of gates, and are volatile. That is, programs are lost in case power is switched off.

The SPLD is typically based on PAL architecture, and uses EPROM technology to implement the switches. Note that PAL is a registered trademark of Advanced Micro Devices, Inc. (AMD). PALs were introduced by Monolithic Memories (a division of AMD) in 1970. The PAL chips are usually identified by a two-digit number followed by a letter and then one or two digits. The first two-digit number specifies the number of inputs whereas the last one or two digits define the number of outputs. The fixed number of AND gates are connected to either an OR or a NOR gate. The letter H indicates that the output gates are OR gates; the letter L is used when the outputs are NOR gates; the letter C is used when the outputs include both OR and NOR gates. Note that OR outputs generate active HIGH whereas NORs provide active LOW outputs. On the other hand, OR-NOR gates include both active HIGH and active LOW outputs.

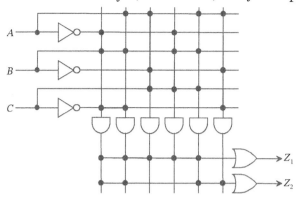

FIGURE 7.27   PLA implementation of Example 7.1

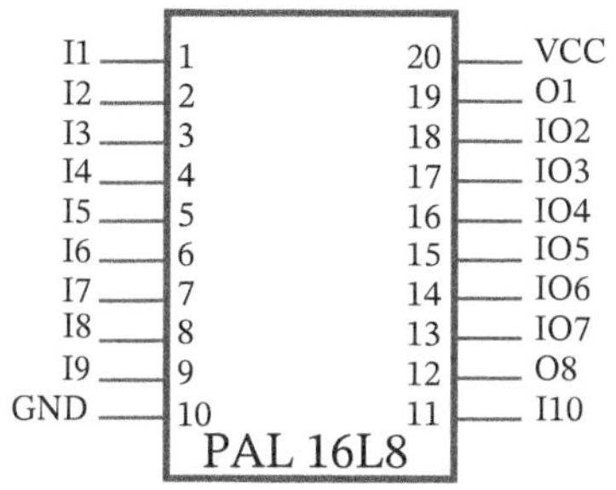

FIGURE 7.28   Pinout for PAL 16L8

For example, the PAL16L8 is a 20-pin chip with a maximum of 16 inputs, up to 8 outputs, one power pin, and one ground pin. The 16L8 contains 10 nonshared inputs, six inputs that are shared by six outputs, and two nonshared outputs. Figure 7.28 shows the pin diagram of the PAL16L8. Note that PEEL (Programmable Electrically Erasable Logic) devices or Erasable PLDs such as 18CV8 or 16V8 are available for instant reprogramming just like an EEPROM. These devices utilize CMOS EEPROM technology. These erasable PLDs use electronic switches (MOS transistors) rather than fuses so that they are erasable and reprogrammable like EEPROMs.

A typical CPLD contains several PLDs. Each PLD Contains AND and OR gates with EEPROM or EPROM or Flash memory (designed using EEPROM and EPROM) to implement the programmable switches along with all the interconnections in the same chip. Altera Corporation's EPM7032LC44-6 (36 user I/O pins) is an example of a typical CPLD.

IC manufacturers such as Altera and Xlinix also took a different approach for handling larger applications. They devised FPGA (Field Programmable Gate Array) chips which can be programmed at the user's location. A typical FPGA chip contains several smaller individual logic blocks (SRAM, multiplexers, gates, and flip-flops) along with all interconnections in a single chip. The FPGA does not use EEPROM technology to implement the switches; the programming information is stored in SRAM. The SRAM is normally programmed to store a look-up table (truth table) containing the combinational circuit functions for the logic block. Note that the concept of FPGA is based on the fact that a truth table (hence, a combinational logic circuit) can be implemented in memory such as SRAM. Finally, products can be developed using FPGA from conceptual design via prototype to production in a very short time since debugging software is faster than debugging hardware. Basics of FPGA along with implementation of simple designs using Verilog and Xlinix software are covered in Chapter 13. Note that FPGAs can be used to implement both combinational and sequential circuits since they contain flip-flops.

QUESTIONS AND PROBLEMS

7.1 Design a combinational logic shifter with 4-bit input and 4-bit output as follows:

$\overline{OE}$	Shift Count		Four- bit output
	S_1	S_0	
1	X	X	High Impedance output lines
0	0	0	No Shift
0	0	1	Right Shift once
0	1	0	Right Shift twice
0	1	1	Right Shift three times

where X means don't care. Using multiplexers and tristate buffers, draw a logic diagram.

7.2 What is a barrel shifter?

7.3 Design a combinational circuit to compute the absolute value of an 8-bit two's complement number. Use 8-bit binary adder and exclusive-OR gates. Draw a schematic.

7.4 Using a 4-bit CLA as the building block, design an 8-bit adder.

7.5 Design:
   (a) a 16-bit adder whose worst-case add-time is 10D using a 4-bit CLA as a building block.

   (b) the fastest 64-bit adder using a 4-bit CLA as the building block. Estimate the worst-case add-time of your design.

   (c) a combinational circuit to compute the function $f(x) = (3/8) * x$ where x is a 4-bit 2's complement number.

7.6 Design and implement a 6×6 array multiplier.

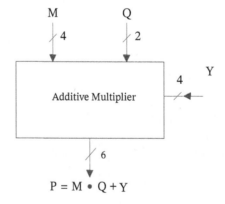

FIGURE P7.7

7.7 Design an unsigned 8×4 non-additive multiplier using the additive-multiplier module whose block diagram is shown in Figure P7.7.
Assume that M, Q, and Y are unsigned integers.

7.8 Design and draw the logic circuit for an arithmetic logic unit to perform the following functions:

S_1	S_0	F
0	0	A plus B
0	1	A minus B
1	0	A AND B
1	1	A OR B

Use multiplexers, binary adders, and gates as needed. Assume that A and B are 4-bit numbers.

7.9   Design a combinational circuit that will perform the following operations:

S_1	S_0	Y
0	0	0
0	1	A
1	0	B
1	1	15_{10}

Assume that A is a 4-bit number and $B = \overline{A_3}\,\overline{A_2}\,\overline{A_1}\,\overline{A_0}$. Draw a logic diagram.

7.10   Design a 4-bit ALU to perform the following operations:

S	F
0	Logical Left Shift A once
1	0

Assume that A is a 4-bit number. Draw a logic diagram using a binary adder, multiplexers, and inverters as necessary.

7.11   Design a 4-bit arithmetic unit as follows:

S	F
0	A plus B
1	A plus 1

Assume that A and B are 4-bit numbers

7.12   Design an ALU to perform the following operations:

S_1	S_0	F
0	0	x plus y
0	1	x
1	0	B
1	1	$x \oplus y$

Assume that x and y are 4-bit numbers, and $B = \overline{Y_3}\,\overline{Y_2}\,\overline{Y_1}\,\overline{Y_0}$. Draw a logic diagram.

7.13   What are the main logic elements/gates in a ROM chip?

7.14   Design a combinational circuit using a 16×4 ROM that will increment a 4-bit unsigned number by 1. Determine the truth table and then draw a block diagram of your implementation showing the addresses and their contents in binary along with one Output Enable (OE) input.

7.15   What are the basic differences among PROM, PLA, PAL and PEEL?

7.16   What is the technology used to fabricate EPROMs and EEPROMs?

7.17   What is the basic difference between CPLD and FPGA?

8

COMBINATIONAL LOGIC USING VERILOG

This chapter describes how to design combinational circuits using Verilog. Topics include basics of Verilog including structural modeling, dataflow modeling, and behavioral modeling. Several examples illustrating the use of Verilog for synthesizing combinational circuits are provided in a simplified manner. Finally, several examples for describing combinational circuits using Verilog are included in Chapter 13 on FPGA-based design.

8.1   Hardware Description Languages (HDLs)

Hardware description languages (HDLs) such as Verilog and VHDL along with CAD (Computer-aided design) tools, allow FPGAs to be programmed with millions of gates in a short time. A CAD system contains a number of programs that are used to design a logic circuit. Some of these tools are discussed in the following.

A "schematic capture" tool utilizes a schematic editor program for entering, modifying and drawing a schematic on a computer screen using menus, keyboard commands, and the mouse. As mentioned before, the word "schematic" means a digital logic circuit in which logic gates along with their interconnections are shown. The schematic capture tool maintains an internal library consisting of graphic symbols for gates. The designer can place these gates on the screen from the library and then connect with lines that represent wires. The "schematic capture" is useful for small design. For larger circuits, the designer normally uses a hardware description language (HDL) to write codes to specify the circuit.

Synthesis is similar in concept to the functions provided by a compiler. The compiler generates the object code. Synthesis, on the other hand, generates a database with instructions on how to integrate the hardware specified by the HDL code. Using "synthesis" software of the CAD system, the designer can produce a circuit either from a schematic or from the HDL code. Using either approach, the synthesis tool generates a set of logic expressions describing the functions required to obtain the circuit. These initial logic expressions are not in minimum form because they are basically devised by the designer using the CAD tools. For larger circuits, it may be difficult for the designer to manually come up with a better circuit. The designer may be able to use the "synthesis" CAD tool to obtain a better circuit automatically based on the designer's original circuit.

A "functional simulator" is a CAD tool that is used to verify the correct operation of the circuit being designed. The "simulator" can be used for simulations that take into consideration the specified inputs and produces the desired outputs. Timing diagrams are used to represent the simulation results. The designer can check these timing diagrams to verify that the circuit performs according to the specifications.

Verilog and VHDL are two popular HDLs for designing both combinational and sequential circuits. Note that Verilog and VHDL are not programming languages like C. Rather, they are hardware description languages used to describe a logic circuit based on its hardware components.

Verilog (developed by Design Automation in 1984 and later acquired by Cadence Design Systems) is a hardware description language. Verilog is not an acronym. Verilog syntax is based mostly on C and some Pascal. Note that Cadence Design Systems made Verilog available to the public during the early 90's. It was then accepted as an IEEE (Institute of Electrical and Electronics Engineers) standard (number 1364) in 1995.

VHDL is an acronym for VHSIC Hardware Description Language, where VHSIC stands for Very High Speed Integrated Circuits. The design of VHDL evolved from the United States Department of Defense (DOD) VHSIC program. VHDL is based on the Ada programming language. The design of VHDL started in 1983, and after going through several versions, was formally accepted as an IEEE standard, number 1076, in 1987.

Verilog includes several reserved keywords such as **not, or, and**. These keywords must be lower case. However, module names are case sensitive. This will be explained later. Like Verilog, VHDL also includes several keywords or reserved words such as **and**, **or**, **not**. However, unlike Verilog, VHDL is not case sensitive. This means that upper case letters are equivalent to lower case letters. Appendices C and D provide step-by-step tutorials for downloading Xilinx Vivado IDE software, and its use for compiling and simulating Verilog code for combinational logic.

Since undergraduate students are usually familiar with C programming, it is easier for them to learn Verilog compared to VHDL. Hence, Verilog is covered in this book.

8.2   Basics of Verilog

In order to design systems using Verilog, three levels of abstractions or their combinations are used. These are structural modeling, behavioral modeling, and dataflow modeling.

Structural modeling can be used to describe a schematic or a logic diagram (gates and interconnections) of a system. This type of modeling makes the designer's task easy for hardware implementation. Structural modeling is used for small systems.

"Hierarchical" structural modeling can be used by the designer to decompose a large digital system into smaller blocks or modules. The designer can define a block that is used repeatedly. This common block can be used by other blocks in the Verilog code to accomplish the desired task. This concept is analogous to function call in C.

The Behavioral modeling, on the other hand, is used to describe a system in terms of what it does and how it behaves rather than in terms of its components and their interconnections. Boolean expressions are used to accomplish this. Behavioral modeling is used for larger systems.

Behavioral modeling is typically used to describe sequential circuits, although it can also be used to describe combinational circuits. The flow of data in behavioral modeling can be represented via concurrent or sequential statements. Concurrent statements are executed in parallel as soon as data is available at the inputs while sequential statements are executed in the order that they are written. The first method is useful in describing complex digital systems. When behavioral model is described by concurrent statements, it is called "Dataflow modeling". The Dataflow modeling describes a digital circuit in terms of its function and flow of data through the circuit. Dataflow modeling utilizes a number of operators that can be used on variables to obtain the outputs.

A Verilog design program can be written and simulated using software tools provided by the manufacturers including Xilinx and Altera. Verilog code called "test bench" can be written to test a Verilog design. A test bench program allows the designer to monitor the output(s) based on the application of appropriate inputs. These outputs can then be verified for correctness. Test results can be represented in terms of both waveform and tabular form. The waveform typically contains timing diagrams to graphically show the relationship between time, inputs, and outputs.

8.2.1   Verilog keywords

Verilog includes approximately 100 predefined identifiers called keywords. These keywords must be lowercase since Verilog is a case-sensitive language. Some of the keywords include **module, endmodule, input, output, not, or, nor, nand, xor,** and **xnor.** The keywords are printed in **bold** for clarity throughout this text. Verilog compilers ignore blank lines, TAB and SPACE keys. Verilog keywords are reserved and cannot be used as user-defined names.

8.2.2   Representing numbers in Verilog

Numbers in Verilog can be expressed in four different bases (radii). They are Binary, Hexadecimal, Octal, and Decimal. The general syntax for using literals in <size in bits><base><value>, in which base is b for binary, h for hexadecimal, o for octal, and d for decimal. For example, the value 12 in decimal can also be written as 4'hC, 4'd12, or 4'o14. If no base is specified, the default is decimal notion. For better readability, underscores '_' can be inserted into the literal to demark nibbles or bytes.

As an example, the number 100 in decimal can be expressed in three other bases supported by Verilog as follows:

8'd100	=	8'h64	(hexadecimal)
	=	8'b0110_0100	(binary)
	=	8''o144	(octal)
	=	100	(decimal, no radix specified)

As another example, the Verilog constant x can be assigned to a value of 668 decimal using both binary and hexadecimal as follows:

$$668_{10} = 1010011100_2$$

Hence, x = 10'b10_1001_1100
          x = 10'h29C

8.2.3   A typical Verilog Segment

Verilog describes a digital system as a set of modules. A module is a basic block in Verilog which contains the statements specifying the circuit. A module can be as simple as a single gate, or a circuit containing several gates or even a microcontroller or a microprocessor. A typical Verilog segment is given below:

```
module  <module name> (<port list>);   // A typical Module
<port declarations>
<module declarations>
<module items>
endmodule
```

Verilog module, port and module declarations   In the above, the module is enclosed by the keyword   **module** and ended by the keyword **endmodule**. An entire circuit can be described in a module.

The module name identifies a module uniquely. This means that a name or an identifier is assigned to a module to identify it. This name must start with an alpha character or an underscore (_) rather than a number. The module name can be an alpha character (upper case or lower case) followed by numbers and/or alpha characters. Module names (identifiers) in Verilog are case sensitive. This means that Full_adder and full_adder are two different variables. The following are some examples of valid and invalid module names:

```
module decoder3to8(<port list>);    VALID
module decoder_3to8(<port list>);    VALID
module  _3to8 decoder(<port list>); VALID

module 3to8decoder(<port list>);    INVALID
module $3to8decoder(<port list>);    INVALID
```

Signals entering or exiting the module are listed in the "port list" section of the module. This means that the <port list> inside the parentheses after the module name contains inputs and outputs called ports. The ports are included in parentheses with commas separating them. Inputs and Outputs can be listed in any order. For example, one may place all inputs followed by all outputs and vice versa as long as the same order is used by another module for calling (instantiating) this module.

Each port in the <port list> needs to be declared as input, output, or inout (for bidirectional signals). A semicolon (;) is used to terminate the module statement. Two slashes (//) shown in the above Verilog module is used before a single line comment. Comments may be added anywhere in a Verilog module and are always preceded by a double forward slash (//) as shown in the initial example. Block comments are also supported by Verilog and begin with /* and end with*/. Different types of comments are shown in the following example:

```verilog
// Comment outside a module
module decoder3to8(...); // Comment after a statement
// Comment inside a module
/* Block comments
   consisting of Multiple
   Lines
*/
...
endmodule
```

The ports for Verilog module are defined by a combination of the items in the module statement and the content of the module declarations. The name of a port must be specified in the port list; however the direction can be specified in either the port list or the port declarations, but not both. All inputs and outputs need to follow the same format. If one is specified in the port list, then all need to be specified in the port list.

There are two basic data types in Verilog: nets and registers. A net represents connections between hardware elements. Nets behave like wires in actual circuits providing connections while registers in Verilog means a variable that can hold a value. Note that Verilog registers differ from hardware registers in real circuits such as those built from flip-flops where the register contents can be changed by a clock. Verilog registers, on the other hand, may not have clock as hardware registers do. The values of Verilog registers can be changed anytime during simulation by assigning a new value to the register.

The keyword **wire** is used for a net type variable while the keyword **reg** is used for register type variable. Keywords **reg** and **wire** are one-bit wide by default. To define a wider **reg** or **wire**, the left and right bit positions are defined in square brackets separated by a colon. For example, "reg [7:0] a,b;" declares two variables a and b as 8 bits with the most significant bit as bit 7 (a[7] or b[7]) and the least significant bit as bit 0 (a[0] or b[0]). By default, all ports are of the **wire** type. This can be changed to a **reg** type. This type can also be specified in the port list or the port declarations, but also not in both at the same time. This topic will be covered later.

Typical examples of port declarations are provided in the following:

1. An example of declaring direction (input or output) of the ports inside the port list is provided below:

```verilog
module decoder3to8 (input A2, input A1, input A0, output [7:0]D );
// no port declarations are needed as everything is in the module
// statement
endmodule
```

Another example of declaring direction (input or output) of the ports inside the port list is provided below:

```verilog
module decoder3to8 (input A2, A1, A0, output [7:0]D );
   ...
endmodule
```

As shown in the last example, the port type (**input** and one-bit size by default in this case) for A1 and A0 remains the same as A2 until it is changed by another direction and/or size (**output** and 8-bit size in this case) for [7:0]D. If the size of the next port differs from the previously listed port, the direction keyword (**input, output, or inout**) must also be included.

2. An example of declaring direction (**input** or **output**) of the ports in the port declaration is provided below:

```
module decoder3to8 (A2, A1, A0,D);
input A2, A1, A0;          //Module declarations for A2, A1, A0
output [7:0]D;             //Module declarations for D[7], D[6], ... , D[0]
 ...
endmodule
```

Most modules require connections between elements instantiated with the module. Nets are required for connections between elements. Note that a "Network" is abbreviated as a "Net". A network provides a common connection among several devices. Note that **wire** net data type is used in structural modeling for connections between gates and modules, while **reg** data type is used for procedural assignments in behavioral modeling. Also, basic logic gates should be connected using wires defined within the module declarations section.

When declaring a vector, the statement needs to specify the type, the size or indices separated by a colon, and the name of the vector. The generic syntax is:

```
<type> [<Left Index>:<Right Index>] <name>
```

For example, to declare a 4-bit **wire** foo and 8-bit **reg** bar, the statements will be:

```
wire [3:0] foo;
reg [7:0] bar;
```

The number before the semi-colon represents the index for the left-most bit, and likewise the number to the right the index of the right-most bit. In the above example, the bit to the left is the MSB (Most Significant Bit). The left index does not necessarily be greater than the right. For example, the same wire could also be declared as:

```
wire [0:3] foo;
```

In this case, the left-most bit is the LSB (Least Significant bit). When the vector is interpreted as a value, the declarations indices become relevant. For example, take the following two code fragments:

```
//Fragment 1                 // Fragment 2
wire [3:0]msb_left;          wire [0:3]lsb_left;
assign msb_left[3] = 1;      assign lsb_left[3] = 1;
assign msb_left[2] = 0;      assign lsb_left[2] = 0;
assign msb_left[1] = 0;      assign lsb_left[1] = 0;
assign msb_left[0] = 0;      assign lsb_left[0] - 0;
```

While the assignments are the same, the two fragments have different values when read as a vector:

```
        msb_left value = 8 ,   lsb_left value = 1
```

Next, the concept of accessing a single bit or a string of bits in a vector will be discussed. Individual bits of a vector can be accessed by specifying either the single bit or by specifying both the left and right indices. Note that when accessing a vector, the bits to be accessed are specified after the vector name. Partial select is valid for any data type such as **wire** and **reg**. For example, consider the vector:

```
wire [15:0]my_vector = 16'b1000_0101_0110_1011;
```

The partial selects below yield the following results:

```
my_vector[2]    = 0         // Bit 2
my_vector[15]   = 1         // Bit 15
my_vector[3:0]  = 1011      // Lower 4 bits
my_vector[11:6] = 010101    // Bits 11 down to 6
my_vector[15:8] = 10000101  // Upper 8 bits
```

As mentioned before, by default **wire** and **reg** declare elements that are one-bit wide. To define wider elements, left and right indexes, also referred to as bit positions, must be specified with the following syntax:

```
<type> [<Left Index>:<Right Index>] <name>
```

For example, **wire** [7:0]a declares 'a' as wire with 8 bits ranging from a[7] through a[0], with a[7] as the most significant bit and a[0] as the least. When declaring nets of larger than one bit width such as **wire** [7:0]a in the above, the size (indexes) must be declared before the net name. However, when referring to the net such as to connect a single bit to a gate, the bit position is specified after the name. For example, consider the statement,

or f(a[2], a[0], a[1]);

where a[2] is the output with a[0] and a[1] as the two inputs of an OR gate.

Module definitions within modules are prohibited. This means that the keyword **module** cannot exist between a **module** and **endmodule** pair. Instead, module instantiation is used to place a module as a component inside another module. The most basic types of module instantiations are those using logic gates. Verilog contains several pre-defined modules called "primitives" for performing logic functions. These primitives are also called reserved keywords. Some of the primitives include **not, and, or, nand, nor, xor, xnor**.

These primitives can be used with the following syntax:

```
<primitive name> [identifier](<output,<input_0>,[input_1],[input_2], ..
,[input_n])
```

The primitive name of the logic gate is listed first, followed by an identifier. An identifier should also be used to distinguish between multiple gates of the same type. While technically not required, it is a good practice to do so. As shown in the syntax example, the logic gate primitives support any number of inputs, excluding the **not** primitive which, obviously, can only have a single input and a single output. To accommodate this, the output is always listed first. For example, the definition of a 5-input nand gate with output g, and inputs f0, f1, f2, f3 and f4 will be:

```
nand my_nand_gate (g, f0, f1, f2, f3, f4);
```

The text my_nand_gate in the above example is the identifier, which can be anything conforming to the same restrictions as the module identifiers. This means that the identifier must be unique and cannot be shared by any two objects in a module.

Other user-defined modules can also be instantiated in a similar fashion. When instantiating modules, the port list in the instantiation must match the port-list provided in the module statement, similar to how function arguments need to be in the same order for C functions. For example, consider the following module called simple:

```
module simple (input x, y, z, output f);
  wire c;
  and and0 (c, x, y);
  or or0 (f, z, c);
endmodule
```

To use a module called "simple" inside another module called "top", the following Verilog codes can be used:

```
module top (input A,B,C, output D);
   wire e;
   simple mysimplemodule (A,B,C,e);
   not not00(D,e);
endmodule
```

In the previous example, the top module contains an instance of the simple module inside it. The connections are made to the "simple module" by matching the order of the signals defined by the "**module** simple (**input** x, y, z, **output** f);" statement. Signal "A" is associated and connected to x, B to y, C to z, and the wire e is connected to the output signal f. This is called "positional association" because the first signal provided in the top module is connected to the first signal in the port list, the second to the second, and so forth. This approach is generally used for small to medium sized modules since it is relatively easy to match the order.

For larger designs, another approach called "named association" can be used. Named association specifies the name of the port with which to make the connection. Using the same example as above, the "simple module" can be instantiated using named association as follows:

```
module top (input A,B,C, output D);
  wire e;
  simple mysimplemodule( .x(A), .y(B), .z(C), .f(e) );
  not not0(D,e);
endmodule
```

In the above, A is associated with x, B with y, z with C, and e with f. The same associations are made, except now the connections are made to the specified ports. The advantage to named association is that the order of the signals is not significant. Since the port to be connected is associated by name, any order can be used. To illustrate this, the following Verilog code is also valid:

```
module top (input A,B,C, output D);
   wire e;
   simple mysimplemodule( .f(e), .y(B), .x(A), .z(C));
   not not0(D,e);
endmodule
```

To leave inputs or outputs unconnected in positional associating, no signal will be specified between the commas, such as **simple mysimplemodule (A,,C,e);** instead of **simple mysimplemodule (A,B,C,e);** which will leave the y signal unconnected. For named association, the associated port will simply be omitted during instantiation. It should be noted that any unconnected input is determined to be in the high impedance (Z) state.

The definition of a **module** keyword always ends with the **endmodule** keyword as shown in all previous examples. The module items are not limited to just basic gates and other modules which are commonly referred to as "structural modeling". Note that structural modeling is used in all the examples just described. Verilog also supports operators, constants, and conditional statements, which are used in "behavioral modeling"; this topic will be discussed later in this chapter.

Note that Structural modeling is the process of describing hardware in Verilog modules using only basic gates as the building blocks, similar to how logic gates and wires would be connected on a breadboard. All examples presented so far have used structural modeling since it is easy to understand and follow from a hardware perspective.

and follow from a hardware perspective.

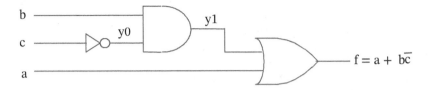

FIGURE 8.1   Schematic for $f = a + b\bar{c}$

Module Items   The <module items> shown as the beginning of section **8.2.3** contain all statements to describe the circuit to be implemented. These differ based on the modeling type used (structural vs. behavioral vs. dataflow) (to be discussed later). Verilog uses keywords **begin** and **end** like Pascal to define a block. Curley brackets { } are not used with **begin** and **end** like C since these brackets are used for concatenation in Verilog.

8.3   Structural Modeling

Structural modeling can be used to write Verilog codes for small designs. In order to describe a combinational logic circuit using structural modeling, consider a simple example of writing the Verilog code for $f = a + b\bar{c}$.

For structural modeling, the schematic for $f = a + b\bar{c}$ must be drawn first. Figure 8.1 shows the schematic. Using the schematic, Verilog code is written as follows:

```
module func(a, b, c, f);
   input a, b, c;          // line #1
   output f;               // line #2
   wire y0,y1;             // line #3
   not g1(y0, c);          // line #4
   and g2(y1, b, y0);      // line #5
   or g3(f, y1, a);        // line #6
endmodule
```

Verilog codes should be written in such a way that they are easy to read. That is why keywords **module** and **endmodule** are aligned properly. The module name "func" is used arbitrarily. In order to explain the above Verilog code, line #1 through line #6 are used as comments after //.

Since there are three inputs (a,b,c) shown in the schematic, line #1 defines them using the **input** keyword. Similarly, line #2 defines one output (f) using the **output** keyword.

As mentioned before, nets specify the connections between gates by using the keyword **wire** in structural modeling. Hence, keyword **wire** (line #3) is used to declare the intermediate outputs y0 and y1 to be connected as shown in the schematic.

The statement in line #4, **not** g1(y0,c), uses the keyword **not**, and specifies 'y0' as the output and 'c' as the input. Hence, this statement means that y0 = NOT c. The statement in line #5, **and** g2(y1, b, y0); uses the keyword **and**, and specifies 'y1' as the output with 'b' and 'y0' as inputs. Hence, this statement means y1 = b AND y0. The statement in line #6, **or** g3(f, y1, a); uses the keyword **or**, and specifies 'f' as the output with 'y1' and 'a' as inputs. Hence, this statement means f = a **or** y1. Hence, f = a + b$\bar{c}$.

Example 8.1

Write a Verilog description for Z1 and Z2 of the circuit shown Figure 8.2. Use structural modeling.

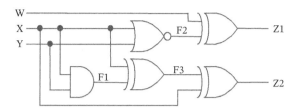

FIGURE 8.2 Figure for Example 8.1

Solution

```
module my_circuit (input W, input X, input Y, output Z1, output Z2);
  wire F1, F2, F3;
  and gate1(F1, X, Y);
  nor gate2(F2, X, Y);
  xor gate3(F3, X, F1);
  xor gate4(Z1, W,F2);
  xor gate5(Z2, F3, X);
endmodule
```

Example 8.2

Write a Verilog description for the 2-to-4 decoder of Figure 8.3 using structural modeling.

Solution

The Verilog description for the decoder using structural modeling is provided below:

```
// Structural description of a 2-to-4 decoder
module decoder2to4 (x1, x0, e, d0, d1, d2, d3);
    input x1, x0, e;
    output d0, d1, d2, d3;
    wire x11, x00;
    not  inv1 (x11, x1),
    not  inv2 (x00, x0);
    and and0(d0, x11, x00,e);
    and and1(d1, x11, x0, e);
    and and2(d2, x1, x00, e);
    and and3(d3, x1, x0, e);
endmodule
```

The above structural description for the 2-to-4 decoder contains three inputs (x1, x0, e), and four outputs (d0 through d3). The **wire** declaration provides internal connections. Keyword **not** is used to obtain complements x11 and x00 of the inputs x1 and x0 respectively while the keyword **and** is used to obtain the outputs d0 through d3. In the gate list such as "**and** and0 (d0, x11, x00, e);" the output d0 is always listed first followed by inputs x11, x00, and e.

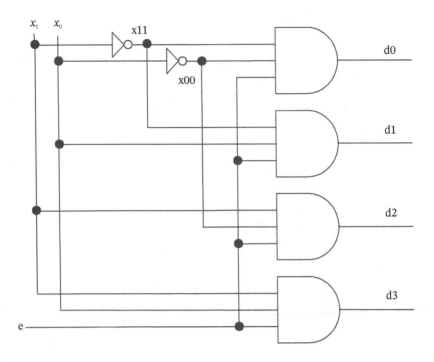

FIGURE 8.3   Schematic of the 2-to-4 decoder

Example 8.3

Write a Verilog description of the 2-to-4 decoder of Example 8.2 using structural modeling with vectored inputs.

Solution

The Verilog description for the decoder using structural modeling is provided below:

```
// Structural description of a 2-to-4 decoder
module decoder2to4 (x, e, d);
    input e;
    input [1:0]x;
    output [0:3] d;
    wire x11, x00;
    not
        inv1 ( x11, x[1] ),
        inv2 ( x00, x[0] );
    and
        and0 ( d[0], x11, x00, e ),
        and1 ( d[1], x11, x[0], e ),
        and2 ( d[2], x[1], x00, e ),
        and3 ( d[3], x[1], x[0], e );
endmodule
```

The above structural description for the 2-to-4 decoder contains three inputs (x1, x0, e), and four outputs (d[0] through d[3]). The **wire** declaration provides internal connections. Keyword **not** is used to obtain complements x11 and x00 of the inputs x[1] and x[0], respectively, while the keyword

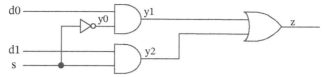

FIGURE 8.4   2-to-1 Multiplexer schematic for Example 8.4

the output d[0] is always listed first followed by inputs x11, x00, and e. The keyword **and** is written once for all AND operations, and in this case provides output d[0] by logically ANDing x11, x00, and e. Note that if a Verilog operation is required several times in a program such as NOT requiring twice in the above, the Verilog code can be written in two ways. The two NOT operations, in the above, are written using the keyword **not** followed by two different labels inv1 and inv2 separated by commas, and terminated by ;. An alternate Verilog code for the two NOT operations can be written the keyword **not** each time as follows:

```
not(x11, x1);
not(x00, x0);
```

Similarly, alternative codes for other logic operations in the above can be written. All four AND gates in the initial code for Example 8.3 are described using only a single **and** keyword, with each gate separated by a comma with its own unique identifier.

Example 8.4

Write a Verilog description for a 2-to-1 multiplexer of Figure 8.4 using structural modeling.

Solution

Using the schematic of Figure 8.4, Verilog description of the 2-to-1 MUX is written as follows:

```
//Structural  modeling  for 2-to-1 mux
module mux2(d0,d1,s,z);
   // I/O port declarations
   output z;
   input d0, d1, s;
   // Internal nets
   wire y0, y1, y2;
   // Instantiate logic gate primitives
   not gate1(y0, s);
   and gate2(y1, d0, y0);
   and gate3(y2, d1, s);
   or gate4(z, y1, y2);
endmodule
```

Example 8.5

Write a Verilog description for a half adder shown in Figure 8.5 using structural modeling.

Solution

This schematic of Figure 8.5 can be used to write the Verilog code for the half adder. The Verilog description is given below:

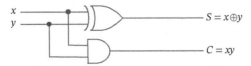

FIGURE 8.5   Half adder schematic

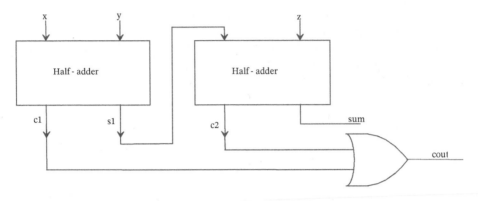

FIGURE 8.6   Figure for Example 8.6

```
// Half  Adder
module half_adder (s,c,x,y);
   output s,c;
   input x,y;
   xor  gate1(s,x,y);
   and  gate2(c,x,y);
endmodule
```

Example 8.6

Using Figure 8.6, write a Verilog description for a full adder using two half adders and an OR gate. Use hierarchical (structural) modeling.

Solution

```
//Verilog code for half adder from Example 8.5
module half_adder (s,c,x,y);
   output s,c;
   input x,y;
   xor  gate1(s,x,y);
   and  gate2(c,x,y);
endmodule

//Obtain full adder
module full_adder(sum, cout, x, y, z);
   input x, y,z;
   output sum, cout;
   wire s1, c1, c2;

// Instantiating half adder module twice
half_adder ha0(s1, c1, x, y);
half_adder ha1(sum, c2, s1, z);
//Perform OR for carry
   or carry1(cout, c1, c2);
endmodule
```

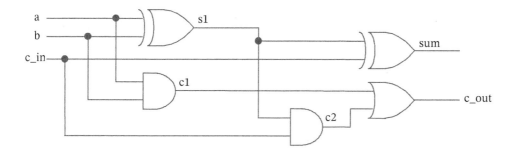

FIGURE 8.7   Full adder schematic

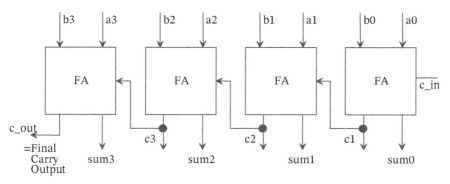

FIGURE 8.8   Figure for four-bit binary adder

Example 8.7

Using Figure 8.7, write a Verilog description for a four-bit binary adder using hierarchical (structural) modeling.

Solution

Verilog description of the full adder is written using the schematic of Figure 8.7.

The full adder module is called fulladd which is then instantiated four times to obtain the four-bit binary adder of Figure 8.8.

Verilog description of the four-bit binary adder using hierarchical modeling is provided below:

```
// Define the full_adder
module fulladd(sum, c_out, a, b, c_in);

    // I/O port declarations
    output sum, c_out;
    input a, b, c_in;

    // Internal nets
    wire s1, c1, c2;

    // Instantiate logic gate primitives
    xor a0(s1, a, b);
    and a1(c1, a, b);
```

```
    xor a2(sum, s1, c_in);
    and a3(c2, s1, c_in);
    or a4(c_out, c2, c1);
endmodule


// Define a 4-bit binary adder
module fulladd4(sum, c_out, a, b, c_in);

    // I/O port declarations
    output sum0, sum1, sum2, sum3;
    output c_out;
    input a0, a1,a2,a3, b0, b1, b2, b3;
    input c_in;

    // wire nets
    wire c1, c2, c3;

    // Instantiate four one-bit full adders.
    fulladd fa0(sum0, c1, a0, b0, c_in);
    fulladd fa1(sum1, c2, a1, b1, c1);
    fulladd fa2(sum2, c3, a2, b2, c2);
    fulladd fa3 (sum3, c_out, a3, b3, c3);
endmodule
```

Note that in Verilog, nesting of modules is not permitted. That is, a module cannot be placed between **module** and **endmodule** of another module. However, modules can be instantiated within other modules. This provides hierarchical modeling of design in Verilog.

In the above program, the full adder is defined by instantiating primitive gates. The fulladd4 module describes the 4-bit binary adder by instantiating four full adders. The instantiation is done by using the name of the module that is instantiated with the same port names in this case.

The statement, "fulladd fa0(sum0, c1, a0, b0, c_in);" in the submodule called "fulladd fa0" instantiates the full adder module called "fulladd". This submodule is given the name fa0 which is a user-defined identifier that must start with an alpha character or the underscore (_). The order in which the ports are listed inside the bracket of the submodule "fulladd fa0" is the same as those of the module "fulladd". The other three submodules with names "fa1", "fa2", and "fa3" can be explained similarly.

Example 8.8

Write a Verilog description for a 74138 3-to-8 decoder shown in Figure 8.9 using structural modeling.

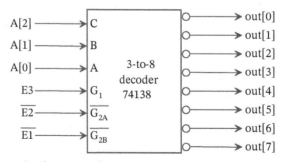

FIGURE 8.9   74138 Decoder for Example 8.8

Solution

```
module decoder_3_8(
   input [2:0]A,
   input E1, E2, E3,
   output [7:0]OUT);

wire [2:0]A_not;
wire enable, E1_not, E2_not;
not E1_inv(E1_not, E1),
    E2_inv(E2_not, E2);

and and_enable(enable, E1_not, E2_not, E3);
  not A_inv2(A_not[2]),
  A_inv1(A_not[1], A[1]),
  A_inv0(A_not[0], A[0]);

nand  o7_nand(OUT[7],  A[2], A[1], A[0], enable),
      o6_nand(OUT[6],  A[2], A[1], A_not[0], enable),
      o5_nand(OUT[5],  A[2], A_not[1], A[0], enable),
      o4_nand(OUT[4],  A[2], A_not[1], A_not[0], enable),
      o3_nand(OUT[3],  A_not[2], A[1], A[0], enable),
      o2_nand(OUT[2],  A_not[2], A[1], A_not[0], enable),
      o1_nand(OUT[1],  A_not[2], A_not[1], A[0], enable),
      o0_nand(OUT[0],  A_not[2], A_not[1], A_not[0], enable;
endmodule
```

In the above, the equation for enable: enable = (E1_not) AND (E2_not) AND (E3). Also, E1_not and E2_not are inverted outputs of E1 and E2 respectively, and enable is the ANDed output of E1_not, E2_not, E3. Therefore, E1_not, E2_not, and enable must be declared as **wire**.

8.4   Dataflow Modeling

Structural modeling is useful for writing Verilog code for small designs. However, it may be cumbersome to use structural modeling for writing Verilog code for large designs. Dataflow modeling can be used for describing the behavior of large circuits. This type of modeling utilizes Boolean operators along with logic expressions. Hence, dataflow modeling in Verilog allows a digital system to be designed in terms of its function.

Dataflow modeling utilizes Boolean equations, and uses a number of operators that can act on inputs to produce outputs. There are approximately 30 Verilog operators. These operators can be used to synthesize digital circuits. Some of the operators are listed in the Table 8.1.

All Boolean equations are executed concurrently whenever any one of the values on the right hand side of one or more equations changes. This is accomplished by using Verilog's continuous assignment statement. This statement uses the keyword **assign**. A continuous assignment statement is used to assign a value to a net. It is used to specify the output (defined by **output** or **wire** using declaration statements) of a gate. For example, consider the following assignment statement:

assign e = (a & b) & (~c | d);

Note that in the above, the keyword **assign** means that the value of 'e' is continuously updated whenever one or more values (a,b,c,d) on the right hand side of the equation change. The Boolean expression on the right hand side of the above equation is first evaluated, and the AND gate output is connected to e.

In order to illustrate dataflow modeling in Verilog, consider writing the Verilog code for $f = a + b\bar{c}$.

Verilog code using dataflow modeling is provided in the following:

```
module function(a,b,c,f);
    input a, b,c;
    output f;
    assign f = a | (b & ~c);
endmodule
```

The above code uses the 'or' operator along with the 'and' operator to implement the circuit.

Some of the Verilog operators shown in Table 8.1 will be discussed next. The arithmetic operators perform the operation on two input signals, producing an output for a third signal. All arithmetic operations are performed bitwise, so it is important to ensure that there are sufficient numbers of bits for the result.

For example, consider the Verilog segment provided below:

```
wire [3:0]X, [3:0]Y;
reg [3:0]Z;
. . .
Z = X + Y;
. . .
```

The binary addition operation is performed using 4-bit unsigned number, X and 4-bit unsigned number, Y with the 4-bit unsigned result in Z. If the result of X + Y is less than 16, then the four-bit size of Z is adequate. However, if the result is greater than 16, a final carry (also called overflow for unsigned numbers) will occur, and the value of signal Z will not be the correct result. This is where behavioral description is quite powerful since the overflow condition can be accounted for by techniques discussed in Chapter 2.

The other arithmetic operators follow the same restrictions, and any bits above and beyond those allocated for the result will be lost. The division operation truncates fractional bits, however the modulo operator can be used to obtain the remainder. For example, consider X = 3, Y =2 in the following:

```
Z = X / Y;          // Z will have the value of 1
W = X % Y;          // W= Remainder of (X/Y). Hence, W will have the value of 1
```

The bitwise operations perform the specified logical operator on a bit-by-bit basis. For example, take the AND operator:
X = 4'b1101; Y = 4'b0110;
Z will have the value of 4'b0110 from the AND operation is shown below:

$$1101$$
$$0110$$
$$----$$
$$0100$$

The same is true for the rest of the bitwise operators, except for the one's complement (also referred to as the negation operation) since that operator is unary only operator, which inverts all bits.

TABLE 8.1 Some of the Verilog operators

Type	Operation	Symbol
Arithmetic	Binary addition	+
	Binary subtraction	-
	Binary multiplication	*
	Binary division	/
	Modulus	%
Bitwise / Reduction	One's compliment	~
	AND	&
	OR	|
	XOR	^
	NAND	~&
	NOR	~ |
	XNOR	~^ or ^~
Boolean Logical	NOT	!
	AND	&&
	OR	||
Shift	Logical Shift Left	<<
	Logical Shift Right	>>
	Arithmetic Shift Left	<<<
	Arithmetic Shift Right	>>>
Relational	Equality	==
	Inequality	!=
	Less than	<
	Greater than	>
	Less than or equal to	<=
	Greater than or equal to	>=
Special	Parenthesis	( )
	Bit-select	[ ]
	Conditional	?:
	Concatenation	{}

Next, Verilog reduction operators will be discussed. The bitwise operators can also be used as reduction operators to convert vectors to scalars. They operate on all bits in a vector, and then convert the result into a single bit. All bitwise operations can also be used as unary (single operand) operators which performs its operation on each of bits of a signal to produce a single-bit result. For example, if V = &X;

Then, from the previous example, the result will be a 1'b0 since the AND operation is performed on X[3] & X[2] & X[1] & X[0]. Similarly, V = ^X will yield a value of 1'b1 since there are an odd-number of 1's in X.

The Boolean logical operators perform logical operations after converting the operators to a one-bit value by assigning a '1' to any non-zero number, and a '0' only if the value is zero. Suppose two 8-bit numbers have the following values:

```
X = 8'b1001_0010
Y = 8'b0000_0000
```

The logical operators interpret the above values of X and Y as true or false. Any non-zero value is considered as TRUE (Logic 1) while a zero value is considered FALSE (Logic 0). This means that X (non-zero value), and Y (zero-value) can be evaluated to a single-bit of '1' (X = 1) and Y to '0' (Y=0) respectively. Therefore, the following results for various Boolean logic operators can be obtained:

```
!X = NOT 1 = 0
```

```
!Y = NOT 0 = 1
X && Y = 1 AND 0 = 0
X || Y = 1  OR 0 = 1
```

Note that for a single bit, !X and ~X will have the same result. However, given that X in the above example is 8-bit, the two operations would produce different results:

```
!X = 1'b0  // Converts to a scalar and inverts
~X = 8'b0110_1101;  // Negation, result is a vector.
```

The Logical shift operators take the given operand and shift it the given number of positions to the left in the case of << or to the right for >>. Logical shift will insert 0's to the vacated bits on the left or right. On the other hand, arithmetic shift right (>>>) will sign extend, padding the left side with the value of the MSB (sign bit) when shifting to right. Left shift is the same between both logical(<<) and arithmetic (<<<), since zeros are inserted in both cases. Both logical and arithmetic shifts are discussed in Chapter 2.

Below are the outcomes of logical and arithmetic shift on a register X:

```
X = 8'b1001_0010;
X >> 1 is 8'b0100_1001;          X <<< 1 is 8'b0010_0100;
X >> 4 is 8'b0000_1001;          X >>> 1 is 8'b1100_1001;
X << 1 is 8'b0010_0100;          X >>> 4 is 8'b1111_1001;
X << 3 is 8'b1001_0000;          X >>> 0 is 8'b1001_0010;
```

The equality operators behave in the same way as any other language, producing either 1'b1 or 1'b0 representing TRUE or FALSE. In Verilog, a double equal sign (==) is used to evaluate if two signals are equivalent. Note that the single equal sign is used for value assignment. Given X = 4'b0101 and Y = 4'b0111, the following are the evaluated results:

```
X == Y : 0 // False
X > Y : 0 // False
X < Y : 1 // True
X >= Y : 0 // False
X <= Y : 0 // False
X != Y : 1 // True
X = Y  : N/A // Not Valid, will have unintended outcome
```

The concatenation operators allows bits for different signals, or the same signal, if needed, to be placed together to form a longer vector. For example, to take the most significant bit of vector [3:0]A and insert in front of vector [6:0], the following can be used:

{A[3], B[6:0]}

The curly-braces indicate the concatenation operation, while the comma is used to separate the signals. There is limit to the number of elements to be concatenated, and the total length of the concatenated vector is the sum of all the lengths of the vectors to be concatenated together.

Example 8.9

Use concatenation to reverse the bits of the vector X[7:0] to form Y[7:0].

Solution

```
Y = { X[0], X[1], X[2], X[3], X[4], X[5], X[6], X[7] }
```

Example 8.10

Use concatenation to change Z[15:0] to swap the upper 8 bits with he lower 8 bits, giving the value to vector W.

Solution

$$W = \{ Z[7:0], Z[15:8] \};$$

Example 8.11

Use dataflow modeling to rewrite the description of the circuit from Example 8.1.

Solution

```
module my_circuit_dataflow(W, X, Y, Z1, Z2);
  input W, X, Y;
  output Z1, Z2;
  assign Z1 = W ^ ~(X | Y);
  assign Z2 = (X & Y) ^ X ^ X;
endmodule
```

Example 8.12

Use dataflow modeling to describe a component that doubles and adds one to the value of a 4-bit input, and generates the result on a 5-bit output:

Solution

```
module doubler(input [3:0]IN, output [4:0]OUT;
  assign OUT = IN*2 + 1;
endmodule
```

The same can also be accomplished using the shift operator:

```
module doubler(input [3:0]IN, output [4:0]OUT);
  assign OUT = (IN << 1) + 1;
endmodule
```

Dataflow modeling can greatly simplify the amount of code needed to implement combinational circuits compared to the structural modeling equivalent. The **assign** keyword is commonly referred to as continuous assignment because the net value on the left of the equal sign is continuously updated whenever any of the nets on the right side of the equal sign changes.

Example 8.13

Write a Verilog description of the 2-to-4 decoder of Figure 8.3 using dataflow modeling.

Solution

The four output equations for the decoder are obtained as follows:
$d_0 = e\overline{x1}\,\overline{x0}$, $d_1 = e\overline{x_1}\,x_0$, $d_2 = ex_1\overline{x_0}$, and $d_3 = ex_1x_0$

```
module decoder2to4 (e, x1, x0, d0, d1, d2, d3);
    input e, x0, x1;
    output d0, d1, d2, d3;
    assign d0 = (e & ~x1 & ~x0);
    assign d1 = (e & ~ x1 & x0);
    assign d2 = (e & x1 & ~x0);
    assign d3 = (e & x1 & x0);
endmodule
```

Example 8.14

Write a Verilog description for the 2-to-1 multiplexer of Figure 8.4 using dataflow modeling.

Solution

Note that the equation for the MUX output is $z = \bar{s}d_0 + sd_1$.
Verilog code using dataflow modeling is provided below:

```
module mux_2to1 (s, d0, d1, z);
    input s, d0, d1;
    output z;
    assign z = (~s & d0) | (s & d1);
endmodule
```

Example 8.15

Write a Verilog description for the 2-to-1 multiplexer of Figure 8.4 using the conditional operator.

Solution

```
module mux 2to1 (s, d0, d1, z);
    input s, d0, d1;
    output z;
    assign z = s ? d1 : d0;
endmodule
```

Note: In the above, the **assign** statement with conditional operator (?:) means that if s = 1 then z = d1, else if s = 0 then z = d0.

Example 8.16

Write a Verilog description using dataflow modeling for the full adder shown in Figure 8.6.

Solution

```
module half_adder_V2 (input a, b, output sum, carry);
 assign sum = a ^ b;
 assign carry = a & b;
endmodule

module full_adder_V2(X, Y, Cin, Sum, Carry);
 input X,Y,Cin;
 output Sum, Carry;
 wire [2:0]w;

 half_adder ha0(    X,    Y, w[0], w[1]);
 half_adder ha1(w[0], Cin, Sum, w[2]);

 assign Carry = w[1] | w[2];
endmodule
```

The half_adder and full_adder modules previously modeled can be further simplified into a single module by using concatenation and addition operators to create an intermediate two-bit vector representing the sum as shown in Example 8.17.

Example 8.17

Write a Verilog description for a full adder using dataflow modeling. Use the concatenation operator.

Solution

```
module full_adder_V3(X, Y, Z, Sum, Carry);
 input X,Y,Z;
 output Sum, Carry;
assign {Carry,Sum} = X + Y + Z;
endmodule
```

Example 8.18

Write a Verilog description for a 4-bit binary adder using dataflow modeling. Use the concatenation operator.

Solution

```
// 4-bit binary adder using the concatenation operator
module adder4 (x, y, cin, s, cout);
  input [3:0] x, y;
  output  cout;
  output  [3:0]s;
  assign {cout, s} = x + y + cin;
endmodule
```

8.5   Behavioral modeling

Behavioral modeling is used to describe a circuit using logic expressions and C-like constructs. Behavioral modeling allows for the description of circuits based on their function rather than their hardware components. This functional description is placed inside an **initial** or **always** block, which can be compared to the **setup()** and **loop()** functions in C respectively. The **begin** and **end** keywords encapsulate the behavioral description, just like the functions in C. If there are more than one statement in the **always** block, then the keywords **begin** and **end** must be used. Keywords **begin** and **end** are not required for a single statement in the **always** block.

A simple example with keywords **begin** and **end** using the equations of the full adder is provided below:

```
always @ (a, b, c)
 begin
      sum = a ^ b ^ c;
      carry = (b & c) | (a & c) | (a & b);
 end
```

The outputs of the procedural statements must be declared by the keyword **reg**. Input ports cannot be declared as **reg** since they do not retain values. Rather, they affect the changes in the external signals they are connected to. Note that a **reg** data type retains its value until a new value is assigned.

Behavioral modeling takes dataflow modeling to the next level by adding support for decision-based statements in software languages. Decision statements are supported in Verilog in the form of **if-else**, **case**, and **conditional** statements. In Verilog, these types of statements are called "procedural statements". These are similar to programming languages, while making it easier to describe the functionality of a module using behavioral modeling. It is an important concept in HDL to always have an outcome in the case of decision statements. For example, it is good practice to always have an **else** statement following an **if** so that signals are always given a value independent of the outcome.

In order to use the decision statements, they must reside with an **always** block to indicate procedural statements are going to be used. The syntax for the **always** block is:

```
always @ (<sensitivity list>)
```

The sensitivity list should contain all of the signals that are used to determine the value of another signal when they change. For example, a simple 3-input AND gate with inputs a, b, and c, with an output d can be modeled as follows:

```
always @ (a, b, c)
begin
  d = a & b & c;
end
```

Since the value of d depends on a, b, and c, all three variables must be present in the sensitivity list. If one is missing, the synthesis step will not include that signal, and the wrong hardware model would be generated. To make the **always** block sensitive to all signals, an asterisk (*) can be used as the sensitivity list. In addition to the sensitivity list requirements, any signal that gets a value driven by an **always** block must be declared as **reg**. With these two requirements, the above three-input AND gate example can be written as follows:

```
module myandgate (input a,b,c, output reg d);
  always @ (*) // Sensitive to changes in all signals.
    d = a & b & c;
endmodule
```

Example 8.19

Describe the circuit from Example 8.1 using behavioral modeling:

Solution

```
module my_circuit_behavioral (W,X, Y, Z1, Z2);
  input W, X, Y;
  output reg Z1, Z2;
  always @ (*)
  begin
    Z1 = W ^ ~(X | Y);
    Z2 = (X & Y) ^ X ^ X;
  end
endmodule
```

Example 8.20

Describe a full adder using behavioral modeling.

Solution

```
module full_adder_V4(X, Y, Z, Sum, Carry);
  input X,Y,Z;
  output Sum, Carry;
  always @ ( X, Y, Z )
  {Carry,Sum} = X + Y + Z;
endmodule
```

Example 8.21

Write a Verilog description for a four-bit adder (Figure 8.8) to add two 4-bit numbers, X and Y, with carry-in (Cin) generating a four-bit Sum and a Carry bit.

Solution

```
module full_adder_4bit (X, Y, Cin, Sum, Carry);
    input [3:0]X,Y;
    input Cin;
    output reg [3:0] Sum;
    output reg Carry;
    always @ (X or Y or Cin )
    {Carry,Sum} = X + Y + Cin;
endmodule
```

8.5.1 if-else block

In addition to the operators listed in Table 8.1, Verilog also supports other procedural constructs to aid in a module's description. The **if-else** block allows for signals values to be determined based on a condition. The syntax for the **if-else** construct is as follows:

```
if (cond)
    <statement1 if cond evaluations to true>;
else
    <statement2 if cond evaluates to false>;
```

      The condition is evaluated to either a value of true or false. Any non-zero value is considered to be true, while zero is false. If the condition is true, the statement1 is executed; else (the condition is false), statement 1 is skipped, and the statement2 is executed. If multiple statements need to be executed for either case, the statements be wrapped in a **begin-end** construct.

For example:

```
if (x==3'b7)
    begin
        y = 0;
        z = 2'b10;
    end
else
    begin
        y = 0;
        z = 0;
    end
```

      Nesting if statements are supported, but care must be taken to ensure that all possible outcomes have valid signal assignments for all nested if-else blocks.

```
if(x == 1)
    if(y == 1)
        z = 3'b111;
    else
        z = 3'b100;
else

    if(y == 1)
        z == 3'b010;
    else
        z = 3'b000;
```

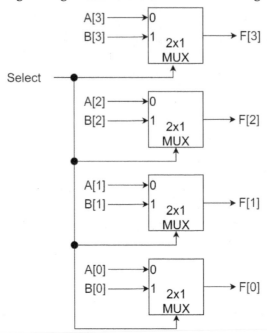

FIGURE 8.10   Figure for Example 8.22

Example 8.22

Write a Verilog description using behavioral modeling for the schematic shown in Figure 8.10. Use if-else statements. Note that in Figure 8.10, if select = 0, then F[3] F[2] F[1] F[0] = A[3] A[2] A[1] A[0], else if   select = 1, then F[3] F[2] F[1] F[0] = B[3] B[2] B[1] B[0].

Solution

```
module mux2to1 (input select, input [3:0]A, B, output [3;0]F);
   reg [3:0]F;
   always @ (*)
   if(select)
      F = B;
   else
      F = A;
endmodule
```

8.5.2   Modeling logical conditions in a circuit
To precisely model all logical conditions in a circuit, each bit in Verilog can be one of the following: 1'b0, 1'b1, 1'bz (high impedance), or 1'bx (don't care). 1'b0 and 1'b1, respectively, correspond to 0 and 1. Verilog includes 1'bz for the situation when the designer needs to define a high impedance state. Furthermore, Verilog includes 1'bx to specify a don't care condition. Sometimes, miswiring of gates may also result into an unknown value of the output in a certain situation.

For example, suppose that the designer makes a mistake and connects outputs of two gates together. In this case, the connected output may want to assume a value of either 0 or 1. This may cause physical damage to certain logic families. In order for the simulator to detect such problems, the 1'bx (don't care) definition can be used for the output.

8.5.3   Case-endcase construct
The **if-else** statement allows one to select an expression based on true or false condition. However, if there are several possible expressions, Verilog code using **if-else** becomes cumbersome. In such a situation, the **case-endcase** construct can be useful.

The syntax for the construct is as follows:

```
case (controlling parameters)
<option_0> : statement_0;
<option_1> : statement_1;
<option_2> : statement_2;
---
---
<option_n> : statement_n;
default: statement_default;
endcase
```

The controlling parameters are compared with each option, the equation with respect to the matched (first) option is executed.

Example 8.23

Describe a 3-to-8 decoder generating a '1' when selected using behavioral modeling with **case -endcase** statements.
Assume no enable input.

Solution

```
module decoder_3_8(input [2:0]x, output reg[7:0]d);

always @ x
  case(x)
    3'b000 : d = 8'b0000_0001;
    3'b001 : d = 8'b0000_0010;
    3'b010 : d = 8'b0000_0100;
    3'b011 : d = 8'b0000_1000;
    3'b100 : d = 8'b0001_0000;
    3'b101 : d = 8'b0010_0000;
    3'b110 : d = 8'b0100_0000;
    3'b111 : d = 8'b1000_0000;
endcase
endmodule
```

When not all possible input permutations are defined in the **case** construct, a default statement should be used as shown in the following example:

Example 8.24

Repeat Example 8.23 using **case-endcas**e with default.

Solution

```
module decoder_3_8(input [2:0]x, output reg[7:0]d);
case( x[2:0] )
    0 : d = 3'b000
    1 : d = 3'b010;
    2 : d = 3'b100;
    default : d = 3'b111;
endcase
endmodule
```

Since x is three-bit, there are eight possible input values. x=0, x=1, and x=2 are defined explicitly, while the other five are covered by the default. For x = 3 through x = 7, d will have a value of 3'b111. The default statement is useful for providing a "catch all" when more complex logic is used for the controlling parameters instead of listing every possible input scenario.

Example 8.25

Write a Verilog description using behavioral modeling to implement a common cathode BCD to seven segment decoder; output low for non-BCD numbers.

Solution

```
module bcd_7seg_CC(input [3:0]x, output reg[0:6]seg);
always @ x
  case(x)
  //            abc_defg  // Segment Order
  0 : seg = 7'b111_1110; // Display 0
  1 : seg = 7'b011_0000; // Display 1
  2 : seg = 7'b110_1101; // Display 2
  3 : seg = 7'b111_1001; // Display 3
  4 : seg = 7'b011_0011; // Display 4
  5 : seg = 7'b101_1011; // Display 5
  6 : seg = 7'b101_1111; // Display 6
  7 : seg = 7'b111_0000; // Display 7
  8 : seg = 7'b111_1111; // Display 8
  9 : seg = 7'b111_1011; // Display 9
  default : seg = 7'b000_0000; // Non-BCD
endcase
endmodule
```

8.5.4 Conditional Operator

The conditional operator listed in Table 8.1 is a one-line implementation of the **if-else** construct, which can be used with dataflow and behavioral modeling, using either the **assign** keyword or used within an **always** block. The conditional operator also supports nesting, which can be used to implement nested **if** statements and **case** statements for dataflow modeling. The syntax for the conditional operator is below:

```
assign <net> = <condition> ? <statement if true> : <statement if false>;
```
                or
```
<net> = <condition> ? <statement if true> : <statement if false>;
```

The condition is evaluated to either true or false just like an **if-else** block, which will select the statement to the left in the case of true, or to the right of the colon when false. Nesting is accomplished by including additional conditional operators within the statements to be executed. As noted before, it is important to always have a value assigned to the net to the left of the equal sign regardless of the path that is taken by the conditional operator. Not doing so can cause latched to be inferred during synthesis when unwanted.

Example 8.26

Repeat Example 8.23 for a 2x1 MUX using the dataflow modeling and the conditional operator.

Solution

```
module mux_2_1_4bit( input select, input [3:0]A, B, output [3:0]F );
  assign F = select ? B: A;
endmodule
```

Example 8.27

Implement a 2-to-4 decoder generating minterms with an active-low enable using behavioral modeling and, conditional operator.

Solution

```
module decoder_2_4_le(input nE, input [1:0]A, output reg [3:0]D);
   always @ (nE, A)
   if(!nE)
      D = (A == 2'b00) ? 4'b0001:
          (A == 2'b01) ? 4'b0010:
          (A == 2'b10) ? 4'b0100:
           4'b1000; // Final else value. If A is not 2'b00, 2'b01, or
                    // 2'b10, must be 2'b11 (3).
   else
      D = 0;         // Decoder disabled
endmodule
```

8.6   Simulation

Modules can be simulated using Verilog itself to test how the module functions as written. A test bench is a Verilog module specifically designed to provide input stimuli and output wires for monitoring purposes. The outputs can be represented as text, tables, or waveforms from the test bench. Verilog has a built-in function called **$time**, represented as integers. The most common unit of time in Verilog is nanoseconds (ns), with a resolution of one pico second (ps). This can be defined at the beginning of a test bench with the line:

```
timescale 1ns / 1ps
```

Creating a Test Bench A verilog test bench generally consists for the following structure:

```
module <test bench name>();
   <reg and wire declarations for inputs and outputs>
   <instantiate module under test>
   <Test bench stimuli using initial and begin>
   [monitor outputs using $monitor]
endmodule
```

A test bench is just another Verilog module, so it requires a module name. There are no ports to a test bench, and it can be thought of similar to a lab bench. Everything exists on the bench, nothing "falls off either side". In order to provide stimuli to the module under test, variables are needed to store values. For each input signal existing in the module to be tested, there must be an associated **reg** datatype to provide data. Similarly, for each output signal of the module to be tested, there must be a **wire** datatype to monitor each output state.

The module to be tested must be instantiated within the test bench, providing the associated **reg** and **wire** signals to each of the module's inputs and outputs respectively. Using the Verilog code from Example 8.1, the test bench can be written as follows:

```
module my_testbench();
   reg input_w, input_x, input_y;
   wire out1, out2;
   my_circuit dut (.W(input_w), .X(input_x), .Y(input_y), .Z1(out1),
   .Z2(out2));
endmodule
```

In the above, "dut" is an abbreviation for "device under test," and is used as the instance name for the module. Also, as shown in the above example, the signal names in the test bench do not need to match those of the module under test. As mentioned before, Verilog is case-sensitive, so **w** is not the same signal as **W**. Hence, either positional or named association can be used. In the above, named association is used.

In order to apply general stimuli for testing the design, **initial** and **begin** procedural blocks are used along with the **$time** function. Units of time can be specified by using the pound symbol (#). For example, to set input_w to 0 for one time unit, and then change it to 1 for 5 time units, before finally changing it back to 0, the following could be used.

```
initial begin
      input_w = 0;
  #1  input_w = 1;
  #5  input_w = 0;
end
```

The #1 operator is not a timestamp, but rather a delay. The initial block starts at time 0 and the statements after a delay operator will only change after that unit of time has completed. Referring to the previous initial block, the following inputs are generated:

At time 0ns: input_w = 0
At time 1ns: input_w = 1
At time 6ns: input_w = 0

To further test the my_circuit module, all the inputs needs to have values, which can be seen in the more complete initial block below. If a new value is not assigned to an input after a delay operator, it will maintain the same value as before. Note that not all the input combinations are tested.

```
initial begin
  #0 input_W = 0; input_X = 0; input_Y = 0; // Give values to W,Y,Z
  #1 input_W = 1; input_X = 0;              // Only change W and X
  #1 input_W = 0; input_X = 1;              // Y remains 0
  #1 input_W = 1; input_X = 1; input_Y = 1; // X remains the same, and
                                            // change W and Y to 1
end
```

Example 8.28

Write a Verilog description for a four-bit adder using dataflow modeling, and then create a test bench.

Solution:

```
module FA(
  input A, B, Cin,
  output Cout, Sum);
  assign Sum = A ^ B ^ Cin;
  assign Cout = ( A & B ) | ( A & Cin ) | ( B & Cin );
endmodule

module FA_4bit(
  input [3:0]A,
  input [3:0]B,
  input Cin,
  output Cout,
  output [3:0]S;
  wire [1:3]C);
  FA FA0 (A[0], B[0],  Cin, C[1], S[0]);
  FA FA1 (A[1], B[1], C[1], C[2], S[1]);
  FA FA2 (A[2], B[2], C[2], C[3], S[2]);
  FA FA3 (A[3], B[3], C[3], Cout, S[3]);
endmodule

//Test Bench
module FA_4Bit_tb();
  reg [3:0]X;
  reg [3:0]Y;
```

```
reg CIN;
wire COUT;
wire [3:0]S;

FA_4bit dut(.A(X), .B(Y), .Cin(CIN), .Cout (COUT), .S(S) );
initial begin
     CIN = 0; X = 0; Y = 0;
  #1 X = 1; Y = 0;
  #1 X = 2; Y = 5;
  #1 X = 4; Y = 6;
  #1 X = 11; Y = 3;
  #1 X = 7; Y = 7; CIN = 1;
  #1 ;
end
endmodule
```

When the simulation is run, it can produce a waveform which shows the value of each signal over time. Figure 8.11 shows the waveform is output of the test bench from Example 8.28.

Most simulators support monitoring of internal signals from the design, not just the inputs and outputs defined in the test bench. For example, the internal carries (from **wire** C[1:3] in FA_4bit) can be added to the waveform window as shown in Figure 8.12 of Example 8.28.

Name	Value	0 ns	1 ns	2 ns	3 ns	4 ns	5 ns
X[3:0]	0	0	1	2	4	11	7
Y[3:0]	0		0	5	6	3	7
CIN	0						
COUT	0						
S[3:0]	0	0	1	7	10	14	15

FIGURE 8.11   Output waveform of the test bench for Example 8.28

Name	Value	0 ns	1 ns	2 ns	3 ns	4 ns	5 ns
X[3:0]	0	0	1	2	4	b	7
Y[3:0]	0		0	5	6	3	7
CIN	0						
COUT	0						
S[3:0]	0	0	1	7	a	e	f
C[1:3]	0		0		1	6	7
[1]	0						
[2]	0						
[3]	0						

FIGURE 8.12   Test bench waveform for Example 8.28 showing internal carries

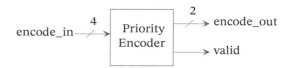

FIGURE 8.13   Figure for Example 8.29

Example 8.29

Design an active-high 4-to-2 priority encoder shown in Figure 8.13 that outputs the encoded value and a valid flag which is high when at least one input is high. Write the Verilog description, create a test bench, and simulate.

Solution

```verilog
module  priority_encoder_4bit(encode_in, encode_out, valid);
  input [3:0] encode_in;
  output reg [1:0] encode_out
  output valid;
  // Use reduction operator for valid (OR all encode_in bits together)
  assign valid = | encode_in; //valid = 1 only if at least one input is 1

  // always and if statements to describe encode_out;
  always @ (encode_in)
  begin
    encode_out = 0; //default value if none below are true
    if(encode_in[3] == 1'b1)
      encode_out = 3;
    else if(encode_in[2] == 1'b1)
      encode_out = 2;
    else if(encode_in[1] == 1'b1)
      encode_out = 1;
    else if(encode_in[0] == 1'b1)
      encode_out = 0;
    else encode_out = 0;
  end
endmodule

module priority_encoder_sim();
  reg [3:0]IN;
  wire [1:0]OUT;
  wire FLAG;
  // Instantiate module to be tested
  priority_encoder_4bit dut(IN, OUT, FLAG);
 // Define test vectors
  initial begin
        IN = 4'b0000;
    #1 IN = 4'b0001;
    #1 IN = 4'b0010;
    #1 IN = 4'b0100;
    #1 IN = 4'b1000;
    #1 IN = 4'b1001;
    #1 IN = 4'b0111;
    #1 IN = 4'b0000;
  end
 endmodule
```

Name	Value	0 ns	1 ns	2 ns	3 ns	4 ns	5 ns	6 ns	7 ns
IN[3:0]	0000	0000	0001	0010	0100	1000	1001	0111	0000
OUT[1:0]	0	0		1	2		3	2	0
FLAG	0								

FIGURE 8.14 Test bench waveform for Example 8.29

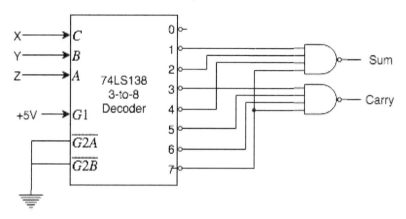

FIGURE 8.15 Schematic for Example 8.30

Figure 8.14 shows the waveform for the test bench of Example 8.29.

Example 8.30

Describe the schematic of Figure 8.15 using a combination of behavioral, structural, and dataflow modeling, create a test bench and then simulate.

Solution

```
module decoder_74138(
   input C, B, A, G1, nG2A, nG2B,
   output reg [7:0]OUT
      );
      always @ (*)
      if ( {G1, nG2A, nG2B} == 3'b100 )
         case ({C,B,A})
         0 : OUT = 8'b1111_1110;
         1 : OUT = 8'b1111_1101;
         2 : OUT = 8'b1111_1011;
         3 : OUT = 8'b1111_0111;
         4 : OUT = 8'b1110_1111;
         5 : OUT = 8'b1101_1111;
         6 : OUT = 8'b1011_1111;
         7 : OUT = 8'b0111_1111;
         default : OUT = 8'bx; //THIS SHOULD NOT HAPPEN IF INPUTS DEFINED
         endcase
      else
         OUT = 8'b1111_1111;
endmodule

module FA_using_decoder(X, Y, Z, Carry, Sum);
   input X, Y, Z;
   output Carry, Sum;
```

```
    wire [7:0]D;
    //Instantiate the 74138 decoder
    decoder_74138 u1 (X, Y, Z, 1'b1, 1'b0, 1'b0, D);
    assign Sum = ~(D[1] & D[2] & D[4] & D[7]);
    assign Carry = ~(D[3] & D[5] & D[6] & D[7]);
endmodule
```

Test Bench / Simulation:

```
module FA_using_decoder_sim();
    reg A,B,Cin;
    wire S, Cout;
    //Header of the module to be tested
    //module FA_using_decoder(X, Y, Z, Carry, Sum);
    FA_using_decoder dut(A,B,Cin, Cout, S);

    initial begin
        A = 0; B = 0; Cin = 0;
    #1 A = 1; B = 0; Cin = 0;
    #1 A = 0; B = 1, Cin = 0;
    #1 A = 1; B = 1, Cin = 0;
    #1 A = 0; B = 0; Cin = 1;
    #1 A = 1; B = 0; Cin = 1;
    #1 A = 0; B = 1; Cin = 1;
    #1 A = 1; B = 1; Cin = 1;
    end
endmodule
```

Figure 8.16 shows the test bench waveform for Example 8.30:

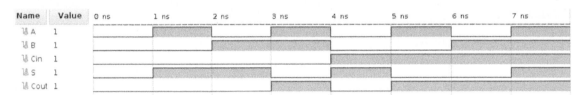

FIGURE 8.16   Test bench waveform for Example 8.30

QUESTIONS AND PROBLEMS

8.1 Write the Verilog module header for the block diagram shown in Figure P8.1.

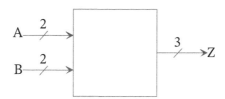

FIGURE P8.1

8.2 Write the Verilog module header for a generic 2-to-4 bit decoder with an active-high enable line.

8.3 Write the Verilog module to implement the circuit in Figure 8.3 using structural modeling.

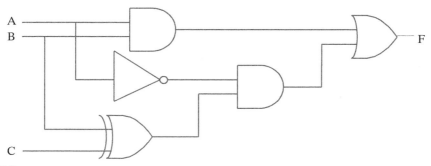

FIGURE P8.3

8.4 Write a Verilog description to implement the circuit of Figure P8.4 using structural modeling.

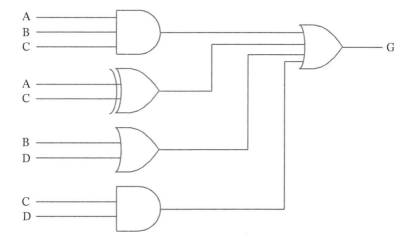

FIGURE P8.4

8.5 Use dataflow modeling to describe the circuit in Figure P8.3.

8.6 Use behavioral modeling to describe the circuit in Figure P8.4.

8.7 Write a Verilog description for 4-to-1 multiplexer using structural modeling.

8.8   Write a Verilog description for 4-to-1 multiplexer using dataflow modeling.

8.9   Write a Verilog description for a 4-bit 2-to-1 multiplexer using behavioral modeling.

8.10   Create a test bench for the 4-to-1 multiplexer from Problems 8.7 and 8.8.

8.11.   Use hierarchical modeling to write the Verilog description for a five-bit adder using a minimum number of full adders. Include carry_in and carry_out.

8.12   Using a multiplexer similar to the one designed in Problem 8.9, write the verilog description for a circuit that takes three five-bit numbers A, B, and C as inputs, and outputs a five-bit sum. The circuit performs A + B or A+ C depending on, if a fourth input S is 0 or 1 respectively. Use hierarchical modeling.

8.13   Use behavioral modeling to write the Verilog description for 8-to-3 priority encoder with an active-low enable. Use **if-else** statements.

8.14   Using behavioral modeling, write the verilog description for a 4-bit binary number (single hex digit 0-F) as an input, and then output the hex digit on a common-anode seven-segment display.

8.15   Using dataflow modeling, write a Verilog description for the block diagram shown in Figure P8.15. The shift circuit in the figure logically shifts the input (8-bit vector A) left or right based on input dir, where dir = 0 for right shift, and dir = 1 for left shift.

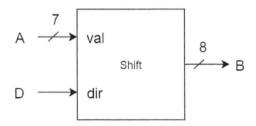

FIGURE P8.15

8.16.   For the 4-bit ALU functions shown below:

Select inputs	Operation
S1S0	performed
0 0	A OR B
0 1	A AND B
1 0	A + B
1 1	A - B

a.   Write a verilog description to implement the design using behavioral modeling
b.   Create a test bench to test each operation.

8.17   Write a Verilog module using dataflow modeling for a converter which swaps the upper and lower bytes of a 16-bit number if an enable signal is set to '1'.

8.18   Repeat Problem 8.15 to be able to shift left or right n-times by adding a two-bit input n to specify the shift count.

8.19   Using conditional operators and hierarchical modeling to design a 4-bit 8-to-1 multiplexer.

      a.   Write the Verilog description using only 2-to-1 multiplexers and conditional statements as building blocks.

      b.   Create a test bench and verify the operation.

8.20   Write the Verilog description for a BCD to seven-segment display converter using a **case-endcase** construct with default. Turn the segments off for non-BCD digits. Use an additional input type to sup-port both common-anode and common-cathode displays.

9

LATCHES AND FLIP-FLOPS

This chapter covers basics of latches and flip-flops. Topics include types of latches and flip-flops. Timing diagrams along with typical timing parameters associated with edge-triggered flip-flops are also included.

9.1 Latches and Flip-Flops

A flip-flop is a one-bit memory. As long as power is available, the flip-flop retains the bit. However, its output (stored bit) can be changed by a clock input. This basic type of a storage device is called a "latch" which uses a level-sensitive clock. Flip-flops are designed using the latches. The most common latch is the Set-Reset (SR) latch. A flip-flop is a latch with an edge-triggered clock input. Synchronous sequential circuits are designed using flip-flops.

9.1.1 SR Latch

Figure 9.1 shows a basic SR latch circuit along with its truth table. The latch circuit uses NOR gates with positive pulse inputs. The SR latch has two inputs, S (Set) and R (Reset), and two outputs Q (true output) and $\bar{Q}$ (complement of Q). To analyze the SR latch of Figure 9.1(a), note that a NOR gate generates an output 1 when all inputs are 0; on the other hand, the output of a NOR gate is 0 if any input is 1. Now assume that $S = 1$ and $R = 0$, the $\bar{Q}$ output of NOR gate #2 will be 0. This places 0 at both inputs of NOR gate #1. Therefore, output Q of NOR gate #1 will be 1. Thus, Q stays at 1. This means that one of the inputs to NOR gate #2 will be 1, producing 0 at the $\bar{Q}$ output regardless of the value of S. Thus, when the pulse at S becomes 0, the output $\bar{Q}$ will still be 0. This will apply 0 at the input of NOR #1. Thus, Q will continue to remain at 1. This means that when the set input $S = 1$ and the reset (clear) input $R = 0$, the SR latch stores a 1 ($Q = 1$, $\bar{Q} = 0$). This means that the SR latch is set to 1.

Consider $S = 0$, $R = 1$; the Q output of NOR gate #1 will be 0. This will apply 0 at both inputs of NOR gate #2. Thus, output $\bar{Q}$ will be 1. When the reset pulse input R returns to zero, the outputs continues to remain at $Q = 0$, and $\bar{Q} = 1$. This means that with set input $S = 0$ and reset input $R = 1$, the SR latch is cleared to 0 ($Q = 0$, $\bar{Q} = 1$).

Next, consider $Q = 1$, $\bar{Q} = 0$. With $S = 0$ and $R = 0$, the NOR gate #1 will have both inputs at 0. This will generate 1 at the Q output. The output $\bar{Q}$ of NOR gate #2 will be zero. Thus, the outputs Q and $\bar{Q}$ are unchanged when $S = 0$ and $R = 0$.

When $S = 1$ and $R = 1$, both Q and $\bar{Q}$ outputs are 0. This is an invalid condition because for the SR latch Q and $\bar{Q}$ must be complements of each other. Therefore, one must ensure that the condition $S = 1$ and $R = 1$ does not occur for the SR latch. This undesirable situation is indicated by a question mark (?) in the truth table. An SR latch can be built from NAND gates with negative pulse set and reset inputs. Figure 9.2 shows the NAND gate implementation using negative pulse inputs of an SR latch.

The SR latch with S and R inputs will store a 1 ($Q = 1$ and $\bar{Q} = 0$) when the S input is a low input (logic 0) and $R = 1$. On the other hand, the latch will be cleared or reset to 0 ($Q = 0$, $\bar{Q} = 1$) when the R input is a low input (logic 0) and $S = 1$.

Note that a negative pulse performs the desired function when it is low or 0. In Figure 9.2, the SR latch stores a 1 when $S = 0$ and $R = 1$; on the other hand, the latch stores a 0 when $R = 0$ and $S = 1$.

Also, note that the NAND gate produces a 0 if all inputs are 1; on the other hand, the NAND gate generates a 1 if at least one input is 0. Now, suppose that $S = 0$ and $R = 1$. This implies that the output of NAND gate #2 is 1. Thus, $Q = 1$. This will apply 1 to both inputs of NAND gate #1. Thus, $\bar{Q} =$

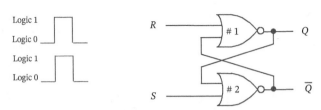

S	R	Q	$\overline{Q}$
0	0	Q	$\overline{Q}$
0	1	0	1
1	0	1	0
1	1	0	0?

(a) NOR gate implementation using positive pulse

(b) Truth table

FIGURE 9.1   SR Latch using NOR gates

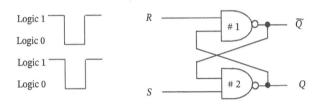

S	R	Q	$\overline{Q}$
0	0	1	1?
0	1	1	0
1	0	0	1
1	1	Q	$\overline{Q}$

(a) NAND gate implementation using negative pulse

(b) Truth table

FIGURE 9.2   SR Latch using NAND gates

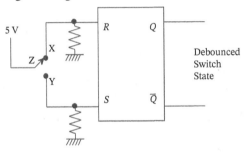

FIGURE 9.3   A debouncing circuit for a mechanical switch

0. Therefore, a 1 is stored in the latch. Similarly, with inputs $S = 1$ and $R = 0$, it can be shown that $Q = 0$ and $\overline{Q} = 1$. The latch stores a 0.

With $S = 1$ and $R = 1$, both outputs of the latch will remain at the previous values. There will be no change in the latch outputs. Finally, $S = 0$ and $R = 0$ will produce an invalid condition ($Q = 1$ and $\overline{Q} = 1$). This is indicated by a question mark (?) in the truth table of Figure 9.2(b).

An SR latch can be used for designing a switch debouncing circuit. Mechanical switches are typically used in digital systems for inputting binary data manually. These mechanical ON-OFF switches (e.g., the keys on a computer keyboard) vibrate or bounce several times such that, instead of changing state once when activated, a key opens and closes several times before settling at its final values. These bounces last for several milliseconds before settling down.

A debouncer circuit, shown in Figure 9.3, can be used with each key to get rid of the bounces. The circuit consists of an SR latch (using NOR gates) and a pair of resistors. In the figure, a single-pole double-throw switch is connected to an SR latch. The center contact (Z) is tied to $+5$ V and outputs logic 1. On the other hand, contacts X or Y provide logic 0 when not connected to contact Z. The values of the resistors are selected in such a way that X is HIGH when connected to Z or Y is HIGH when connected to Z.

When the switch is connected to X, a HIGH is applied at the R input, and $S = 0$, then $Q = 0$, $\overline{Q} = 1$. Now, suppose that the switch is moved from X to Y. The switch is disconnected from R and $R = 0$ because the ground at the R input pulls R to 0. The outputs Q and $\overline{Q}$ of the SR latch are unchanged because both R and S inputs are at 0 during the switch transition from X to Y. When the switch touches

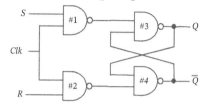

(a) NAND gate implementation

S	R	Clk	Q+	$\bar{Q}+$
0	0	1	Q	$\bar{Q}$
0	1	1	0	1
1	0	1	1	0
1	1	1	?	?
X	X	0	Q	$\bar{Q}$

(b) Truth table

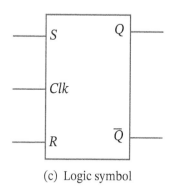

(c) Logic symbol

FIGURE 9.4 Gated SR latch

Y, the S input of the latch goes to HIGH and thus $Q = 1$ and $\bar{Q} = 0$. If the switch vibrates, temporarily breaking the connection, the S input of the the SR latch becomes 0, leaving the latch outputs unchanged. If the switch bounces back connecting Z to Y, the S input becomes 1, the latch is set again, and the outputs of the SR latch do not change. Similarly, the switch transition from Y to X will get rid of switch bounces and will provide smooth transition.

9.1.2 Gated SR Latch
Figure 9.4 shows the NAND gate implementation, the truth table, and the logic symbol of the Gated SR latch. This latch includes an additional level-sensitive clock input. When a change in the level of the clock pulse occurs, the outputs of the latch change.

The gated SR latch contains the basic SR latch with two more NAND gates. It has three inputs (S, Clk, R) and two outputs (Q and $\bar{Q}$). When $S = 0$ and $R = 0$ and $Clk = 1$, the outputs of both NAND gates #1 and #2 are 1. This means that the output of NAND gate #3 is 0 if $\bar{Q} = 1$ and is 1 if $\bar{Q} = 0$. Hence, Q is unchanged as long as $S = 0$ and $R = 0$. On the other hand, the output of NAND gate #4 is 0 if $Q = 1$ and is 1 if $Q = 0$. Thus, $\bar{Q}$ is also unchanged.

Suppose $S = 1$, $R = 0$, and $Clk = 1$. This will produce 0 and 1 at the outputs of NAND gates #1 and #2 respectively. This in turn will generate 1 and 0 at the outputs of NAND gates #3 and #4, respectively. Thus, the flip-flop is set to 1. When the clock is zero, the outputs of both NAND gates #1 and #2 are 1. This, in turn, will make the outputs of NAND gates #3 and #4 unchanged.

The other conditions in the function table can similarly be verified. Note that $S = 1, R = 1$, and $Clk = 1$ is combination of invalid inputs because this will make both outputs, Q and $\bar{Q}$ equal to 1. Also, Q and $\bar{Q}$ must be complements of each other in the gated SR latch. Q+ and $\bar{Q} +$ are outputs of the gated SR latch after the clock (Clk) is applied.

9.1.3 Gated D Latch
Figure 9.5 shows the logic diagram, the truth table, and the logic symbol of a gated D latch. This type of latch ensures that the invalid input combinations $S = 1$ and $R = 1$ for the gated SR latch can never occur. The gated D latch has two inputs (D and Clk) and two outputs (Q and $\bar{Q}$). The D input is the same as the S input and the complement of D is applied to the R input. Thus, R and S can never be equal to 1 simultaneously. Note that the Clk input is level sensitive.

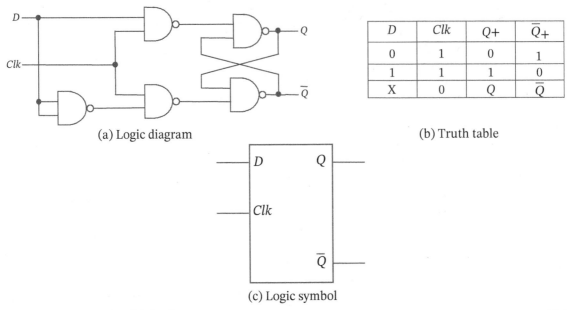

D	Clk	Q+	$\overline{Q}+$
0	1	0	1
1	1	1	0
X	0	Q	$\overline{Q}$

(a) Logic diagram   (b) Truth table

(c) Logic symbol

FIGURE 9.5   Gated D latch

The gated D latch transfers the *D* input to output *Q* when *Clk* = 1. Note that if *Clk* = 0, one of the inputs to each of the last two NAND gates will be 1; thus, outputs of the D flip-flop remain unchanged regardless of the values of the *D* input. The gated D latch is also called a "transparent latch." The term "transparent" is based on the fact that the output *Q* follows the *D* input when *Clk* = 1. Therefore, transfer of input to outputs is transparent, as if the gated D latch were not present.

9.1.4   Edge-Trigerred D Flip-Flop

As mentioned before, sequential circuits contain combinational circuits and flip-flops. These flip-flops generate outputs at the clock based on the inputs from the combinational circuits. This can create an undesirable situation if level-sensitive latches are used instead of edge-triggered flip-flops. For example, assume that a positive pulse is used as the clock input of a gated D latch.

With *D* input = 1, the output of the latch will become 1 when the clock pulse reaches logic 1. Now, suppose that the *D* input changes to zero but the clock pulse is still at 1. This means that the flip-flop will have a new output, 0. In this situation, the output of one latch cannot be connected to the input of another latch when both latches are enabled simultaneously by the same clock input. This situation can be avoided if the latch outputs do not change until the clock pulse goes back to 0.

One way of accomplishing this is to ensure that the outputs of the latches are affected by the pulse transition (flip-flop) rather than the pulse duration (latch) of the clock input. To understand this concept, consider the clock pulses shown in Figure 9.6. There are two types of clock pulses: positive and negative. A positive pulse includes two transitions: logic 0 to logic 1 and logic 1 to logic 0. A negative pulse also goes through two transitions: logic 1 to logic 0 and logic 0 to logic 1.

Since flip-flops are constructed using latches, the multiple-transition can be avoided in the flip-flops if they are clocked by either the positive (leading) edge or the negative (trailing) edge transition, rather than the level of the pulses as with the latches. A master–slave flip-flop is used to accomplish this. Figure 9.7 shows the logic diagram, truth table, and the logic symbol of a typical master-slave D flip-flop (or simply D flip-flop). A master-slave flip-flop contains two independent gated D latches. Gated D-latch #1 (GDL #1) works as a master flip-flop, whereas the gated D-latch #2 GDL #2) is a slave. An inverter is used to invert the clock input to the slave gated D-latch.

Assume that the *Clk* is a positive pulse. Suppose that the *D* input of the GDL #1 is 1 and the *Clk* input = 1 (leading edge). The output of the inverter will apply a 0 at the *Clk* input of the GDL #2. Thus, GDL #2 is disabled. The GDL #1 will transfer a 1 to its *Q* output. Thus, *X* will be 1.

At the trailing edge of the *Clk* input, the *Clk* input of the master GDL #1 is 0. Thus, GDL #1 is disabled. The inverter will apply a 1 at the *Clk* input of the GDL #2. Thus, 1 at the *X* input (*D* input of

GDL #2) will be transferred to the *Q* output of GDL #2. When the *Clk* goes back to 0, the master gated D-latch is separated. This avoids any change in the other inputs to affect the master gated D-latch. The slave gated D-latch will have the same output as the master.

     The D flip-flop of Figure 9.7(a) is negative edge-triggered since the outputs change at the negative edge of the clock. The triggering at the negative edge is indicated by a bubble with a triangular symbol at the *Clk* input of the logic symbol of the D flip-flop of Figure 9.7. The logic symbol for the positive edge-triggered flip-flop, on the other hand, includes only the triangular symbol without any circle for the clock. Finally, note that the logic diagram of Figure 9.7(a) can be converted to a positive edge-triggered flip-flop by removing the inverter connected between the *Clk input* of GDL#2, and the connecting point x, and then placing an inverter between the *Clk input* of GDL#1 and the connecting point x.

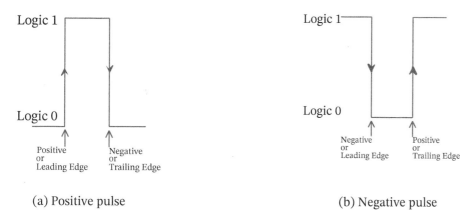

(a) Positive pulse

(b) Negative pulse

FIGURE 9.6   Clock pulses

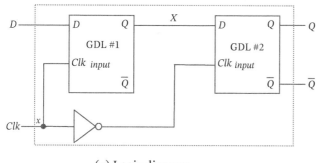

(a) Logic diagram

D	Clk	Q+	$\overline{Q}+$
0	1	0	1
1	1	1	0
X	0	Q	$\overline{Q}$

(b) Truth table

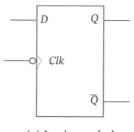

(c) Logic symbol

FIGURE 9.7   Typical D flip-flop

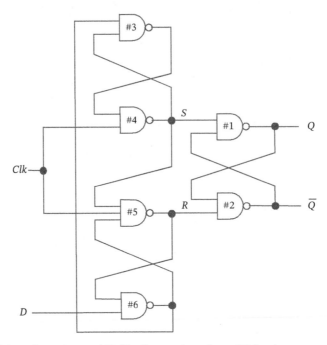

FIGURE 9.8   Positive edge-triggered D flip-flop using three SR latches

Master-slave flip-flops provide a simple way of understanding the meaning of edge-triggered flip-flops. A more efficient edge-triggered D flip-flop can be obtained by using three SR latches as shown in Figure 9.8. This implementation requires six NAND gates while the master-slave D flip-flop needs eleven gates (10 gates for GDL#1 and GDL#2 plus one inverter). In Figure 9.8, when $Clk = 0$, then $S = R$ = 1. The outputs of NAND gate #1 and NAND gate # 2 are maintained at the present outputs regardless of input D (Figure 9.2 (b)). When the clock changes form LOW to HIGH, and $D = 0$, then the output of NAND gate #6 is 1. With $S = 1$, R will be 0. Thus, $Q = 0$ and $\overline{Q} = 1$. Next, if $D = 1$ and clock = 1, then with $S = 0$, R will be 1. Hence, $Q = 1$ and $\overline{Q} = 0$.

Note that as long as $Clk = 1$, the output Q stays the same regardless of any changes in the D input. Hence, the output Q is the same as the D input for a positive or a leading-edge clock. Therefore, this is a positive-edge or leading-edge triggered D flip-flop.

Similarly, a negative-edge (trailing edge-triggered) D flip-flop can be obtained using NOR gates.

9.1.5   JK Flip-Flop

The JK flip-flop was popular during the 1970's when small scale integrated circuits with flip-flops using TTL were available. The JK flip-flops are now replaced by D flip-flops. This is because equations of D flip-flops are simpler and they are widely used by FPGA.

The JK flip-flop can be obtained from a D flip-flop and four logic gates (two AND, one OR, and one inverter) as shown in Figure 9.9 (a). From the figure, $D = J\overline{Q} + \overline{K}Q$. Let us now verify the truth table of Figure 9.9 (b) by determining the outputs (Q and $\overline{Q}$) by substituting the various combinations of the inputs (J, K) in the preceding equation as follows:

(i)   **For $J = K = 0$**

$$D = 0.\overline{Q} + \overline{0}.Q = Q$$

Hence, the D input will be Q. Therefore, the outputs (Q and $\overline{Q}$) of the flip-flop will remain the same at the leading edge of Clk.

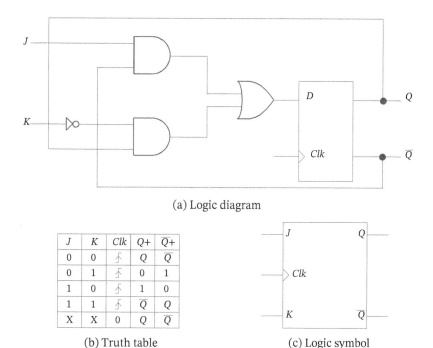

(a) Logic diagram

J	K	Clk	Q+	$\overline{Q}$+
0	0	⤒	Q	$\overline{Q}$
0	1	⤒	0	1
1	0	⤒	1	0
1	1	⤒	$\overline{Q}$	Q
X	X	0	Q	$\overline{Q}$

(b) Truth table　　　　　　(c) Logic symbol

FIGURE 9.9　　Logic diagram, Truth table, and logic symbol of a JK flip-flop

(ii)　　**For J =1 and K = 0**

$$D = 1.\overline{Q} + \overline{0}.Q = 1$$

Hence, the *D* input will be 1 which will be transferred to the *Q* output at the leading edge of *Clk*. Therefore, $Q = 1$ and $\overline{Q} = 0$. Thus the flip-flop is set to 1.

(iii)　　**For J =0 and K = 1**

$$D = 0.\overline{Q} + \overline{1}.Q = 0$$

Hence, the *D* input will be 0 which will be transferred to the *Q* output at the leading edge of *Clk*. Therefore, $Q = 0$ and $\overline{Q} = 1$. Thus the flip-flop is reset to 0.

iv)　　**For J =1 and K = 1**

$$D = 1.\overline{Q} + \overline{1}.Q = \overline{Q}$$

Hence, the *D* input will be $\overline{Q}$ which will be transferred to the output at the leading edge of *Clk*. Therefore, the flip-flop outputs will be complemented.

9.1.6　T Flip-Flop

The Toggle (T) flip-flop complements its output when the clock input is applied with $T = 1$; the output remains unchanged when $T = 0$. The name "toggle" is based on the fact that the T flip-flop toggles or complements its output when the clock input is 1 with $T = 1$.

The T flip-flop is not available commercially. That is, one cannot buy T flip-flop. One needs to build it using other flip-flops such as the JK flip-flop. For example, T flip-flop can be obtained from JK flip-flop in two ways as shown in Figure 9.10 as follows:

(i) In the first approach [Figure 9.10(a)], the *J* and *K* inputs of the JK flip-flop can be tied together to provide the *T* input; the output is complemented when $T = 1$ at the clock while the output remains unchanged when $T = 0$ at the clock.

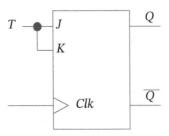

(a) T flip-flop by connecting JK input together

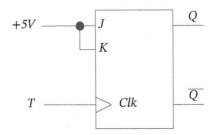

(b) T flip-flop by connecting JK to high

FIGURE 9.10   T flip-flop from JK flip-flop

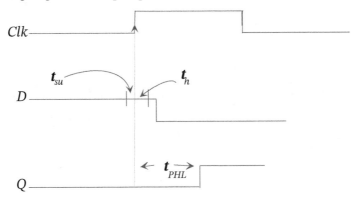

FIGURE 9.11   D flip-flop timing parameters

(ii) In the second approach, the *J* and *K* inputs can be tied to high. In this case, *T* is the clock input. This is shown in Figure 9.10(b).

9.2   Timing parameters for edge-triggered flip-flops

Certain timing parameters of an edge-triggered flip-flop must be considered when using the flip-flop. These are setup time (t_{su}), hold time (t_h), and propagation delay time of the flip-flop (t_{PHL}). These parameters are shown in the timing diagram of Figure 9.11 for a typical D flip-flop.

The setup time (t_{su}) is the minimum amount of time for which the input(s) of the flip-flop must remain stable before arrival of the clock edge. The hold time (t_h), on the other hand, is the minimum amount of time for which the input(s) of the flip-flop must remain stable after arrival of the clock edge. Finally, the propagation delay (t_{PHL}) is the time for a signal to travel from the flip-flop's input to output when the output changes its value; this delay is mainly due to the time associated with the internal transistors of the flip-flop to turn them ON and OFF.

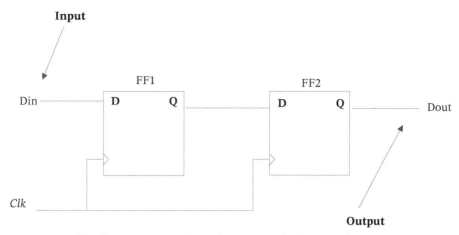

FIGURE 9.12 Two D flip-flops connected in series to get rid of metastability

As an example, consider a 74HC74 chip containing two D flip-flops. The timing parameters (t_{su}, t_h, and t_{PHL}) for each D-ff in the 74HC74, according to the manufacturers' data sheet, are provided in the following: t_{su} = 2ns, t_h = 3ns, and t_{PHL} = 14ns. The designer should ensure that the flip-flop input (D in this case) is stable (for either logic 0 or logic 1) at the clock edge so that Q will have a stable value for the system being designed. If the minimum setup and hold times specified by the manufacturers are not satisfied in a circuit, the flip-flop enters an undefined state (between 0 and 1) called the "metastable" state. If the setup and hold times are violated on the input of a flip flop, then the output will be unpredictable for certain amount of time.

When the output is unpredictable, it could be high or low or somewhere in between, or it could oscillate. After this metastable period, the output will be high or low; but it is unknown which way it will go until it happens.

Most of the metastable times are quite short. The best way to deal with metastability is to make all of the logic synchronous, and not violate any of the setup and hold times. This is, of course, difficult or impossible for circuits of any complexity. So what needs to be done is to try to limit the places where metastability could be an issue and then deal with those places. The normal method to get rid of metastability is to "double-clock" the data. This means that two D flip-flops can be connected in series with the output of the first feeding the input of the second . This is shown in Figure 9.12.

It is expected that if the first flip-flop goes to metastable state, then the metastable period would be over before it violates the setup/hold time of the second flip-flop.

9.3   Preset and Clear Inputs

Commercially available flip-flops include separate inputs for setting the flip-flop to 1 or clearing the flip-flop to 0. These inputs are called "preset" and "clear" inputs respectively. These inputs are useful for initializing the flip-flops without the clock pulse. When the power is turned ON, the output of the flip-flop is in an undefined state. The preset and clear inputs can directly set or clear the flip-flop as desired prior to its clocked operation.

Figure 9.13 shows a D flip-flop with clear inputs. As mentioned before, the triangular symbol indicates that the flip-flop is clocked at the positive (leading) edge of the clock pulse. In Figure 9.13, a circle (inverter) is used with the triangular symbol. This means that the flip-flop is enabled at the negative (trailing) edge of the clock pulse. The circle at the clear input means that clear input must be 1 for normal operation. If the clear input is tied to ground (logic 0), the flip-flop is cleared to 0 ($Q = 0$, $\overline{Q}$ = 1) irrespective of the clock pulse and the D input. The CLR input should be connected to 1 for normal operation. Some flip-flops may have a preset input that sets Q to 1 and $\overline{Q}$ to 0 when the preset input is tied to ground. The preset input is connected to 1 for normal operation.

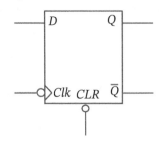

FIGURE 9.13   D flip-flop with clear input

9. 4   Summary of Flip-Flops

Figures 9.14 through 9.17 summarize operations of all four flip-flops along with the symbolic representations, characteristic and excitation tables. In the figures, X represents don't care whereas $Q+$ indicates output Q after the clock pulse is applied.

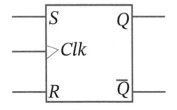

S	R	Q+	
0	0	Q	Unchanged
0	1	0	Reset
1	0	1	Set
1	1	?	Invalid

Q	Q+	S	R
0	0	0	X
0	1	1	0
1	0	0	1
1	1	X	0

(a) Symbolic representation   (b) Characteristic table   (c) Excitation table

FIGURE 9.14   RS flip-flop

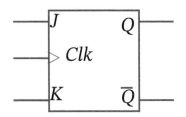

J	K	Q+	
0	0	Q	Unchanged
0	1	0	Reset
1	0	1	Set
1	1	$\overline{Q}$	Complement

Q	Q+	J	K
0	0	0	X
0	1	1	X
1	0	X	1
1	1	X	0

(a) Symbolic representation   (b) Characteristic table   (c) Excitation table

FIGURE 9.15   JK flip-flop

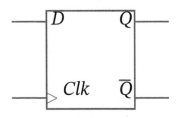

D	Q+	
0	0	Reset
1	1	Set

Q	Q+	D
0	0	0
0	1	1
1	0	0
1	1	1

(a) Symbolic representation   (b) Characteristic table   (c) Excitation table

FIGURE 9.16   D flip-flop

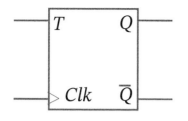

T	Q+	
0	Q	Unchanged
1	$\overline{Q}$	Complement

Q	Q+	T
0	0	0
0	1	1
1	0	1
1	1	0

(a) Symbolic representation   (b) Characteristic table   (c) Excitation table

FIGURE 9.17 T flip-flop

The characteristic table of a flip-flop is similar to its truth table. It contains the input combinations along with the output after the clock pulse. The characteristic table is useful for analyzing a flip-flop. The present state (present output), the next state (next output) after the clock pulse, and the required inputs for the transition are included in the excitation table. This is useful for designing a sequential circuit, in which one normally knows the transition from the present to next state and wants to determine the required flip-flop inputs for the transition.

The D flip-flop is widely used in digital systems for transferring data. Several D flip-flops can be combined to form a register in the CPU of a computer. The 74HC374 is a 20-pin chip containing eight independent D flip-flops. It is designed using CMOS. The flip-flops are enabled at the leading edge of the clock. The 74LS374 is the same as the 74HC374 except that it is designed using TTL.

The JK flip-flop is in a declining stage and is sometimes used for general applications. Typical commercially available JK flip-flop includes the 74HC73 (or 74LS73A). The 74HC73 is a 14-pin chip. It contains two independent JK flip-flops in the same chip, designed using CMOS. Each flip-flop is enabled at the trailing edge of the clock pulse. Each flip-flop also contains a direct clear input. The 74HC73 is cleared to zero when the clear input is LOW. The 74LS73A is the same as the 74HC73 except that it is designed using TTL. The T flip-flop is normally used for designing binary counters because binary counters require complementation. The T flip-flop is not commercially available. One way of obtaining a T Flip-flop is by connecting the *J* and *K* inputs of a JK flip-flop together which is covered earlier in this section.

An example of a commercially available level-triggered flip-flop is the 74HC373 (or 74LS373). The 373 (20-pin chip) contains eight independent D latches with one enable input.

Sometimes, the characteristic equation of a flip-flop is useful in analyzing the flip-flop's operation. The characteristic equations for the flip-flops can be obtained from the truth tables. Figure 9.18 through 9.20 show how these equations are obtained using K-maps for RS, JK, T, and D flip-flops.

Q	S	R	Q+
0	0	0	0
0	0	1	0
0	1	0	1
0	1	1	Invalid
1	0	0	1
1	0	1	0
1	1	0	1
1	1	1	Invalid

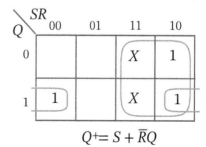

$$Q+ = S + \overline{R}Q$$

(a) Truth Table for RS-FF   (b) K-map for characteristic equation of RS-FF

FIGURE 9.18 Truth table and K-map for the characteristic equation of RS flip-flop

Q	J	K	Q+
0	0	0	0
0	0	1	0
0	1	0	1
0	1	1	1
1	0	0	1
1	0	1	0
1	1	0	1
1	1	1	0

(a) Truth table for JK-FF

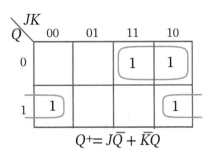

$$Q+ = J\bar{Q} + \bar{K}Q$$

(b) K-map for characteristic equation of JK-FF

Q	T	Q+
0	0	0
0	1	1
1	0	1
1	1	0

(c) Truth table for T-FF

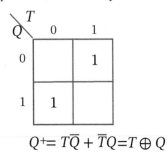

$$Q+ = T\bar{Q} + \bar{T}Q = T \oplus Q$$

(d) K-map for characteristic equation of T-FF

FIGURE 9.19   Truth table and K-map for the characteristic equation of JK and T flip-flops

Q	D	Q+
0	0	0
0	1	1
1	0	0
1	1	1

(a) Truth table for D-FF

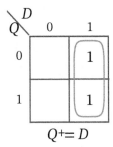

$$Q+ = D$$

(b) K-map for characteristic equation of D-FF

FIGURE 9.20   Truth table and K-map for the characteristic equation of D flip-flop

Example 9.1

Using the characteristic equations for T-FF and D-FF shown in Figures 9.19 (d) and 9.20 (b), obtain the schematic for a T-FF using a D-FF and a minimum number of logic gates. Use a rising edge-triggered FF.

Solution

Note that a T-FF can be obtained from D-FF using the equations for Q+ in Figures 9.19 (d) and 9.20 (b). For T-FF from Figure 9.19 (d), $Q+ = T\bar{Q} + \bar{T}Q = T \oplus Q$. Also, from Figure 9.20 (b), $Q+ = D$. Hence, $D = T \oplus Q$.

Figure 9.21 shows the T-FF obtained using a D-FF and an XOR gate.

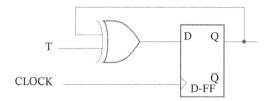

FIGURE 9.21   T-FF using a D-FF and an XOR gate

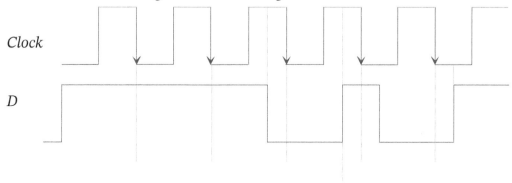

FIGURE 9.22   Figure for Example 9.2

Example 9.2

Given the clock and the *D* inputs for a negative-edge-triggered D flip-flop shown in Figure 9.22, draw the timing diagram for the *Q* output for the first five cycles shown. Assume *Q* is preset to 1 initially.

Solution

Figure 9.23 shows the solution for Example 9.2.

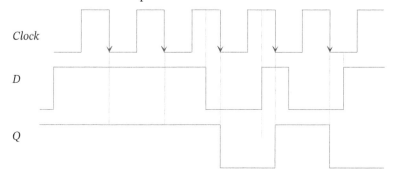

FIGURE 9.23   Solution for Example 9.2

QUESTIONS AND PROBLEMS

9.1   What is the basic difference between a combinational circuit and a sequential circuit?

9.2   Identify the main characteristics of a synchronous sequential circuit and an asynchronous sequential circuit.

9.3   What is the basic difference between a latch and a flip-flop?

9.4   Draw the logic diagram of a D flip-flop using OR gates and inverters.

9.5   Assume that initially $x = 1$, $A = 0$, and $B = 1$ in Figure P9.5. Determine the values of A and B after the positive edge of Clk.

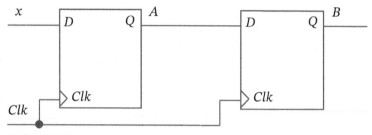

FIGURE P9. 5

9.6   Draw the logic diagram of a JK flip-flop using AND gates and inverters.

9.7   Assume that initially $X = 1$, $A = 0$, and $B = 1$ in Figure P9.7. Determine the values of A and B after one Clk pulse. Note that the flip-flops are triggered at the clock level.

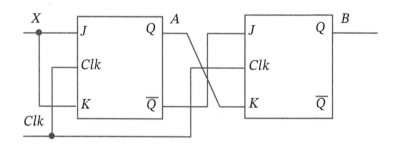

FIGURE P9.7

9.8   Given Figure P9.8, draw the timing diagram for Q and $\overline{Q}$ assuming a negative-edge triggered JK flip-flop. Assume Q is preset to 1 initially.

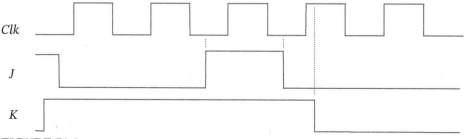

FIGURE P9.8

FIGURE P9.9

FIGURE P9.10

9.9   Given the timing diagram for a positive-edge triggered D flip-flop in Figure P9.9, draw the timing diagrams for Q and $\overline{Q}$. Assume Q is cleared to zero initially.

9.10   Given the timing diagram for a negative-edge-triggered T flip-flop in Figure P9.10, draw the timing diagram for Q. Assume Q is preset to 1 initially.

9.11   Why would you use an edge-triggered flip-flop rather than a level-triggered flip-flop?

9.12   What are the advantages of a master–slave flip-flop?

9.13   Draw the block diagram of a T flip-flop using (a) JK-FF (b) D-FF.

9.14   Draw a logic circuit of the switch debouncer circuit using NAND gates.

9.15   Analyze the circuit shown in Figure P9.15 and show that it is equivalent to a T flip-flop.

9.16   Using the characteristic equation of JK-FF of Figure 9.19 (b) and the characteristic equation of D-FF of Figure 9.20 (b), draw the schematic for a D flip-flop using a JK flip-flop and a minimum number of logic gates.

9.17   Draw the timing diagram for the Figure P.9.17 for six clock cycles. Assume that $Q_A \, Q_B \, Q_C = 000$ initially.

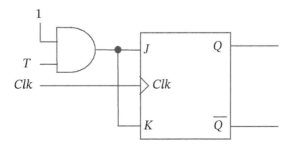

FIGURE P9.15

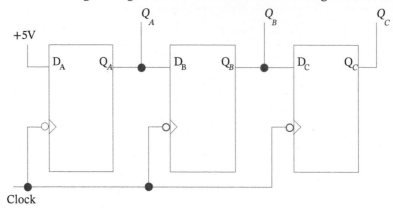

FIGURE P9.17

10

ANALYSIS AND DESIGN OF SEQUENTIAL CIRCUITS

This chapter describes basic concepts associated with sequential circuits. Topics include analysis and design of synchronous sequential circuits using gates, design of a sequence detector, SRAM, state machine design using ASM, and an introduction to asynchronous sequential circuit. Note that ASM chart was widely used in the past for designing synchronous sequential circuits. However, with the popularity of hardware description languages, use of ASM chart has declined. Hence, a brief coverage of ASM is provided in this chapter.

10.1   Introduction

So far we have considered the design of combinational circuits. The main characteristic of these circuits is that the outputs at a particular time t are determined by the inputs at the same time t. This means that combinational circuits require no memory. However, in practice most digital systems contain combinational circuits along with memory. These circuits are called "sequential." There are two types of sequential circuits: synchronous and asynchronous.

In a synchronous sequential circuit, a clock signal is used at discrete instants of time to ensure that all desired operations are initiated only by a train of synchronizing clock pulses. A timing device called the "clock generator" produces these clock pulses. The desired outputs of the memory elements are obtained upon application of the clock pulses and some other signal at their inputs. This type of sequential circuit is also called a "clocked sequential circuit." Flip-flops are used as memory elements in clocked sequential circuits. Since the flip-flop stores only one bit, a clocked sequential circuit usually utilizes several flip-flops to store a number of bits as required. Synchronous sequential circuits are also called "state machines."

A synchronous sequential circuit is basically a combinational circuit with memory. As mentioned before, a combinational circuit does not require any memory (flip-flops), whereas sequential circuits require flip-flops to remember the present states. A counter is a typical example of a synchronous sequential circuit.

To illustrate the operation of a synchronous sequential circuit, suppose that it is desired to count in the sequence 0, 1, 2, 3, and repeat. In binary, the sequence is 00, 01, 10, 11, 00, 01, ..., and so on. This means that a two-bit memory using two flip-flops is required for storing the two bits of the counter because each flip-flop stores one bit.

Let us call these flip-flops with outputs A and B. Note that initially $A = 0$ and $B = 0$. The flip-flop changes outputs upon application of a clock pulse. With appropriate inputs to the flip-flops and then applying the clock pulse, the flip-flops change the states (outputs) to $A = 0$, $B = 1$. Thus, the count to 1 can be obtained. The flip-flops store (remember) this count. Upon application of appropriate inputs along with the clock, the flip-flops will change the status to $A = 1$, $B = 0$; thus, the count to 2 is obtained. The flip-flops remember (store) this count at the outputs until a common clock pulse is applied to the flip-flops. The inputs to the flip-flops are manipulated by a combinational circuit based on A and B as inputs. For example, consider $A = 1$, $B = 0$. The inputs to the flip-flops are determined in such a way that the flip-flops change the states at the clock pulse to $A = 1$, $B = 1$; thus, the count to 3 is obtained. The process is repeated.

Digital Logic with an Introduction to Verilog and FPGA-Based Design. First Edition. M. Rafiquzzaman and Steven A. McNinch.
© 2019 John Wiley & Sons, Inc. Published 2019 by John Wiley & Sons, Inc.

In an asynchronous sequential circuit, completion of one operation starts the operation that is next in sequence. Synchronizing clock pulses are not required. Instead, time-delay devices are used in asynchronous sequential circuits as memory elements. Logic gates are typically used as time delay devices, because the propagation delay time associated with a logic gate is adequate to provide the required delay. A combinational circuit with feedback among logic gates can be considered as an asynchronous sequential circuit. One must be careful while designing asynchronous systems because feedback among logic gates may result in undesirable system operation. The logic designer is normally faced with many problems related to the instability of asynchronous system, so they are not commonly used. Most of the sequential circuits encountered in practice are synchronous because it is easy to design and analyze such circuits.

10.2   Analysis of Synchronous Sequential Circuits

A synchronous sequential circuit can be analyzed by determining the relationships between inputs, outputs, and flip-flop states. A state table or a state diagram illustrates how the inputs and the states of the flip-flops affect the circuit outputs. Boolean expressions can be obtained for the inputs of the flip-flops in terms of present states of the flip-flops and the circuit inputs. As an example, consider analyzing the synchronous sequential circuit of Figure 10.1.

The logic circuit contains two D flip-flops (outputs X, Y), one input A and one output B. The equations for the next states of the flip-flops can be written as

$$D_x = X{+} = \overline{(X + Y)} \cdot A$$
$$D_y = Y{+} = A + \overline{X}$$

Here $X{+}$ and $Y{+}$ represent the next states of the flip-flops after the clock pulse. The right side of each equation denotes the present states of the flip-flops (X, Y) and the input (A) that will produce the next state of each flip-flop. The Boolean expressions for the next state are obtained from the combinational circuit portion of the sequential circuit. The outputs of the combinational circuit are connected to the D inputs of the flip-flops. These D inputs provide the next states of the flip-flops after the clock pulse. The present state of the output B can be derived from Figure 10.1 as follows:

$$B = A \oplus \overline{Y}$$

A state table listing the inputs, outputs, and states of the flip-flops along with the required flip-flop inputs can be obtained for Figure 10.1. Table 10.1 depicts a typical state table. The state table is formed by using the following equations (shown earlier):

$$X{+} = \overline{(X + Y)} \cdot A$$
$$Y{+} = A + \overline{X}$$

To derive the state table, all combinations of the present states of the flip-flops and input A are tabulated. There are eight combinations for three variables from 000 to 111. The values for the flip-flop inputs (next states of the flip-flops) are determined using the equations. For example, consider the top row with $X = 0$, $Y = 0$, and $A = 0$. Substituting in the equations for next states, the following values for $X{+}$ and $Y{+}$ can be obtained:

$$X{+} = \overline{(X + Y)} \cdot A = \overline{(0 + 0)} \cdot 0 = 1$$
$$Y{+} = A + \overline{X} = 0 + \overline{0} = 1$$

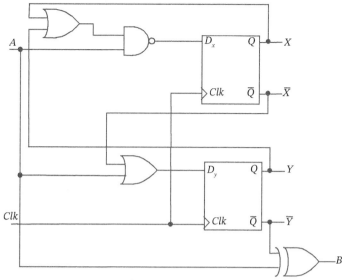

FIGURE 10.1   Analysis of a sequential circuit

TABLE 10.1   State table for Figure 10.1

| Present State | | Input | Next State | | Flip Flop Inputs | | Output |
X	Y	A	X+	Y+	D_x	D_y	B
0	0	0	1	1	1	1	1
0	0	1	1	1	1	1	0
0	1	0	1	1	1	1	0
0	1	1	0	1	0	1	1
1	0	0	1	0	1	0	1
1	0	1	0	1	0	1	0
1	1	0	1	0	1	0	0
1	1	1	0	1	0	1	1

Now, to find the flip-flop inputs, one should consider each flip-flop separately. Two D flip-flops are used. Note that for a D flip-flop, the input at D is same as the next state. The D input is transferred to the output Q at the clock pulse. Therefore, $X+ = D_x$ and $Y+ = D_y$.

The characteristic table of a D flip-flop, discussed in Chapter 9, is used to determine the flip-flop inputs that will change present states of the flip-flops to next state. The characteristic table of D flip-flop is provided here for reference:

D	Q^+
0	0
1	1

Therefore, for D flip-flops, the next states and the flip-flop inputs will be the same in the state table. By inspecting the top row of the state table (Table 10.1), it can be concluded that $D_x = 1$ and $D_y = 1$ because the next states $X+ = 1$ and $Y+ = 1$.

Finally, the output B can be obtained from the equation,

$$B = A \oplus \overline{Y}$$

For example, consider the top row of the state table. $A = 0$ and $Y = 0$. Thus,
$$B = 0 \oplus \overline{0} = 0 \oplus 1 = 1$$

TABLE 10.2   Another form of the state table for Figure 10.1

Present State		Next State				Flip Flop Inputs				Outputs	
		A=0		A=1		A=0		A=1		A=0	A=1
X	Y	X+	Y+	X+	Y+	D_X	D_Y	D_X	D_Y	B	B
0	0	1	1	1	1	1	1	1	1	1	0
0	1	1	1	0	1	1	1	0	1	0	1
1	0	1	0	0	1	1	0	0	1	1	0
1	1	1	0	0	1	1	0	0	1	0	1

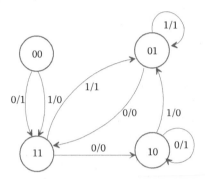

FIGURE 10.2   State diagram for Table 10.1

All other rows of the state table can similarly be verified. The state table of Table 10.1 can be shown in a slightly different manner. Table 10.2 depicts another form of the state table of Table 10.1.

A state table can be depicted in a graphical form. All information in the state table can be represented in the state diagram. A circle is used to represent a state in the state diagram. A straight line with an arrow indicator is used to show direction of transition from one state to another. Figure 10.2 shows the state diagram for Table 10.1.

Because there are two flip-flops (X, Y) in Figure 10.1, there are four states: 00, 01, 10 and 11. These are shown in the circle of the state diagram. Also, transition from one state to another is represented by a line with an arrow. Each line is assigned with a/b where a is input and b is output. From the example in Figure 10.2, with present state 10 and an input of 1, the output is 0 and the next state is 01. If the input (and/or output) is not defined in a problem, the input (and/or output) will be deleted in the state table and the state diagram.

The inputs of the flip-flops (D_x and D_y) in the state table are not necessary to derive the state diagram. In analyzing a synchronous sequential circuit, the logic diagram is given. The state equation, state table, and state diagram are obtained from the logic diagram. However, in order to design a sequential circuit, the designer has to derive the state table and the state diagram from the problem definition. The flip-flop inputs will be useful in the design. One must express the flip-flop inputs and outputs in terms of the present states of the flip-flops and the inputs. The minimum forms of these expressions can be obtained using a K-map. From these expressions, the logic diagram can be drawn.

Analysis of a synchronous sequential circuit can be summarized into a three-step process, and is provided below:

Step 1: Derive the equations for the flip-flop inputs, and the circuit output(s) if any, from the given circuit.

Step 2: Obtain the present and the next states based on the type of flip-flop used in the circuit.

Step 3: Obtain the state table and the state diagram.

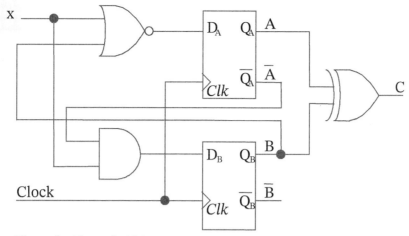

FIGURE 10.3 Figure for Example 10.1

TABLE 10.3 State table for Example 10.1

Present State		Input	Next State		FF Inputs		Output
A	B	x	A+	B+	D_A	D_B	C
0	0	0	1	0	1	0	0
0	0	1	0	1	0	1	0
0	1	0	0	0	0	0	1
0	1	1	0	1	0	1	1
1	0	0	1	0	1	0	1
1	0	1	0	0	0	0	1
1	1	0	0	0	0	0	0
1	1	1	0	0	0	0	0

Example 10.1

For the synchronized sequential circuit shown in Figure 10.3, obtain the flip-flop input equations for D_A, D_B, and the output equation for output, C. Derive the state table, and the state diagram.

Solution

Following the three steps for analyzing a circuit:

Since, D-ff, Q+ = D,

Hence, $A+ = D_A = \overline{x + B}$, $B+ = D_B = x\,\overline{A}$. Also, output, $C = A \oplus B$.

Using these equations, the state table of Table 10.3, and the state diagram of Figure 10.4 can be obtained.

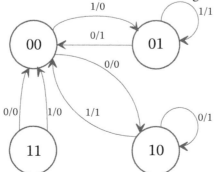

FIGURE 10.4 State diagram for Example 10.1

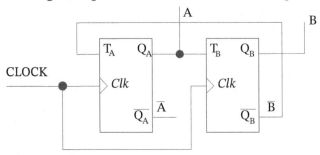

FIGURE 10.5   Figure for Example 10.2

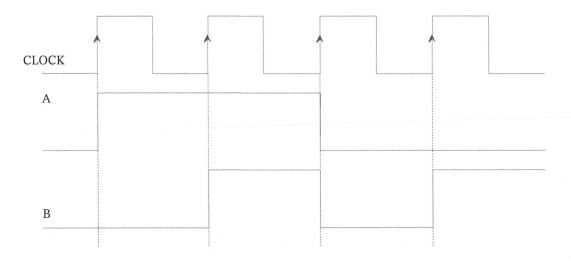

FIGURE 10.6   Timing diagram for Example 10.2

Example 10.2

Consider the synchronous sequential circuit of Figure 10.5. Assume the flip-flop outputs (A, B) are zero initially. Draw a timing diagram for A and B for the first four clock pulses.

Solution

Figure 10.6 shows the timing diagram. For the first four clock pulses, the following transitions occur:
At the first rising clock pulse, since T_A is connected to $\overline{B}$ and $\overline{B} = 1$, A goes from 0 to 1. Also, at the first rising pulse, since $T_B = A$, B = 0. Similarly, transitions of the T-FF outputs (A,B) for other three rising clock edges can be obtained.

Example 10.3

Analyze the synchronous sequential circuit shown in Figure 10.7.

Solution

Step 1: Derive the equations for the flip-flop inputs, and the circuit output(s) if any, from the given circuit.
$D_A = \overline{B}, D_B = A$
There is no circuit output.

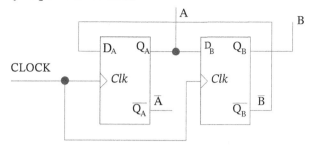

FIGURE 10.7   Figure for Example 10.3

TABLE 10.4   State table for Example 10.3

Present State		Next State		FF Inputs	
A	B	A+	B+	D_A	D_B
0	0	1	0	1	0
0	1	0	0	0	0
1	0	1	1	1	1
1	1	0	1	0	1

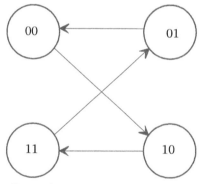

FIGURE 10.8   State diagram for Example 10.3

Step 2: Obtain the present and the next states based from the type of flip-flop used in the circuit.

Since D flip-flop is used, Q+ = D. Hence, A+ = $\bar{B}$, B+ = A
Based on present state values of 00, 01, 10, and 11, the values of the next states A+ and B+ will be determined. For example, for the present states A = 0 and B = 0, the next states will be A+ = 1, and B+ = 0. Similarly, transitions to next states can be determined. All state transitions are listed below:

Step 3: Obtain the state table and the state diagram.

Table 10.4 shows the state table. Figure 10.8 shows the state diagram.

10.3   Types of Synchronous Sequential Circuits

There are two types of synchronous sequential circuits: the Mealy circuit and the Moore circuit. A synchronous sequential circuit typically contains inputs, outputs, and flip-flops. In the Mealy circuit, the outputs depend on both the inputs and the present states of the flip-flops. Hence, the outputs may change asynchronously if the inputs change. In the Moore circuit, on the other hand, the outputs are obtained from the flip-flops, and depend only on the present states of the flip-flops. Hence, the outputs in a Moore circuit change synchronously with the state transition at the active clock edge. Therefore, the only difference between the two types of circuits is how the outputs are produced.

The state table of a Mealy circuit must contain an output column. The state table of a Moore circuit may contain an output column, which is dependent only on the present states of the flip-flops. A Moore machine normally requires more states to generate identical output sequence compared to a Mealy machine. This is because the transitions are associated with the outputs in a Mealy machine.

Note that the Mealy machines respond faster to changes in inputs; they normally react at the same clock. The Moore machines usually need more logic for decoding the outputs; hence, require more hardware resulting into more circuit delays. The Moore circuits normally respond one clock cycle later. Finally, as mentioned before, the Mealy machine normally requires fewer states than the Moore machine.

Note that in a Mealy circuit, next states of the Flip-flops are determined by the input at the preceding active clock edge. Any input changes between two consecutive clock edges may produce "false outputs" or "glitches". One should discard the false outputs, and only consider the outputs at the active clock edge without any problem. Moore circuits, on the other hand, do not generate any false outputs.

Next, an example is provided to illustrate the concept of Mealy and Moore machines. Suppose it is desired to derive the state diagram for a sequence detector that will output a '1' when three consecutive 1's are received at the input for three clock pulses, and outputs a '0' otherwise. The state diagram can be obtained using both Mealy and Moore machines. Figures 10.9 and 10.10 show the state diagrams using Mealy and Moore implementations, respectively. In Figure 10.9, three states (00, 01, 10) are required, and the Mealy machine outputs a '1' in state 10 when three consecutive 1's are detected.

The state diagram of the Moore machine in Figure 10.10, on the other hand, requires four states (00, 01, 10, 11), and the Moore machine outputs a '1' when three consecutive 1's are detected in state 11. Note that XY/Z shown inside each circle indicates the state number XY with Z as the output. Note that design of sequence detectors is covered in more detail later in this chapter.

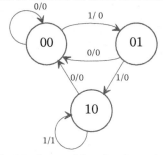

FIGURE 10.9   State diagram for the Mealy machine for detecting 111

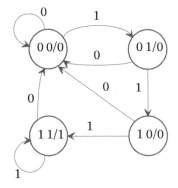

FIGURE 10.10   State diagram for the Moore Machine for detecting 111

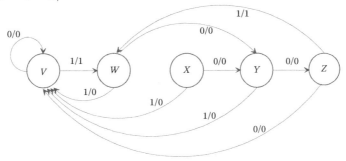

FIGURE 10.11 State diagram for minimization

10.4 Minimization of States

A simplified form of a synchronous sequential circuit can be obtained by minimizing the number of states. This will reduce the number of flip-flops and simplify the complexity of the circuit implementations. However, logic designers rarely use the minimization procedures. Also, there are sometimes instances in which design of a synchronous sequential circuit is simplified if the number of states is increased. The techniques for reducing the number of states presented in this section are merely for illustrative purposes.

The number of states can be reduced by using the concept of equivalent states. Two states are equivalent if both states provide the same outputs for identical inputs, and have the same next states. One of the states can be eliminated if two states are equivalent. Thus, the number of states can be reduced.

For example, consider the state diagram of Figure 10.11. Each state is represented by a circle with transition to the next state based on either an input of 0 or 1 generating an output.

Next, consider that a string of input data bits (d) in the sequence 0100111101 is applied at state V of a synchronous sequential circuit. For the given input sequence, the output and the state sequence can be obtained as follows:

State	V	V	W	Y	Z	W	V	W	V	V	W
Input	0	1	0	0	1	1	1	1	0	1	
Output	0	1	0	0	1	0	1	0	0	1	

With the sequential circuit in initial state V, a 0 input generates a 0 output and the circuit stays in state V, whereas in state V, an input of 1 produces an output 1 and the circuit will move to the next state W. In state W and input = 0, the output is 0 and the next state is Y. The process thus continues. The state table shown in Table 10.5 for the state diagram in Figure 10.11 can be obtained. Next, the equivalent states will be determined to reduce the number of states. V and Z are equivalent because they have same next states of V and W with identical inputs $d = 0$ and $d = 1$. Similarly, W and X are equivalent states. Table 10.6 shows the process of replacing of a state by its equivalent.

Because V and Z are equivalent, one of the states can be eliminated. Hence, Z is removed. Also, W and X are equivalent, so one of the states can be removed. Thus, X is eliminated from the state table. The row with present states X and Z is also eliminated. If they appear in the next state columns, they must be replaced by their equivalent states. In our case, the row for state Y contains Z in the next column. This is replaced its equivalent state V. By inspecting the modified state table further, no more equivalent states are found. The state table after elimination of equivalent states is shown in Table 10.7.

TABLE 10.5   State table for minimization of states

Present State	Next State		Output	
	d=0	d=1	d=0	d=1
V	V	W	0	1
W	Y	V	0	0
X	Y	V	0	0
Y	Z	V	0	0
Z	V	W	0	1

TABLE 10.6   Replacing states by their equivalents

Present State	Next State		Output	
	d=0	d=1	d=0	d=1
V	V	W	0	1
W	Y	V	0	0
X̶	Y	V	0	0
Y	Z̶ V	V	0	0
Z̶	V	W	0	1

TABLE 10.7   State table after the elimination of equivalent states

Present State	Next State		Output	
	d=0	d=1	d=0	d=1
V	V	W	0	1
W	Y	V	0	0
Y	V	V	0	0

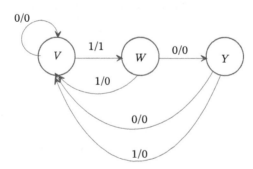

FIGURE 10.12   Reduced form of the state diagram

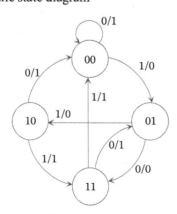

FIGURE 10.13   State diagram for Example 10.4

Note that the original state diagram in Figure 10.11 requires five states. Figure 10.12 shows the reduced form of the state diagram with only three states. Three flip-flops are required to represent five states whereas two flip-flops will represent three states. Thus, one flip-flop is eliminated and the complexity of implementation may be reduced. Note that a synchronous sequential circuit can be minimized by determining the equivalent states, provided the designer is only concerned with the output sequences due to input sequences.

10.5   Design of Synchronous Sequential Circuits

Like the combinational circuit design, the procedure for designing the synchronous sequential circuit is standardized, and divided into three steps. This will make it easier to design a sequential circuit. The procedure for designing a synchronous sequential circuit is provided below:

Step 1   *Obtain state table and state diagram:* Derive the state table and state diagram from the problem definition. If the state diagram is given, determine the state table.

Step 2   *Minimization:* Obtain the minimum form of the Boolean equations for flip-flop inputs and outputs, if any, using K-maps.

Step 3   *Schematic or Logic diagram:* Draw the logic diagram. Note that a combinational circuit is designed using a truth table whereas the synchronous sequential circuit design is based on the state table.

Example 10.4

Design a synchronous sequential circuit for the state diagram of Figure 10.13 using D flip-flops.

Solution

Step 1   *Obtain the state table and the state diagram:* Derive the state table.

The state table is derived from the state diagram (Figure 10.13) and the excitation table of the D flip-flop. Table 10.8 shows the state table. The state table is obtained directly from the state diagram. In the state table, the next states are the same as the flip-flop inputs because D flip-flops are used. This is evident from the excitation table of D flip-flop provided in Chapter 9.

Step 2   *Minimization:* Obtain the minimum forms of the equations for the flip-flop inputs and the output. Using K-maps and the output, the equations for flip-flop inputs are simplified as shown in Figure 10.14.

Step 3   *Schematic or Logic diagram:* The logic diagram is shown in Figure 10.15.

TABLE 10.8   State table for Example 10.4

Present State		Input	Next State		Flip Flop Inputs		Output
X	Y	A	X+	Y+	D_X	D_Y	Z
0	0	0	0	0	0	0	1
0	0	1	0	1	0	1	0
0	1	0	1	1	1	1	0
0	1	1	1	0	1	0	0
1	0	0	0	0	0	0	1
1	0	1	1	1	1	1	1
1	1	0	0	1	0	1	1
1	1	1	0	0	0	0	1

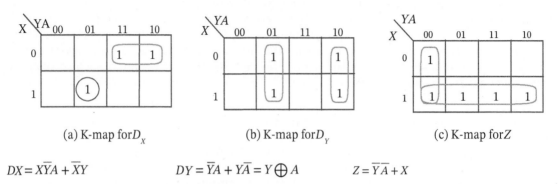

(a) K-map for D_X (b) K-map for D_Y (c) K-map for Z

$$DX = X\overline{Y}A + \overline{X}Y \qquad DY = \overline{Y}A + Y\overline{A} = Y \oplus A \qquad Z = \overline{Y}\,\overline{A} + X$$

FIGURE 10.14   K-maps for Example 10.4

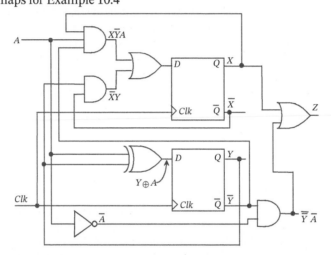

FIGURE 10.15   Logic diagram for Example10.4

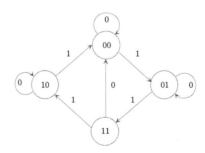

FIGURE 10.16   State diagram for Example 10.5

Example 10.5

Design a synchronous sequential circuit for the state diagram of Figure 10.16 using JK flip-flops.

Solution

Step 1   *Obtain state table and state diagram:* Derive the state table.

The state table can be directly obtained from the state diagram (Figure 10.16) and the excitation table [Table 10.9 (a)] of JK flip-flop. Table 10.9 (b) shows the state table. For convenience, the excitation table of JK flip-flop [Table 10.9 (a)] is also included.

Let us explain how the state table is obtained. The input A is 0 or 1 at each state, so the left three columns show all eight combinations for X, Y, and A. The next state column is obtained from the state diagram.

The flip-flop inputs are then obtained using the excitation table for the JK flip-flop. For example, consider the top row. From the state diagram, the present state (00) remains in the same state (00) when input $A = 0$ and the clock pulse is applied. The output of flip-flop X goes from 0 to 0 and the output of flip-flop Y goes from 0 to 0. From the excitation table of the JK flip-flop, $J_x = 0$, $K_x = X$, $J_x = 0$, and $K_x = X$. The other rows are obtained similarly.

Step 2 *Minimization:* Obtain the minimum forms of the equations for the flip-flop inputs.

Using K-maps, the equations for flip-flop inputs are simplified as shown in Figure 10.17.

Step 3 *Schematic or Logic diagram:*
Figure 10.18 shows the schematic.

TABLE 10.9   Excitation and state tables for Example 10.5

(a) Excitation table of JK flip-flop

Q	$Q+$	J	K
0	0	0	X
0	1	1	X
1	0	X	1
1	1	X	0

(b) State table for Example 10.5

Present State		Input	Next State		Flip Flop Inputs			
X	Y	A	$X+$	$Y+$	J_x	K_X	J_Y	K_Y
0	0	0	0	0	0	X	0	X
0	0	1	0	1	0	X	1	X
0	1	0	0	1	0	X	X	0
0	1	1	1	1	1	X	X	0
1	0	0	1	0	X	0	0	X
1	0	1	0	0	X	1	0	X
1	1	0	0	0	X	1	X	1
1	1	1	1	0	X	0	X	1

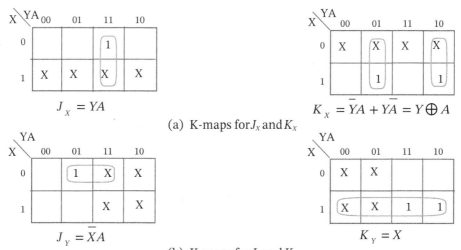

$$J_X = YA$$

$$K_X = \overline{Y}A + Y\overline{A} = Y \oplus A$$

(a) K-maps for J_X and K_X

$$J_Y = \overline{X}A$$

$$K_Y = X$$

(b) K-maps for J_Y and K_Y

FIGURE 10.17   K-maps for Example 10.5

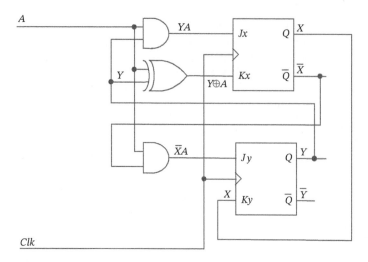

FIGURE 10.18   Logic diagram for Example 10.5

10.6   Serial Adder

Designs of parallel adders are presented in Chapter 6. Parallel adders are faster and require more hardware. Serial adders, on the other hand, are slower, and require less hardware. If speed is not important, then the cost-effective choice is a serial adder.

Parallel adders are designed using combinational logic while serial adders are designed using sequential logic. Therefore, flip-flops are needed to design a serial adder. Also, in a serial adder, a pair of bits along with the carry bit is added at a time in one clock cycle.

Figure 10.19 shows the block diagram of an 8-bit serial adder. In Figure 10.19, X and Y are 8-bit numbers where $X = x_7 x_6 .....x_0$ and $Y = y_7 y_6 .....y_0$. Also, the sum (S) is an 8-bit number where $S = s_7 s_6 .....s_0$. The input and output shift registers shift 8-bit parallel data for X, Y, and S serially one bit at a time at each clock pulse into the serial adder while the 8-bit sum, S is obtained from s_i by shifting s_i serially using a shift register. Note that design of shift registers is covered in Chapter 11. However, the basics of shift operations are covered in Chapter 2. Note that C_{out} in Figure 10.19 needs to be stored in a flip-flop. Hence, Serial adder is designed using sequential circuit design procedure.

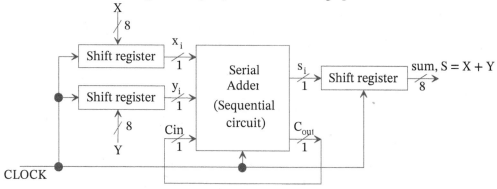

FIGURE 10.19   Block diagram of a serial adder

Example 10.6

Design a serial adder of Figure 10.19. Do not design any shift registers. The serial adder will add two 8-bit numbers (X and Y) entered serially bit-by-bit via the shift registers, and then add the bits as follows:

$$c_6 \, c_5 \, c_4 \, c_3 \, c_2 \, c_1 \, c_0 \, 0$$
$$X_7 \, X_6 \, X_5 \, X_4 \, X_3 \, X_2 \, X_1 \, X_0$$
$$\text{plus } \underline{Y_7 \, Y_6 \, Y_5 \, Y_4 \, Y_3 \, Y_2 \, Y_1 \, Y_0}$$
$$S_7 \, S_6 \, S_5 \, S_4 \, S_3 \, S_2 \, S_1 \, S_0$$

The serial adder will add three bits at a time. Note that in the above, $c_{in} = 0$ while adding the least significant bits x_0 and y_0, and any carry generated will be reflected to higher order addition for correct result. Use D-ff for sequential design.

Solution

Step1   *Obtain state table and state diagram:*   Derive the state table and state diagram from the problem definition. If the state diagram is given, determine the state table.
In this case, the state table needs to be determined.
Table 10.10 shows the state table.

Step2   *Minimization:* Obtain the minimum form of the Boolean equations for flip-flop inputs and outputs, if any, using K-maps. Minimization is obtained as follows:
S_i column of Table 10.10 is the same as the S column of the truth table of the full adder of Table 6.12 with inputs as $C_{in} = x$, $x_i = y$, and $y_i = z$, and outputs as S_i and C_{out}. Hence, this part of the schematic shown in Step 3 can be replaced by a full adder. Note that minimization for the sum and the carry of the full adder is provided in Chapter 6.

TABLE 10.10   State table for the serial adder of Example 10.6

Present State	Inputs	Next State	Sum	D-ff inputs
C_{in}	x_i y_i	C_{out}	S_i	D_A
0	0 0	0	0	0
0	0 1	0	1	0
0	1 0	0	1	0
0	1 1	1	0	1
1	0 0	0	1	0
1	0 1	1	0	1
1	1 0	1	0	1
1	1 1	1	1	1

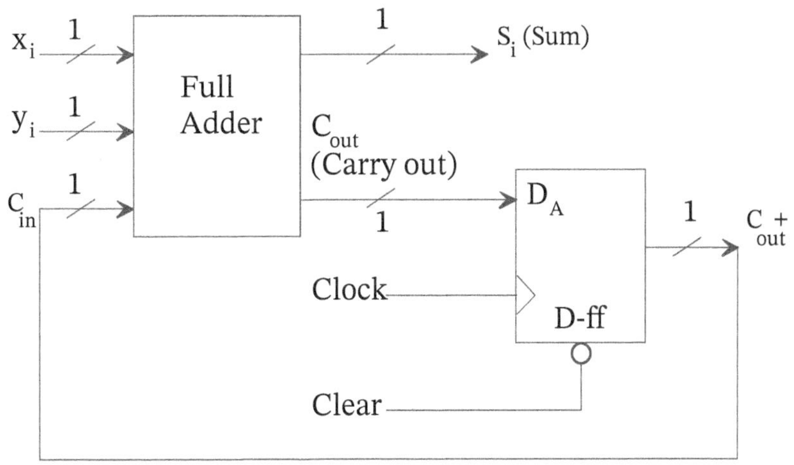

FIGURE 10.20   Schematic for the serial adder

Also, since Q+ = D, the columns for $C_{out}+$ and D_A in the state table of the serial adder are the same. Hence, C_{out} output of the full adder is connected to the D_A input of the D-ff.

Step3 *Schematic or Logic diagram:* Draw the logic diagram.

Figure 10.20 shows the schematic. Note that the D-ff will be cleared to 0 initially so that $C_{in} = 0$ for adding the least significant bits, and C_{in}'s will be the previous carries for all subsequent additions.

10.7   Sequence Generator/Detector

The sequence generator is a sequential circuit which produces a predefined sequence of output bits. A binary counter is an example of a special type of sequence generator. A sequence detector, on the other hand, is a sequential circuit that outputs a one when a specific serial bit pattern arrives at the input. A sequence detector can be used in a remote control for TV or in a garage door opener. For example, the bit pattern might correspond to a specific key being pressed. Note that the steps used for designing synchronous sequential circuits will be used in designing sequence detectors.

The sequence detector can be of two types. They are overlapping and non-overlapping. In the overlapping sequence detector, the last bit of a sequence can be the first bit of the next sequence. In a non-overlapping sequence detector, the last bit of a sequence is not the first bit of the next sequence. As an   example, suppose that the sequence to be detected is 101. Note that the sequence detector inputs a string of bits serially as 0 or 1 starting with the most significant bit, and the detector generates an output of 1 when the target sequence 101 (in this case) is detected.

For example, in order to detect the sequence 101, if   input = 0 0 1 0 1 0 1 1 1 0 1 0 0 0101, then the detector will generate the output as:

Overlapping sequence detector output   = 0 0 0 0 1 0 1 0 0 0 1 0 0 0 0 0 1

Non-overlapping sequence detector output = 0 0 0 0 1 0 0 0 0 0 1 0 0 0 0 0 1

In the above, 17-bit data string is arbitrarily chosen. For the overlapping sequence detector, data is entered into the detector starting with the most significant bit (bit 16). The sequence to be detected is 101. The detector generates a '1' as soon as the sequence 101 is detected. Since the overlap detector includes the last bit of a sequence as the first bit of the next sequence, the sequence detector generates an output of '1' as follows: detects the sequence 101, first time at bit #12 of the input sequence, next at bit #10, next at bit #6, and finally at bit # 0.

The non-overlapping sequence detector, on the other hand, does not include the last bit of a sequence as the first bit of the next sequence. Hence, the detector generates an output of '1' after detecting 101 in the input sequence. In this case, the sequence detector generates an output of '1' as follows: detects the sequence 101, first time at bit #12 of the input sequence, next at bit #6, and finally at bit #0.

Next, an overlapping sequence detector will be designed.

Example 10.7

Design a sequence detector with one input X and an output Z. The input X is a serial message and the system reads X one bit at a time. The output $Z = 1$ whenever the pattern 101 is encountered in the serial message. As shown before,   if input: 0 0 1 0 1 0 1 1 1 0 1 0 0 0 1 0 1
then output: 0 0 0 0 1 0 1 0 0 0 1 0 0 0 0 0 1

Use T flip-flops.

Solution

Step 1 *Obtain state table and state diagram:*

Figure 10.21 shows the state diagram. In this diagram, each node represents a state. The labeled arcs (lines joining two nodes) represent state transitions. For example, when the system is in state C, if it receives an input 1, it produces an output 1 and makes a transition to the state D after the clock.

Similarly, when the system is in state C and receives a 0 input, it generates a 0 output and moves to state A after the clock. This type of sequential circuit is called a Mealy machine because the output generated depends on both the input X and the present state of the system. It should be emphasized that each state in the state diagram actually performs a bookkeeping operation; these operations are summarized as follows:

State	Interpretation
A	Looking for a new pattern
B	Received the first 1
C	Received a 1 followed by a 0
D	Recognized the pattern 101

Note that states B and D are equivalent since both states provide the same outputs for identical inputs, and have the same next states. In Figure 10.21, since B and D are equivalent, one of the states could have been eliminated. For simplicity, minimization of states is not done.

Next, the state diagram can be translated into a state table, as shown in Table 10.11. Each state can be represented by the binary assignment as follows:

Symbolic State	Binary State	
	y_1	y_0
A	0	0
B	0	1
C	1	1
D	1	0

The state table in Table 10.11 can be modified to reflect this state assignment, as illustrated in Table 10.12. Note that the excitation table actually describes the required excitation for a particular state transition to occur. For example, with respect to a T flip-flop, for the transition $0 \rightarrow 1$ or $1 \rightarrow 0$, a 1 must be applied to the T input. Similarly, for transitions $0 \rightarrow 0$ or $1 \rightarrow 1$ (that is, no change of state), the T input must be made 0. Using this excitation table, the flip-flop input equations can be derived as illustrated in Table 10.13.

In this figure, the entries corresponding to the flip-flop inputs T_y and T_{y0} are directly derived using the T flip-flop excitation table. For example, consider the present state $y_1 y_0 = 00$. When the input $X = 1$, the next state is 01. This means that flip-flop y_1 should not change its states and flip-flop y_0 must change its state to 1. It follows that $T_{y1} = 0$ (because a $0 \rightarrow 0$ transition is required) and $T_{y0} = 1$ (because a $0 \rightarrow 1$ transition is required). The other entries for T_{y1} and T_{y0} can be obtained in a similar manner.

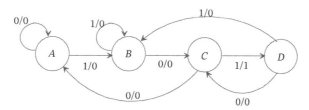

FIGURE 10.21   State diagram for Example 10.7

TABLE 10.11   State table for Example 10.7

Present State	Next State		Output Z	
	$X=0$	$X=1$	$X=0$	$X=1$
A	A	B	0	0
B	C	B	0	0
C	A	D	0	1
D	C	B	0	0

TABLE 10.12   Modified state table for Example 10.7

Present State		Next State		Output Z	
		$y_{1+} y_{0+}$	$y_{1+} y_{0+}$	Input	Input
y_1	y_0	X=0	X=1	X=0	X=1
0	0	0 0	0 1	0	0
0	1	1 1	0 1	0	0
1	1	0 0	1 0	0	1
1	0	1 1	0 1	0	0

Step 2 *Minimization:* Derive the minimum forms of the equations for the flip-flop inputs and the output. Using K-maps, the simplified equations for the flip-flops inputs and the output can be obtained as shown in Figure 10.22.

Step 3 *Schematic or Logic diagram:*
Figure 10.23 shows the schematic.

TABLE 10.13   Another form of the state table for Example 10.7

Present State		Input	Next State		Flip Flop Inputs		Ouput
y_1	y_0	X	y_{1+}	y_{0+}	T_{y0}	T_{y0}	Z
0	0	0	0	0	0	0	0
0	0	1	0	1	0	1	0
0	1	0	1	1	1	0	0
0	1	1	0	1	0	0	0
1	0	0	1	1	0	1	0
1	0	1	0	1	1	1	0
1	1	0	0	0	1	1	0
1	1	1	1	0	0	1	1

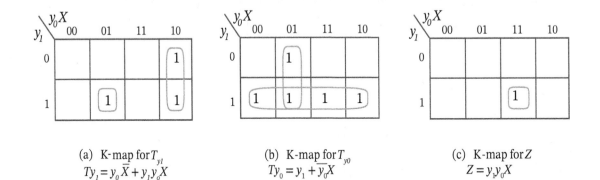

(a) K-map for T_{y1}
$$Ty_1 = y_0 \bar{X} + y_1 y_0 X$$

(b) K-map for T_{y0}
$$Ty_0 = y_1 + \bar{y_0} X$$

(c) K-map for Z
$$Z = y_1 y_0 X$$

FIGURE 10.22   K-maps for Example 10.7

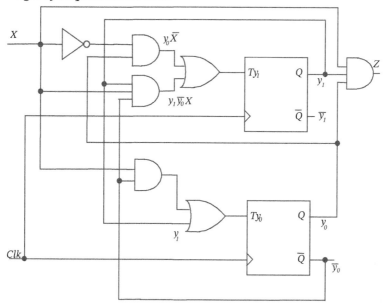

FIGURE 10.23 Logic diagram for Example 10.7

10.8 Random-Access Memory (RAM)

As mentioned before, a RAM is read/write volatile memory. RAM can be classified into two types: static RAM (SRAM) and dynamic RAM (DRAM). A static RAM stores each bit in a flip-flop, whereas the dynamic RAM stores each bit as charge in a capacitor. As long as power is available, the static RAM retains information. Because the capacitor can hold charge for a few milliseconds, the dynamic RAM must be refreshed every few milliseconds. This means that a circuit must rewrite that stored bit in a dynamic RAM every few milliseconds. Let us now discuss a typical SRAM implementation using D flip-flops. Figures 10.24 (a) and 10.24 (b) show a cell and the block diagram of a typical one-bit RAM.

In Figure 10.24 (a), $R/\overline{W} = 1$ means READ whereas $R/\overline{W} = 0$ indicates a WRITE operation. Select = 1 indicates that the one-bit RAM is selected. In order to read the cell, $R/\overline{W} = 1$ and select = 1. A '1' appears at the input of AND gate 3. This will transfer Q to the output. This is a READ operation. Note that the inverted $R/\overline{W}$ to the input of AND gate 2 is 0. This will apply a 0 at the input of the *Clk* input of the D flip-flop. The output of the D flip-flop is unchanged. In order to write into the one-bit RAM, $R/\overline{W} = 0$ must be zero.

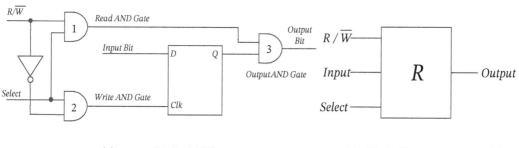

(a) A one-bit RAM (R) (b) Block diagram of the one bit RAM

FIGURE 10.24 A typical SRAM cell

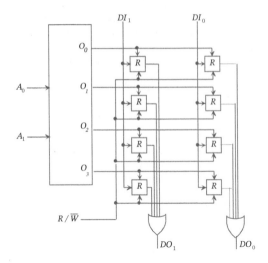

FIGURE 10.25   4 × 2 RAM

This will apply a '1' at the input of AND gate 2. The output of AND gate 2 (*Clk* input) is 1. The D input is connected to the value of the bit (1 or 0) to be written into the one-bit RAM. With *Clk* = 1, the input bit is transferred at the output. The one-bit RAM is, therefore, written into with the input bit. Figure 10.25 shows a 4 × 2 RAM. It includes 8 RAM cells providing two-bit output and 4 locations.

The RAM contains a 2 × 4 decoder and 8 RAM cells implemented with D flip-flops and gates. In contrast, a ROM consists of a decoder and OR gates. The four locations (00, 01, 10, 11) in the RAM are addressed by two bits (A_1, A_0). In order to read from location 00, the address A_1A_0 = 00 and R/$\overline{W}$ = 1. The decoder selects O_0 high. R/$\overline{W}$ = 1 will apply 0 at the clock inputs of the two RAM cells of the top row and will apply 1 at the inputs of the output AND gates, thus transferring the outputs of the two D flip-flops to the inputs of the two OR gates. The other inputs of the OR gate will be 0. Thus, the outputs of the two RAM cells of the top row will be transferred to DO_1 and DO_0, performing a READ operation. On the other hand, consider a WRITE operation: The 2-bit data to be written is presented at DI_1 DI_0. Suppose A_1A_0 = 00. The top row is selected (O_0 = 1). Input bits at DI_1 and DI_0 will respectively be applied at the inputs of the D flip-flops of the top row. Because R/$\overline{W}$ = 0, the clock inputs of both the D flip-flops of the top row are 1; thus, the *D* inputs are transferred to the outputs of the flip-flops. Therefore, data at DI_1 DI_0 will be written into the RAM.

10.9   Algorithmic State Machines (ASM) Chart

The performance of a synchronous sequential circuit (also referred to as a state machine) can be represented in a systematic way by using a flowchart called the Algorithmic State Machines (ASM) chart. This is an alternative approach to the state diagram. In the previous sections, it was shown how state diagrams could be used to design a synchronous sequential circuit. An ASM chart was widely used in the past along with the state diagram for designing a synchronous sequential circuit. However, with the popularity of hardware description languages, use of ASM chart has been reduced significantly. Note that HDLs provide a lot more structured features including C-constructs. Hence, a brief coverage of ASM is provided in this section.

An ASM chart is similar to a flowchart for a computer program. The main difference is that the flowchart for a computer program is translated into software, whereas an ASM chart is used to implement hardware. An ASM chart specifies the sequence of operations of the state machine along with the conditions required for their execution. Three symbols are utilized to develop the ASM chart: the state symbol, the conditional output symbol, and the decision symbol (Figure 10.26).

The ASM chart utilizes one state symbol for each state. The state symbol includes the state name, binary code assignment, and outputs (if any) that are asserted during the specified state. The decision symbol indicates testing of an input and then going to an exit if the condition is true and to another exit if the condition is false. The entry of the conditional output symbol is connected to the exit of the decision symbol.

The ASM chart and the state diagram are very similar. Each state in a state diagram is basically similar to the state symbol. The decision symbol is similar to the binary information written on the lines connecting two states in a state diagram. Figure 10.27 shows an example of an ASM chart for a modulo-7 counter (counting the sequence 000, 001, ..., 111 and repeat) with an enable input. Q_2, Q_1, and Q_0 at the top of the ASM chart represent the three flip-flop states for the three-bit counter.

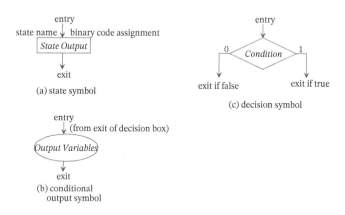

FIGURE 10.26 Symbols for an ASM Chart

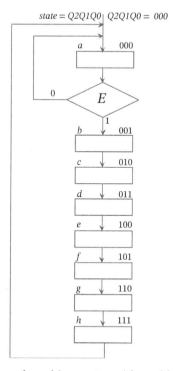

FIGURE 10.27 An ASM chart for a three-bit counter with enable input

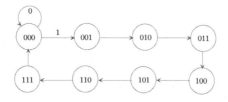

FIGURE 10.28   State diagram for the three-bit counter

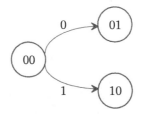

FIGURE 10.29   ASM chart illustrating timing relationships between states

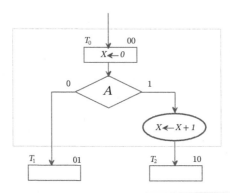

FIGURE 10.30   State diagram for the ASM chart of Figure 10.27

Each state symbol is given a symbolic name at the upper left corner along with a binary code assignment of the state at the upper right corner. For example, the state 'a' is assigned with a binary value of 000. The enable input E can only be checked at state a, and the counter can be stopped if $E = 0$; the counter continues if $E = 1$. This is illustrated by the decision symbol. Figure 10.28 shows the equivalent state diagram of the ASM chart for the three bit counter.

The ASM chart describes the sequence of events and the timing relationship between the states of a synchronous sequential circuit and the operations that occur for transition from one state to the next. An arbitrary ASM chart depicted in Figure 10.29 illustrates this. The chart contains three ASM blocks. Note that an ASM block must contain one state symbol and may include any number of decisions and conditional output symbols connected to the exit. The three ASM blocks are the ASM block for T_0 surrounded by the dashed lines and the simple ASM block defined by T_1 and T_2. Figure 10.30 shows the state diagram.

From the ASM chart of Figure 10.27, there are three states: T_0, T_1, and T_2. A ring counter can be used to generate these timing signals. During T_0, register X is cleared and flip-flop A is checked. If $A = 0$, the next state will be T_1. On the other hand, if $A = 1$, the circuit increments register X by 1 and then moves to the next state, T_2.

Note that the following operations are performed by the circuit during state T_0:
1. Clear register X.
2. Check flip-flop A for 1 or 0.
3. If A = 1, increment X by 1.

On the other hand, state machines do not perform any operations during T_1 and T_2. Note that in contrast, state diagrams do not provide any timing relationship between states. ASM charts are utilized in designing the controller of digital systems such as the control unit of a CPU. It is sometimes useful

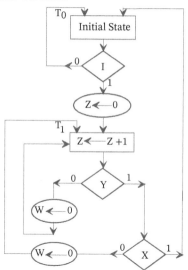

FIGURE 10.31   ASM Chart showing the sequence of operations for the binary counter

to convert an ASM chart to a state diagram and then utilize the procedures of synchronous sequential circuits to design the control logic.

State Machine Design using ASM chart   As mentioned before, an ASM chart is used to define digital hardware algorithms which can be utilized to design and implement state machines. This section describes a procedure for designing state machines using the ASM chart. This is a three step process as follows:

1. Draw the ASM chart from problem definition.
2. Derive the state transition table representing the sequence of operations to be performed.
3. Derive the logic equations and draw the hardware schematic. The hardware can be designed using either classical sequential design or PLAs as illustrated by the examples provided below.
    In the following, a digital system is designed using an ASM chart that will operate as follows:
    The system will contain a two-bit binary counter. The binary counter will count in the sequence 00, 01, 10, and 11. The most significant bit of the binary count XY is X while Y is the least significant bit. The system starts with an initial count of 3. A start signal I (represented by a switch) initiates a sequence of operations. If $I = 0$, the system stays in the initial state T_0 with count of 3. On the other hand, $I = 1$ starts the sequence.

When $I = 1$, counter Z (represented by XY) is first cleared to zero. The system then moves to state T_1. In this state, counter Z is incremented by 1 at the leading edge of each clock pulse. When the counter reaches 3, the system goes back to the initial state T_0, and the process continues depending on the status of the start switch I. The counter output will be displayed on a seven-segment display. An LED will be connected at the output of flip-flop W. The system will turn the LED ON for the count sequence 1, 2 by clearing flip-flop W to 0.

The flip-flop W will be preset to 1 in the initial state to turn the LED OFF. This can be accomplished by using input I as the PRESET input of flip-flop W. Use D flip-flops for the system.

***Step* 1:   Draw the ASM chart**.   Figure 10.31 shows the ASM chart. The symbol T_n is used without its binary value for the state boxes in all ASM charts in this section.

In the ASM chart of Figure 10.31, when the system is in initial state T_0, it waits for the start signal (I) to become HIGH. When I=1, Counter Z is cleared to zero and the system goes to state T_1. The counter is incremented at the leading edge of each clock pulse.

In state T_1, one of the following possible operations occurs after the next clock pulse transition:

Either, if counter Z is 1 or 2, flip-flop W is cleared to zero and control stays in state T_1;
         or
If the Counter Z counts to 3, the system goes back to initial state T_0.

The ASM chart consists of two states and two blocks. The block associated with T_0 includes one state box, one decision box, and one conditional box. The block in T_1 consists of one state box, two decision boxes and two conditional boxes.

***Step* 2: Derive the state transition table representing the sequence of operations.**
One common clock pulse specifies the operations to be performed in every block of an ASM chart. Table 10.14 shows the state transition table.

The binary values of the counter along with the corresponding outputs of flip-flop W is shown in the transition table. In state T_0, if I = 1, Counter Z is cleared to zero (XY = 00) and the system moves from state T_0 to T_1. In state T_1, Counter Z is first incremented to XY = 01 at the leading edge of the clock pulse; Counter Z then counts to XY = 10 at the leading edge of the following clock pulse. Finally, when XY = 11, the system moves to state T_0. The system stays in the initial state T_0 as long as I = 0; otherwise the process continues.

The operations that are performed in the digital hardware, as specified by a block in the ASM chart, occur during the same clock period and not in a sequence of operations following each other in time, as is usually interpreted in a conventional flowchart. For example, consider state T_1. The value of Y to be considered in the decision box is taken from the value of the counter in the present state T_1. This is because the decision boxes for flip-flop W belong to the same block as state T_1. The digital hardware generates the signals for all operations specified in the present block before arrival of the next clock pulse.

***Step* 3: Derive the logic equations and draw the hardware.**
The system can be divided into two sections. These are data processor and controller. The requirements for the design of the data processor are defined inside the state and conditional boxes. The logic for the controller, on the other hand, is determined from the decision boxes and the necessary state transitions.

The design of the data processor is typically implemented by using digital components such as registers, counters, multiplexers, and adders. The system can be designed using the theory of sequential logic already discussed. Figure 10.32 shows the hardware block diagram. The controller is shown with the required inputs and outputs. The data processor includes a 2-bit counter, one flip-flop, and one AND gate. The counter is incremented by one at the positive edge of every clock pulse when control is in state T_1. The counter is assumed to be in count 3 initially. It is cleared to zero only when control is in state T_0 and I=1. Therefore, T_0 and I are logically ANDed. The D input of Flip-flop W is connected to output X of the counter to clear flip-flop W during state T_0. This is because if present count is 00 (X=0), the counter will be 01 after the next clock. On the other hand, if the present count is 01 (X=0), the count will be 10 after the next clock. Hence, X is connected to the D input of flip-flop W to turn the LED ON for count sequence 1, 2. A common clock is used for all flip-flops in the system including the flip-flops in the counter and flip-flop W.

TABLE 10.14   State transition table

COUNTER		FLIP-FLOP W	CONDITIONS	STATE
X	Y	(Q)		
0	0	1	X = 0, Y = 0	T_0
0	1	0	X = 0, Y = 1	T_1
1	0	0	X = 1, Y = 0	T_1
1	1	1	X = 1, Y = 1	T_0

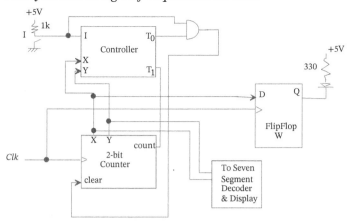

FIGURE 10.32 Hardware schematic for the two-bit counter along with associated blocks

TABLE 10.15 State table for the controller

Present State (Controller)	Present States (counter)		Inputs (Controller)			Next States (counter)		Next Output States (controller)	
	X	Y	I	X	Y	X+	Y+	T_1	T_0
T_0	1	1	0	1	1	1	1	0	1
T_0	1	1	1	1	1	0	0	0	1
T_0	0	0	1	0	0	0	1	1	0
T_1	0	1	1	0	1	1	0	1	0
T_1	1	0	1	1	0	1	1	0	1

This example illustrates a technique of designing digital systems using the ASM chart. The two-bit counter can be designed using the concepts already described. In order to design the controller, a state table for the controller must be derived. Table 10.15 shows the state table for the controller. There is a row in the table for each possible transition between states. Initial state stays in T_0 or goes from T_0 to T_1 depending on the status of the switch input (I). The same procedure for designing a sequential circuit can be utilized. Since there are two controller outputs (T_1, T_0) and three inputs (I, X, Y), a three-variable K-map is required. The design of the final hardware schematic is left as an exercise to the reader. The system will contain D flip-flops with the same common clock and a combinational circuit. The design of the system using classical sequential design method may be cumbersome. Hence, other simplified methods using PLAs can be used as illustrated below.

A second example is provided below for designing a digital system using an ASM chart. The system has three inputs (X, Y, Z) and a 2-bit MOD-4 counter (W) to count from 0 to 3. The four counter states are T_0, T_1, T_2 and T_3. The operation of the system is initiated by the counter clear input, C. When $C = 0$, the system stays in initial state T_0. On the other hand, when $C = 1$, state transitions to be handled by the system are as follows:

INPUTS	STATE TRANSITIONS
$X = 0$	The system moves from T_0 to T_1
$X = 1$	The system stays in T_0
$Y = 0$	The system moves back from T_1 to T_0
$Y = 1$	The system goes from T_1 to T_2
$Z = 0$	The system stays in T_2
$Z = 1$	The system moves from T_2 to T_3 and then stays in T_3 indefinitely (for counter clear input $C=1$ until counter W is reset to zero (state T_0) by activating the counter clear input C to 0 to start a new sequence.

Use counter, decoder, and a PAL. Figure 10.33 shows the block diagram of the MOD-4 counter to be used in the design.

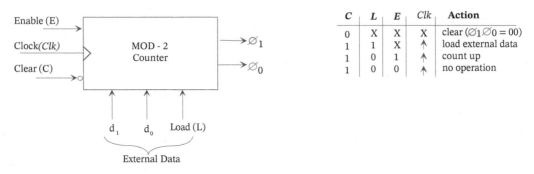

C	L	E	Clk	Action
0	X	X	X	clear ($\varnothing_1\varnothing_0 = 00$)
1	1	X	↑	load external data
1	0	1	↑	count up
1	0	0	↑	no operation

FIGURE 10.33 Block diagram and truth table of the two-bit counter

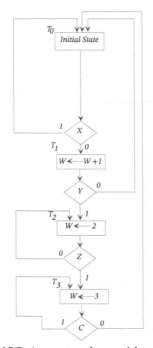

FIGURE 10.34 ASM chart for the MOD-4 counter along with transitions

Step 1: **Draw an ASM chart.**

The ASM chart is shown in Figure 10.34

Step 2: **Derive the inputs, outputs, and a sequence of operations.**

The system will be designed using a PAL, a MOD-4 counter, and a 2 to 4 decoder. The MOD-4 counter is loaded or initialized with the external data if the counter control inputs C and L are both ones. The counter load control input L overrides the counter enable control input E.

The counter counts up automatically in response to the next clock pulse when the counter load control input $L = 0$ and the enable input E is tied to HIGH. Such normal activity is desirable for the situation (obtained from the ASM chart) when the counter goes through the sequence T_0, T_1, T_2, T_3 for the specified inputs.

However, if the following situations occur, the counter needs to be loaded with data out of its normal sequence: If the counter is in initial state T_0 (counter W=0 with C= 0) , it stays in T_0 for $X = 1$. This means that if the counter output is 00 and if $X = 1$, the counter must be loaded with external data dd = 00. Similarly, the other out of normal sequence count includes transitions ($C = 1$) from T_1 to T_0 ($X = 0, Y = 0$), T_2 to T_2 ($X = 0, Y=1, Z = 0$) with count 2, and T_3 to T_3 ($X = 0, Y = 1, Z = 1$); C is assumed to be HIGH during these transitions. Finally, if $C = 0$, transition from T_3 to T_0 occurs regardless of the values of X, Y, Z and the process continues. The appropriate external data must be loaded into the counter for out of normal count sequence by the PLA using the L input of the counter.

Step 3: **Derive the logic equations and draw a hardware schematic**.

Figure 10.35 depicts the logic diagram. Figure 10.36 shows the truth table and hardware schematic for PLA-based implementation.

The equations for the product terms are: $P_0 = XT_0C$, $P_1 = \bar{X}\,\bar{Y}T_1C$, $P_2 = \bar{X}YZT_2C$, $P_3 = \bar{X}YZT_3C$, $P_4 = T_3\bar{C}$, $L = P_0 + P_1 + P_2 + P_3 + P_4$, $d_1 = P_2 + P_3$, $d_0 = P_3$

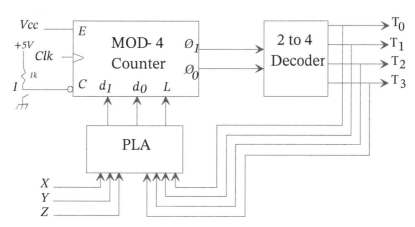

FIGURE 10.35 Hardware schematic of the MOD-4 counter with PLA and decoder

	Inputs								Outputs		
C	X	Y	Z	T$_0$	T$_1$	T$_2$	T$_3$	L	d$_1$	d$_0$	
1	1	X	X	1	X	X	X	1	0	0	
1	0	0	X	X	1	X	X	1	0	0	
1	0	1	0	X	X	1	X	1	1	0	
1	0	1	1	X	X	X	1	1	1	1	
0	X	X	X	X	X	X	1	1	0	0	
X = don't cares											

(a)   Truth table for out of normal count sequence

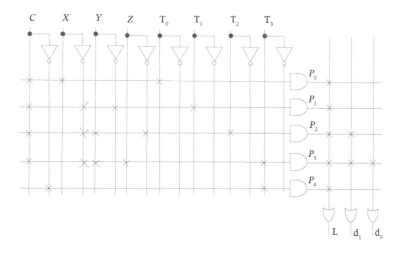

(b)   PLA implementation

FIGURE 10.36 PLA-based system

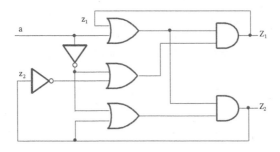

FIGURE 10.37   Asynchronous sequential circuit

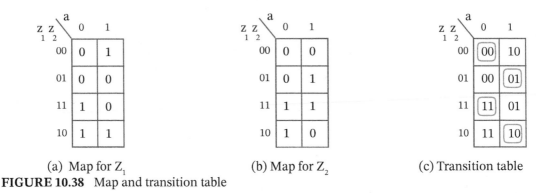

(a) Map for Z_1 (b) Map for Z_2 (c) Transition table

FIGURE 10.38   Map and transition table

10.10   Asynchronous Sequential Circuits

Asynchronous sequential circuits do not require any synchronizing clocks. As mentioned before, a sequential circuit basically consists of a combinational circuit with memory. In synchronous sequential circuits, memory elements are clocked flip-flops. In contrast, memory in asynchronous sequential circuits includes either unclocked flip-flop or time-delay devices. The propagation delay time of a logic gate (finite time for a signal to propagate through a gate) provides its memory capability. Note that a sequential circuit contains inputs, outputs, and states. In synchronous sequential circuits, changes in states take place due to clock pulses. On the other hand, asynchronous sequential circuits typically contain a combinational circuit with feedback. The timing problems in the feedback may cause instability. Asynchronous sequential circuits are, therefore, more difficult to design than synchronous sequential circuits.

Asynchronous sequential circuits are used in applications in which the system must take appropriate actions to input changes rather than waiting for a clock to initiate actions. For proper operation of an asynchronous sequential circuit, the inputs must change one at a time when the circuit is in a stable condition (called the "fundamental mode of operation"). The inputs to the asynchronous sequential circuits are called "primary variables" whereas outputs are called "secondary variables."

Figure 10.37 shows an asynchronous sequential circuit. In the feedback loops, the uppercase letters are used to indicate next values of the secondary variables and the lowercase letters indicate present values of the secondary variables. For example, Z_1, and Z_2 are next values whereas z_1 and z_2 are present values. The output equations can be derived as follows:

$$Z_1 = (a + z_1)(\bar{a} + \bar{z}_2)$$
$$Z_2 = (a + z_1)(a + z_2)$$

The delays in the feedback loops can be obtained from the propagation delays between z_1 and Z_1 or z_2 and Z_2. Let us now plot the functions Z_1 and Z_2 in a map, and a transition table as shown in Figure 10.38.

Figures 10.38 (a) and (b) show maps for Z_1 and Z_2. The map for Z_1 in Figure 10.38(a) is obtained by substituting the values z_1, z_2, and a for each square into the equation for $Z1$. For example, consider

$z_1 z_2 = 11$ and $a = 0$.

$$Z_1 = (a + z_1)(\overline{a} + \overline{z}_2)$$
$$= (0 + 1)(\overline{0} + \overline{1})$$
$$= 1$$

$$Z_2 = (a + z_1)(\overline{a} + z_2)$$
$$= (0 + 1)(\overline{0} + 1)$$
$$= 1$$

Similarly, values for all other sequences can be obtained similarly. The transition table of Figure 10.38(c) can be obtained by combining the binary values of two squares in the same position and placing them in the corresponding square in the transition table. Thus, the variable $Z = Z_1 Z_2$ is placed in each square of the transition table. For example, from the first square of Figures 10.38(a) and (b), $Z = 00$. This is shown in the first square of Figure 10.38(c). The squares in the transition table in which $z_1 z_2 = Z_1 Z_2$ are circled to show that they are stable. The uncircled squares are unstable states.

Let us now analyze the behavior of the circuit due to change in the input variable. Suppose $a = 0$, $z_1 z_2 = 00$, then the output is 00. Thus, 00 is circled and shown in the first square of Figure 10.38(c). Z is the next value of $z_1 z_2$ and is a stable state. Next, suppose that a goes from 0 to 1 and the value of Z changes from 00 to 01. Note that this causes an interim unstable situation because $Z_1 Z_2$ is initially equal to $z_1 z_2$. This is because as soon as the input changes from 0 to 1, this change in input travels through the circuit to change $Z_1 Z_2$ from 00 to 01. The feedback loop in the circuit eventually makes $z_1 z_2$ equal to $Z_1 Z_2$; that is, $z_1 z_2 = Z_1 Z_2 = 01$. Because $z_1 z_2 = Z_1 Z_2$, the circuit attains a stable state. The state 01 is circled in the figure to indicate this. Similarly, it can be shown that as the input to an asynchronous sequential circuit changes, the circuit goes to a temporary unstable condition until it reaches a stable state when $Z_1 Z_2 =$ present state, $z_1 z_2$. Therefore, as the input moves between 0 and 1, the circuit goes through the states 00, 01, 11, 10, and repeats the sequence depending on the input changes. A state table can be derived from the transition table. This is shown in Table 10.16, which is the state table for Figure 10.38(c).

A flow table obtained from the transition table is normally used in designing an asynchronous sequential circuit. A flow table resembles a transition table except that the states are represented by letters instead of binary numbers. The transition table of Figure 10.38(c) can be translated into a flow table as shown in Figure 10.39. Note that the states are represented by binary numbers as follows: $w = 00$, $x = 01$, $y = 11$, $z = 10$. The flow table in Figure 10.39 is called a "primitive flow table" because it has only one stable state in each row.

An asynchronous sequential circuit can be designed using the primitive flow table from the problem definition. The flow table is then simplified by combining squares to a minimum number of states. The transition table is then obtained by assigning binary numbers to the states. Finally, a logic diagram is obtained from the transition table. The logic diagram includes a combinational circuit with feedback.

The design of an asynchronous sequential circuit is more difficult than synchronous sequential circuit because of the timing problems associated with the feedback loop. This topic is beyond the scope of this book.

TABLE 10.16 Transition table

Present State		Next State			
		a=0		a=1	
0	0	0	0	1	0
0	1	0	0	0	1
1	0	1	1	1	0
1	1	1	1	0	1

FIGURE 10.39   Flow table

QUESTIONS AND PROBLEMS

10.1   Name typical steps for analyzing and designing a synchronous sequential circuit.

10.2   Analyze the clocked synchronous circuit shown in Figure P10.2. Express the next state in terms of the present state and inputs, derive the state table, and draw the state diagram.

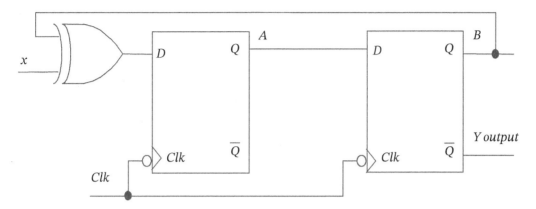

FIGURE P10.2

10.3   A synchronous sequential circuit with two D flip-flops (Da, Db), present states (a and b), next states (a+, b+), one input (x), *and* an output (y) is expressed by the following equations:
$$y = a + b \qquad Da = abx \qquad Db = \bar{a}x + bx$$
(a)   Derive the state table and state diagram for the circuit.
(b)   Draw a schematic.

10.4   A synchronous sequential circuit with two D flip-flops *(a,b as outputs)*, one input *(x)*, and an output *(y)* is expressed by the following equations:
$$Da = a\bar{b}x + \bar{a}b, \ Db = \bar{x}b + \bar{b}x$$
$$y = \bar{b}\bar{x} + a$$
(a)   Derive the state table and state diagram for the circuit.
(b)   Draw a schematic.

10.5   Analyze the synchronous sequential circuit shown in Figure P10.5.

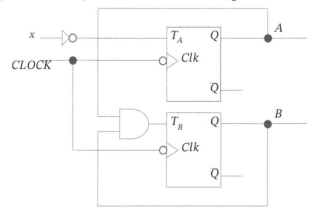

FIGURE P10.5

10.6   In Figure P10.6, assume the flip-flop outputs (A, B) are zero initially. Draw a timing diagram for A and B for the first four clock pulses.

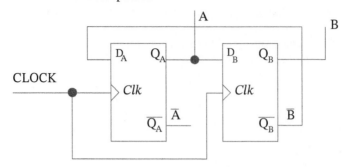

FIGURE P10.6

10.7   A synchronous sequential circuit is represented by the state diagram shown in Figure P10.7. Using JK flip-flops and undefined states as don't-cares:
(a)   derive the state table.
(b)   minimize the equation for flip-flop inputs using K-maps.
(c)   draw a logic diagram.

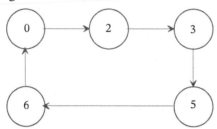

FIGURE P10.7

10.8   A sequential circuit contains two D flip-flops (A, B), one input (x), and one output (y), as shown in Figure P10.8.
Derive the state table and the state diagram of the sequential circuit.

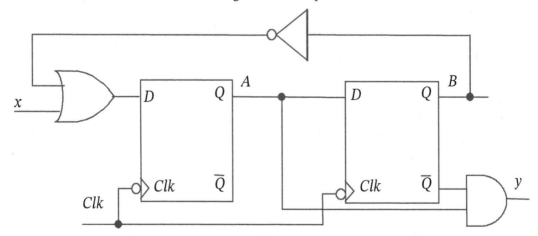

FIGURE P10.8

10.9   Design the Mealy circuit for the state diagram shown in Figure P10.9. Use D flip-flops.

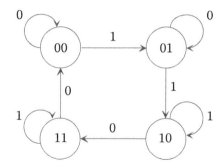

FIGURE P10.9

10.10   Design the Mealy circuit using T flip-flops for the state diagram shown in Figure P10.10.

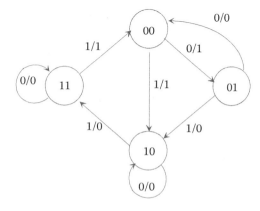

FIGURE P10.10

10.11   Design a Moore circuit that will go through the following sequence: 00, 11, 10, 01, and repeat.

Using T flip-flops:
    (a)   Draw a state diagram.
    (b)   Derive a state table.
    (c)   Draw the schematic.

10.12   Design a Moore circuit that will go through the following sequence: 000, 001, 100, 110, 111, and repeat.

Using T flip-flops:
    (a)   Draw a state diagram.
    (b)   Derive a state table.
    (c)   Draw the schematic.

10.13   What is the difference between combinational adder and sequential adder?

10.14   Name an example of a sequence generator.

10.15   What is a sequence detector? Name an application where sequence detector is used.

10.16 Given the following 8-bit data input for a sequence director: 0101 1010, find the detector outputs for both overlapping and non-overlapping sequence detectors for detecting the two-bit sequence 01.

10.17 Design a synchronous sequential circuit with one input x and one output y. The input x is a serial message, and the system reads x one bit at a time. The output y is 1 whenever the binary pattern 000 is encountered in the serial message. For example: If the input is 01000000, then the output will be 00001010. Use T flip-flops.

10.18 What is the basic difference between SRAM and DRAM?

10.19 Given a memory with a 24-bit address and 8-bit word size,
   (a) how many bytes can be stored in this memory?
   (b) if this memory were constructed from 1K × 1-bit RAM chips, how many memory chips would be required?

10.20 Draw an ASM chart for the following: Assume three states (a, b, c) in the system with one input x and two registers R_1 and R_2. The circuit is initially in state a. If $x = 0$, the control goes from state a to state b and, clears registers R_1 to 0 and sets R_2 to 1, and then moves to state c. On the other hand if $x = 1$, the control goes to state c. In state c, R_1 is subtracted from R_2 and the result is stored in R_1. The control then moves back to state a and the process continues.

10.21 Draw an ASM chart for each of the following sequence of operations:
   (a) The ASM chart will define a conditional operation to perform the operation $R_2 \leftarrow R_2 - R_1$ during State T^0 and will transfer control to State T_1 if the control input c is 1; if c=0, the system will stay in T_0. Assume that R_1 and R_2 are 8-bit registers.
   (b) The ASM chart in which the system is initially in State T_0 and then checks a control input c. If c=1, control will move from State T_0 to State T_1; if c=0, the system will increment an 8-bit register R by 1 and control will return to the initial state.

10.22 Draw an ASM chart for the following state diagram of Figure P10.22. Assume that the system stays in initial state T_0 when control input c = 0 and input X = 1. The sequence of operations is started from T_0 when X = 0. When the system reaches state T_3, it stays in T_3 indefinitely as long as c = 1; the system returns to state T_0 when c = 0.

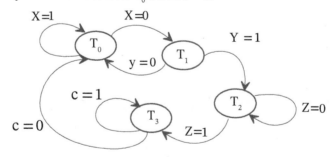

FIGURE P10.22

10.23   Derive the output equations for the asynchronous sequential circuit shown in Figure P10.23. Also, determine the state table and flow table.

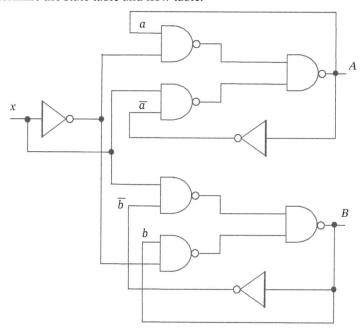

FIGURE P10.23

11

COUNTERS AND REGISTERS

This chapter describes design of counters and registers. Note that D flip-flop is popular these days. This is because equations for D flip-flop are simple and also D flip-flop is widely used by FPGA. Hence, D flip-flop will be mostly used for designing counters and registers. Topics include design of counters, shift registers, and General-Purpose Register (GPR).

11.1   Design of Counters

A counter is a synchronous sequential circuit that moves through a predefined sequence of states upon application of clock pulses. A binary counter, which counts binary numbers in sequence at each clock pulse, is the simplest example of a counter. An n-bit binary counter contains n flip-flops and can count binary numbers from 0 to 2^{n-1}. Other binary counters may count in an arbitrary manner in a nonbinary sequence. The following examples will illustrate the binary sequence and nonbinary sequence counters.

Example 11.1

Design a two-bit counter to count in the sequence 00, 01, 10, 11, and repeat. Use T flip-flops.

Solution

Step 1   *Obtain state table and state diagram:* Derive the state table and state diagram from the problem definition. If the state diagram is given, determine the state table.

Figure 11.1 shows the state diagram. Note that state transition occurs at the clock pulse. No state transitions occurs if there is no clock pulse. Therefore, the clock pulse does not appear as an input. Table 11.1 shows the state table.

Step 2   *Minimization:* Obtain the minimum form of the Boolean equations for flip-flop inputs and outputs, if any, using K-maps.

Using K-maps, the simplified equations for the flip-flop inputs can be obtained as shown in Figure 11.2.

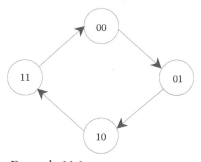

FIGURE 11.1   State diagram for Example 11.1

TABLE 11.1   Stable table for Example 11.1

Present State		Next State		Flip Flop inputs	
a_1	a_0	a_1+	a_0+	T_{A1}	T_{A0}
0	0	0	1	0	1
0	1	1	0	1	1
1	0	1	1	0	1
1	1	0	0	1	1

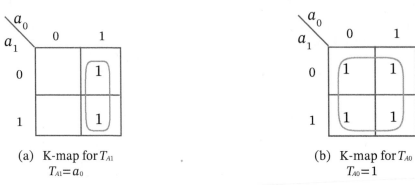

(a)   K-map for T_{A1}
$T_{A1} = a_0$

(b)   K-map for T_{A0}
$T_{A0} = 1$

FIGURE 11.2   K-maps for Example 11.1

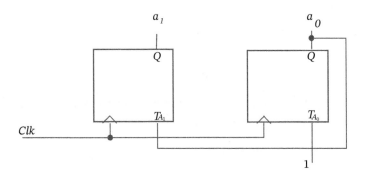

FIGURE 11.3   Schematic for two-bit counter of Example 11.1

The excitation table of the T flip-flop is used for deriving the state table. For example, consider the top row of the state table of Table 11.1. The state remains unchanged ($a_1 = 0$ and $a_{1+} = 0$) requiring a T input of 0 and thus, $T_{A1} = 0$. State a_0 is complemented from the present state (0) to the next state (1), and thus $T_{A0} = 1$.

Step 3   *Schematic or Logic diagram:*   Draw the logic diagram.

The schematic as shown in Figure 11.3.

Example 11.2

Design a three-bit counter to count in the sequence 000 through 111, return to 000 after 111, and then repeat the count. Use JK flip-flops.

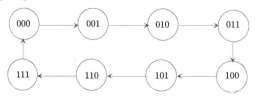

FIGURE 11.4   State diagram for Example 11.2

Step 1 *Obtain state table and state diagram:* Derive the state table and state diagram from the problem definition. If the state diagram is given, determine the state table.

Figure 11.4 shows the state diagram. Table 11.2 shows the JK-FF excitation table, and the state table. Consider the top row. The present state of a_2 changes from 0 to 0 at the clock, a_1 changes from 0 to 0, and a_0 changes from 0 to 1. From the JK flip-flop excitation table, for these transitions, $Ja2 = 0$, $Ka2 = X$, $Ja1 = 0$, $Ka1 = X$, and $Ja0 = 1$, $Ka0 = X$.

TABLE 11.2   JK-FF excitation table and State Table for Example 11.2

(a) Excitation table of JK-FF

Q	$Q+$	J	K
0	0	0	X
0	1	1	X
1	0	X	1
1	1	X	0

(b) State Table for Example 11.2

Present State			Next State			Flip-Flop Inputs					
$a2$	$a1$	$a0$	$a2+$	$a1+$	$a0+$	$Ja2$	$Ka2$	$Ja1$	$Ka1$	$Ja0$	$Ka0$
0	0	0	0	0	1	0	X	0	X	1	X
0	0	1	0	1	0	0	X	1	X	X	1
0	1	0	0	1	1	0	X	X	0	1	X
0	1	1	1	0	0	1	X	X	1	X	1
1	0	0	1	0	1	X	0	0	X	1	X
1	0	1	1	1	0	X	0	1	X	X	1
1	1	0	1	1	1	X	0	X	0	1	X
1	1	1	0	0	0	X	1	X	1	X	1

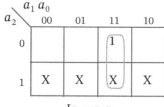

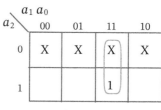

$$Ja_2 = a_1 a_0 \qquad\qquad Ka_2 = a_1 a_0$$

(a)   K-Maps for Ja_2 and Ka_2

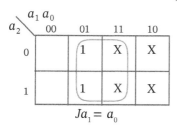

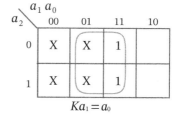

$$Ja_1 = a_0 \qquad\qquad Ka_1 = a_0$$

(b) K-Maps for Ja_1 and Ka_1

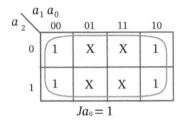
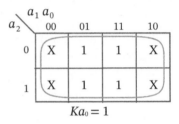

(c) K-Maps for Ja_0 and Ka_0

FIGURE 11.5   K-Maps for Example 11.2

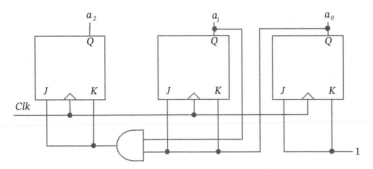

FIGURE 11.6   Schematic for Example 11.2

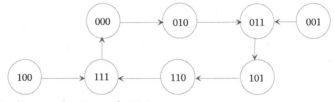

FIGURE 11.7   State diagram for Example 11.3

Step 2   *Minimization:* Obtain the minimum form of the Boolean equations for flip-flop inputs and outputs, if any, using K-maps.

     Derive the minimum forms of the equations for the flip-flop inputs. Using K-maps, the simplified equations for the flip-flop inputs can be obtained as shown in Figure 11.5

Step 3   *Schematic or Logic diagram:*   Draw the logic diagram.

     Figure 11.6 shows the schematic.

Example 11.3

Design a three-bit counter that will count in the sequence 000, 010, 011, 101, 110, 111, and repeat the sequence. The counter has two unused states. These are 001 and 100. Implement the counter as a self-correcting such that if the counter happens to be in one of the unused states (001 or 100) upon power-up or due to error, the next clock pulse puts it in one of the valid states and the counter provides the correct count. Use T Flip-flops. Note that the initial states of the flip-flops are unpredictable when power is turned ON. Therefore, all the unused (don't care) states of the counter should be checked to ensure that the counter eventually goes into the desirable counting sequence. This is called a self-correcting counter.

Solution

Step 1   *Obtain state table and state diagram:*   Derive the state table and state diagram from the problem definition. If the state diagram is given, determine the state table.

TABLE 11.3 T-FF excitation table and state table for Example 11.3

(a) Excitation Table for T Flip-flop

Q	Q+	T
0	0	0
0	1	1
1	0	1
1	1	0

(b) State Table for Example 11.3

Present State			Next State			Flip Flop Inputs		
a2	a1	a0	a2+	a1+	a0+	Ta2	Ta1	Ta0
0	0	0	0	1	0	0	1	0
0	1	0	0	1	1	0	0	1
0	1	1	1	0	1	1	1	0
1	0	1	1	1	0	0	1	1
1	1	0	1	1	1	0	0	1
1	1	1	0	0	0	1	1	1

Figure 11.7 shows the state diagram. Note that in the state diagram, it is shown that if the counter goes to an invalid state such as 001 upon power-up, the counter will then go to the valid state 011 and will count correctly. Similarly, for the invalid state 100, the counter will be in state 111 and the correct count will continue. This self-correcting feature will be verified from the counter's state table using T flip-flops as shown in Table 11.3.

Step 2 *Minimization:* Obtain the minimum form of the Boolean equations for flip-flop inputs and outputs, if any, using K-maps.

Using K-maps, the simplified equations for the flip-flop inputs can be obtained, as shown in Figure 11.8. The unused states 001 and 100 are invalid and can never occur, so they are don't care conditions.

Now, let us verify the self-correcting feature of the counter. The flip-flop input equations are:

$$Ta_2 = a_1 a_0$$
$$Ta_1 = \overline{a_1} + a_0$$
$$Ta_0 = a_2 + a_1 \overline{a_0}$$

Suppose that the counter is in the invalid state 001 upon power-up or due to error, therefore, in this state, $a_2 = 0$, $a_1 = 0$, and $a_0 = 1$. Substituting these values in the flip-flop input equations, we get

$$Ta_2 = 0 \cdot 1 = 0$$
$$Ta_1 = \overline{0} + 1 = 1$$
$$Ta_0 = 0 + 0 \cdot \overline{1} = 0$$

Note that with $a_2 a_1 a_0 = 001$ and $Ta_2 Ta_1 Ta_0 = 010$, the state changes from 001 to 011. Therefore, the next state will be 011. The correct count will resume. Next, if the flip-flop goes to the invalid state 100 due to error or when power is turned ON. Substituting $a_2 = 1$, $a_1 = 0$, and $a_0 = 0$ gives:

$$Ta_2 = 0 \cdot 0 = 0$$
$$Ta_1 = \overline{0} + 0 = 1$$
$$Ta_0 = 1 + 0 \cdot \overline{0} = 1$$

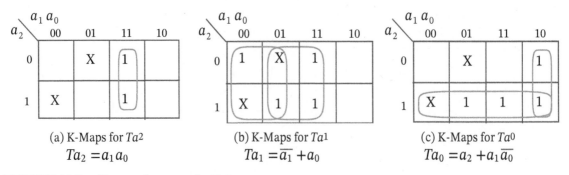

(a) K-Maps for $Ta2$
$$Ta_2 = a_1 a_0$$

(b) K-Maps for $Ta1$
$$Ta_1 = \overline{a_1} + a_0$$

(c) K-Maps for $Ta0$
$$Ta_0 = a_2 + a_1 \overline{a_0}$$

FIGURE 11.8   K-maps for example 11.3

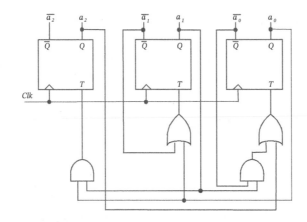

FIGURE 11.9   Schematic for Example 11.3

Note that with $a_2 a_1 a_0 = 100$ and $Ta_2 Ta_1 Ta_0 = 011$, the state changes from 100 to 111. Hence, the next state for the counter will be 111. The correct count will continue. Therefore, the counter is self-correcting.

Step 3   *Schematic or Logic diagram:*   Draw the logic diagram.
Figure 11.9 shows the schematic.

11.2   Design of Registers

A flip-flop can store one-bit of data. Several flip-flops are needed in order to store several bits of data. This means that eight flip-flops are required to store 8-bit data. A register uses a number of flip-flops and stores a string of bits. The register is an important part of any CPU. A CPU with several registers reduces the number of accesses to the main memory, therefore simplifying the programming task and shortening execution time.

Two types of registers namely, Shift registers and General-Purpose Register (GPR) will be covered in this section. Note that there are four types of shift registers: Serial In-Serial Out, Serial In-Parallel Out, Parallel In-Serial Out and Parallel In-Parallel Out. Data may be entered in or out of a shift register serially one bit after another from either to the left or to the right. Data can also be entered into a shift register in a parallel configuration. A General-Purpose Register, on the other hand, can provide multiple functions including clear operation, serial shift and parallel shift operations. Design of a Serial In-Serial Out shift register and a typical GPR will be provided in the section.

11.2.1   Shift Register

A three-bit serial-in/serial-out right shift register will be designed in this section. This means that the shift register will receive binary data from the Most Significant Bit (MSB) to the Least Significant Bit (LSB). As an example, consider three-bit data 110 to be shifted into a three-bit right shift register containing three negative edge-trigerred D flip-flops with Q2 as the output of the MSB, Q1 as the next, and Q0 as the LSB. Assume that Q2Q1Q0 = 000 initially. Table 11.4 shows how each bit of data 110 will be entered serially into the three-bit right shift register starting with the LSB.

The table shows that the LSB (0) is shifted first into Q2 of the three-bit register at the negative edge of the clock pulse #1, next data (1) is then shifted into Q2 while the previous bit in Q2 (0) is shifted one bit to the right into Q1 at the negative clock pulse #2. The MSB (1) of three-bit data 110 is then shifted to Q2 at the negative edge of the clock pulse #3. At this point, register Q2Q1Q0 will contain data 110. Continuing this way, data 110 will be completely shifted out of the register at the negative edge of the clock pulse #6. Hence, the three-bit serial-in/serial-out right shift register needs six clock pulses to transfer three-bit data (110 in this case) to the output. Note that the output may be connected to another register.

The three-bit right shift register will now be designed using the three steps for the sequential circuit design of Chapter 10 as follows.

Step 1 *Obtain state table and state diagram:* Derive the state table and state diagram from the problem definition. If the state diagram is given, determine the state table.

Derive the state diagram as shown Figure 11.10. Obtain the state table shown in Table 11.5 from the state diagram. Next, consider the state diagram of Figure 11.10. At state 000, if the input is 0, then 0 is shifted to the MSB of the three-bit right shift register discarding the LSB. Thus, the circuit stays in state 000 with input 0. Next, with input 1, a 1 is shifted to the MSB of the register. Hence, the circuit goes to state 100. Thus, transitions for all other states can similarly be obtained.

TABLE 11.4 Contents of three-bit Serial right shift register with input binary data 110

Number of negative clock pulses	Serial data input	Q2	Q1	Q0
0	---	0	0	0
1	0 (LSB)	0	0	0
2	1	1	0	0
3	1 (MSB)	1	1	0 (LSB)
4	---	---	1	1
5	---	---	---	1 (MSB)
6	---	---	---	---

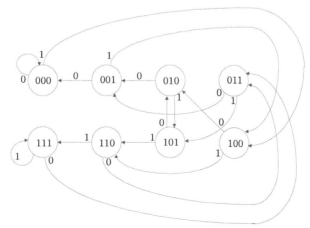

FIGURE 11.10 State diagram for the three-bit right shift register

TABLE 11.5   State table for the three-bit right shift register

Present State Q2 Q1 Q0			Input x	Next State Q2+ Q1+ Q0+			FF inputs D2 D1 D0		
0	0	0	0	0	0	0	0	0	0
0	0	0	1	1	0	0	1	0	0
0	0	1	0	0	0	0	0	0	0
0	0	1	1	1	0	0	1	0	0
0	1	0	0	0	0	1	0	0	1
0	1	0	1	1	0	1	1	0	1
0	1	1	0	0	0	1	0	0	1
0	1	1	1	1	0	1	1	0	1
1	0	0	0	0	1	0	0	1	0
1	0	0	1	1	1	0	1	1	0
1	0	1	0	0	1	0	0	1	0
1	0	1	1	1	1	0	1	1	0
1	1	0	0	0	1	1	0	1	1
1	1	0	1	1	1	1	1	1	1
1	1	1	0	0	1	1	0	1	1
1	1	1	1	1	1	1	1	1	1

Step 2   *Minimization:* Obtain the minimum form of the Boolean equations for flip-flop inputs and outputs, if any, using K-maps. Obtain the minimum forms of the equations for the flip-flop inputs.

Using K-maps, the equations for flip-flop inputs are simplified as shown in Figure 11.11.

Step 3   *Schematic or Logic diagram:*   Draw the logic diagram.

Figure 11.12 shows the schematic.

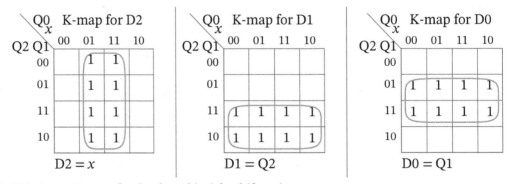

$$D2 = x \qquad\qquad D1 = Q2 \qquad\qquad D0 = Q1$$

FIGURE 11.11   K-maps for the three-bit right shift register

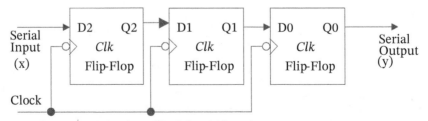

FIGURE 11.12   Schematic of the three-bit right shift register

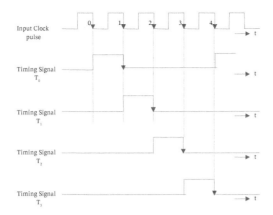

FIGURE 11.13 Timing signals

11.2.2 "Shift register" Counters

The "Shift register" counters are modulo-n counters that count in a fixed sequence via shifting, and then repeat the count. Hence, these types of counters go through a fixed sequence of states. There are two types of "Shift register" counters. They are Ring counter and Johnson counter.

The ring counter is a shift register with feedback connected from the true output (Q) of the least significant bit flip-flop to the D input of the most significant bit flip-flop. The Johnson counter, also called a shift register, is similar to the ring counter but with inverted feedback. The Johnson counter is also called "Twisted ring counter", "Switch-tail counter" or "Mobius counter". These shift registers will be designed later in this section.

Note that the control unit inside the CPU of a computer translates instructions. The control unit utilizes timing signals that determines the time sequences in which the operations required by an instruction are executed. These timing signals, shown in Figure 11.13, can be generated normally by the ring counter. For proper operation, a ring counter must be initialized with one flip-flop in the high state (Q=1) and all other flip-flops in the zero state (Q=0). Ring counters are also used for providing time delays.

An n-bit ring counter transfers a single bit among the flip-flops to provide n unique states. The n-bit ring counter requires no decoding but contains n flip-flops for an n-bit ring counter. A four-bit ring counter will count in the sequence 1000, 0100, 0010, 0001, and repeat. Although the ring counter does not count in the usual binary counting sequence, it is still called a counter because each count corresponds to a unique set of flip-flop states. The four-bit ring counter will now be designed using the three steps for the sequential circuit design of Chapter 10 as follows.

Step 1 *Obtain state table and state diagram:* Derive the state table and state diagram from the problem definition. If the state diagram is given, determine the state table.
Derive the state diagram (Figure 11.14). Obtain the state table (Table 11.6) from the state diagram.

Step 2 *Minimization:* Obtain the minimum form of the Boolean equations for flip-flop inputs and outputs, if any, using K-maps.
Using K-maps, the equations for flip-flop inputs are simplified as shown in Figure 11.15.

Step 3 *Schematic or Logic diagram:* Draw the logic diagram.

The schematic is shown in Figure 11.16.

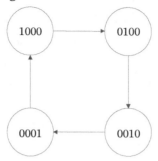

FIGURE 11.14 State diagram for the four-bit ring counter

TABLE 11.6   State table for the four-bit ring counter

Present State				Next State				FF Inputs			
w	x	y	z	w+	x+	y+	z+	Dw	Dx	Dy	Dz
1	0	0	0	0	1	0	0	0	1	0	0
0	1	0	0	0	0	1	0	0	0	1	0
0	0	1	0	0	0	0	1	0	0	0	1
0	0	0	1	1	0	0	0	1	0	0	0

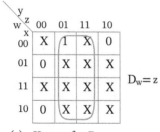

(a)   K-map for D_w

(b)   K-map for D_x

(c)   K-map for D_y

(d)   K-map for D_z

FIGURE 11.15   K-maps for 4-bit ring counter

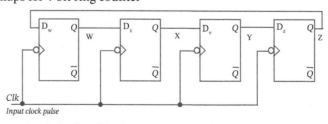

FIGURE 11.16 Schematic of the four-bit ring counter

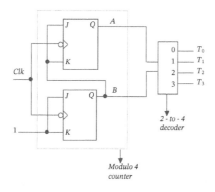

FIGURE 11.17 Modulo-4 counter with a decoder

Note that from the state table of Table 11.6, using the present states along with the unused present states as don't cares, the following equations are obtained from four K-maps (one for each FF input, Figure 11.15) : $D_w = z$, $D_x = w$, $D_y = x$, $D_z = y$. This circuit is also known as a *circular shift register*, because the least significant bit shifted is not lost. This is the simplest shift-register counter. Thus, the schematic of Figure 11.16 is obtained.

In Figure 11.16, the output z from the last flip-flop is connected to the input D_w of the first flip-flop. This creates a closed loop circuit. This means that the same data bit is transferred around the loop continuously, thus creating a ring-type operation. Hence, this type of counter is called the "ring counter". Note that the modulo of a counter means that the counter sequences through a count before repeating. The schematic of Figure 11.16 is a mod-4 ring counter requiring four flip-flops. Sixteen states are possible with four flip-flops although only four states are used as shown in the truth table of Table 11.6. Hence, the ring counter is inefficient as far as the generation of the output states is concerned.

However, the main advantages of this circuit are design simplicity and the ability to generate timing signals without a decoder. Nevertheless, n flip-flops are required to generate n timing signals. This approach is not economically feasible for large values of n. To generate timing signals economically, a new approach is used. A modulo-n counter is first designed using n flip-flops. The n outputs from this counter are then connected to a n-to-2^n decoder as inputs to generate 2^n timing signals. The circuit depicted in Figure 11.17 shows how to generate four timing signals using a modulo-4 counter and a 2-to-4 decoder.

From Figure 11.17 the Boolean equation for each timing signal can be derived as follows:

$$T_0 = \overline{A}\,\overline{B}$$

$$T_1 = \overline{A}B$$

$$T_2 = A\overline{B}$$

$$T_3 = AB$$

These equations show that four two-input AND gates are needed to derive the timing signals (assuming single-level decoding). The main advantage of this approach is that 2^n timing signals using only n flip-flops are generated. In this method, 2^n (n-input) AND gates are required to decode the n-bit output from the flip-flops into 2^n different timing signals. However, the ring counter approach requires 2^n flip-flops to accomplish the same task.

Typical modulo-n counters provide trade-offs between the number of flip-flops and the amount of decoding logic needed. The binary counter uses the minimum number of flip-flops but requires a decoder. On the other hand, the ring counter uses the maximum number of flip-flops but requires no decoding logic.

Next, design of the Johnson counter will be provided. The Johnson counter is very similar to a ring counter. Figure 11.20 shows a 4-bit Johnson counter using four D flip-flops. Note that the $\overline{Q}$ output of the right-hand flip-flop is connected to the D input of the leftmost flip-flop.

A Johnson counter requires the same hardware as a ring counter of the same size but can represent twice as many states. Assume that the flip-flops are initialized at 1000. The counter will count in the sequence 1000, 1100, 1110, 1111, 0111, 0011, 0001, 0000, and repeat.

The four-bit Johnson counter will be designed using the following steps:

Step 1 *Obtain state table and state diagram*: Derive the state table and state diagram from the problem definition. If the state diagram is given, determine the state table.
Figure 11.18 shows the state diagram while Table 11.7 shows the state table.

Step 2 *Minimization:* Obtain the minimum form of the Boolean equations for flip-flop inputs and outputs, if any, using K-maps.
Using K-maps as shown in Figure 11.19, the equations for flip-flop inputs are simplified as follows: $D_w = \bar{z}$, $D_x = w$, $D_y = x$, $D_z = y$

Step 3 *Schematic or Logic diagram:* Draw the logic diagram.

The schematic or logic diagram is shown in Figure 11.20.

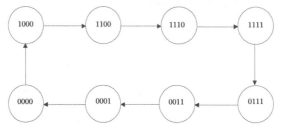

FIGURE 11.18 State diagram for the four-bit Johnson counter

TABLE 11.7 State table for the four-bit Johnson counter

Present State				Next State				FF inputs			
W	X	Y	Z	W+	X+	Y+	Z+	D_w	D_x	D_y	D_z
1	0	0	0	1	1	0	0	1	1	0	0
1	1	0	0	1	1	1	0	1	1	1	0
1	1	1	0	1	1	1	1	1	1	1	1
1	1	1	1	0	1	1	1	0	1	1	1
0	1	1	1	0	0	1	1	0	0	1	1
0	0	1	1	0	0	0	1	0	0	0	1
0	0	0	1	0	0	0	0	0	0	0	0
0	0	0	0	1	0	0	0	1	0	0	0

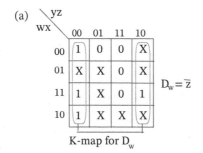

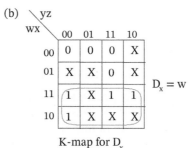

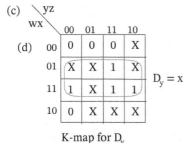

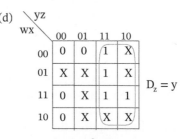

FIGURE 11.19 K-maps for the four-bit Johnson counter

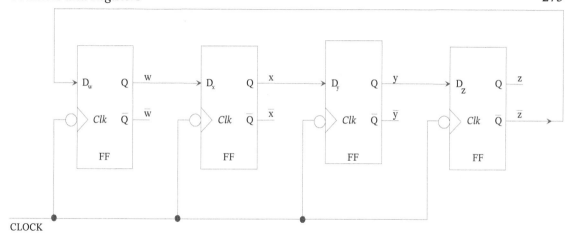

FIGURE 11.20 Schematic of the Four-bit Johnson counter

Note that the Johnson counter, shown in Figure 11.20, is very similar to a ring counter except that the inverted output $(\bar{z})$ of the last flip-flop is connected to the D_w input of the first flip-flop. The main advantage of the Johnson counter over the ring counter is that the 4-bit Johnson counter will circulate a single bit through the ring providing a sequence of eight states (Table 11.7). The four-bit ring counter, on the other hand, requires four flip-flops to generate a sequence of four states. Johnson counters can be used to divide the frequency of a clock by an integer. Since the speed of a stepper motor depends mainly on the clock frequency, Johnson counter is typically used in stepper motor control. However, explanation of this concept is beyond the scope of this book.

11.2.3 General-Purpose Register (GPR)

A general-purpose register (GPR) is designed in this section. The primary task of the GPR is to store addresses or data for an indefinite amount of time, then to be able to retrieve the data when needed.

To design a GPR, the internal organization of a basic cell, S shown in Figure 11.21(a) is used. Figure 11.21(b) shows the block diagram of the basic cell S. A 4-input multiplexer selects one of the external inputs as the D flip-flop input, and the selected input appears as the flip-flop output Q after the clock pulse. The $\overline{CLR}$ input is an asynchronous clear input, and whenever this input is asserted (held low), the flip-flop is cleared to zero. Using the basic cell S as the building block, a 4-bit GPR can be designed. Its schematic representation is shown in Figure 11.22.

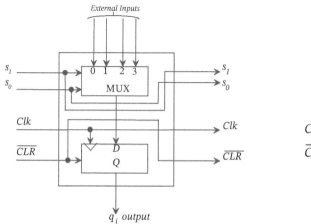

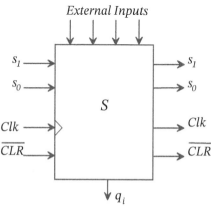

(a) Internal organization of the basic cell S (b) Block diagram of the basic cell S

FIGURE 11.21 A basic cell for designing a GPR

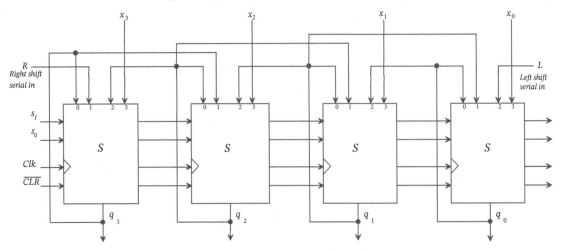

FIGURE 11.22　A 4-bit General Purpose Register

TABLE 11.8　　Truth table for the General Purpose Register

Selection Input		Clock Input	Clear Input	Operation
s_1	s_0	Clk	$\overline{CLR}$	
X	X	X	0	Clear
0	0	⤒	1	No operation
0	1	⤒	1	Shift Right
1	0	⤒	1	Shift Left
1	1	⤒	1	Parallel Load

x means "don't care"

The truth table illustrating the operation of this register is shown in Table 11.8. This table shows that when the selection inputs s_1 and s_0 =11, the external inputs x_3 through x_0 are selected as the D inputs for the flip-flops. This means that the output q_i will follow the input x_i after the clock. By choosing the correct values for the serial shift inputs R and L, right and left shifts can be achieved.

This register can be loaded with any desired data in a serial fashion. For example, after four successive right shift operations, data $a_3\,a_2\,a_1\,a_0$ will be loaded into the register if the register is set in the right shift mode and the required data $a_3\,a_2\,a_1\,a_0$ is applied serially to input R.

11.1   Design a BCD counter to count in the sequence 0000, 0001, 0010, 0011, 0100, 0101, 0110, 0111, 1000, 1001, and repeat. Use T flip-flops.

11.2   Design the following nonbinary sequence counter using JK flip-flop. Assume the unused states as don't cares. Is the counter self-correcting? Justify your answer.
Counting sequence 0, 1, 3, 4, 5, 6, 7, and repeat.

11.3   Design the following nonbinary sequence counter using D flip-flop. Assume the unused states as don't cares. Is the counter self-correcting? Justify your answer.
Counting sequence 0, 2, 3, 4, 6, 7, and repeat.

11.4   Design the following nonbinary sequence counter using T flip-flop. Assume the unused states as don't cares. Is the counter self-correcting? Justify your answer.
 Counting sequence 0, 1, 2, 4, 5, 6, 7, and repeat.

11.5   Design the following nonbinary sequence counter using T flip-flop:
Counting sequence 0, 1, 3, 5, 7, 9, and repeat.
Assume the unused states as don't cares. Is the counter self-correcting? Justify your answer. Also, draw a block diagram connecting the counter schematic to a 7447 along with a common-anode 7-segment display to display the current count and then turn ON an LED each time the odd count is displayed; Turn OFF the LED for the even count of 0. Assume that a '1' will turn the LED ON while a '0' will turn it OFF.

11.6   Design a logic diagram that will generate 19 timing signals. Use a ring counter with JK flip-flops.

11.7   Consider the two-bit Johnson counter shown in Figure P11.7. Derive the state diagram. Assume the D flip-flops are initialized to $A = 0$ and $B = 0$.

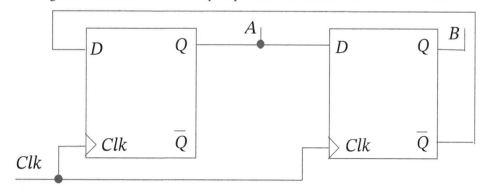

FIGURE P11.7

11.8   Assuming $AB = 10$, verify that the two-bit counter shown in Figure P11.8 is a ring counter. Derive the state diagram.

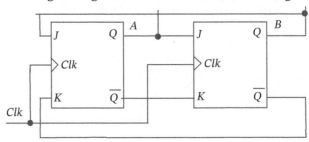

FIGURE P11. 8

11.9   Design a three-bit left shift serial in/serial out register. Show all steps.

11.10   A four-bit left shift register contains 1100. Four-bit data 0011 is waiting to be enetered on the serial data input line starting with the most significant bit. What will be the contents of the shift register after two clock pulses?

11.11   What is the basic difference between Johnson counter and ring counter.

11.12   Name an application of the ring counter and the Johnson counter.

11.13   What are the total number of states in a four-bit Johnson counter and in a four-bit ring counter?

11.14   Consider the two-bit Johnson counter shown in Figure P11.14. Derive the state table. Assume the D flip-flops are initialized to $A = 0$ and $B = 0$.

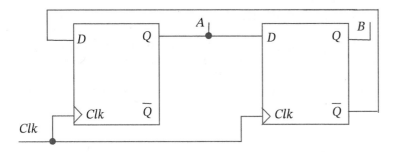

FIGURE P11.14

11.15   Assuming $AB = 10$, verify that the two-bit counter shown in Figure P11.15 is a ring counter. Derive the state table.

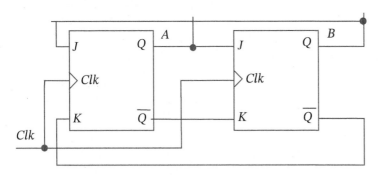

FIGURE P11.15

11.16   Design a 4-bit general-purpose register as follows:

S_1	S_0	Function
0	0	Load external data
0	1	Rotate left; ($A_0 \leftarrow A_3$, $A_i \leftarrow A_{i-1}$ for $i = 1,2,3$)
1	0	Rotate right; ($A_3 \leftarrow A_0$, $A_i \leftarrow A_{i+1}$ for $i = 0,1,2$)
1	1	Increment

Use Figure P11.16 as the building block:

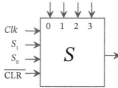

FIGURE P11. 16

12

SEQUENTIAL LOGIC DESIGN USING VERILOG

This chapter describes the basics of sequential logic design using Verilog. An introduction to Verilog for combinational logic design was covered in Chapter 8. This chapter provides a basic coverage of writing Verilog code for flip-flops and synchronous sequential circuits. Finally, several examples for describing synchronous sequential circuits using Verilog are included in Chapter 13 on FPGA-based design. Appendices C and D provide step-by-step tutorials for downloading Xilinx Vivado IDE software, and its use for compiling and simulating Verilog code for sequential logic.

12.1   Basics

An introduction to Verilog is provided in Chapter 8. Topics such as Verilog syntax, module structure, and various modeling types for creating Verilog code for combinational circuits were included. This section describes the essentials for describing sequential logic circuits and their basic components.

While it is possible to model sequential circuits using structural modeling, this approach is very limited and time consuming. Because of this, synchronous sequential circuits are typically described using behavioral modeling and the use of **always** blocks to describe how the circuit behaves. RTL (register transfer level) description is commonly used to provide a high-level behavioral abstraction to describe a circuit.

The behavior is defined in a module using the keyword **always.** A typical structure for the **always** block is provided below:

```
always @ (sensitivity list)
  <Procedural statements>
```

The **always** statement specifies certain events in the sensitivity list. Any changes in these events will initiate execution of the procedural statements that follow. The events can be either level-sensitive (combinational circuits and latches) or edge-sensitive (flip-flops).

The level-sensitive latch can be accomplished by the following statement:

```
always @ (x,enable)
  <Procedural statements>
```

As soon as a change in 'x' or 'enable' occurs, the procedural statements in the **always** block will be executed. Note that Verilog also allows separation of events 'x' or 'enable' by the keyword **or** rather than by commas. This implies that **always** @ (x,enable) and **always** @ (x **or** enable) mean the same thing. Also, note that "@ (x,enable)" specifies the procedural control.

Just like behavioral modeling for combinational logic, sequential modeling "always" blocks require a sensitivity list which triggers the execution of the procedure. The sensitivity list may be level triggered to describe latches and combinational circuits as previously shown, or event triggered. Event triggered "always" blocks are used to describe flip flops which are edge-sensitive devices. It is important to distinguish between them since using the wrong type will cause flip-flop designs to be interpreted as latches and vice versa.

Digital Logic with an Introduction to Verilog and FPGA-Based Design. First Edition. M. Rafiquzzaman and Steven A. McNinch.

Whenever the clock transitions occur from low to high (positive-edge) or high to low (negative edge), the events corresponding to Verilog keywords **posedge** and **negedge** events are triggered, which are used to describe flip-flops. They trigger the code execution at the rising edge or the falling edge of the signal respectively. The syntax for a rising-edge, also known as positive-edge triggered flip-flop is provided below:

```
always @ ( posedge <signal> )
   <procedural statements>
```

will initiate execution of the procedural statements in the **always** block for positive edge clock.

The syntax for a falling-edge, also known as negative-edge triggered Flip-flop provided below:

```
always @ ( negedge <signal> )
   <procedural statements>
```

will initiate execution of the procedural statements in the **always** block for negative edge clock.

Since a sequential circuit is comprised of flip-flops and combinational circuits, it can be represented using behavioral and dataflow modeling. Flip-flops can be described with behavioral modeling using **always** keyword while the combinational circuit part can be assigned with dataflow modeling using **assign** keyword and Boolean equations. It is important to note that the **assign** keyword can also be referred to as continuous procedural assignment. However, it should only be used outside the **always** block and be of type **wire**. Because of this, it will not be referred to as procedural.

Note that a behavioral model in Verilog is defined using the keyword **always** followed by one or several procedural statements. The final output of these statements must be of the **reg** data type rather than **wire** (normally used for structural) data type. As mentioned before, **wire** continuously updates the output while the **reg** stores the value until a new value is provided.

Next, the meaning of "procedural statement" in the previous examples will be discussed. A procedural statement is an assignment inside the context of an **always** statement. Also, Procedural statement assigns value to a register (data objects of type **reg**). There are two types of procedural assignments used within always blocks. The blocking procedural assignment (uses = as the operator), and non-blocking procedural assignment (uses <= as the operator). The right-hand side of a procedural assignment is an expression which must evaluate to a value while the left-hand side is of type **reg**. The procedural assignment can be used to retain the last output (when a digital circuit is disabled) until it is enabled again by one of the events in the sensitivity list. This is useful in modeling latches and flip-flops. The blocking procedural assignment that uses the = operator executes the statements sequentially. This means that after a blocking assignment, the next procedural assignment must wait until the present one is completed. This also means that these types of procedural statements are executed sequentially in the order they are listed in the source code. Note that the continuous assignment statements using the **assign** keyword outside an always block can only be used for level-sensitive behavior such as combinational design and latches. They cannot be used for modeling edge-triggered behavior such as flip-flops. Modeling of flip-flop circuits generally uses non-blocking procedural assignments as will be shown later.

Next, consider the following two procedural blocking assignments (uses '=' as the operator) included in the **always** block:

```
b = 0;
x = y;
```

In the above, the statement x = y is executed only after b = 0 is executed. The statements in the **always** block are executed in sequence since blocking statements are used.

In non-blocking procedural assignment, the right hand side of each expression is evaluated first using the values at the beginning of the **always** block and the new values are then updated concurrently at the end of the **always** block as soon as changes in the condition in the sensitivity list occurs. Next, consider an example of the following non-blocking assignments included in the **always** block:

```
z <= y;
a <= b;
```

In the above, variables 'z' and 'a' have certain values when the **always** block is entered. The new values of 'z' and 'a' are then calculated and assigned simultaneously at the end of the **always** block as soon as one or more conditions in the sensitivity list change.

Non-blocking assignments are used in digital design where multiple concurrent data transfers, such as in a register transfer, take place after a common event (positive- or negative-edge triggered clock). For state machines, the inputs including clock, and outputs can be declared at the beginning of a Verilog module. The states can be defined using **parameter** keyword in Verilog which defines constants in a module. Statement using **always** along with **posedge** or **negedge** can be used for the clock. Statements using **case** and **if-else** can then be used to implement various state transitions.

12.2   Examples Illustrating Non-blocking and Blocking Assignments
Several examples with non-blocking and non-blocking assignments are provided in this section.

Example 12.1

Write a Verilog description for the gated D latch of Figure 12.1 (re-drawn from Figure 9.5 (a)). Use conditional operator.

Solution

```
// Gated D latch
module dlatch(q,nq, d, clk);
   input clk, d;
   output q, nq;
   reg q, nq;
   assign q = clk ? d:q;
   assign nq = !q;
endmodule
```

Example 12.2

Write a Verilog description for a positive edge-triggered D flip-flop.

Solution

```
module DFF(Q, D, CLK)
   output reg Q;
   input D, CLK;

   always @ ( posedge CLK )
      Q <= D;
endmodule
```

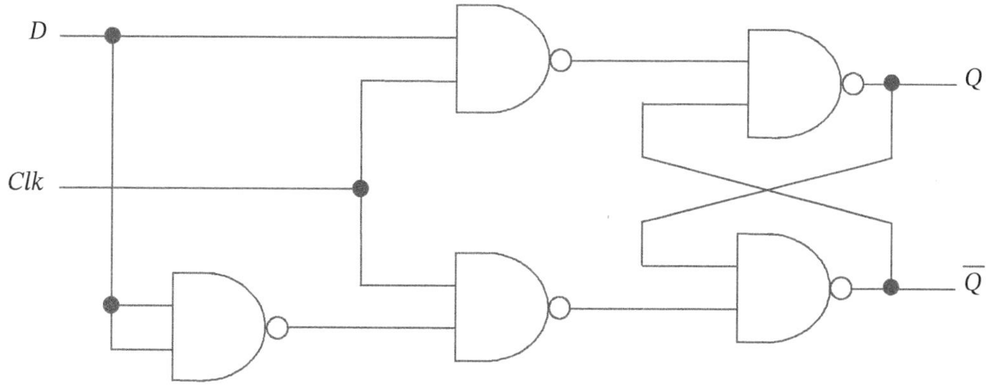

FIGURE 12.1   Gated D-latch for Example 12.1

In Example 12.2, the output Q of the flip-flop will change whenever the CLK signal changes from 0 to 1. The non-blocking assignment is used since the sensitively list is edge triggered, inferring a flip-flop. Non-blocking assignments are named as such since they do not block subsequent statements. When the triggering event occurs, all the non-blocking assignments are evaluated simultaneously at the time the event occurs.

Example 12.3

Write a Verilog description for a 4-bit register using D flip-flops.

Solution

Method 1:

```verilog
module DFF_4bit(Q, D, CLK)
   output reg [3:0] Q;
   input [3:0]D;
   input CLK;

   always @ (posedge CLK)
   begin
      Q[3] <= D[3];
      Q[2] <= D[2];
      Q[1] <= D[1];
      Q[0] <= D[0];
   end
endmodule
```

Method 2:

```verilog
module DFF_4bit(Q, D, CLK)
   output reg [3:0] Q;
   input [3:0]D;
   input CLK;

   always @ (posedge CLK)
      Q <= D;
   endmodule
```

Both methods describe the same 4-bit register. Since non-blocking assignments are used, the values of Q[3], Q[2], Q[1], and Q[0] are updated at the same time. Q[2] does not wait for Q[3] to be updated, and similarly Q[0] does not need to wait for the other three. This property of the non-blocking assignment ensures that all flip-flops and signals are kept synchronous with the clock which is used to trigger them. Note that more than one event signal may be specified in the **always** sensitivity list. For example, either

```verilog
always @  (posedge clk, negedge reset)
```
                                            or
```verilog
always @  (posedge clk or negedge reset)
```

describes the event which triggers when either the clk changes from 0 to 1 or the reset signal changes from 1 to 0. When the trigger occurs, it does not specify which of the two events caused the trigger. The logic to deduce which event caused the trigger must be done in the procedural statements.

Example 12.4

Write a Verilog description for a D flip-flop with an asynchronous active-low clear input.

Solution

```
module DFF_CLR(Q, D, CLK, CLR);
  output reg Q;
  input D, CLK, CLR;

  always @ (posedge CLK or negedge CLR)
  if(CLR == 0) //If CLR is low, then negedge CLR, reset the flipflop
      Q = 0;
  else          //If CLR is NOT low, must be a posedge CLK
      Q = D;
endmodule
```

Example 12.4 implements the clear function of the flip-flop by checking if the trigger was caused by the CLR signal or the CLK signal. If **negedge** CLR is the event, then the value of CLR must be low since **negedge** is defined as transition from high to low, and Q = 0. If CLR is not low, then the **posedge** of the CLK must have been the event to trigger the execution. Note that blocking assignments (=) are used. This is a valid design since there is only one statement executed for each of the **if-else** branches, so there is nothing to be blocked. The non-blocking assignment will also be valid in this design.

Example 12.5

Write a Verilog description for a postive edge-triggered JK flip-flop.

Solution

```
module JK_FF(Q, Qnot, J, K, CLK);
  input J, K, CLK;
  output Q, Qnot;
  reg Q;

  assign Qnot = ~Q;

  always @ (posedge CLK)
  case( {J,K} )
    2'b00 : Q <= Q;  // Hold
    2'b01 : Q <= 0;  // Reset
    2'b10 : Q <= 1;  // Set
    2'b11 : Q <= ~Q; // Toggle
  endcase
endmodule
```

In Example 12.5, only Q is defined as a **reg**. Since Qnot is just the inversion of Q, there is no need to include it in the procedural statement since the continuous assignment using **assign** will always update the value of Qnot whenever Q changes. The other way to interpret the Qnot assignment as an inverted value which has input Q and output Qnot.

The blocking assignment is normally used to describe latches using level triggered **always** blocks. While it is possible to represent flip-flops using blocking assignments and event-triggered **always** block, it is discouraged since it is not guaranteed to be translated to flip-flops by the Verilog compiler.

Blocking assignments get their name in the same way that non-blocking does. As mentioned before, blocking assignment will "block" the execution of subsequent statements until completed. The = operator defines blocking assignments when used inside an **always** construct. Consider the following blocking assignment:

```verilog
always @ ( X )
begin
  A = 0;
  B = C;
end
```

The value of A will be updated to 0, and then the value of B will be updated to the value of C. The same result would occur if the **always** block is event-triggered. This may not seem to be a problem; however, one should be careful when using blocking assignments to describe sequential logic. Examples 12.6 and 12.7 show how the same circuits shown in the previous examples can be modeled with blocking assignments instead of non-blocking.

Example 12.6

Write a Verilog description for D flip-flop with a low clear input using blocking assignments.

Solution

```verilog
module DFF_blocking(Q, Qnot, D, CLK, CLR);
  output Q, Qnot;
  input D, CLK, CLR;
  reg Q;  // Q needs to be a reg since it used in procedural block

  assign Qnot = ~Q;

  always @ (posedge CLK or negedge CLR)
    if(CLR == 0) //If CLR is low, then reset the flipflop
      begin
        Q = 0;
      end
    else           //If CLR is NOT low, must be a posedge clk
      begin
        Q = D;
      end
endmodule
```

Example 12.7

Write a Verilog description for JK Flip flop using blocking assignments.

Solution

```verilog
module JK_FF(Q, Qnot, J, K, CLK);
  input J, K, CLK;
  output Q, Qnot;
  reg Q;

  assign Qnot = ~Q;

  always @ (posedge CLK)
    case( { J, K} )
    2'b00 : Q = Q;   // Hold
    2'b01 : Q = 0;   // Reset
    2'b10 : Q = 1;   // Set
    2'b11 : Q = ~Q;  // Toggle
    endcase
endmodule
```

Examples 12.6 and 12.7 show how the blocking assignments can be used instead of non-blocking without any consequences. However, if the design contains connections among multiple flip-flops, non-blocking assignments are better suited for the design. Examples 12.8 and 12.9 show how the Verilog code is interpreted by the use of blocking assignments vs. non-blocking assignments.

Example 12.8

Write a Verilog description for a three-bit left shift register using non-blocking assignment. Use positive-edge triggered flip-flops.

Solution

```
module shiftreg_3bit_nonblock(Q, X, CLK)
   output reg [0:2] Q;
   input X, CLK;

   always @ (posedge CLK)
   begin
     Q[0] <= X;
     Q[1] <= Q[0];
     Q[2]<= Q[1];
   end
endmodule
```

In the shift register of Example 12.8, the simultaneous evaluation behavior is used to describe all three flip-flops. At the positive edge of the clock, all three statements are executed using the values at the time of the posedge event. For example, if the content of Q before the CLK event is 3'b010 and X = 1'b1, Q[2] gets the value from Q[1] which is '1', Q[1] gets the value from Q[0] which is '0' and Q[0] gets the value of X which is '1'. The resulting hardware shifts each bit at the edge of the clock. This is an important distinction between non-blocking and blocking assignments since blocking will result in a different hardware interpretation as shown in Example 12.9.

Example 12.9

Repeat Example 12.8 using blocking assignment.

Solution

```
module shiftreg_3bit_blocking(Q, X, CLK)
   output reg [0:2] Q;
   input X, CLK;

   always @ (posedge CLK)
   begin
     Q[0] = X;
     Q[1] = Q[0];
     Q[2] = Q[1];
   end
endmodule
```

Example 12.10

Perform simulations for Examples 12.8 and 12.9, compare the simulation results, and obtain the hardware for both non-blocking and blocking assignments.
Solution

Simulation results for both non-blocking and blocking assignments are shown in Figure 12.2.

The simulation results shown in Figure 12.2 compare the function of the non-blocking design with the blocking design when shifting 3'b101 once to the left. Instead of creating a shift register, the blocking assignment code synthesizes the design into a three-bit parallel register. At each rising edge of the clock, the blocking design loads the value of X into all three registers, instead of shifting the value. Blocking assignment, which uses the = operator, execute each statement sequentially. Because of this, the value of Q[0] gets updated to X, and then Q[1] gets updated with the new value of Q[0], which is also now X. The same goes for Q[2], which also gets the value of X. Thus, a single register is loaded with the same data. Figures 12.3 and 12.4 show the difference between non-blocking and blocking synthesis results.

Name	Value	0 ns	1 ns	2 ns	3 ns	4 ns	5 ns	6 ns
X	1							
CLK	0							
Q_nonblocking[0:2]	000	000	100		010		101	
[0]	0							
[1]	0							
[2]	0							
Q_blocking[0:2]	000	000	111		000		111	
[0]	0							
[1]	0							
[2]	0							

FIGURE 12.2   Non-blocking vs. blocking simulation results

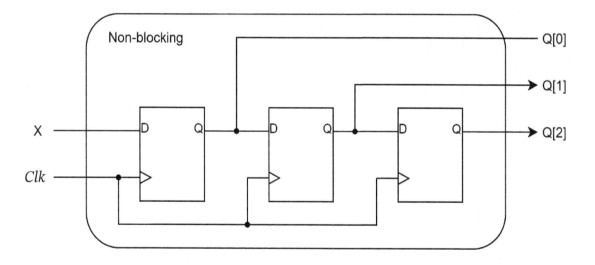

FIGURE 12.3   Non-blocking synthesis result (shift register)

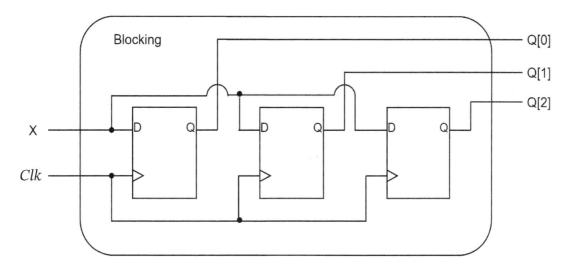

FIGURE 12.4 Blocking synthesis result (parallel register)

12.3   RTL (Register Transfer Level) modeling

RTL is an acronym for "Register Transfer Level". It is mainly used for modeling synchronous sequential circuits in terms of data flow from one register to another, and the logical operations performed on those signals. RTL can be used by HDL such as Verilog to describe how data is transformed from one register to another register. Data transfer is performed by the combinational logic connecting the registers.

Three levels of design levels namely, systems level, logic level, and device level are discussed in Chapter 1. Systems level will be re-named as RTL design in this discussion. As mentioned before, the CPU consists of registers, ALU, and the control unit. In a CPU, data is typically transferred from registers via the datapath units such as the ALU (combinational logic) to registers again. RTL is normally used for this type of register transfer. Modern CAD tools allow the designers to produce RTL-based system-level design in a very short period of time.

RTL is used in HDLs such as Verilog to obtain a high-level representation of a circuit. Lower-level representation of the circuit, and eventually, actual wiring can also be obtained. RTL design is typically used in modern digital design for synchronous sequential circuits. Note that a synchronous sequential circuit consists of registers implemented using flip-flops, and combinational logic. Registers synchronize the circuits operation at the rising or falling edges of the clock while the combinational logic consisting of logic gates that performs all logic operations. When RTL is used for designing a synchronous sequential circuit, the designer declares the registers, and describes combinational logic by using **if-else** and **case** constructs.

RTL description is normally converted to a gate-level description of the circuit by a synthesis tool. The synthesis can then be used by placement and routing tools to create a physical layout.

Modeling using non-blocking assignments are commonly referred to as Register transfer level (RTL) modeling because they can be used to describe how data is transferred between registers. The general RTL syntax is:

$$A \leftarrow B$$

where data from register B is transferred to register A. The $\leftarrow$ symbol is referred to as the transfer operator, and this is equivalent to using the non-blocking operator $<=$ in Verilog. Non-blocking assignment is used since any number of flip-flops can be described without needing to worry about the interactions as shown in the shift register Examples 12.9 and 12.10 where all values are calculated simultaneously (Example 12.10) rather than statement-by-statement (Example 12.9).

The theory behind RTL is to describe register behavior based on when and how the data in registers change. Behavioral modeling is used for RTL since **if-else** and **case** statements allow for high-level abstraction of how the register is intended to function. Note that **if-else** or **case** will be used for combinational parts of the circuit while the non-blocking operator $<=$ is used for sequential elements. Also, register values may need to come from a variety of sources and have some combinational logic performed in order to calculate the final value to be stored. While this can be done using other types of modeling, behavioral modeling is substantially more efficient in doing so due to the availability of **if-else**, **case**, and non-blocking constructs.

Sometimes a register will have a multiplexer connected to its input so that it can store a number from more than one source. For example, consider a simple schematic of Figure 12.5 which keeps a running sum of the input data. Figure 12.5 shows the register SUM (Sequential logic) along with a multiplexer (Combinational logic). Note that the register SUM keeps a running sum of the input data. If the enable signal is high, then the value of X is added to the current value in register SUM.

The schematic can be modeled using RTL and Verilog for the SUM register as follows:

```
if(clear)
   SUM <= 0;
else if(enable)
        SUM <= SUM + X;
     else
        SUM <= SUM;
```

At a basic level, RTL describes how data gets transferred to registers. This is useful for counters, finite state machines, or any other designs which use registers to store data. As another example, an up-down counter with load can be modeled with RTL using Verilog in only a few lines as follows:

```
case(operation)
0 : count <= count;       // Hold Operation
1 : count <= count + 1;   // Increment Operation
2 : count <= count - 1;   // Decrement Operation
3 : count <= load;        // Load external value
endcase
```

The above RTL generates the design of Figure 12.6.

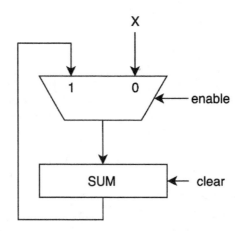

FIGURE 12.5   Register SUM along with a multiplexer to keep track of the running total

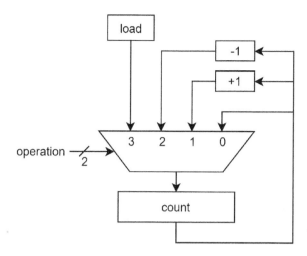

FIGURE 12.6   Up-down counter

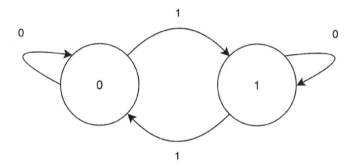

FIGURE 12.7   State diagram for Example 12.11

Example 12.11

Write the Verilog description of a parity checker. Use RTL modeling.

Solution

Figure 12.7 shows the state diagram of the parity checker. Note that the parity checker counts the number of 1's in a string of bits, and determines whether the total number of 1's is even (even parity with 0 being even), or odd (odd parity). For example, consider a 4-bit number 0111 whose parity needs to be determined by the parity checker. Assume that data 0111 is entered into the parity checker with the least significant bit first. Data is entered into the parity checker one bit at a time at the clock. The parity of 0111 is odd since there are odd number of 1's (three 1's in 0111) in 0111. Next, consider the state diagram of Figure 12.7 to verify this. The state diagram has two states state 0 for even parity and state 1 for odd parity.

Let us assume that the parity checker is initially in state 0 after clearing or resetting the flip-flop to 0. Note that '0' is considered even. Since the first bit (least significant bit) entered is a '1' (odd parity), the parity checker moves from state 0 to state 1. The next bit (bit 1) entered is a '1', the parity checker moves from state 1 to state 0 (even parity with two 1's). Bit 2 with a '1' is entered next. The count will be three 1's (odd parity). Hence, the parity checker moves from state 0 to state 1. Finally, bit 3 with a '0' is entered next. The count will still be three 1's (odd parity). The parity checker stays in state 1 indicating odd parity. The parity checker can be represented by a T flip-flop whose output is the output of the parity checker, and the data entered at the T input of the flip-flop bit-by-bit at the clock. The flip-flop output will toggle if the input is a '1' while the output will remain the same if the input is a '0'. The flip-flop output will eventually indicate even parity if '0', and odd parity if '1'.

Verilog code for the parity checker is provided in the following:

```verilog
module parity_checker(clk, X, reset, parity);
  input clk, X, reset;
  output reg parity = 0;

  always @ (posedge clk or posedge reset)
  if(reset)
    parity <= 0;
  else
    case(parity)
    0 : if(X) parity <= 1;
        else parity <= 0;
    1 : if(X) parity <= 0;
        else parity <= 1;
    endcase
endmodule
```

The parity checker module in Example 12.11 uses RTL to describe the T Flip-flop hardware. The reset signal is asynchronous, therefore the **always** block needs to be sensitive to both the positive edge of the clock and the positive edge of the reset signal. The procedural statement "**if** (reset)" checks if the reset signal caused the procedural execution. If the reset signal is high, then the parity state is reset to zero. If reset is not high, then posedge of the clk must have triggered the execution. The **case** statement checks for the value of the X input to determine the next state of the parity checker. If the parity is currently 0 and the input X is 1, then the parity needs to be changed to 1. If X is 0, then the parity should remain at 0. If the current parity is 1, the parity state will change back to 0 if the X input is also 1 since an even number of 1's would be even parity represented by 0. If the input were 0, then the parity would remain the same. Essentially, the parity state toggles if input X is equal to 1 since the parity would be changing from even to odd or vice versa.

Simulation of sequential Verilog circuits often requires additional elements to the test bench compared to those for combinational circuits. In most cases, it is beneficial to have a free running clock that toggles at a set period rather than manually specifying the clock state in the same initial block as the rest of the inputs. Example 12.12 shows how to simulate the parity checker of Example 12.11 without using a free running clock.

Example 12.12

Write a test bench for the parity checker of Example 12.11, without using a free running clock, and then run the simulation. Note that a free running clock means the on-board clock upon power-up.

Solution

Verilog test bench without using a free running clock:

```verilog
module parity_checker_sim();
reg clk,reset,X;
wire P;

//Define 8bit serial strings to test
 parameter [7:0] string_odd = 8'b1110_1100;
 parameter [7:0] string_even = 8'b1010_1100;

parity_checker dut(clk,X,reset,P);

initial begin
clk = 0; reset = 0; X = string_odd[0];
  #1 clk = 1;
```

```
    #1 clk = 0; reset = 0; X = string_odd[1];
    #1 clk = 1;
    #1 clk = 0; reset = 0; X = string_odd[2];
    #1 clk = 1;
    #1 clk = 0; reset = 0; X = string_odd[3];
    #1 clk = 1;
    #1 clk = 0; reset = 0; X = string_odd[4];
    #1 clk = 1;
    #1 clk = 0; reset = 0; X = string_odd[5];
    #1 clk = 1;
    #1 clk = 0; reset = 0; X = string_odd[6];
    #1 clk = 1;
    #1 clk = 0; reset = 0; X = string_odd[7];
    #1 clk = 1;
    #1 clk = 0; reset = 0;
    #1 clk = 0; reset = 1;
    #1 clk = 0; reset = 0; X = string_even[0];
    #1 clk = 1;
    #1 clk = 0; reset = 0; X = string_even[1];
    #1 clk = 1;
    #1 clk = 0; reset = 0; X = string_even[2];
    #1 clk = 1;
    #1 clk = 0; reset = 0; X = string_even[3];
    #1 clk = 1;
    #1 clk = 0; reset = 0; X = string_even[4];
    #1 clk = 1;
    #1 clk = 0; reset = 0; X = string_even[5];
    #1 clk = 1;
    #1 clk = 0; reset = 0; X = string_even[6];
    #1 clk = 1;
    #1 clk = 0; reset = 0; X = string_even[7];
    #1 clk = 1;
    #1 clk = 0;
    #1 $finish;
  end
endmodule
```

Figure 12.8 shows the simulation waveform using a manual clock for Example 12.12. In the test bench and simulation from Example 12.12, the clock is toggled in the same initial block used to create the input conditions. Two parameters string_odd and string_even are used to create strings representing binary 0's and 1's, with odd and even parity, respectively. The test bench shifts though the strings, and toggles to clock to represent the string being shifted into the parity checker. At time 16ns, the parity of the oddstring can be read and shows that the parity is 1, as expected since the string contains an odd number of 1's. After this, the FSM (Finite State Machine) is reset by toggling the reset signal, and then the even parity string is shifted in. The parity of the even string is finished calculating at time= 35ns, which is 0 as expected for an even parity value.

While manually toggling the clock is a valid approach, it can become long and tedious for complex designs. A more practical approach is to define a clock using a **forever** statement which creates an infinite loop. A **forever** loop initiates continuous execution of one or more procedural statements during simulation. For example, consider the following:

```
initial begin
clk = 0;
forever #0.5 clk = ~clk;
end
```

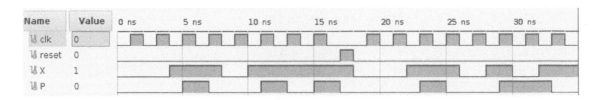

FIGURE 12.8   Simulation results for Example 12.12 without using a free running clock

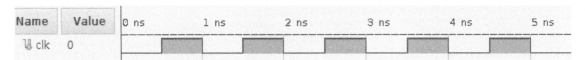

FIGURE 12.9   Clock generated using a forever loop

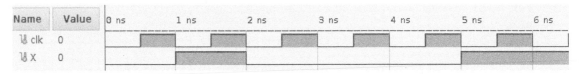

FIGURE 12.10   Clock and input timing relationship using the $\#(n + 0.5)$ technique.

The initial block above creates a clock that being at 0 and toggles with a period of one delay unit (#1). The clock will have a rising edge at #0.5, #1.5, #2.5, etc, or more generically, at $\#(n + 0.5)$, where n is a positive integer. Figure 12.9 shows the clock generated by the forever loop.

Since the clock toggles from low to high at $\#(n + 0.5)$, all inputs can be set at integer multiples of #1 for positive-edge triggered designs since the clock will always rise #0.5 after that. For example, the following initial block can be used with the previous forever statement to provide input stimuli for a positive-edge triggered design:

```
initial begin
     X = 0;
  #1 X = 1;
  #1 X = 0;
  #3 X = 1;
end
```

Using integer values for the delays ensures that the inputs change before and remain constant until after the rising edge of the clock, simulating sufficient setup and hold times for the flip-flops in the design. This also avoids any potential pitfalls during simulation with signals changing at the exact same time as the clock. Figure 12.10 shows the relationship between the inputs and the clock edges.

Example 12.13

Design a vending machine, shown Figure 12.11, that dispenses items that cost $1. The machine accepts nickels, dimes, and quarters, and has inputs for vend and cancel. Outputs are the total amount inserted, an output for dispensing items, and an output to return change. Assume only one input will be high at a time. Use RTL modeling.

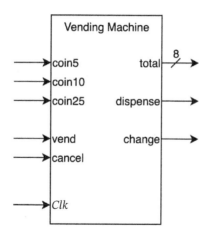

FIGURE 12.11 Figure for Example 12.13

Solution

The vending machine shown in Figure 12.11 can be modeled using synchronous RTL to describe the function of the total, dispense, and change outputs. At the positive edge of the clock, if one of the coin inputs are set to high, the value of that coin should be added to the value of total. If the vend input is set to 1 and the total amount is greater than 100 (representing $1), the dispense output will toggle high to control a dispensing mechanism in the machine, while subtracting 100 from the sum amount. If the cancel input is set to 1, the change output will be set to 1 to control a coin return. Since the design is being modeled in using RTL, no state register needs to be explicitly described as it is handled by the RTL description.

Verilog description is provided below:

```verilog
module vending_machine(clk, coin5, coin10, coin25, vend, cancel, total,
dispense, change);
input clk, coin5, coin10, coin25, vend, cancel;
output reg [7:0]total = 0;
output reg dispense = 0, change = 0;

always @ (posedge clk)
begin
    // default conditions for change and dispense.
    change <= 0; dispense <= 0;
if(cancel)
begin
change <= 1;
total <= 0;
end
else  if(coin5)
total <= total + 5;
    else if(coin10)
    total <= total + 10;
else if(coin25)
    total <= total + 25;
        else if(vend && total >= 100)
            begin
        total <= total - 100;
```

```
        dispense <= 1;
            end
    else
        total <= total;
end
endmodule
```

All registers in the vending machine are rising edge-triggered. At the beginning of the **always** block, both change and dispense are both set to 0. This is valid because everything is modeled using non-blocking assignments, so the value will not change until the entire procedural block has been run. Using this technique, the default value will only be applied if and only if no other statements change the value. The signal with the highest priority is the cancel input, represented by it being the first **if** statement. If the value of cancel is 1, the change output is set to 1. Since the rest of the procedural statements are gated by the else condition, no other statements will be executed. The coin inputs are analyzed using **else-if**. This is valid approach since only one coin can be inserted at a time; hence, only one of the inputs will be 1 at a time.

The last input to check is the vend input, which controls the dispense output. If vend $== 1$ and total $>= 100$, then the total amount should be decreased by 100 and the dispense output should be set to 1. If no inputs are set to 1, then the value of total remains as total, and the dispense and change outputs are also 0.

Simulation

```
module vending_machine_sim();
reg clk = 0, coin5, coin10, coin25 , vend, cancel;
wire [7:0] total;
wire dispense, change;

vending_machine dut(clk, coin5, coin10, coin25, vend, cancel, total,
dispense, change);

initial forever # 0.5 clk = ~clk;

initial begin
  {coin5, coin10, coin25, vend, cancel} = 5'b00000;  #1 // Initial state
  {coin5, coin10, coin25, vend, cancel} = 5'b10000;  #1 // Insert Nickel
  {coin5, coin10, coin25, vend, cancel} = 5'b01000;  #1 // Insert Dime
  {coin5, coin10, coin25, vend, cancel} = 5'b00100;  #1 // Insert
  // Quarter
  {coin5, coin10, coin25, vend, cancel} = 5'b00000;  #1 // Wait
  {coin5, coin10, coin25, vend, cancel} = 5'b00010;  #1 // Try to vend
  // Insert three Quarters
  {coin5, coin10, coin25, vend, cancel} = 5'b00100;  #3
  {coin5, coin10, coin25, vend, cancel} = 5'b00000;  #2 // Wait
  {coin5, coin10, coin25, vend, cancel} = 5'b00010;  #1 // Vend
  {coin5, coin10, coin25, vend, cancel} = 5'b00000;  #2 // Wait
  {coin5, coin10, coin25, vend, cancel} = 5'b00001;  #1 // Change
  {coin5, coin10, coin25, vend, cancel} = 5'b00000;
end
endmodule
```

Figure 12.12 shows the simulation results for Example 12.13. The test bench for the vending machine simulates coins various coin values being inserted which increased the value of total. The vend operation (both before the total is greater than 100 and after) and the change return operation are also simulated and verified. The total output is shown as decimal radix instead of binary or hexadecimal, which can be changed in the simulation options that can be used to increase the simulation readability.

RTL is used in Example 12.13 to describe the function of the total, change, and dispense registers simultaneously. Register transfer level allows for modeling of all the input logic, register behavior, and output logic to be condensed to a handful of **if-else** clauses which handle all the possible states of the design.

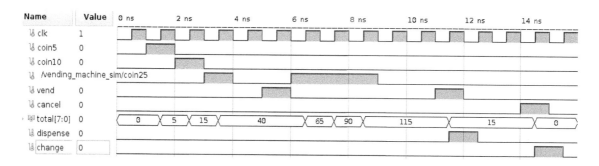

FIGURE 12.12 Simulation waveform for Example 12.13

QUESTIONS AND PROBLEMS

12.1   What is the difference between combinational **always** statements and sequential **always** statements?

12.2   Write the always block statement for a T flip-flop with a positive-edge triggered clock and with active-high clear.

12.3   Write the Verilog module for a D-flip-flop with an active-low preset. When preset goes low, it changes the value of the Flip-flop to '1'.

12.4   Write the Verilog description of a 4-bit register with asynchronous clear input.

12.5   Write the Verilog description for a D flip-flop with a positive-edge triggered clock with active-low clear and active-low preset. Give the clear function priority over preset.

12.6   Write the Verilog description of a 4-bit counter with synchronous clear input.

12.7   Create a 4-bit left-shift register that shifts in the value of input X at the positive edge of the clock.

12.8   Write the Verilog description of an 8-bit right shift register that shifts data at the positive edge of the clock with asynchronous negative-edge triggered reset.

12.9   Create a test bench and simulate the 4-bit shift register from Problem #7.

12.10   Write the Verilog description for the 4-bit ripple counter shown in Figure P12.10. Include an asynchronous clear input.

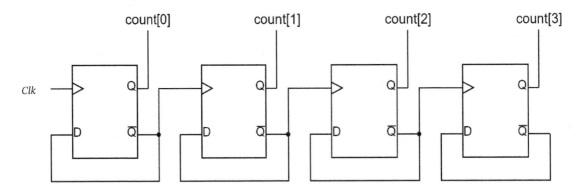

FIGURE P12.10

12.11   Create and simulate the ripple counter from Figure P12.10. Ensure that the clear input functions as intended.

12.12   Implement the finite state machine shown in Figure P12.12. Output Z is equal to '1' when in state D. Note: Output Z should not be in the procedural statements since it is a Moore state machine.

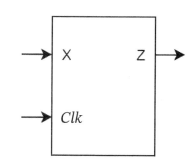

(a) Block diagram

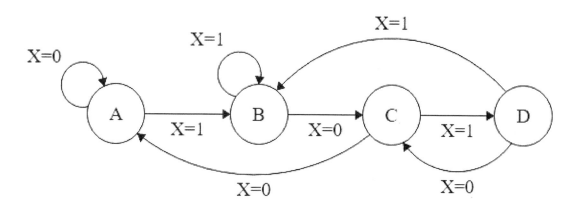

(b) State diagram

FIGURE P12.12

12.13   Implement the Mealy version of the finite state machine shown in Figure P12.13.

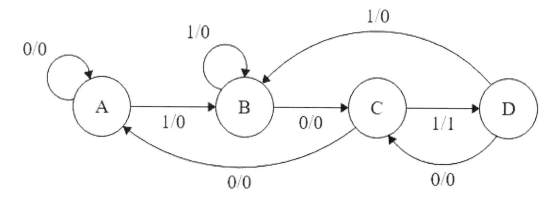

FIGURE P12.13

12.14   Design a BCD counter that counts 0 through 9, and then repeats. Include a reset input. Simulate and verify the design.

12.15 Expand the design from P12.13 and design a 2-digit BCD counter able to count to a value of 99 BCD. Create a test bench and simulate the design.

13

IMPLEMENTATION OF DIGITAL DESIGN USING FPGA

This chapter describes the basics of Verilog-based digital design using FPGA (Field programmable Gate Array) in a simplified manner. An introduction to FPGA is provided in Chapter 7. Designers have the option of implementing digital circuits in various types of Integrated Circuits (ICs). Typical IC chips include full-custom, semi-custom, CPLDs, and FPGAs. Because of the popularity of FPGAs, a simplified explanation of a typical FPGA's internal architecture is covered. Furthermore, typical steps for implementing an FPGA-based design using CAD tools are provided. Finally, several successfully-implemented examples on FPGA-based design are also included.

13.1   Basics of FPGA

In the past, industries developed products for specific applications. It was difficult for the users to redesign these products according to their requirements. This led to the introduction of a flexible IC chip called the FPGA. An FPGA-based design would mean that it can be programmed and re-configured according to the user's specification. In contrast, ASIC (Application Specific Integrated Circuit) chips are custom-designed   for specific applications at higher frequencies. Although FPGA-based products were slower in the past, FPGAs can now run at a speed in the range of 500 MHz.

Note that FPGAs do not contain any CPU to execute programs. The end user is responsible for designing the circuit. An FPGA can be configured as a simple combinational circuit containing logic gates to a more complex circuit containing logic gates and flip-flops (sequential circuit). In order to develop an FPGA-based design, code can be written using either Verilog or VHDL. The compiled code can then be synthesized to program the FPGA.

The concept of FPGA is based on the fact that a truth table which describes a combinational logic circuit can be stored in memory as a table called the Look-Up Table (LUT). Flip-flops are needed to implement a sequential circuit. Hence, an FPGA contains three main blocks namely, Look-Up Tables (LUTs), flip-flops, and switch matrices (programmable interconnects). These switch matrices connect various LUTs and flip-flops to obtain a very flexible design which can be modified and reprogrammed in a very short period of time. This topic will be covered in more detail the next section.

Altera and Xilinx are two leading manufacturers of FPGA chips. Altera, founded in 1981, introduced the first EPROM-based reprogrammable logic device in 1984. Altera became a leading manufacturer of FPGA later on. Note that Intel acquired Altera in 2015. Xilinx invented the first commercially available FPGA in 1985. With the rapid growth of the FPGA applications primarily in telecommunications and networking, FPGAs were eventually used in consumer, automative, and industrial applications during the early 2000's. FPGAs are widely used these for simulating a design. This means that designers can develop prototype hardware on FPGAs first, and then manufacture the final product on the ICs in a very short period of time.

In the past, FPGAs were slower, less energy efficient, and achieved less functionality than ASIC (Application Specific Integrated Circuit). An ASIC is a custom chip designed for a specific application. Also in the past, an FPGA chip required 40 times as much area, consumed 12 times as much power, and ran at one third the speed of a comparable ASIC chip. At present, FPGAs consume significantly reduced power usage, increased speed, lower material cost, minimal real estate, and very flexible re-programmable features. One of the main advantages of FPGAs over ASICs is that FPGAs are field-programmable while ASIC designs are fixed. Also, FPGAs can be programmed basically anywhere in minutes while ASICs will require weeks to fabricate a new design in a lab.

Next, the features of CPLDs will be compared with FPGAs. The main difference between CPLD and FPGA is architectural. A CPLD has a comparatively limited structure consisting of one or more sum-of-products logic arrays outputting into a relatively small number of registers. Hence, CPLDs are less flexible. FPGAs, on the other hand, have the far more flexibility of interconnecting various digital blocks. CPLDs are typically used in smaller applications while FPGAs are used in larger applications. Both CPLDs and FPGAs may be used in a single application. In such a system, CPLDs usually perform "glue logic" functions including booting the FPGA and controlling the reset and boot sequence of the complete circuit board. Note that glue logic is a special form of digital circuitry that allows different types of logic circuits to work together by acting as an interface between them.

An FPGA chip contains several same-sized smaller LUTs and programmable routing matrices (Switch matrices or Programmable interconnects) to implement combinational circuits. Note that the programmable routing matrices can be programmed to connect various LUTs. In addition, an FPGA chip also contains flip-flops to implement sequential circuits. These elements work together to create a very flexible device such as the FPGA.

13.1.1 LUTs (Look-Up Tables)

A LUT typically contains several inputs and one or more outputs based on the truth table. A memory such as a SRAM (Static RAM) can be used to store a LUT. Note that a memory consists of addresses and their contents. The content of a memory (word) is identified by an address. The inputs in the truth table are the addresses of the LUT while the output(s) of the truth table are the contents.

A 4x1 SRAM can be used to store the truth table of any two-input logic gate such as OR, AND, and XOR. For example, the truth table for an OR gate shown in Table 13.1 can be stored in a 4x1 memory as shown in Figure 13.1. The 'a' and 'b' inputs of the truth table can be connected to A1 and A0 address inputs of the SRAM . The one-bit outputs of the truth table can be programmed at the corresponding addresses of the SRAM. The content of a specific address can be outputted to the output SRAM (Dout) by connecting R/$\overline{\text{W}}$ to +5V. For example, when ab = 10, then Dout will be 1. Thus, the OR gate truth table can be implemented in a SRAM.

TABLE 13.1   An OR gate truth table

	Address in SRAM	
Inputs		Output
a	b	c
0	0	0
0	1	1
1	0	1
1	1	1

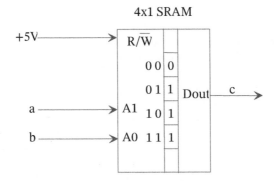

FIGURE 13.1   A 4x1 SRAM containing the OR gate truth table of Table 13.1

TABLE 13.2   Truth table for F2, F1, F0

Address in SRAM				
Inputs		Outputs		
a	b	F2	F1	F0
0	0	0	0	0
0	1	0	1	0
1	0	0	1	1
1	1	1	1	0

4x3 SRAM

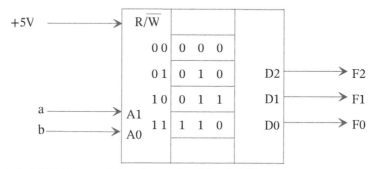

FIGURE 13.2   A 4x3 SRAM containing the truth table of Table 13.2

Next, consider three Boolean functions provided below:

$$F2 = ab, F1 = a + b, F0 = a\bar{b}$$

Table 13.2 depicts the truth table with two inputs (a, b) and three outputs (F2, F1, F0).

A 4x3 SRAM shown in Figure 13.2 can be used to implement the truth table of Table 13.2. In Figure 13.2, when address inputs ab = 11, then the outputs F2F1F0 = 110. Note that in both Figure 13.1 and Figure 13.2, address inputs to the SRAM are inputs of the truth table while output(s) of the SRAM are the output(s) of the truth table. These examples imply that a combinational logic circuit can be implemented in memory using a table called the Look-Up Table (LUT) in memory. The addresses to the LUT are inputs of the truth table while the contents of the LUT are outputs of the truth table. Note that LUTs are specified by the number of address input bits and the number of output bits rather than the memory size. Also, an "m-input n-output LUT" is called an "m x n LUT". For example, a "3-input 2-output LUT" will be called "3x2 LUT".

As the number of inputs in the truth table increases, the size of the LUT becomes large. For example, 16 inputs in a truth table will need 65,536 (2^{16}) bytes in memory while 20 inputs in a truth table will require one megabyte (2^{20}) of memory. Hence, it is impractical to implement a Boolean function with a large number of inputs using a single LUT. Therefore, a large LUT is divided into several small-sized LUTs such as two-input one-output LUT and three-input one-output LUT to represent a Boolean function in an efficient manner.

For example, a single truth table with five inputs must be subdivided into smaller LUTs. Note that subdividing a single LUT into smaller LUTs in the FPGA is handled by the CAD tools. The smaller-sized LUTs can be used to implement a truth table with numerous inputs and multiple outputs.

Next, consider implementing the Boolean function, v = wx + yz using 2x1 LUTs. Figure 13.3 shows the schematic for 'v' using AND/OR. Figure 13.4, on the other hand, shows the block diagram using 2x1 LUT's. The implementation using 2x1 LUTs of Figure 13.3 will require 12 ($2^2 + 2^2 + 2^2$) one-bit words using 2x1 LUTs. On the other hand, using a single LUT (with 4 inputs w, x, y, z), implementation will require 16 (2^4) one-bit words which is higher than using three 2x1 LUTs. With numerous inputs, large memory savings can be obtained using small-sized LUTs. Table 13.3 shows the truth table for u1, u2, and v.

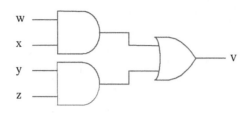

FIGURE 13.3   Schematic for 'v' using AND/OR

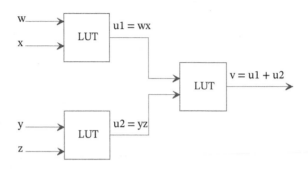

FIGURE 13.4   Block diagram for a partitioned to be represented by 2x1 LUTs

TABLE 13.3   Truth tables for u1, u2, and v

Truth table for u1 or u2				Truth table for $v = u1 + u2$		
Inputs		Output		Inputs		Output
w	x	u1 or u2		u1	u2	v
0	0	0		0	0	0
0	1	0		0	1	1
1	0	0		1	0	1
1	1	1		1	1	1

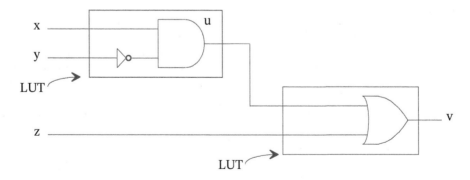

FIGURE 13.5   Schematic for 'v'

If the inputs of the original (single) truth table are not even multiples of the inputs of the smaller LUTs, then the schematic for the Boolean function(s) must be partitioned so that smaller sized LUTs can be used. For example, consider implementing the Boolean function, $v = x\overline{y} + z$ using 2x1 LUT's. In this case, three inputs (x,y,z) are not even multiples of two inputs of the 2x1 LUT. Hence, partitioning of the schematic for 'v' is done in such a way that 2x1 LUTs can be used. Figure 13.5 shows how the schematic for 'v' can be partitioned. Table 13.4 shows the truth table for 'v' before partitioning. Table 13.5 (a) and Table 13.5 (b) show the truth tables after partitioning. Figure 13.6 shows how the schematic is represented using two 2x1 LUT's. Note that this challenging task of converting a circuit to subcircuits is performed by the CAD tools.

It will be shown that the truth table for 'v' of Table 13.4 is equivalent to two partitioned truth tables of Table 13.5 (a) and Table 13.5 (b). For example, from Table 13.4, the output $v = 1$ for inputs $x\bar{y} = 1$ or $z = 1$. From Table 13.5 (a), $u = 1$ for $x = 1$ and $y = 0$. Finally, from Table 13.5 (b), $v = 1$ for $u = x\bar{y} = 1$ or $z = 1$. Hence, the 3x1 truth table of Figure 13.4 is equivalent to two same-sized (2x1) smaller truth tables. This concept is used by the CAD tools for mapping a large truth table into smaller-sized truth tables in an FPGA.

TABLE 13.4   Truth table for v

Inputs			Output
x	y	z	$v = x\bar{y} + z$
0	0	0	0
0	0	1	1
0	1	0	0
0	1	1	1
1	0	0	1
1	0	1	1
1	1	0	0
1	1	1	1

TABLE 13.5   Truth table after partitioning the schematic for 'v'

(a) Truth table for u

Inputs		Output
x	y	$u = x\bar{y}$
0	0	0
0	1	0
1	0	1
1	1	0

(b) Truth table for v

Inputs		Output
u	z	$v = u + z$
0	0	0
0	1	1
1	0	1
1	1	1

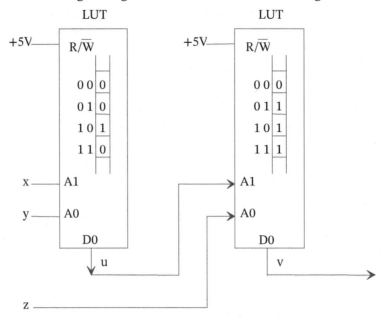

FIGURE 13.6   Implementing 'v' using two 2x1 LUT's

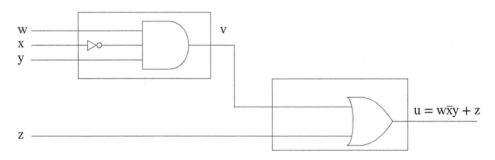

FIGURE 13.7   Schematic for 'u' along with partitioning

Note that commercial FPGAs contain thousands of LUTs, numerous I/O (Input/Output), and other pins namely power, ground, programming, and clock pins. As an example, Xilinx Spartan 6 (XC756 device) is an FPGA-based board containing 100 I/O pins and provides support for both hardware and software. Next, consider implementing u = w̄xy + z in an FPGA. Figure 13.7 shows the schematic. Table 13.6 (a), Table 13.6 (b), and Table 13.6 (c) show the truth tables for the output 'u' before and after partitioning along with partitioned output 'v'.

TABLE 13.6   Truth tables for 'u' and 'v' before and after partitioning

Inputs				Output
w	x	y	z	u
0	0	0	0	0
0	0	0	1	1
0	0	1	0	0
0	0	1	1	1
0	1	0	0	0
0	1	0	1	1
0	1	1	0	0
0	1	1	1	1
1	0	0	0	0
1	0	0	1	1
1	0	1	0	1
1	0	1	1	1
1	1	0	0	0
1	1	0	1	1
1	1	1	0	0
1	1	1	1	1

(a) Truth table for 'u' before partitioning

Inputs			Output
w	x	y	$v = w\bar{x}y$
0	0	0	0
0	0	1	0
0	1	0	0
0	1	1	0
1	0	0	0
1	0	1	1
1	1	0	0
1	1	1	0

(b) Truth table for 'v' after partitioning

Inputs		Output
v	z	$u = v + z$
0	0	0
0	1	1
1	0	1
1	1	1

(c) Truth table for 'u' after partitioning

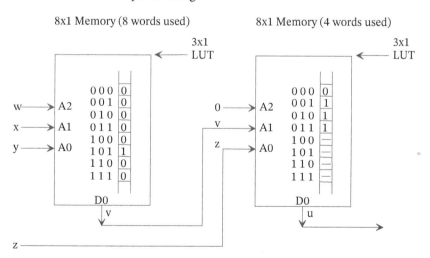

FIGURE 13.8   Implementation of 'u' using two 3x1 LUTs

Figure 13.8 shows implementation of 'u' using two 3x1 LUTs. These two 3x1 LUTs are implemented in the simplified FPGA configuration of Figure 13.9.

13.1.2   Programmable Switch Matrix

The FPGA of Figure 13.9 shows five input pins (A through E) and one output pin (Dout). The FPGA contains two 3x1 LUTs and one programmable switch matrix. The programmable switch matrix contains three 4x1 multiplexers. Each multiplexer is selected by a two-bit internal register. The CAD tools program these multiplexers and provide the contents of each S1S0 with appropriate values – S1S0 (top MUX) = 00, S1S0 (middle MUX) = 01, and S1S0 (bottom MUX) = 10. The selected S1S0 values will send IN0 of the top MUX, IN1 of the middle MUX, and IN2 of the bottom MUX to the outputs. Note that the pins of the FPGA can be programmed to connect D = 0 to IN0 of the top MUX, 'v' (output from the left LUT) to IN1 of the middle MUX, and E = z to IN2 of the bottom MUX. The pins A = w, B = x, and C = y can be programmed to be connected to the address pins of the left 3x1 LUT. Hence, the switch matrix can be programmed to connect the left LUT output (v) and the FPGA pins (D, E), and then provide the appropriate inputs (A2 = 0, A1 = v, A0 = z) to the right LUT.

After programming the FPGA of Figure 13.9, the successful implementation can be verified by connecting the input pins A, B, C, E to DIP swiches (A = w, B = x, C = y, E = z) and the D input pin to 0. An LED can be connected to the Dout pin of the FPGA. The truth table of Table 13.6 (a) can be used to verify the successful operation of the implementation.

13.1.3   Configurable Logic Blocks (CLBs)

As mentioned before, flip-flops are needed with LUTs and switch matrix to implement sequential circuits. A CLB is the basic functional unit of a FPGA. The CLB consists of a LUT, one or more flip-flops, and one or more 2-to-1 multiplexer. Figure 13.10 shows a CLB with a 3x1 LUT, one flip-flop, and a 2-to-1 multiplexer. The number of flip-flops and multiplexers depends on the word size of the LUT. For example, Figure 13.11 shows a CLB with two words in the 3x2 LUT.

Note that in Figure 13.10, when s = 0, the combinational circuit output is transferred directly (without the flip-flop) to the CLB output. On the other hand,when s = 1, the sequential circuit output with the flip-flop is selected and transferred to the CLB output.

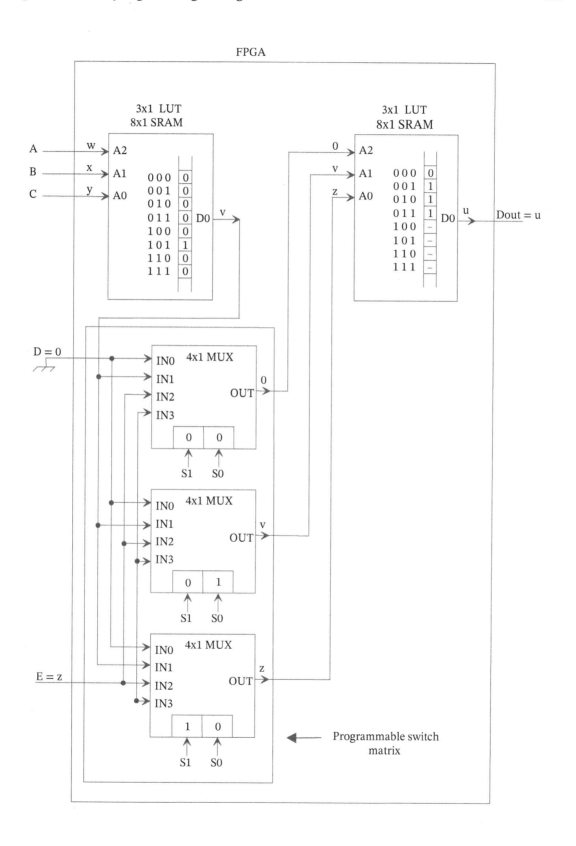

FIGURE 13.9 FPGA implementation of the schematic of Figure 13.7 with LUTs and programmable switch matrix.

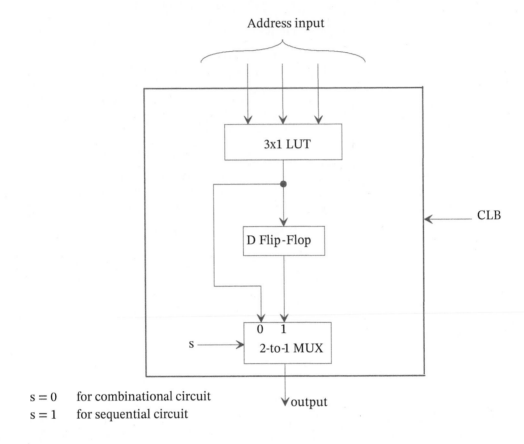

FIGURE 13.10   A typical CLB

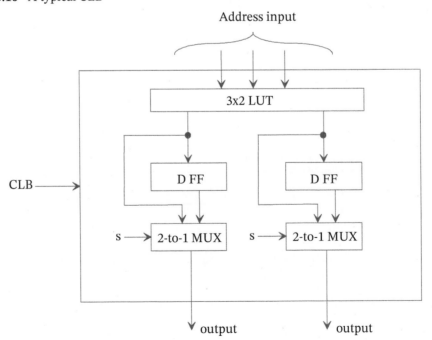

FIGURE 13.11   CLB for a 3x2 LUT

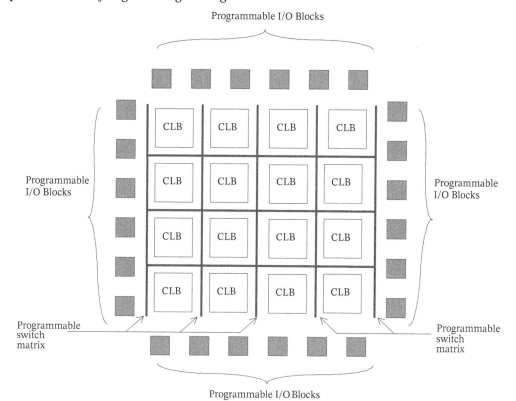

FIGURE 13.12   Generic FPGA architecture

13.1.4   FPGA Architecture

Figure 13.12 shows a generic FPGA architecture. An FPGA mainly contains CLBs, Programmable switch matrices, and Programmable I/O blocks. As mentioned before, a basic CLB includes a LUT, flip-flops, and multiplexers to implement the logic functions. The Programmable switch matrix, on the other hand, provides connections between CLBs and Programmable I/O blocks to obtain a user-specified design.

The Programmable I/O blocks connect the CLBs and Programmable switch matrices to external devices via the I/O pins. A typical FPGA contains over 250,000 CLBs and over 1000 inputs and outputs. With technological advancements, modern CLBs contain special functions such as ALU (Arithmetic Logic Unit) and DSP (Digital Signal Processing).

13.1.5   FPGA Programming

CAD tools are used to program the FPGA with a "bitfile". The bitfile contains all information needed to program the FPGA including all bits in the LUTs, flip-flop select bits, and mux select bits of the switch matrix. To illustrate this concept, consider Figure 13.13 which is obtained by modifying Figure 13.9.

Figure 13.9 contains the CLBs along with switch matrix and the programs for LUTs, FFs, and the switch matrix. The bitfile is formed as follows:

Eight one-bit contents of the left LUT (00000100) followed by the select input s = 0 (combinational logic) of the 2x1 MUX, followed by 00 01 10 (select inputs of the Switch matrix, followed by four one-bit contents (0111) of the right LUT, followed by the select bit (s = 0) of the 2-to-1 MUX selecting combinational logic. Hence, the contents of bitfile will be 00000100000011001110.

These bits in the bitfile are scattered throughout the chip. The FPGA chip is programmed using its programming pin. The bits in the bitfile are shifted via a shift register to the appropriate places inside the FPGA chip.

FPGA

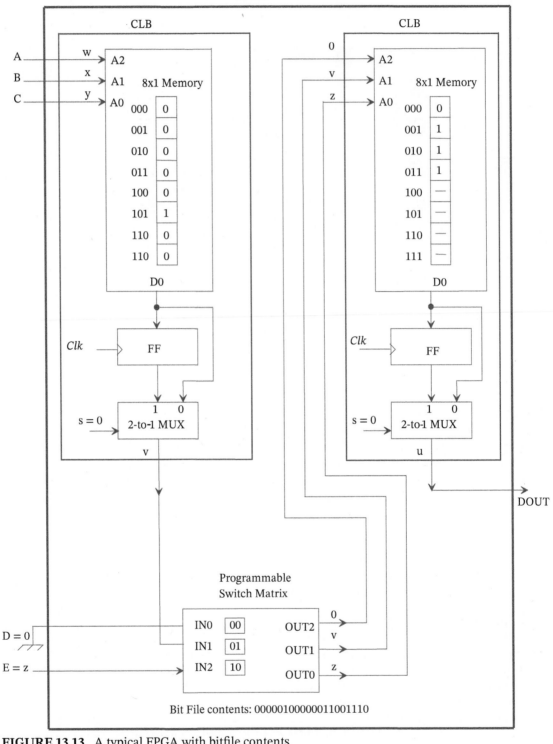

FIGURE 13.13 A typical FPGA with bitfile contents

13.2   A Typical FPGA Chip

A typical FPGA chip, such as the Xilinx Artix 7, provides numerous user I/O pins and a JTAG port.
The user I/O pins are used to connect simple I/O devices such as switches and LEDs in our case for

performing meaningful experiments after programming the FPGA chip with Verilog code. The JTAG port, on the other hand, is primarily used for programming and testing. The JTAG port is utilized for downloading the compiled HDL (Verilog or VHDL) codes, configuration data for CLBs, and data for testing and debugging the FPGA chip from the laptop or Personal Computer.

JTAG stands for "Joint Test Action Group" formed in 1985 to develop a technique for verifying designs and testing printed circuit boards after manufacturing. The Institute of Electrical and Electronics Engineers (IEEE) adopted this as a standard, and named this "IEEE Standard 1149.1-1990". Note that Intel was the first manufacturer to use JTAG in the Intel 80486 microprocessor in 1989. The JTAG standards have been eventually accepted by FPGA manufacturers to perform various tests such as continuity test.

A JTAG port is comprised of four pins. They are TCK (Test Clock), TMS (Test Mode Select), TDI (Test Data Input), and TDO (Test Data Output). The TCK pin synchronizes the internal state machine operations. The TMS pin is sampled at the rising edge of TCK to determine the next state. The TDI pin represents the data shifted into the device's test or programming logic. It is sampled at the rising edge of TCK when the internal state machine is in the correct state. The TDO pin represents the data shifted out of the device's test or programming logic, and is valid on the falling edge of the TCK when the internal state machine is in the correct state.

The four pins in the JTAG port can be used for testing certain features such as connectivity between signals (Continuity test). A PC (Personal computer) or a Laptop can be used for performing these tests by connecting the FPGA and the ICs in a daisy chain configuration. Figure 13.14 shows a simplified diagram for a FPGA chip with two ICs connected to a PC or a Laptop for testing. Note that the FPGA chip is connected to the ICs in a daisy chain configuration since TDO of one device connected to the next device. For example, the TDO pin of the FPGA chip is connected to the TDI pin of the Chip #1, and so on. The loop created in the figure is called a "Daisy chain loop" or "JTAG loop". In practice, there will be many more ICs connected to an FPGA. An FPGA with two ICs is shown here merely for illustrative purposes. Note that the PC or Laptop can be connected to the FPGA and the ICs using a USB-to-JTEC cable.

In addition to having the four pins for JTAG, each device in the JTAG loop must have a register called the "Boundary-scan register." The main advantage of boundary scan technology is the ability to read the values on the pins without direct physical address. This register can be used, for example, to check interconnection between the devices. Continuity checks may be performed by serially outputting a known pattern of data on the TDO pin of the PC or Laptop, and then receiving the same pattern of data serially at the TDI pin of a device in the JTAG loop. Indication of a failed IC or non-connectivity will occur if a matching test signal or a bit pattern is not received.

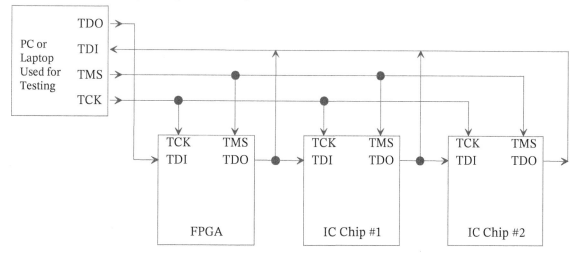

FIGURE 13.14 Simplified diagram of a PC or Laptop connected to a FPGA with two IC chips for testing in a daisy chain

FPGAs are usually high pin count devices with plenty of I/O pins which can be used to implement digital circuits. Modern FPGAs also contain other specialized elements that help with implementing more complex and high-speed designs. Those resources are more advanced and outside the scope of this text, but it should still be noted that they exist. A typical FPGA has three classes of pins: configuration pins, power/ground pins, and general purpose I/O pins. Each of these types of pins have its own specific function, and an FPGA must have all three types. Some FPGA may have other specialty classes of pins to support more advanced functions.

13.2.1 Configuration Pins

The configuration pins of a FPGA chip are used to setup and configure the device. The JTAG port is used to allow for the configuration (connecting LUTs , programming I/O) of the entire FPGA chip. This port is used to shift in the bitstream file data serially. The same port is also used to shift data out of the FPGA for debugging purposes.

Figure 13.15 shows the typical JTAG port in an FPGA. Since the FPGA configuration is stored in RAM, the configuration data is lost when the power is switched off, and thus must be configured at every power-up. To rectify this problem, most FPGAs store configuration data in a non-volatile external flash memory. The flash memory is usually located on the same board as the FPGA chip. Being non-volatile, the flash memory chip holds the entire FPGA configuration, and automatically re-loads the FPGA's RAM upon power-up. During configuration, the FPGA acts as the master and the flash acts as the slave.

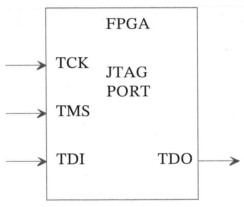

FIGURE 13.15   FPGA JTAG Port

FIGURE 13.16 Xilinx Artix 7 FPGA chip-based Digilent Nexys A7 FPGA trainer board

13.2.2 User I/O Pins

One of the major advantages to using FPGA in designs is the high user I/O count. The I/O count on the Xilinx 7-Series line of FPGAs ranges from 100 user I/O pins to over 1000 on the high-end devices. Most pins can be configured as inputs or outputs, or both in the case of bidirectional signals. The I/O pins in FPGAs are divided into groups called banks which can be connected to 5V or 3.3V as long as all pins in the same bank use the same settings. For example, two pins in the same bank cannot be configured for 3.3V and 1.8V respectively since they share a common power supply rail.

13.2.3 Power/Ground Pins

FPGAs require several power supply rails in order to power the different internal elements. Several power and ground pins are provided for distributing power in order to reduce noise and provide sufficient current.

13.3 A Typical FPGA Board

While an FPGA chip can be used to implement complex digital circuits, it requires external supporting circuitry such as flash memory to store the FPGA configuration, LEDs or displays to indicate the status of outputs, and switches to provide inputs. FPGA PCBs (Printed Circuit Boards) or simply boards are commonly used to accommodate these circuits.

The Digilent Nexys A7 is an excellent example of an FPGA board containing a Xilinx Artix 7 FPGA chip providing several switches, LEDs, ports, and external devices. Figure 13.16 shows a pictorial view of the Nexys A7 FPGA board that will be used for performing meaningful experiments for all the examples in this book.

The Nexys A7, from henceforth, will be referred to as the "FPGA Board". The terms "Nexys A7" and "FPGA Board" will be used interchangeably in the following. The FPGA board has all external circuitry required to generate all power supply rails and configuration pin connections to successfully implement the FPGA designs. A single USB cable providing 5V can be used. Figure 13.17 shows the connections for various I/O devices including switches, LEDs, push buttons, and seven-segment displays. Note that the Nexys A7 board has 16 switches connected to I/O of the FPGA to be used as inputs, as well as 16 LEDs connected to another 16 I/O to be used as outputs. The board also contains push buttons for inputs. Eight 7-segment displays are also included which can be used to display results. The switch/LED connections are depicted in Figure 13.18 while Figure 13.19 shows the push button connections.

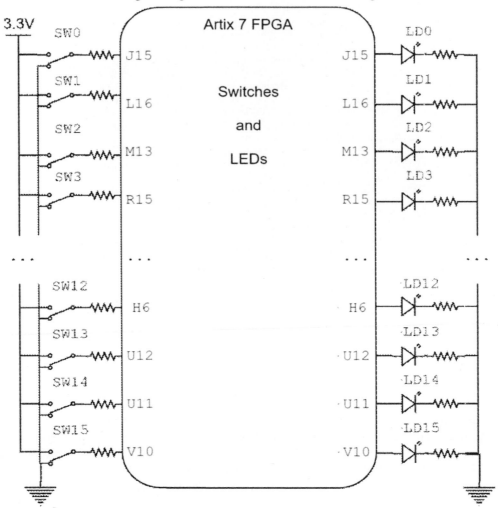

FIGURE 13.17   Switches, push buttons, LEDs, and seven-segment connections of Artix 7 of the
Nexys A7 board

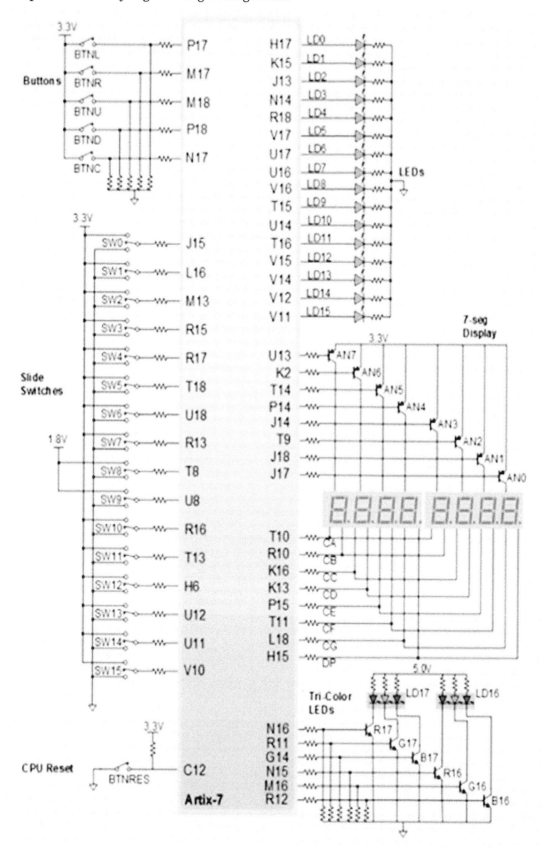

FIGURE 13.18 Switch/LED connections of the Artix 7 of the Nexys A7 board

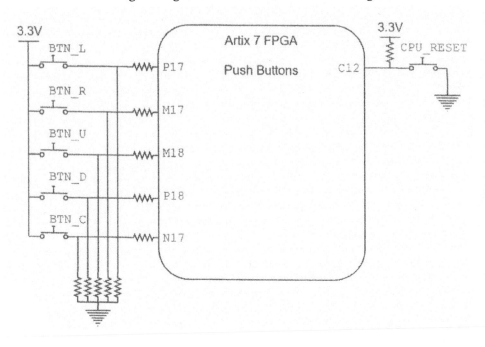

FIGURE 13.19 Push button connections of the ArtIx 7 of the Nexys A7 board

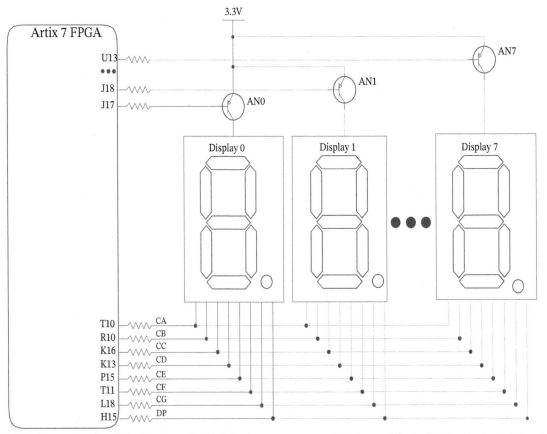

FIGURE 13.20 Simplified connections of the seven-segment displays with the Xilinx Artix 7 chip of the Digilent Nexys A7 board

Figure13.20 shows the Nexys A7 connections to eight seven-segment common-anode displays (Display 0 through Display 7). In order to provide enough current for each of the seven-segment displays, a PNP transistor is used as a buffer (current amplifier) for each display. The emitter of each display (Display 0 through Display 7) is connected to 3.3V while the base of each transistor is connected to an FPGA pin. The FPGA can output a '0' to the base of each PNP transistor to turn it ON, and a '1' to turn it OFF. In the figure, the bases of transistors AN0, AN1, AN7 are connected to FPGA pins J17, J18, and U13, respectively. Note that the bases of transistors AN2 through AN6 (not shown in the figure) are connected to the FPGA pins as follows: pin T9 to the base of AN2, pin J14 to the base of AN3, pin P14 to the base of AN4, pin T14 to the base of AN5, and pin K2 to the base of AN6.

In Figure 13.20, the collector of each transistor is connected to the cathode segment of each display. Also, in the figure, CA stands for Cathode A, CB stands for Cathode B, and so on. All CAs (segment A) are tied together, all CBs (segment B) are tied together, and so on.

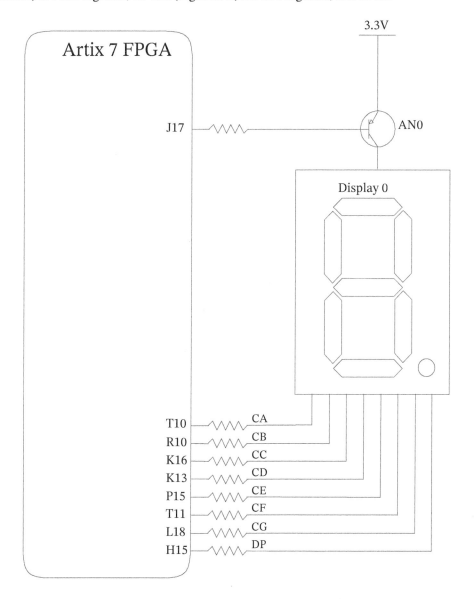

FIGURE 13.21 Simplified diagram of the Xilinx Artix 7 FPGAchip of the Nexys7 board to a single seven-segment display 0

For simplicity, a single display is used in all the examples of this chapter. Figure 13.21 shows FPGA connections to a single display such as Display 0. Now in order to enable segment 'A' of Display 0, the output pin J17 needs to be a '0' to turn ON transistor AN0 to provide 3.3V to the anode of Display 0, and the output pin T10 also needs to be a '0' to turn the segment 'A' ON.

13.4   FPGA-based Design and Implementation

As mentioned before, there is no processor in the FPGA to execute any programs, the end-user is responsible for designing the circuit. The designer can configure an FPGA as a simple OR gate to any complex sequential circuit. In order to create a design, Verilog or VHDL code is written for the design. This code is synthesized into a bitfile using a BITGEN to configure the FPGA. As mentioned before, the FPGA chip stores the configuration in an external RAM. Since RAMs are volatile, the configuration data will be lost in case the power is switched off. This means that the FPGA must be configured by the end-user each time power is turned on. In order to avoid this, FPGAs are provided with internal flash memory to store the configuration. Since the flash memory is nonvolatile, the configuration is never lost.

In summary, CAD tools are used for developing FPGA-based systems. Typical steps include:

*   Design

*   Synthesis

*   Implementation, programming, and verification

13.4.1   Design

Design phase can be based on hardware schematic or hardware description language (Verilog or VHDL). Synthesis translates Verilog or VHDL code into a netlist format. Hence, a circuit with logic gates is generated. The netlist is stored in a file called "NGF" (Native Generic File).

13.4.2   Synthesis

The first step of configuring an FPGA from a Verilog design is called synthesis. This makes sure that the Verilog modules are first checked for syntax errors. Once syntax checking is complete, the Verilog code is translated into structures such as LUTs, multiplexers, and flip-flops which are present within the FPGA CLBs. The synthesized design consisting of the LUTs, MUXs, and Flip-flops, and the connections between the three are how the entire design gets implemented within the FPGA.

13.4.3   Implementation, Programming, and Verification

In the Digilent Nexys A7 FPGA board, Verilog module inputs and outputs are mapped to FPGA IOBs and the pins connected to those IOBs using a file called the "constraint file". In the Xilinx Vivado software, this file type has the extension .xdc, and is thus referred to as the XDC file. The XDC file is used to link the input and output signals from the Verilog module to the physical I/O on the FPGA device. For example, the switches connected to FPGA I/O pins J15 and L16 can be used as inputs to a circuit, while the LED connected to pin H17 can be used as an output. To aid in FPGA design implementation, a master XDC file is provided by the board manufacturer with all the I/O pins listing their connections to external circuitry, which can be used as a template and modified to fit user designs. Constraint files are also used to define the voltage standard.

The minimum constraint for assigning a signal to an I/O is the location; however, it is always good practice to define the I/O voltage at the same time as most tools will give warnings or errors for unspecified voltages. For example, to assign the signal 'X' from a Verilog module to FPGA I/O pin N17 with a voltage of 3.3V, the following would be used:

```
set_property -dict {PACKAGE_PIN N17 IOSTANDARD LVCMOS33} [get_ports X ]
```

From the previous statement, there are two properties being set: PACKAGE_PIN and IOSTANDARD. These are being set to the pin location N17, and the 3.3 voltage standard as indicated by the 33 following LVCMOS. Note that the direction of the pin is not specified, as this is set by the direction of the port in the Verilog module. These two properties are associated with the signal name from the Verilog following the **get_ports** keyword.

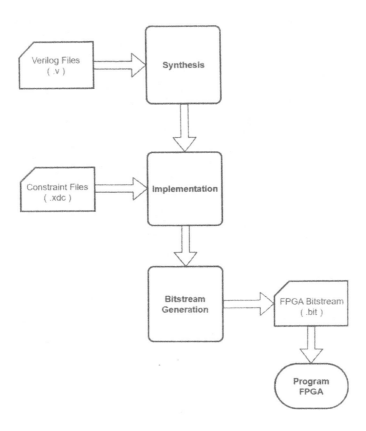

FIGURE 13.22 Basic design flow from Verilog to FPGA

Consider the following Verilog module header and constraints:

```
module my_module(input A, input B, output F);
```

```
set_property -dict {PACKAGE_PIN J15 IOSTANDARD LVCMOS33} [get_ports A]
set_property -dict {PACKAGE_PIN L16 IOSTANDARD LVCMOS33} [get_ports B]
set_property -dict {PACKAGE_PIN H17 IOSTANDARD LVCMOS33} [get_ports F]
```

The first constraint maps input A to FPGA pin J15 and specifies 3.3V voltage levels, while input B is mapped to pin L16. Referring to Figure 13.17, these are both connected to switches on the FPGA board. The last constraint maps the output of the module to pin H17 which is connected to LED0 on the board.

Once a Verilog design has been both synthesized (converted to FPGA structures) and implemented (mapped to device pins), the programming file needs to be generated which is to be sent to the FPGA. This process is called bitstream generation which creates a binary file which is then shifted into the FPGA via JTAG to configure the CLBs, IOBs, and switching matrices required to configure the FPGA. The Verilog development tools are preconfigured for all the FPGA models which they support, since generated FPGA bitstreams will differ in their structure between FPGAs of different models and definitely from different vendors. Figure 13.22 shows the basic Verilog to FPGA design flow.

Several examples for FPGA-based design and implementation using the Digilent Nexys A7 are provided in the following. The steps are listed below:

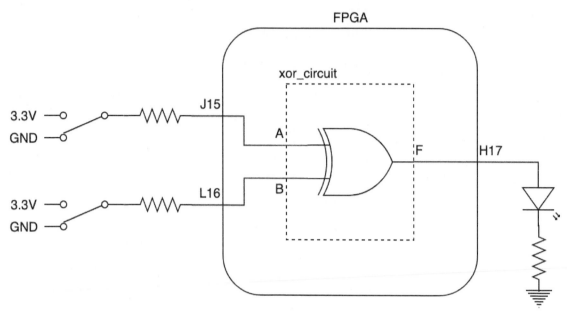

FIGURE 13.23   Figure for Example 13.1

Step 1: Create the Verilog module
Step 2: Create a test bench and run the simulation
Step 3: Assign signals to FPGA I/O pins by adding constraints
Step 4: Generate bitstream, program, and test

13.5   FPGA Examples

Several examples illustrating the FPGA design and implementation for both combinational and sequential logic are included in this section. These examples are designed and implemented successfully using the Digilent Nexys 7 FPGA board. These examples are presented in a very simplified manner, and illustrate the concept of FPGA design and implementation. Appendix E shows step-by-step procedure for downloading Xilinx Vivado IDE software and its usage for FPGA-based design and implementation of combinational and seqential circuits using Verilog.

Example 13.1

Using the Nexys 7 FPGA board, design and implement an Exclusive-OR gate with the XOR equation. Do not use the XOR primitive or operation. Use two input switches and a LED for output on the FPGA board to supply inputs and outputs as shown in Figure 13.23.

Solution

Step 1: Create the Verilog module

```
xor_circuit.v
------------------------------------------------------------------------
module xor_circuit(input A, input B, output F);

   assign F = (A & ~B) | (~A & B);

endmodule
```

Step 2: Create a test bench and run the simulation

```
xor_circuit_sim.v
-----------------------------------------------------------------------
module xor_circuit_sim();
  reg sw_A, sw_B;
  wire LED_F;


xor_circuit dut(sw_A, sw_B, LED_F);

  initial begin
sw_A = 0; sw_B = 0;
  #1  sw_A = 0; sw_B = 1;
  #1  sw_A = 1; sw_B = 0;
  #1  sw_A = 1; sw_B = 1;
  end

endmodule
```

Simulation result for Example 13.1:

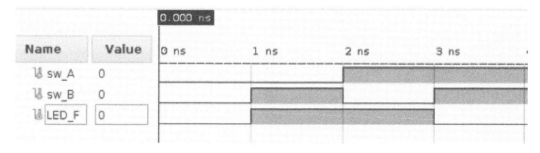

Step 3: Assign signals to FPGA I/O by adding constraints

```
xor_circuit.xdc:
-----------------------------------------------------------------------
set_property -dict {PACKAGE_PIN J15 IOSTANDARD LVCMOS33} [get_ports A]
set_property -dict {PACKAGE_PIN L16 IOSTANDARD LVCMOS33} [get_ports B]
set_property -dict {PACKAGE_PIN H17 IOSTANDARD LVCMOS33} [get_ports F]
```

Step 4: Generate bitstream, program, and test

Once the FPGA is programmed, the XOR function can be tested. Screenshots below show the results of settings the switches to different input combinations and the result is displayed on the output LED.

Screenshots illustrating Example 13.1:

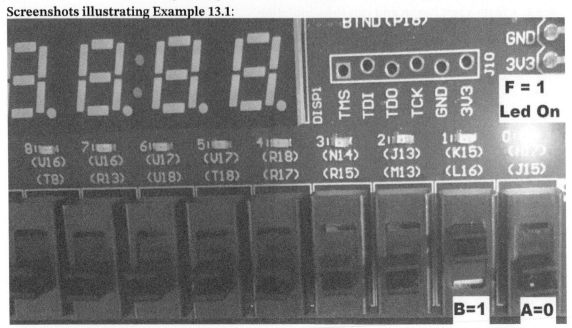

Screenshot   illustrating the XOR operation with switches A = 0 and B =1 generating an output, F = 1 (LED ON)

Screenshot for illustrating the XOR operation with switches A = 1 and B =1 generating an output F = 0 (LED OFF)

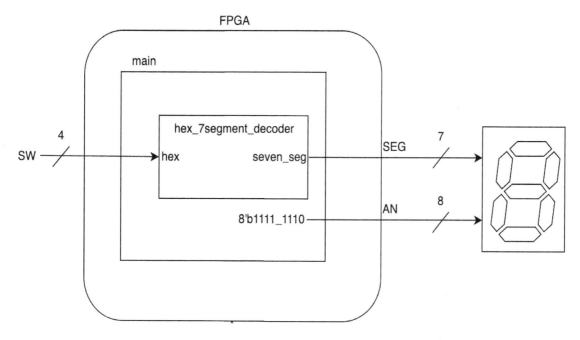

FIGURE 13.24 Figure for Example 13.2

Example 13.2

Using the Nexys 7 FPGA board, design and implement a binary to seven segment converter that takes a 4-bit binary value from SW[3:0] and displays the corresponding hexadecimal value on a seven-segment display (Display 0) as shown in Figure 13.24.

Solution

Step 1: Create the Verilog module

```
hex_segment_decoder.v:
-----------------------------------------------------------------------
module hex_7segment_decoder(
    input [3:0]hex,
    output reg [0:6]seven_seg
    );
    always @ hex
    case(hex)
    4'h0:seven_seg = 7'b000_0001;
    4'h1:seven_seg = 7'b100_1111;
    4'h2:seven_seg = 7'b001_0010;
    4'h3:seven_seg = 7'b000_0110;
    4'h4:seven_seg = 7'b100_1100;
    4'h5:seven_seg = 7'b010_0100;
    4'h6:seven_seg = 7'b010_0000;
    4'h7:seven_seg = 7'b000_1111;
    4'h8:seven_seg = 7'b000_0000;
    4'h9:seven_seg = 7'b000_0100;
    4'hA:seven_seg = 7'b000_1000;
    4'hB:seven_seg = 7'b110_0000;
    4'hC:seven_seg = 7'b011_0001;
```

```
    4'hD:seven_seg = 7'b100_0010;
    4'hE:seven_seg = 7'b011_0000;
    4'hF:seven_seg = 7'b011_1000;
endcase
endmodule
```

For the Nexys 7 FPGA board, each segment cathodes for all of the eight displays are connected together. In order to illuminate only the seven-segment display on the right, its common-anode pin must be driven with a '0' to enable and the other seven displays can be driven with a '1' to disable. This is done by creating outputs for each of the common anodes which are driven by the outer-most Verilog module.

Hex_7seg_main.v:

```
module hex_7seg_main (
  input [3:0]SW,   // Input switches
  output [0:6]SEG,// 7-segment cathodes
  output [7:0]AN   // 7-segment anodes
  );

  // Enable only the right-most display
  assign AN = 8'b1111_1110;

  // Instantiate the decoder
  hex_7segment_decoder sub0(SW,SEG);

endmodule
```

Step 2: Create a test bench and run the simulation

hex_7_segment_sim.v:

```
module hex_7segment_sim();
  reg [3:0]SW;
  wire [0:6]SEG;
  wire [7:0]AN;

  hex_7seg_main dut(SW,SEG,AN);

  initial begin
      SW = 4'h0;
   #1 SW = 4'h5;
   #1 SW = 4'h7;
   #1 SW = 4'h8;
   #1 SW = 4'hF;
   end
endmodule
```

Simulation result for Example 13.2:

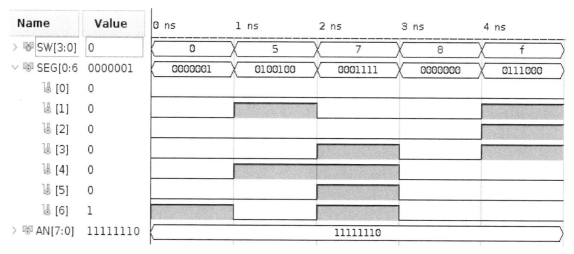

Step 3: Assign signals to FPGA I/O pins by adding constraints

```
hex_segment_decoder.xdc:
-------------------------------------------------------------------
##Switches
set_property -dict {PACKAGE_PIN J15  IOSTANDARD LVCMOS33} [get_ports SW[0]];
set_property -dict {PACKAGE_PIN L16  IOSTANDARD LVCMOS33} [get_ports SW[1]];
set_property -dict {PACKAGE_PIN M13  IOSTANDARD LVCMOS33} [get_ports SW[2]];
set_property -dict {PACKAGE_PIN R15  IOSTANDARD LVCMOS33} [get_ports SW[3]];

##Cathodes
set_property -dict {PACKAGE_PIN T10  IOSTANDARD LVCMOS33} [get_ports SEG[0]];
set_property -dict {PACKAGE_PIN R10  IOSTANDARD LVCMOS33} [get_ports SEG[1]];
set_property -dict {PACKAGE_PIN K16  IOSTANDARD LVCMOS33} [get_ports SEG[2]];
set_property -dict {PACKAGE_PIN K13  IOSTANDARD LVCMOS33} [get_ports SEG[3]];
set_property -dict {PACKAGE_PIN P15  IOSTANDARD LVCMOS33} [get_ports SEG[4]];
set_property -dict {PACKAGE_PIN T11  IOSTANDARD LVCMOS33} [get_ports SEG[5]];
set_property -dict {PACKAGE_PIN L18  IOSTANDARD LVCMOS33} [get_ports SEG[6]];

##Anodes
set_property -dict {PACKAGE_PIN J17  IOSTANDARD LVCMOS33} [get_ports AN[0] ];
set_property -dict {PACKAGE_PIN J18  IOSTANDARD LVCMOS33} [get_ports AN[1] ];
set_property -dict {PACKAGE_PIN T9   IOSTANDARD LVCMOS33} [get_ports AN[2] ];
set_property -dict {PACKAGE_PIN J14  IOSTANDARD LVCMOS33} [get_ports AN[3] ];
set_property -dict {PACKAGE_PIN P14  IOSTANDARD LVCMOS33} [get_ports AN[4] ];
set_property -dict {PACKAGE_PIN T14  IOSTANDARD LVCMOS33} [get_ports AN[5] ];
set_property -dict {PACKAGE_PIN K2   IOSTANDARD LVCMOS33} [get_ports AN[6] ];
set_property -dict {PACKAGE_PIN U13  IOSTANDARD LVCMOS33} [get_ports AN[7] ];
```

Step 4: Generate bitstream, program, and test

Screenshots illustrating Example 13.2:

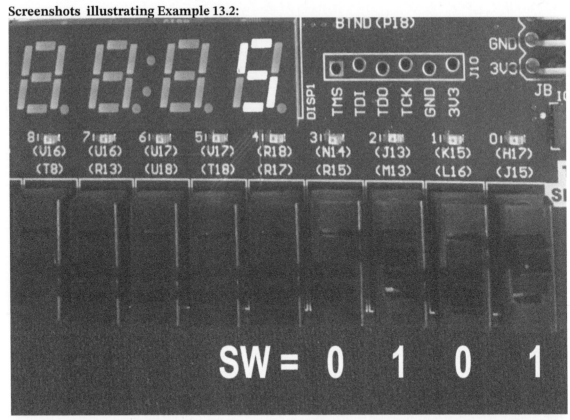

Screenshot illustrating Example 13.2 with switch values = 0101 generating a 7-segment output = 5

Screenshot illustrating Example 13.2 with switch values = 1010 generating a 7-segment output = A

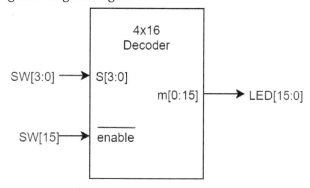

FIGURE 13.25 Figures for Example 13.3

Example 13.3

Using the Nexys 7 FPGA board, design and implement a 4-to-16 binary decoder with an active-low enable signal as shown in Figure 13.25.

Solution

Step 1:   Create the Verilog module

```
decoder4x16.v:
```

```
module decoder4x16(
  input enableb,
  input [3:0]SW,
  output reg [15:0]m
  );

  always @ (*)
  if (enableb)
    m = 15'd0;
  else
    m = 1'b1 << SW;
endmodule
```

Step 2:   Create a test bench and run the simulation

```
module decoder4x16_sim();
  reg E;
  reg [3:0]SW;
  wire [15:0]m;

  decoder4x16 dut(E,SW,m);

  initial begin
    E = 1;
    for(SW = 0; SW<15; SW = SW+1)
      #1;
    #1 E = 0;
    for(SW = 0; SW<15; SW = SW+1)
      #1;
  end
endmodule
```

Simulation result for Example 13.3:

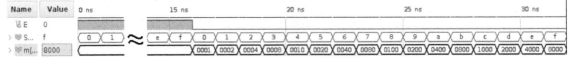

Step 3: Assign signals to FPGA I/O pins by adding constraints

```
decoder4x16.xdc:
--------------------------------------------------------------------------
##Switches
set_property -dict { PACKAGE_PIN J15   IOSTANDARD LVCMOS33 } [get_ports { SW[0]
set_property -dict { PACKAGE_PIN L16   IOSTANDARD LVCMOS33 } [get_ports { SW[1]
set_property -dict { PACKAGE_PIN M13   IOSTANDARD LVCMOS33 } [get_ports { SW[2]
set_property -dict { PACKAGE_PIN R15   IOSTANDARD LVCMOS33 } [get_ports { SW[3]
set_property -dict { PACKAGE_PIN V10   IOSTANDARD LVCMOS33 } [get_ports { enable
## LEDs
set_property -dict { PACKAGE_PIN H17   IOSTANDARD LVCMOS33 } [get_ports m[0] ];
set_property -dict { PACKAGE_PIN K15   IOSTANDARD LVCMOS33 } [get_ports m[1] ];
set_property -dict { PACKAGE_PIN J13   IOSTANDARD LVCMOS33 } [get_ports m[2] ];
set_property -dict { PACKAGE_PIN N14   IOSTANDARD LVCMOS33 } [get_ports m[3] ];
set_property -dict { PACKAGE_PIN R18   IOSTANDARD LVCMOS33 } [get_ports m[4] ];
set_property -dict { PACKAGE_PIN V17   IOSTANDARD LVCMOS33 } [get_ports m[5] ];
set_property -dict { PACKAGE_PIN U17   IOSTANDARD LVCMOS33 } [get_ports m[6] ];
set_property -dict { PACKAGE_PIN U16   IOSTANDARD LVCMOS33 } [get_ports m[7] ];
set_property -dict { PACKAGE_PIN V16   IOSTANDARD LVCMOS33 } [get_ports m[8] ];
set_property -dict { PACKAGE_PIN T15   IOSTANDARD LVCMOS33 } [get_ports m[9] ];
set_property -dict { PACKAGE_PIN U14   IOSTANDARD LVCMOS33 } [get_ports m[10] ];
set_property -dict { PACKAGE_PIN T16   IOSTANDARD LVCMOS33 } [get_ports m[11] ];
set_property -dict { PACKAGE_PIN V15   IOSTANDARD LVCMOS33 } [get_ports m[12] ];
set_property -dict { PACKAGE_PIN V14   IOSTANDARD LVCMOS33 } [get_ports m[13] ];
set_property -dict { PACKAGE_PIN V12   IOSTANDARD LVCMOS33 } [get_ports m[14] ];
set_property -dict { PACKAGE_PIN V11   IOSTANDARD LVCMOS33 } [get_ports m[15] ];
```

Step 4: Generate bitstream, program, and test

Screenshot illustrating Example 13.3:

Example 13.4

Using the Nexys 7 FPGA board, design and implement a 4-bit adder shown in Figure 13.26 . Use full adder module as the building block. Display the 4-bit result and carry using 5 LEDs. Figure 13.27 shows a block diagram of the FPGA implementation.

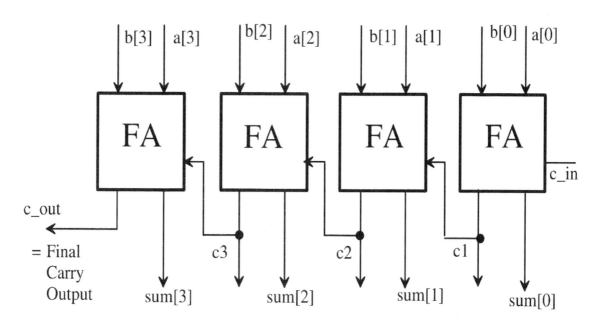

FIGURE 13.26 Four-bit adder block diagram

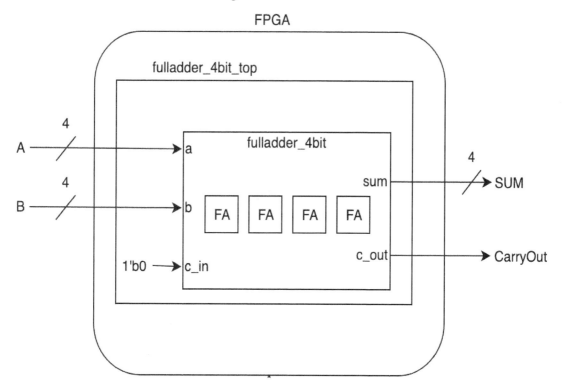

FIGURE 13.27 FPGA implementation block diagram

Solution

Step 1: Create the Verilog module

full_adder.v:
```
-------------------------------------------------------------------
module full_adder(c_out, sum, a, b, c_in);
  output sum, c_out;
  input a, b, c_in;

  // Internal nets
  wire w1, w2, w3;

  // Gate pimitives
xor(sum,a,b,c_in);
  and (w1,a,b);
  and (w2,a,c_in);
  and (w3,b,c_in);
  or (c_out,w1,w2,w3);

endmodule
-------------------------------------------------------------------
```

full_adder_4bit.v:
```
-------------------------------------------------------------------
module adder_4bit(
  output c_out,
  output [3:0]sum,
  input [3:0]a,b,
  input c_in
  );
  //internal nets
  wire c[3:1];

  // Instantiate 4 instances of full_adder
full_adder fa0 ( c[1], sum[0], a[0], b[0], c_in),
            fa1 ( c[2], sum[1], a[1], b[1], c[1]),
            fa2 ( c[3], sum[2], a[2], b[2], c[2]),
            fa3 (c_out, sum[3], a[3], b[3], c[3]);
endmodule
-------------------------------------------------------------------
```

fulladder_4bit_top.v:
```
-------------------------------------------------------------------
module fulladder_4bit_top(
input [3:0]A, input [3:0]B,
output CarryOut, output [3:0]SUM
);

  //Instantiate the 4-bit full adder with the carry-in set to 0;
  adder_4bit adder_inst(CarryOut, SUM, A, B, 1'b0);

endmodule
-------------------------------------------------------------------
```

Step 2: Create a test bench and run the simulation

adder_4bit_sim.v

```verilog
module adder_4bit_top_sim();
  reg [3:0] A, B;
  wire [3:0] SUM;
  wire CarryOut;

  // Instantiate fulladder_4bit_top
  fulladder_4bit_top dut(A,B,CarryOut,SUM);

  initial begin
      A = 0; B = 0;
    #1 A = 4; B = 7;
    #1 A = 10; B = 7;
    #1 A = 15; B = 15;
    #1;
  end
endmodule
```

Simulation result of Example 13.4:

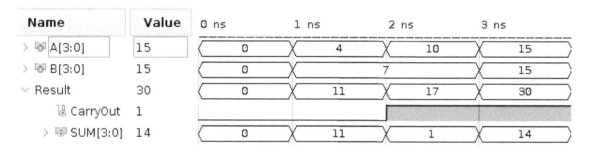

Step 3: Assign signals to FPGA I/O pins by adding constraints

fulladder_4bit.xdc

```
##Switches
set_property -dict { PACKAGE_PIN J15    IOSTANDARD LVCMOS33 } [get_ports  B[0] ];
set_property -dict { PACKAGE_PIN L16    IOSTANDARD LVCMOS33 } [get_ports  B[1] ];
set_property -dict { PACKAGE_PIN M13    IOSTANDARD LVCMOS33 } [get_ports  B[2] ];
set_property -dict { PACKAGE_PIN R15    IOSTANDARD LVCMOS33 } [get_ports  B[3] ];
set_property -dict { PACKAGE_PIN R17    IOSTANDARD LVCMOS33 } [get_ports  A[0] ];
set_property -dict { PACKAGE_PIN T18    IOSTANDARD LVCMOS33 } [get_ports  A[1] ];
set_property -dict { PACKAGE_PIN U18    IOSTANDARD LVCMOS33 } [get_ports  A[2] ];
set_property -dict { PACKAGE_PIN R13    IOSTANDARD LVCMOS33 } [get_ports  A[3] ];

## LEDs
set_property -dict { PACKAGE_PIN H17    IOSTANDARD LVCMOS33 } [get_ports  SUM[0] ];
set_property -dict { PACKAGE_PIN K15    IOSTANDARD LVCMOS33 } [get_ports  SUM[1] ];
set_property -dict { PACKAGE_PIN J13    IOSTANDARD LVCMOS33 } [get_ports  SUM[2] ];
set_property -dict { PACKAGE_PIN N14    IOSTANDARD LVCMOS33 } [get_ports  SUM[3] ];
set_property -dict { PACKAGE_PIN R18    IOSTANDARD LVCMOS33 } [get_portsCarryOut ];
```

Step 4: Generate bitstream, program, and test

Screenshot illustrating Example 13.4:

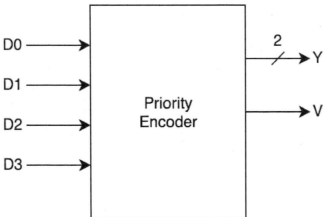

FIGURE 13.28 Figure for Example 13.5

Example 13.5

Using the Nexys 7 FPGA board, design and implement the priority encoder shown in Figure 13.28, with input D0 being the highest priority and D3 being the lowest. Display the value of Y on the seven segment display if valid, display a dash (segment G only) if no input is high.

Solution

Step 1: Create the Verilog module

```
----------------------------------------------------------------------
priority_encoder_4.v
----------------------------------------------------------------------
module priority_encoder_4(input [3:0]D, output reg [1:0]Y, output V);

    // V is '1' if any bit of D is '1'
    assign V = |D;
```

```
    always @ (D)
    if(D[0])
      Y = 0;
    else if(D[1])
      Y = 1;
    else if(D[2])
      Y = 2;
    else if(D[3])
      Y = 3;
    else
     Y = 0;

endmodule
```

----
display_driver.v

```
module display_driver(input [1:0]value, input valid, output reg [0:6]
SEG, output [7:0]AN);

   assign AN = 8'b1111_1110;

   always @ (value,valid)
   if(valid)
     case(value)
     0: SEG = 7'b000_0001;
     1: SEG = 7'b100_1111;
     2: SEG = 7'b001_0010;
     3: SEG = 7'b000_0110;
endcase
   else // No input is activated. Display (-)
     SEG = 7'b111_1110;

endmodule
```

----
priority_encoder_top.v

```
module priority_encoder_top(input [3:0]D, output [0:6]SEG, output [7:0]
AN);

    wire [1:0]line;
    wire valid;

    //Priority Encoder
    priority_encoder_4 u0(D, line, valid);

    // Dispay controller
display_driver u1(line, valid, SEG, AN);

endmodule
```

Step 2: Create a test bench and run the simulation

```
----------------------------------------------------------------------
priority_encoder_4_sim.v
----------------------------------------------------------------------
module priority_encoder_4_sim();
  reg [3:0]D;
  wire [1:0] Y;
  wire V;

  priority_encoder_4 dut(D,Y,V);

  initial begin
     D = 4'b0000;
  #1 D = 4'b1000;
  #1 D = 4'b0100;
  #1 D = 4'b0010;
  #1 D = 4'b0001;
  #1 D = 4'b0000;
  #1 $finish;
  end

endmodule
----------------------------------------------------------------------
```

Simulation result for Example 13.5:

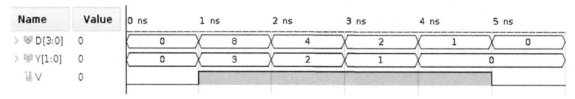

Step 3: Assign signals to FPGA I/O pins by adding constraints

```
----------------------------------------------------------------------
priority_encoder_4.xdc
----------------------------------------------------------------------
##Switches
set_property -dict { PACKAGE_PIN J15    IOSTANDARD LVCMOS33 } [get_ports { D[0] }];
set_property -dict { PACKAGE_PIN L16    IOSTANDARD LVCMOS33 } [get_ports { D[1] }];
set_property -dict { PACKAGE_PIN M13    IOSTANDARD LVCMOS33 } [get_ports { D[2] }];
set_property -dict { PACKAGE_PIN R15    IOSTANDARD LVCMOS33 } [get_ports { D[3] }];

##7 segment displa
set_property -dict { PACKAGE_PIN T10    IOSTANDARD LVCMOS33 } [get_ports { SEG[0] }]
set_property -dict { PACKAGE_PIN R10    IOSTANDARD LVCMOS33 } [get_ports { SEG[1] }]
set_property -dict { PACKAGE_PIN K16    IOSTANDARD LVCMOS33 } [get_ports { SEG[2] }]
set_property -dict { PACKAGE_PIN K13    IOSTANDARD LVCMOS33 } [get_ports { SEG[3] }]
set_property -dict { PACKAGE_PIN P15    IOSTANDARD LVCMOS33 } [get_ports { SEG[4] }]
set_property -dict { PACKAGE_PIN T11    IOSTANDARD LVCMOS33 } [get_ports { SEG[5] }]
set_property -dict { PACKAGE_PIN L18    IOSTANDARD LVCMOS33 } [get_ports { SEG[6] }]
```

```
set_property -dict { PACKAGE_PIN J17    IOSTANDARD LVCMOS33 } [get_ports { AN[0] }]
set_property -dict { PACKAGE_PIN J18    IOSTANDARD LVCMOS33 } [get_ports { AN[1] }]
set_property -dict { PACKAGE_PIN T9     IOSTANDARD LVCMOS33 } [get_ports { AN[2] }]
set_property -dict { PACKAGE_PIN J14    IOSTANDARD LVCMOS33 } [get_ports { AN[3] }]
set_property -dict { PACKAGE_PIN P14    IOSTANDARD LVCMOS33 } [get_ports { AN[4] }]
set_property -dict { PACKAGE_PIN T14    IOSTANDARD LVCMOS33 } [get_ports { AN[5] }]
set_property -dict { PACKAGE_PIN K2     IOSTANDARD LVCMOS33 } [get_ports { AN[6] }]
set_property -dict { PACKAGE_PIN U13    IOSTANDARD LVCMOS33 } [get_ports { AN[7] }]
```

Step 4: Generate bitstream, program, and test

Screenshots illustrating Example 13.5:

With the input D = 4'b0000, the output is expected to be (-) since none of the inputs are '1' and the valid output from the encoder is '0'. On the other hand, when D is set to an input with the zero-bit set to a '1', the display shows a zero. Similarly, when the input is 1 0 1 0 in which bit one is the '1' with the highest priority, the display shows a one. Finally, the display only shows a '3' when D3, the lowest priority, is the only input set to '1'.

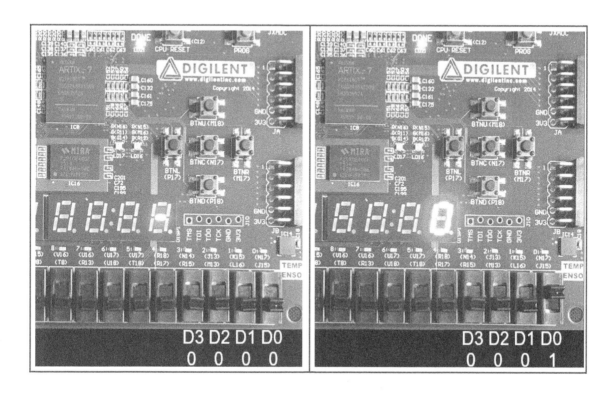

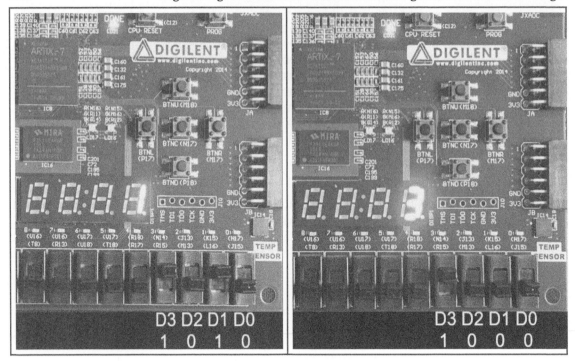

D3	D2	D1	D0
1	0	1	0

D3	D2	D1	D0
1	0	0	0

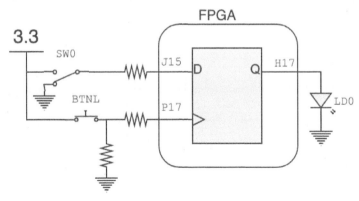

FIGURE 13.29   Figure for Example 13.6

Example 13.6

Using the Nexys 7 FPGA board, design and implement a D flip-flip as shown in Figure 13.29.

Solution

Since the switches, push buttons, and LEDs on the Nexys 7 FPGA board are already connected, no external hardware is required.

Step 1: Create the Verilog module

D_flipflop.v

```
module D_flipflop(input clk, input D, output reg Q);

  always @ (posedgeclk)
    Q <= D;

endmodule
```

Step 2: Create a test bench and run the simulation

```
----------------------------------------------------------------------
D_flipflop.v
----------------------------------------------------------------------
module D_flipflop_sim();

  reg clk, D;
  wire Q;

D_flipflop dut(clk, D, Q);

  initial begin
clk = 0; D = 1;
  #1 clk = 1;
  #0.5clk = 0; D = 0;
  #1clk = 1;
  #0.5clk = 0; D = 1;
  #1clk = 1;
  #0.5clk = 0;
  end
endmodule
----------------------------------------------------------------------
```

Simulation result for Example 13.6:

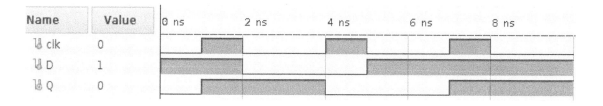

Step 3: Assign signals to FPGA I/O pins by adding constraints

```
----------------------------------------------------------------------
D_flipflop.xdc
----------------------------------------------------------------------
#Switch for D input
set_property -dict { PACKAGE_PIN J15    IOSTANDARD LVCMOS33 } [get_portsD ];

#Button for clk - P17 is a valid FPGA clk pin
set_property -dict { PACKAGE_PIN P17    IOSTANDARD LVCMOS33 } [get_portsclk ];

## LED for Q output
set_property -dict { PACKAGE_PIN H17    IOSTANDARD LVCMOS33 } [get_portsQ ];
----------------------------------------------------------------------
```

Step 4: Generate bitstream, program, and test

Screenshots illustrating Example 13.6:

Initially, Q is set to '0'. With input D set to '1', the *Clk* is pulsed by pressing button BTNL which is mapped to the *Clk* input of the flip-flop. The value of Q changes to '1'.

1. Initial State Q = 0 (LED OFF)	2. Clock pulse with D = 1 Q = 1(LED ON)

3. Second clock pulse with D = 1 Q = 1(LED ON)	4. Third Clock pulse with D = 0 Q = 0 (LED OFF)

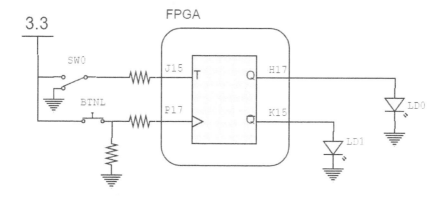

FIGURE 13.30 Figure for Example 13.7

Example 13.7

Using the Nexys 7 FPGA board, design and implement a T flip-flop as shown in Figure 13.30.

Solution

Step 1:   Create the Verilog module

```
------------------------------------------------------------------------
T_flipflop.v
------------------------------------------------------------------------
module T_flipflop(clk, T, Q, Qnot);

   input clk, T;
   // Need to give Q an initial value for simulation to work
   output reg Q = 0;
   output Qnot;

   assign Qnot = ~Q;
   always @ (posedgeclk)
   if(T)
     Q <= Qnot;
   else
     Q <= Q;

endmodule
------------------------------------------------------------------------
```

Step 2: Create a test bench and run the simulation

```
------------------------------------------------------------------------
T_flipflop_sim.v
------------------------------------------------------------------------
module T_flipflop_sim();
   reg clk, T;
   wire Q, Qnot;

T_flipflop dut(clk, T, Q, Qnot);
```

```
   initial begin
clk = 0; T = 1;
  #1    clk = 1;
  #0.5 clk = 0;
  #1    clk = 1;
  #0.5 clk = 0;
  #1    clk = 1;
  #0.5 clk = 0; T = 0;
  #1    clk = 1;
  #0.5 clk = 0;
  #1    clk = 1;
  #0.5 clk = 0;
  end
endmodule
```

- -

Simulation result for Example 13.7:

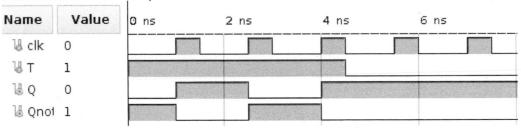

Step 3: Assign signals to FPGA I/O pins by adding constraints

- -

```
T_flipflop.xdc
```
- -
```
#Switch for T input
set_property -dict { PACKAGE_PIN J15    IOSTANDARD LVCMOS33 } [get_ports T ]

#Button for clk - P17 is a valid FPGA clk pin
set_property -dict { PACKAGE_PIN P17    IOSTANDARD LVCMOS33 } [get_portsclk ]

## LED for Q and Qnot outputs
set_property -dict { PACKAGE_PIN H17    IOSTANDARD LVCMOS33 } [get_ports Q ]
set_property -dict { PACKAGE_PIN K15    IOSTANDARD LVCMOS33 } [get_portsQnot ]
```

- -

Step 4: Generate bitstream, program, and test

Screenshots illustrating Example 13.7:
The T-flip flop toggles whenever the clk rises when input T is '1'. Initially, Q =0 and T = 1, so when the CLK button is pressed, the flip flop transitions from 0 to 1, as shown on the LEDs for Q and Qnot. When T = 0 and the clock is pulsed, no change occurs.

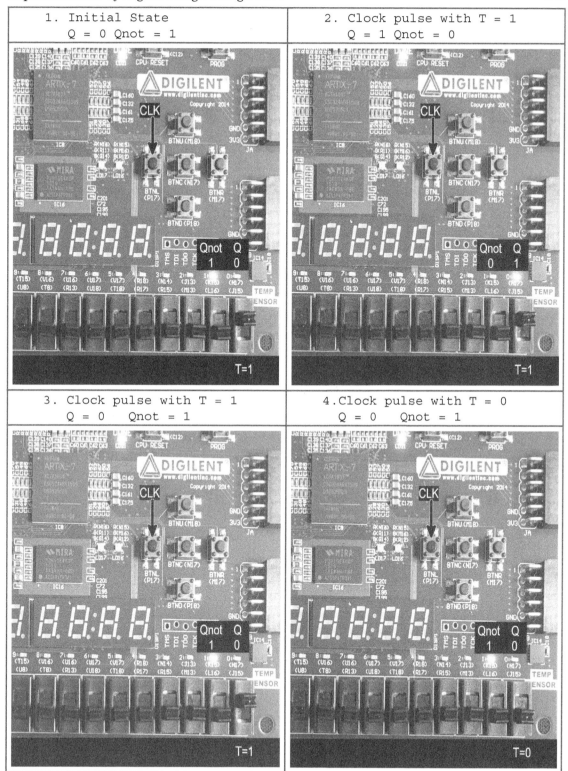

Example 13.8

Using the Nexys 7 FPGA board, design and implement a D flip-flop as shown in Figure 13.31 with an asynchronous CLR input.

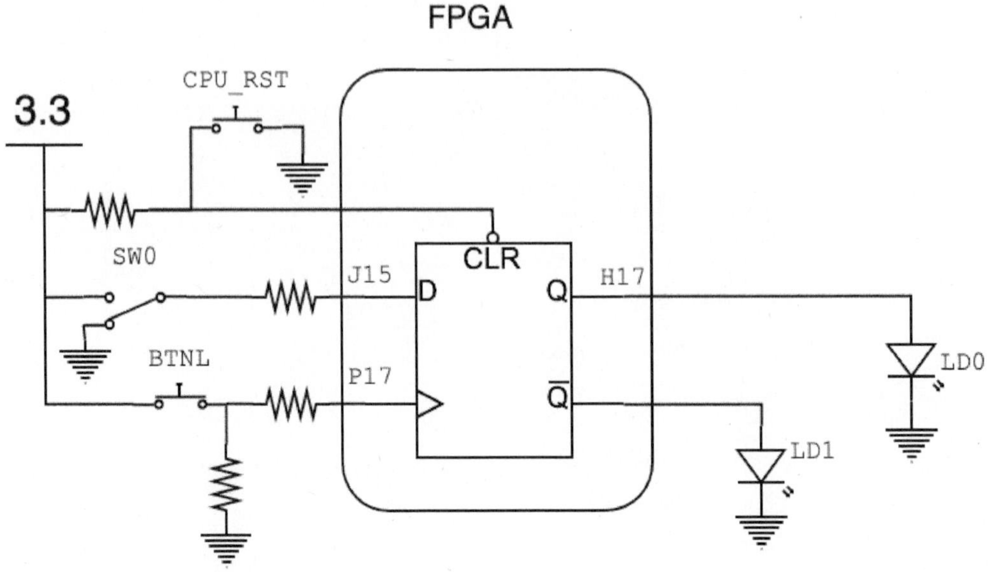

FPGA

FIGURE 13.31 Figure for Example 13.8

Solution

Step 1:   Create the Verilog module

```
------------------------------------------------------------------------
D_flipflop_v2.v
------------------------------------------------------------------------

module D_flipflop(CLK, CLR, D, Q, Qnot);
   input CLK, CLR, D;
   output reg Q = 0;
   output Qnot;

   assign Qnot = ~Q;

   always @ (posedge CLK or negedge CLR)
   // Negedge of CLR implies CLR will be '0'
   if(CLR == 0)
       Q <= 1'b0;

   // PosedgeCLK, CLR not enabled.
   else
       Q <= D;

endmodule
------------------------------------------------------------------------
```

Step 2:   Create a test bench and run the simulation

```
------------------------------------------------------------------
D_flipflop_sim.v
------------------------------------------------------------------------
module D_flipflop_sim();
   reg CLK=0, CLR, D;
```

```
  wire Q, Qnot;

D_flipflop dut(CLK,CLR,D,Q,Qnot);

  // Create CLK
  initial forever #5 CLK = ~CLK;

  // Input stimuli
  initial begin
  #0   CLR = 1; D = 0;
  #10            D = 1;
  #10            D = 0;
  #10            D = 1;
  #10 CLR = 0;
  #10 CLR = 1;
  #10 $finish;
  end
endmodule
```

Simulation result for Example 13.8:

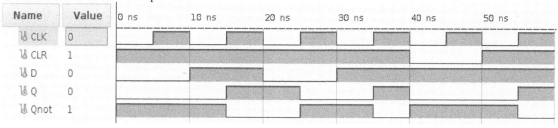

Step 3: Assign signals to FPGA I/O pins by adding constraints

----

```
D_flipflop.xdc
```

```
# Switch for D
set_property -dict { PACKAGE_PIN J15    IOSTANDARD LVCMOS33 } [get_ports D ]
#LEDs for Q and Qnot
set_property -dict { PACKAGE_PIN H17    IOSTANDARD LVCMOS33 } [get_ports Q ]
set_property -dict { PACKAGE_PIN K15    IOSTANDARD LVCMOS33 } [get_portsQnot ]

# Button for CLK - P17 is a valid FPGA CLK pin
set_property -dict { PACKAGE_PIN P17    IOSTANDARD LVCMOS33 } [get_ports CLK ]
#Button for CLR
set_property -dict { PACKAGE_PIN C12    IOSTANDARD LVCMOS33 } [get_ports CLR ]
```

Step 4: Generate bitstream, program, and test

Screenshots illustrating Example 13.8:

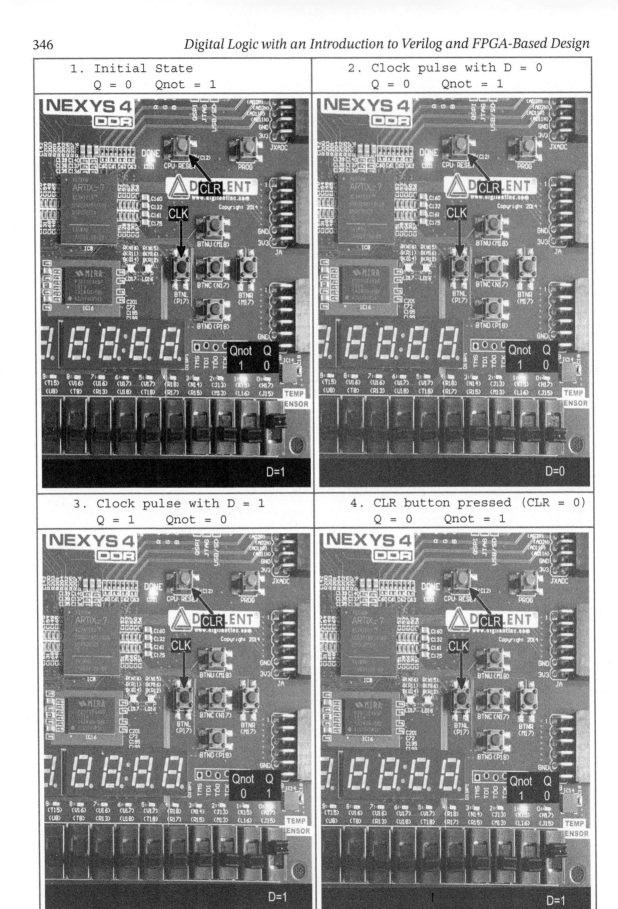

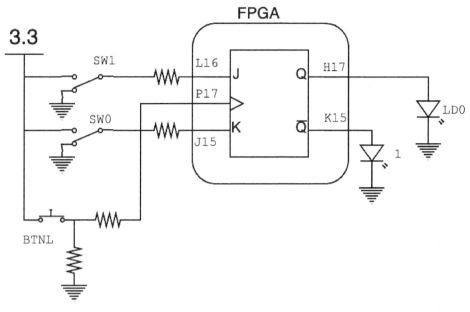

FIGURE 13.32 Figure for Example 13.8

<u>**Example 13.9**</u>

Using the Nexys 7 FPGA board, design and implement a JK flipflop shown in Figure 13.32 using slide switches on the board for J and K, and a push button for CLK. Display both Q and Qnot on LEDs.

Solution

Step 1: Create the Verilog module

```
----------------------------------------------------------------------
JK_flipflop.v
----------------------------------------------------------------------
module JK_flipflop(input CLK, J, K, output reg Q, output Qnot);

   assign Qnot = ~Q;

   always @ (posedge CLK)
   case({J,K})
   2'b00 : Q <=   Q;
   2'b01 : Q <=   0;
   2'b10 : Q <=   1;
   2'b11 : Q <=  ~Q;
Endcase

endmodule
----------------------------------------------------------------------
```

Step 2: Create a test bench and run the simulation

```
----------------------------------------------------------------------
JK_flipflop_sim.v
----------------------------------------------------------------------
```

```
module JK_flipflop_sim();
  reg CLK = 0, J,K;
  wire Q, Qnot;

JK_flipflop dut(CLK, J, K, Q, Qnot);

  initial forever #1 CLK = ~ CLK;

  initial begin
     {J,K} = 2'b01;
  #2 {J,K} = 2'b10;
  #4 {J,K} = 2'b11;
  #4 {J,K} = 2'b00;
  #4 $finish;
  end

endmodule
```

Simulation result for Example 13.9:

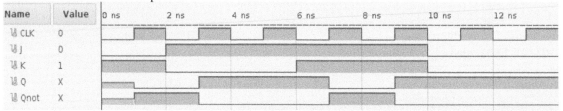

Step 3: Assign signals to FPGA I/O pins by adding constraints

----

```
JK_flipflop.xdc
```

```
# Button for CLK ? P17 is a valid FPGA CLK pin
set_property -dict { PACKAGE_PIN P17    IOSTANDARD LVCMOS33 } [get_ports CLK ]

# Switches for J and K
set_property -dict { PACKAGE_PIN L16    IOSTANDARD LVCMOS33 } [get_ports J ]
set_property -dict { PACKAGE_PIN J15    IOSTANDARD LVCMOS33 } [get_ports K ]

#LEDs for Q and Qnot
set_property -dict { PACKAGE_PIN H17    IOSTANDARD LVCMOS33 } [get_ports Q ]
set_property -dict { PACKAGE_PIN K15    IOSTANDARD LVCMOS33 } [get_portsQnot ]
```

Step 4: Generate bitstream, program, and test

Screenshot illustrating Example 13.9

With J=1 and K=0, Q transitions from low to high. Likewise, with J = 0 and K = 1, Q transitions to low. With both J=K=1, the output toggles from 0 to 1.

1. Initial State Q = 0 Qnot = 1	2. Clock pulse J = 1 K = 0 Q = 1 Qnot = 0

3. Clock pulse J = 0 K = 1 Q = 0 Qnot = 1	4. Clock pulse with J = 1 K = 1 Q = 1 Qnot = 0

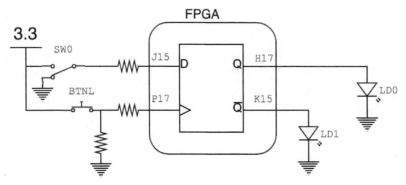

FIGURE 13.33 Figure for Example 13.10

Example 13.10

Write the Verilog description of a gated-D latch. Use dataflow modeling and the conditional operator. Finally, design and implement using the Nexys 7 FPGA board as shown in Figure 13.33.

Solution

Step 1: Create the Verilog module

```
----------------------------------------------------------------------
D_latch.v
----------------------------------------------------------------------

module D_latch(CLK,D,Q,Qnot);
input CLK,D;
output Q,Qnot;

assign Q = CLK? D:Q;
assign Qnot = ~Q;
endmodule
----------------------------------------------------------------------
```

Step 2: Create a test bench and run the simulation

```
----------------------------------------------------------------------
D_latch_sim.v
----------------------------------------------------------------------
module D_latch_sim();
   reg CLK, D;
   wire Q, Qnot;

D_latchDlatch(CLK,D,Q,Qnot);

   initial begin
   #0 CLK = 0; D = 0;
   #1 CLK = 1;
   #1 D = 1;
   #1 D = 0;
   #1 D = 1;
   #1 CLK = 0;
   #1 D = 0;
   #1 D = 1;
```

```
  #1 D = 0;
  #1 CLK = 1;
  end
endmodule
```

Simulation result for Example 13.10:

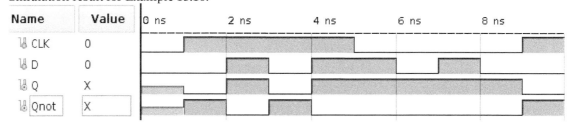

Step 3: Assign signals to FPGA I/O pins by adding constraints

----
```
D_latch.xdc
```

```
# Switch for D
set_property -dict { PACKAGE_PIN J15   IOSTANDARD LVCMOS33 } [get_ports D ]

# Button for CLK - P17 is a valid FPGA CLK pin
set_property -dict { PACKAGE_PIN P17   IOSTANDARD LVCMOS33 } [get_ports CLK ];

#LEDs for Q and Qnot
set_property -dict { PACKAGE_PIN H17   IOSTANDARD LVCMOS33 } [get_ports Q ]
set_property -dict { PACKAGE_PIN K15   IOSTANDARD LVCMOS33 } [get_ports Qnot ]
```

Step 4: Generate bitstream, program, and test

Screenshots illustrating Example 13.10:

While the *Clk* button is not pressed, changes to D do not change the output Q. When the *Clk* input is activated, the value on the D switch is latched into Q.

1. Initial State	2. D set to 1 while CLK = 0
Q = 0 Qnot = 1	No change in Q

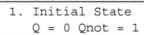

D=0

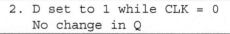

D=1

3. D set to 1 while CLK = 1	4. D = 0 while CLK = 1
Q = 1 Qnot = 0	Q = 0 Qnot = 1

D=1

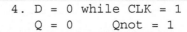

D=0

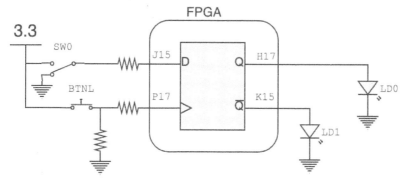

FIGURE 13.34 Figure for Example 13.11

Example 13.11

Write the Verilog description of a gated-D latch from Example 13.10 using behavioral modeling. Implement the design shown in Figure 13.34 on the Nexys 7 FPGA board.

Step 1: Create the Verilog module

```
--------------------------------------------------------------------------
D_latch_behav.v
--------------------------------------------------------------------------
module D_latch_behav(CLK,D,Q,Qnot);
input CLK,D;

output reg Q = 0;
output Qnot;

assign Qnot = ~Q;

always @ (CLK,D)
  if(CLK)
    Q = D;
  else
    Q = Q;

endmodule
--------------------------------------------------------------------------
```

Step 2: Create a test bench and run the simulation

```
--------------------------------------------------------------------------
D_latch_behav_sim.v
--------------------------------------------------------------------------

module D_latch_behav_sim();
  reg CLK, D;
  wire Q, Qnot;

D_latch dut(CLK,D,Q,Qnot);

  initial begin
  #0 CLK = 0; D = 0;
```

```
    #1 CLK = 1;
    #1 D = 1;
    #1 D = 0;
    #1 D = 1;
    #1 CLK = 0;
    #1 D = 0;
    #1 D = 1;
    #1 D = 0;
    #1 CLK = 1;
    #1 $finish;
    end
endmodule
```

Simulation result for Example 13.11:

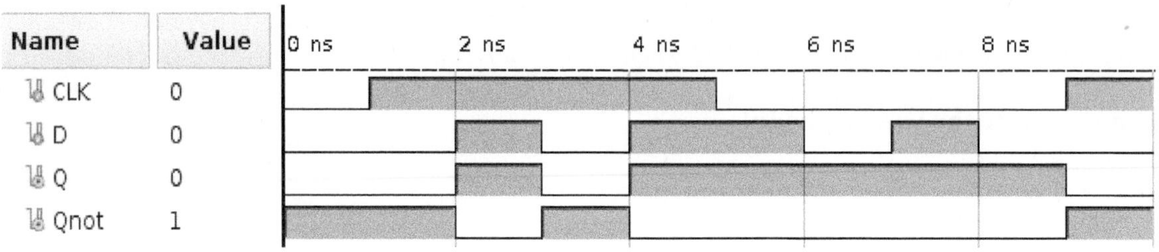

Name	Value	0 ns	2 ns	4 ns	6 ns	8 ns
CLK	0					
D	0					
Q	0					
Qnot	1					

Step 3: Assign signals to FPGA I/O pins by adding constraints

----
D_latch.xdc

```
# Switch for D
set_property -dict { PACKAGE_PIN J15    IOSTANDARD LVCMOS33 } [get_ports D ]

# Button for CLK - P17 is a valid FPGA CLK pin
set_property -dict { PACKAGE_PIN P17    IOSTANDARD LVCMOS33 } [get_ports CLK ];

#LEDs for Q and Qnot
set_property -dict { PACKAGE_PIN H17    IOSTANDARD LVCMOS33 } [get_ports Q ]
set_property -dict { PACKAGE_PIN K15    IOSTANDARD LVCMOS33 } [get_portsQnot ]
```

Step 4: Generate bitstream, program, and test

Screenshots illustrating Example 13.11:

While the *Clk* button is not pressed, changes to D do not change the output Q. When the *Clk* input is activated, the value on the D switch is latched into Q.

1. Initial State Q = 0 Qnot = 1	2. D set to 1 while CLK = 0 No change in Q
 D=0	 D=1
3. D set to 1 while CLK = 1 Q = 1 Qnot = 0	4. D = 0 while CLK = 1 Q = 0 Qnot = 1
 D=1	 D=0

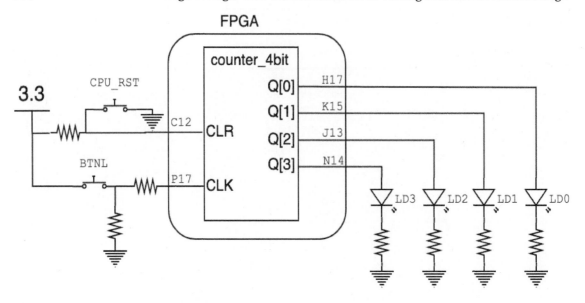

FIGURE 13.35   Figure for Example 13.12

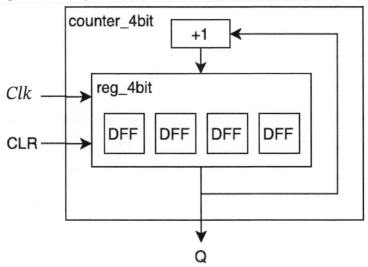

FIGURE 13.36   Figure for hierarchical modeling

Example 13.12

Using the Nexys board, design and implement a 4-bit counter with a CLR input. Use a push button for the CLK and CLR inputs as shown in Figure 13.35. Display the count on four LEDs. Use Figure 13.36 for hierarchical modeling.

Solution

Step 1:   Create the Verilog module

```
--------------------------------------------------------------------------------
D_flipflop.v
--------------------------------------------------------------------------------
module D_flipflop(CLK, CLR, D, Q, Qnot);
  input CLK, CLR, D;
  output reg Q = 0;
```

```
  output Qnot;

  assign Qnot = ~Q;

  always @ (posedge CLK or negedge CLR)
  // Negedge of CLR implies CLR will be '0'
  if(CLR == 0)
      Q <= 1'b0;

  // PosedgeClk and CLR not enabled.
  else
      Q <= D;
endmodule
```

----
reg_4bit.v

```
module reg_4bit(
  input CLK,
  input CLR,
  input [3:0]D,
  output [3:0]Q
    );

D_flipflop DFF0(CLK,CLR, D[0],Q[0],);
D_flipflop DFF1(CLK,CLR, D[1],Q[1],);
D_flipflop DFF2(CLK,CLR, D[2],Q[2],);
D_flipflop DFF3(CLK,CLR, D[3],Q[3],);

endmodule
```

----
counter_4bit.v

```
module counter_4bit(input CLK, CLR, output [3:0]Q);
  wire [3:0]D_next;

  assign D_next = Q[3:0] + 4'b0001;

  reg_4bit fourbitreg(CLK,CLR, D_next,Q[3:0]);

endmodule
```

Step 2: Create a test bench and run the simulation

----
counter_4bit_sim.v

```
module counter_4bit_sim();
  reg CLK, CLR;
  wire [3:0]Q;
```

```
  counter_4bit dut(CLK,CLR,Q);

  // Create a clock
  initial begin CLK = 0; forever #1 CLK = ~CLK; end

  initial begin
      CLR = 1;
  #8 CLR = 0;
  #2 CLR = 1;
  #6 $finish;
  end
endmodule
```

Simulation result for Example 13.12:

Step 3: Assign signals to FPGA I/O pins by adding constraints

----
counter_4bit.v

```
##Button - P17 is a CLK capable FPGA pin
set_property -dict { PACKAGE_PIN P17    IOSTANDARD LVCMOS33 } [get_ports CLK ];
set_property -dict { PACKAGE_PIN C12    IOSTANDARD LVCMOS33 } [get_ports CLR ];

## LEDs
set_property -dict { PACKAGE_PIN H17    IOSTANDARD LVCMOS33 } [get_ports  Q[0] ];
set_property -dict { PACKAGE_PIN K15    IOSTANDARD LVCMOS33 } [get_ports  Q[1] ];
set_property -dict { PACKAGE_PIN J13    IOSTANDARD LVCMOS33 } [get_ports  Q[2] ];
set_property -dict { PACKAGE_PIN N14    IOSTANDARD LVCMOS33 } [get_ports  Q[3] ];
```

Step 4: Generate bitstream, program, and test

Screenshots illustrating Example 13.12:

Initial State Q = 4'b0000	1st clk pulse Q = 4'b0001

2nd clk pulse Q = 4'b0010	CLR set to 0 Q = 4'b0000

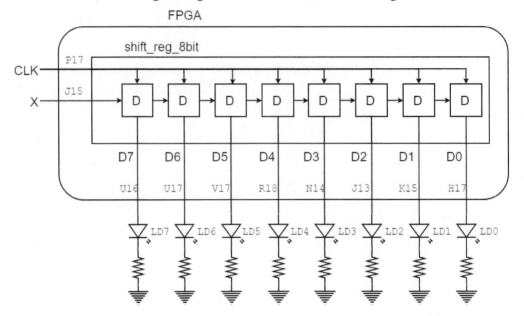

FIGURE 13.37 Figure for Example 13.13

Example 13.13

Using Nexys board, design and implement an 8-bit shift register shown in Figure 13.37 which shifts in an input to the MSB (Most Significant Bit) of the register on the positive edge of the clock.

Solution

Step 1:   Create the Verilog module

```
--------------------------------------------------------------------------
shift_reg_8bit.v
--------------------------------------------------------------------------
module shift_reg_8bit(input CLK, input X, output reg [7:0]D);
  wire [7:0] next_data;

  assign next_data = {X, D[7:1]};

  always @ (posedge CLK)
    D <= next_data;

endmodule
--------------------------------------------------------------------------
```

Step 2: Create a test bench and run the simulation

```
--------------------------------------------------------------------------
shift_reg_sim.xdc
--------------------------------------------------------------------------
module shift_reg_sim();
  reg CLK=0, X=0;
  wire [7:0]Q;

  shift_reg_8bit dut(CLK,X,Q);
```

```
    initial forever # 1 CLK = ~CLK;

    initial begin
    X = 0;
    #6 X=1;
    #8 X=0;
    end
endmodule
```

Simulation result for Example 13.13:

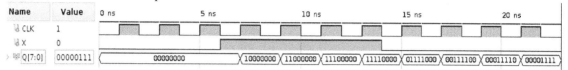

Step 3:   Assign signals to FPGA I/O pins by adding constraints

----

shift_reg.xdc

```
set_property -dict { PACKAGE_PIN P17   IOSTANDARD LVCMOS33 } [get_ports CLK]

##Switches
set_property -dict { PACKAGE_PIN J15   IOSTANDARD LVCMOS33 } [get_ports X ]

## LEDs
set_property -dict { PACKAGE_PIN H17   IOSTANDARD LVCMOS33 } [get_ports D[0] ]
set_property -dict { PACKAGE_PIN K15   IOSTANDARD LVCMOS33 } [get_ports D[1] ]
set_property -dict { PACKAGE_PIN J13   IOSTANDARD LVCMOS33 } [get_ports D[2] ]
set_property -dict { PACKAGE_PIN N14   IOSTANDARD LVCMOS33 } [get_ports D[3] ]
set_property -dict { PACKAGE_PIN R18   IOSTANDARD LVCMOS33 } [get_ports D[4] ]
set_property -dict { PACKAGE_PIN V17   IOSTANDARD LVCMOS33 } [get_ports D[5] ]
set_property -dict { PACKAGE_PIN U17   IOSTANDARD LVCMOS33 } [get_ports D[6] ]
set_property -dict { PACKAGE_PIN U16   IOSTANDARD LVCMOS33 } [get_ports D[7] ]
```

Step 4:   Generate bitstream, program, and test

Screenshots illustrating Example 13.13:

When the *Clk* is pulse, the value on the X switch is shifted into the shift register from the left.

Initial State Q = 8'b0000_0000	1st clk pulse and X = 1 Q = 8'b1000_0000

After shifting in serial data 0 0 0 1 1 0 0 1 Q = 8'b1001_1000

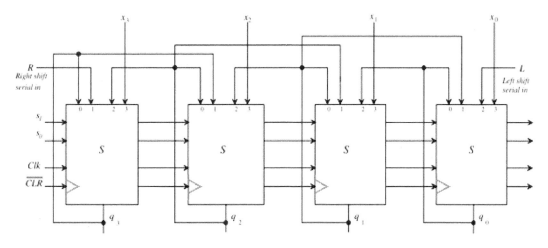

Selection Input		Clock Input	Clear Input	Operation
S_1	S_0	*Clk*	*CLR*	
X	X	X	0	Clear
0	0	⬆	1	No operation
0	1	⬆	1	Shift Right
1	0	⬆	1	Shift Left
1	1	⬆	1	Parallel Load

X means "don't care"

FIGURE 13.38 Figure for Example 13.14

Example 13.14

Using the Nexys board, design and implement a general purpose register shown in Figure 13.38. FPGA–based implementation for hierarchical modeling using basic cell S is shown in Figure 13.39. The structure of the basic cell S is shown in Figure 13.40.

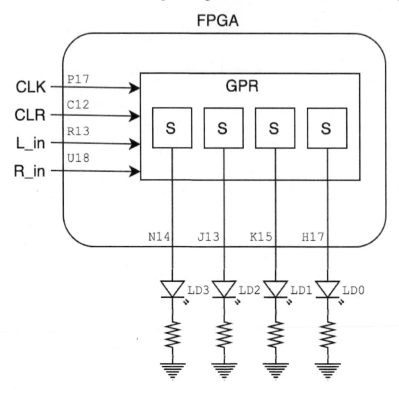

FIGURE 13.39 FPGA – based Implementation using hierarchical modeling for basic cell S

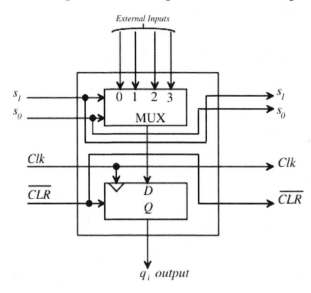

FIGURE 13.40 The structure of the basic cell S

Step 1: Create the Verilog module

Describe the basic cell:

```
-------------------------------------------------------------------------
basic_cell.v:
-------------------------------------------------------------------------
module basic_cell(
  output reg Q,
  input CLR, CLK,
  input [1:0]Sel,
  input [3:0]I
  );

  //Internal nets
  wire data;

  //D Flip Flop
  always @ (posedge CLK or negedge CLR)
  if(!CLR)
    Q <= 0;
  else
    Q <= data;

  //Mux
  assign data = I[Sel];
endmodule
-------------------------------------------------------------------------
```

Instantiate 4 instances of the basic cell to form the GPR:

```
-------------------------------------------------------------------------
GPR.v
-------------------------------------------------------------------------
module GPR(
  output [3:0]Q,
  input [1:0]S,
  input [3:0]D,
  input CLR, CLK, L_in, R_in
  );

  /*

  _____
  |  S    |   Operation          |
  |_____|_____|
  |  00   |   Hold               |
  |  01   |   Shift Right        |
  |  10   |   Shift Left         |
  |  11   |   Parallel Load      |
  |_____|_____|
  */
  //Instantiate 4 basic cells
```

```
basic_cell cell3( Q[3], CLR, CLK, S, { D[3], Q[2], L_in, Q[3] } ),
           cell2( Q[2], CLR, CLK, S, { D[2], Q[1], Q[3], Q[2] } ),
           cell1( Q[1], CLR, CLK, S, { D[1], Q[0], Q[2], Q[1] } ),
           cell0( Q[0], CLR, CLK, S, { D[0], R_in, Q[1], Q[0] } );
endmodule
```

Step 2: Create a test bench and run the simulation

GPR_sim.v

```
module GPR_sim();
  reg [3:0] D;
  reg [1:0] S;
  reg L_in, R_in, CLK=0, CLR;
  wire [3:0]Q;

  GPR dut(Q, S, D, CLR, CLK, L_in, R_in);

  // Create simulation clock
  initial forever #5 CLK = ~CLK;

  initial begin
      S = 0; D = 4'b1100;         //Clear
  CLR = 0; L_in = 0; R_in = 0; //Clear
    #10 S = 3; CLR = 1;  // Parallel Load
    #10 S = 1;           // Shift Right
    #10 S = 2;           // Shift Left
    #10 S = 1; L_in = 1; // Shift Right inserting '1'
    #10 S = 2; R_in = 1; // Shift Left inserting '1'

    end
endmodule
```

Simulation result for Example 13.14:

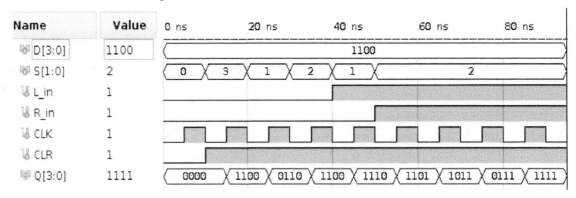

Step 3: Assign signals to FPGA I/O pins by adding constraints

----
GPR.xdc

```
##Switches
set_property -dict { PACKAGE_PIN J15   IOSTANDARD LVCMOS33 } [get_ports  D[0] ];
set_property -dict { PACKAGE_PIN L16   IOSTANDARD LVCMOS33 } [get_ports  D[1] ];
set_property -dict { PACKAGE_PIN M13   IOSTANDARD LVCMOS33 } [get_ports  D[2] ];
```

```
set_property -dict { PACKAGE_PIN R15    IOSTANDARD LVCMOS33 } [get_ports   D[3] ];
set_property -dict { PACKAGE_PIN R17    IOSTANDARD LVCMOS33 } [get_ports   S[0] ];
set_property -dict { PACKAGE_PIN T18    IOSTANDARD LVCMOS33 } [get_ports   S[1] ];
set_property -dict { PACKAGE_PIN U18    IOSTANDARD LVCMOS33 } [get_portsR_in ];
set_property -dict { PACKAGE_PIN R13    IOSTANDARD LVCMOS33 } [get_portsL_in ];

##Button - P17 is a valid FPGA CLK pin
set_property -dict { PACKAGE_PIN P17    IOSTANDARD LVCMOS33 } [get_ports BTN_EXEC ];
set_property -dict { PACKAGE_PIN C12    IOSTANDARD LVCMOS33 } [get_ports CLR ];

## LEDs
set_property -dict { PACKAGE_PIN H17    IOSTANDARD LVCMOS33 } [get_ports   Q[0] ];
set_property -dict { PACKAGE_PIN K15    IOSTANDARD LVCMOS33 } [get_ports   Q[1] ];
set_property -dict { PACKAGE_PIN J13    IOSTANDARD LVCMOS33 } [get_ports   Q[2] ];
set_property -dict { PACKAGE_PIN N14    IOSTANDARD LVCMOS33 } [get_ports   Q[3] ];
```

Step 4: Generate bitstream, program, and test Screenshots illustrating Example 13.14:
The same sequence of operations as shown in the simulation is verified on the FPGA board.

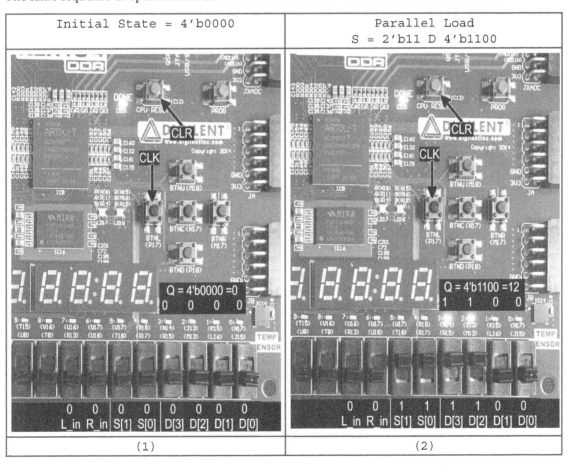

Right Shift S = 2'b01 L_in = 0 R_in = 0	Left Shift S = 2'b10 L_in = 0 R_in = 0
 Q = 4'b0110 = 6	Q = 4'b1110 = 12

Right Shift
S = 2'b01 L_in = 0 R_in = 0

L_in	R_in	S[1]	S[0]	D[3]	D[2]	D[1]	D[0]
0	0	0	1	1	1	0	0

(3)

Left Shift
S = 2'b10 L_in = 0 R_in = 0

L_in	R_in	S[1]	S[0]	D[3]	D[2]	D[1]	D[0]
0	0	1	0	1	1	0	0

(4)

Right Shift inserting 1
S = 2'b01 L_in = 1 R_in = 0

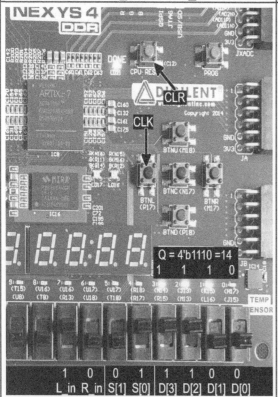

Q = 4'b1110 = 14

L_in	R_in	S[1]	S[0]	D[3]	D[2]	D[1]	D[0]
1	0	0	1	1	1	0	0

(5)

Left Shift inserting 1
S = 2'b10 L_in = 0 R_in = 1

Q = 4'b1101 = 13

L_in	R_in	S[1]	S[0]	D[3]	D[2]	D[1]	D[0]
0	1	1	0	1	1	0	0

(6)

Figures (1) through (6) show the operation of the general purpose register from Example 13.14. Figure (1) shows the initial state of the 4-bit register with a value of 4'b0000. Figure (2) shows the result after the parallel load function (S = 2'b11) with D = 4'b1100, to give an output of 4'b1100. Next, the right-shift operation (S = 2'b01) is performed on the 4-bit value 4'b1100, resulting in the 4'b0110 value shown in Figure (3). The left-shift operation (S = 2'b10) is then applied on the 4'b0110 value from Figure (3) to give the output of 4'b1100 shown in Figure (4). The L_in and R_in functionality is tested by first performing a right-shift with L_in = 1 on the result shown in Figure (4) of 4'b1100. The result is 4'b1110 as shown in Figure (5) since a '1' is inserted as the MSB from the left. Lastly, a left-shift with R_in = 1 on the value 4'b1110 from Figure (5) results in the value 4'b1101 shown in Figure (6).

Example 13.15

Using the Nexys board, design and implement the state diagram shown in Figure 13.41. Display the current state on a seven segment display. Figure 13.42 shows the block diagram for FPGA implementation.

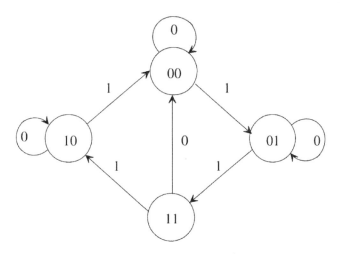

FIGURE 13.41 State diagram for Example 13.15

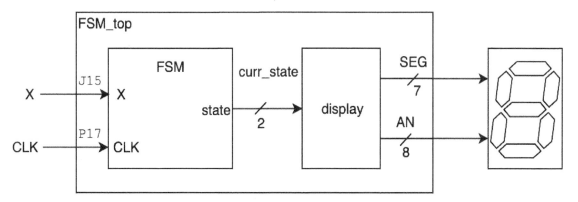

FIGURE 13.42 Block diagram of the FPGA implementation for Example 13.15

Solution

Step 1: Create the Verilog module

```
-------------------------------------------------------------------------------
FSM.v
-------------------------------------------------------------------------------
```

```verilog
module FSM(CLK, X, state);
input CLK, X;
output reg [1:0]state = 2'b00;
reg [1:0]next_state;

always @ (posedge CLK)
  state <= next_state;

always @ (X or state)
begin
next_state = state;
  case(state)
  0: if(X) next_state<= 1;
  1: if(X) next_state<= 3;
  2: if(X) next_state<= 0;
  3: if(X) next_state<= 2; else next_state<= 0;
endcase
end
endmodule
```

---

display.v

```verilog
module display(input [1:0]state,
output reg [0:6]SEG, output [7:0]AN);
assign AN = 8'b1111_1110;
always @ (state)
    case(state)
    0:SEG = 7'b000_0001;
    1:SEG = 7'b100_1111;
    2:SEG = 7'b001_0010;
    3:SEG = 7'b000_0110;
endcase
endmodule
```

FSM_top.v

```verilog
module FSM_top(input CLK, input X, output [0:6]SEG, output [7:0]AN);
  wire [1:0]curr_state;

  //FSM
  FSM u0(CLK,X,curr_state);

  //Display
  display u1(curr_state,SEG,AN);
endmodule
```

Step 2: Create a test bench and run the simulation

FSM_sim.v

```verilog
module FSM_sim();
  reg CLK = 0, X;
```

```
    wire [1:0]state;

    FSM dut(CLK,X,state);

    initial forever #0.5 CLK = ~CLK;

    initial begin
        X = 1;
      #6 X = 0;
      #2 $finish;
      end

endmodule
```

Simulation result for Example 13.15:

Name	Value	0 ns	2 ns	4 ns	6 ns
CLK	0				
X	1				
state[1:0]	0	0 X 1 X 3 X 2 X 0 X 1 X 3 X 0			

Step 3: Assign signals to FPGA I/O pins by adding constraints

----

FSM.xdc

```
## Button for CLK - P17 is a FPGA clk input
set_property -dict { PACKAGE_PIN P17   IOSTANDARD LVCMOS33 } [get_ports CLK ]
##Switch for X
set_property -dict { PACKAGE_PIN J15   IOSTANDARD LVCMOS33 } [get_ports X ]
##7 segment display
set_property -dict { PACKAGE_PIN T10   IOSTANDARD LVCMOS33 } [get_ports SEG[0] ]
set_property -dict { PACKAGE_PIN R10   IOSTANDARD LVCMOS33 } [get_ports SEG[1] ]
set_property -dict { PACKAGE_PIN K16   IOSTANDARD LVCMOS33 } [get_ports SEG[2] ]
set_property -dict { PACKAGE_PIN K13   IOSTANDARD LVCMOS33 } [get_ports SEG[3] ]
set_property -dict { PACKAGE_PIN P15   IOSTANDARD LVCMOS33 } [get_ports SEG[4] ]
set_property -dict { PACKAGE_PIN T11   IOSTANDARD LVCMOS33 } [get_ports SEG[5] ]
set_property -dict { PACKAGE_PIN L18   IOSTANDARD LVCMOS33 } [get_ports SEG[6] ]
set_property -dict { PACKAGE_PIN J17   IOSTANDARD LVCMOS33 } [get_ports { AN[0] }]
set_property -dict { PACKAGE_PIN J18   IOSTANDARD LVCMOS33 } [get_ports { AN[1] }]
set_property -dict { PACKAGE_PIN T9    IOSTANDARD LVCMOS33 } [get_ports { AN[2] }]
set_property -dict { PACKAGE_PIN J14   IOSTANDARD LVCMOS33 } [get_ports { AN[3] }]
set_property -dict { PACKAGE_PIN P14   IOSTANDARD LVCMOS33 } [get_ports { AN[4] }]
set_property -dict { PACKAGE_PIN T14   IOSTANDARD LVCMOS33 } [get_ports { AN[5] }]
set_property -dict { PACKAGE_PIN K2    IOSTANDARD LVCMOS33 } [get_ports { AN[6] }]
set_property -dict { PACKAGE_PIN U13   IOSTANDARD LVCMOS33 } [get_ports { AN[7] }]
```

Step 4: Generate bitstream, program, and test

Screenshots illustrating Example 13.15:

The FSM is tested using the same conditions as shown in the simulation.

1. Initial State = 0	2. 1st clk pulse X = 1 State <= 1

3. 2nd clk pulse X = 1 State <= 3	4. 3rd clk pulse X = 1 State <= 2

5. When in Step 4, FSM is in State 2 (Figure 13.41). Applying appropriate inputs and clocks, the FSM can be in State 3. With X = 0, next State will be State 0 rather than State 2 as shown in Step 4.	6. Result after Step 5. FSM transitions from State 3 to State 0 when imput X = 0.

QUESTIONS AND PROBLEMS

13.1   What are the basic differences between CPLD and FPGA?

13.2   Name a single application where both CPLD and FPGA is used.

13.3   Store a two-input XOR gate in a 4x1 SRAM.

13.4   Implement f = abc + de using a minimum number of 2x1 LUTs.

13.5   What are the purposes of switch matrix and CLB in a typical FPGA CHIP?

13.6   Name pins on a typical FPGA chip, and then briefly describe their functions.

13.7   What are meant by design, synthesis, and bitstrem programming in a FPGA-based design and implementation?

13.8   Summarize the steps for FPGA-based design and implementation. Implement the schematic shown in Figure P13.8 on the Nexys A7 FPGA board. Use switches for inputs and LEDs for outputs.

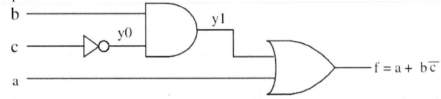

FIGURE P13.8

13.9   Implement a 3-to-8 decoder shown in Figure P13.9. Use switches SW2, SW1, and SW0 for the inputs and LD7 through LD0 for the outputs.

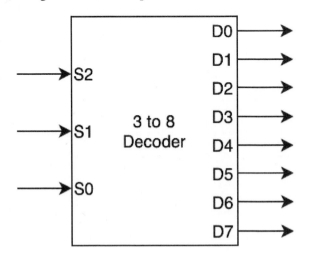

FIGURE P13.9

13.10 Implement a BCD to seven-segment converter. Turn OFF all the segments for non-BCD numbers

13.11 Design a 4-bit comparator shown in Figure P13.12 which compares A to B. If A > B, GT = '1' for example.

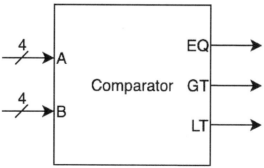

FIGURE P13.11

13.12 Design and implement a 4-bit full adder and subtractor shown in Figure P13.12 which performs A+B or A-B depending on a Mode switch. Mode=0 performs addition, and Mode=1 performs subtraction. Display the result on four LEDs LD3 to LD0, and use LD4 for the final carry. Use SW3 to SW0 for A, SW7 to SW4 for B, and SW16 for Mode.

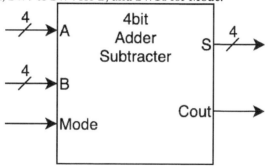

FIGURE P13.12

13.13 Expand on Problem 13.12 by displaying the 4-bit number on a seven segment display. Use the RED led connected to FPGA pin N15 to indicate a negative number. For example, a result of negative 3 should show a '3' on the display and illuminate the RED led.

13.14 Design and implement a 4-bit D Flip-flop register which loads the data from SW3 through SW0 at the positive edge of the clock. Use BTN_L for the clock since it is connected to a FPGA pin P17 which can be used as a clock.

13.15 Improve the functionality of Problem 13.14 by adding asynchronous reset and preset (load 1) to the 4-bit register.

13.16 Design a counter that counts in the following sequence and repeats. Use the BTN_L for the clock. Display the current value on the seven segment display.

$$0 \rightarrow 2 \rightarrow 1 \rightarrow 3 \rightarrow 4 \rightarrow 6 \rightarrow 5 \rightarrow 7$$

13.17 Implement a 4-bit Johnson counter using four LEDs.

13.18   Design and implement an 8-bit shift register with asynchronous clear that shifts RIGHT at the positive edge of the clock. Use BTN_L for the clock, and the CPU_RESET button for the clear that happens whenever clear is low.

13.19   Design the 4-bit serial adder shown in Figure P13.19.

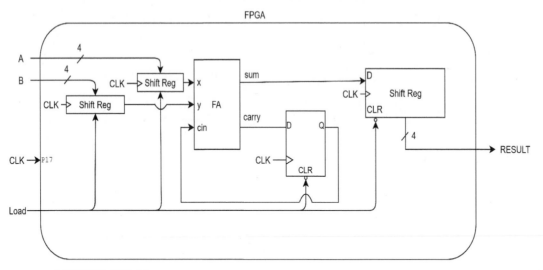

FIGURE P13.19

13.20   Implement a "Blinky" circuit which turns on and off an LED per second. Use the 100MHz clock input to the FPGA.

13.21   Design a circuit which uses an RGB LED on the FPGA board to perform the following:
Green for 5 seconds
Yellow for 2 seconds
Red for 5 seconds
Repeat.

13.22   Design a "Blinky 2.0" circuit which blinks depending on two switch inputs:

00: Always Off

01: Once per second

10: Twice per second

11: Four times per second

13.23 Design a 4-bit hex counter that counts once per second. Implement an enable signal using a switch which allows the counter to be halted. Display the current counter value on one of the seven-segment displays. Figure P13.23 shows the counter. Use the Nexys 7 board.

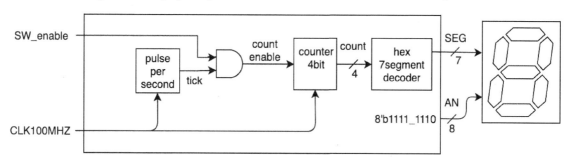

FIGURE P13.23

APPENDIX A: ANSWERS TO SELECTED PROBLEMS

Chapter 2

2.1(b) $1101.101_2 = 13.625_{10}$

2.2(b) $343_{10} = 101010111_2$

2.3(a) $1843_{10} = 3463_8$

2.4(b) $3072_{10} = C00_{16}$

2.6(c) $-48_{10} = 1101\ 0000_2$

2.11(c) $61440_{10} = 1001\ 0100\ 0111\ 0111\ 0011_2$

2.16(b) $0011\ 1110_2$

2.19(b) 0; no overflow

2.19(d) overflow

2.22(a) $0001\ 0000\ 0010_2 = 102$ in BCD

Chapter 3

3.1 $36_{16} \oplus 2A_{16} = 1C_{16}$

3.3 1's Complement of $A7_{16}$

3.6(d) $\overline{(A + \overline{A}B)} = \overline{A}(\overline{\overline{A}B})$

$= \overline{A}(A + \overline{B})$

$= \overline{A}\overline{B}$

3.6(f) $\overline{B}\overline{C} + ABC + \overline{A}\overline{C} = \overline{C}(\overline{B}+\overline{A}) + ABC$

$= \overline{C}(\overline{AB}) + (AB)C$

$= \overline{C \oplus (AB)}$

3.7(c) BC

3.7(i) 1

3.11(a) X + Y

3.13 $f = A + B$

Chapter 4

4.1(a) $F = \Sigma m(0, 1, 5, 7, 10, 14, 15)$
$\overline{F} = \Sigma m(2, 3, 4, 6, 8, 9, 11, 12, 13)$

4.3 (c) $F = \overline{Z}$

4.4 (c) $F = \overline{C}$

4.6 (a) $F = \overline{W} \oplus Y$

4.8 (a) $\overline{F} = \overline{W}X + \overline{Y} + \overline{Z}$

4.10 (a) $f = A + B \oplus C$

Chapter 5

5.1 $F = 0$

5.7 $f = \overline{A \oplus C}$

5.10 $f_3 = \overline{ABC}$ $f_2 = B \oplus C$ $f_1 = C$ $F_0 = \overline{D}$

5.13   a through $g = \overline{w}$

Chapter 6

6.3 $F0 = \Sigma m(0, 4, 5)$ $F1 = \Sigma m(4, 6)$ $F2 = \Sigma m(0, 7)$ $F3 = \Sigma m(2, 3, 6)$

6.6 $Z = 1$

       $Y = 0$

       $X = m5$

       $W = m9$

6.9 $d0 = 0$ $d1 = 1$

6.12   Add the 4-bit unsigned number to itself using full adders.

6.15   For a 4-Bit signed number, A
         $A + 1111_2 = A - 1$, decrement by 1.
         $A + 0001_2 = A + 1$, increment by 1.
         Manipulate C_{in} to accomplish the above.

Chapter 7

7.1

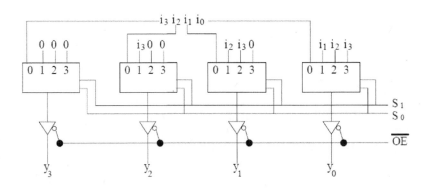

7.9

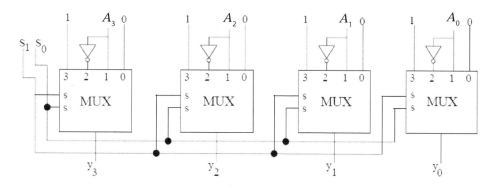

Note: In the diagram above, $B = A = \overline{A}_3\,\overline{A}_2\,\overline{A}_1\,\overline{A}_0 = $ 1's complement of A.

7.10

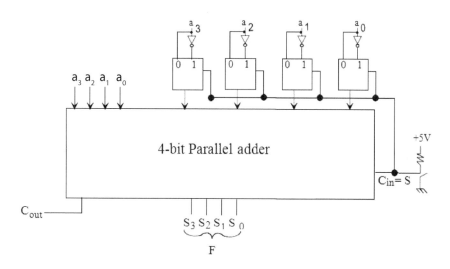

$S = C_{in} = 0$, $F = 2 * A = $ logical left shift once.
$S = C_{in} = 1$, $F = A - A = 0$

7.11

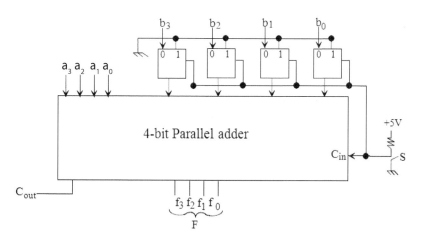

$S = 0$, $F = A + B$
$S = 1$, $F = A + 1$

Chapter 8

8.1   `module circuit_8_1(input [1:0] A, B, output [2:0] Z);`

8.5   ```
module circuit_8_3(input A, B, C, output F);
        wire w1, w2, w3, w4;
        assign w1 = A & B;
        assign w2 = ~A;
        assign w3 = B ^ C;
        assign w4 = w2 & w3;
        assign F = w1 | w4;
endmodule
```

8.7     ```
module mux_4x1(input [1:0] S, input [3:0]D, output M);
        wire [0:3]W;

        and and0(W[0], ~S[1], ~S[0], D[0]),
        and (W[1], ~S[1],  S[0], D[1]),
        and (W[2],  S[1], ~S[0], D[2]),
        and (W[3],  S[1],  S[0], D[3]);
        or(M, W[0], W[1], W[2], W[3]);
endmodule
```

8.11   ```
module adder_5bit(A,B,Cin,Cout,S);
input [4:0]A,B;
input Cin;
output Cout;
output [4:0]S;
        wire [4:0]C;

FA FA0 (A[0], B[0], Cin, C[1], S[0]),
FA1 (A[1], B[1], C[1], C[2], S[1]),
FA2 (A[2], B[2], C[2], C[3], S[2]),
FA3 (A[3], B[3], C[3], C[4], S[3]),
FA4 (A[4], B[4], C[4], Cout, S[4]);
endmodule
```

8.15    ```
module logical_shift(input [6:0] A, input D, output [7:0]B);
assign B = (D == 1) ? A << 1 : A >> 1;
endmodule
```

Chapter 9

9.5 $A = 1, B = 0$
9.7 $A = 1, B = 1$

9.10

9.13 (a) Tie JK inputs to HIGH; Clock is the T input.

9.15   Truth table:

T	Q
0	$\overline{Q}$
1	Q

Hence, T-ff.

Chapter 10

10.2 $B_+ = A$, output $y = \overline{B}$
$A_+ = B \oplus x$

10.7(b) $Jx = z, kx = y$
$Jy = 1, ky = x + z$
$Jz = xy, kz = x$

10.8 $A+ = D_A = \overline{B} + x, B+ = D_B = A$, output, $y = A\overline{B}$

10.10 $D_A = \underline{\ }(A \oplus x) + \overline{B}x$ $Y = \overline{A}\overline{B} + ABx$ where x is the input
$D_B = x(A \oplus B) + AB\overline{x}$

Chapter 11

11.1 $T_3 = Q_3Q_0 + Q_2Q_1Q_0$
$T_2 = \overline{Q_1}Q_0$
$T_1 = \overline{Q_3}Q_0$
$T_0 = 1$

11.2 $J_A = B, K_A = BC, J_B = C, K_B = C, J_C = 1, K_C = A + B$
self correcting

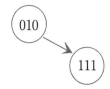

11.14

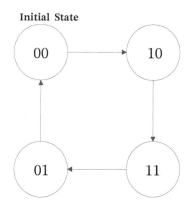

11.15

$$
\begin{array}{cc}
\text{Present State} & \text{Next State} \\
\text{A B} & \text{A+ B+} \\
1\ 0 & 0\ 1 \\
0\ 1 & 1\ 0
\end{array}
$$

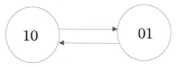

Chapter 12

12.3
```
module DFF_preset(CLK, PRE, D, Q, Qnot);
input CLK, PRE, D;
 output reg Q;
 output Qnot;

assign Qnot = ~Q;

always @ (posedge CLK or negedge PRE)
  if(PRE == 0)
 Q <= 1;
else
 Q <= D;

endmodule
```

12.4
```
module reg_4bit(CLK, CLR, D, Q);
input CLK, CLR;
input [3:0] D;
output reg [3:0] Q;

always @ (posedge CLK or posedge CLR)
if(CLR)
Q <= 4'h0;
    else
Q <= D;

endmodule
```

12.8
```
module shiftreg_8bit(CLK, RST, X, D);
input CLK, RST, X;
output reg [7:0] D = 0;

always @ (posedge CLK or negedge RST)
if(!RST)
D <= 8'b0000_0000;
 else
D <= { X, D[7:1] };
endmodule
```

12.12
```verilog
module FSM_12p12(CLK, X, Z);
input CLK, X;
output Z;

parameter A = 2'b00;
parameter B = 2'b01;
parameter C = 2'b10;
parameter D = 2'b11;

reg [1:0] state = 0;

assign Z = (state == D)? 1: 0;

always @ (posedge CLK)
case(state)
A : if(X == 1)
state <= B;
else
state <= A;
B : if(X == 0)
state <= C;
else
state <= B;
 C : if(X == 1)
state <= D;
else
state <= A;
D : if(X == 0)
state <= C;
else
state <= B;
endcase
endmodule
```

12.14
```verilog
module BCD_counter(CLK, RST, COUNT);
input CLK, RST;
output reg [3:0] COUNT;

always @ (posedge CLK or posedge RST)
if(RST)
COUNT <= 0;
else
 if(COUNT == 9)
      COUNT <= 0;
       else
COUNT <= COUNT + 1;
endmodule
```

Chapter 13

13.3

Address	Data
00	0
01	1
10	1
11	0

```
13.8    module problem_13p8(input a, b, c, output f);
            wire y0, y1;

            not(y0, c);
            and(y1, b, y0);
            or(f, y1, a);

        endmodule

        ########## Constraints #########
        #switches
        set_property -dict { PACKAGE_PIN J15    IOSTANDARD LVCMOS33 } [get_ports  c ];
        set_property -dict { PACKAGE_PIN L16    IOSTANDARD LVCMOS33 } [get_ports  b ];
        set_property -dict { PACKAGE_PIN M13    IOSTANDARD LVCMOS33 } [get_ports  a ];

        # LED
        set_property -dict { PACKAGE_PIN H17    IOSTANDARD LVCMOS33 } [get_ports  f ];


13.10   module bcd_sevenseg(
        input [3:0]BCD,
            output reg [0:6]segments
            );
            always @ BCD
            case(BCD)
            4'h0:segments = 7'b000_0001;
            4'h1:segments = 7'b100_1111;
            4'h2:segments = 7'b001_0010;
            4'h3:segments = 7'b000_0110;
            4'h4:segments = 7'b100_1100;
            4'h5:segments = 7'b010_0100;
            4'h6:segments = 7'b010_0000;
            4'h7:segments = 7'b000_1111;
            4'h8:segments = 7'b000_0000;
            4'h9:segments = 7'b000_0100;
            default: segments = 7'b111_1111;
        endcase
        endmodule

        ########## Constraints #########
        ##Switches
        set_property -dict { PACKAGE_PIN J15    IOSTANDARD LVCMOS33 } [get_ports  BCD[0] ];
        set_property -dict { PACKAGE_PIN L16    IOSTANDARD LVCMOS33 } [get_ports  BCD[1] ];
        set_property -dict { PACKAGE_PIN M13    IOSTANDARD LVCMOS33 } [get_ports  BCD[2] ];
        set_property -dict { PACKAGE_PIN R15    IOSTANDARD LVCMOS33 } [get_ports  BCD[3] ];

        #Seven Seg
        set_property -dict { PACKAGE_PIN T10   IOSTANDARD LVCMOS33 } [get_ports segments[0] ]
        set_property -dict { PACKAGE_PIN R10   IOSTANDARD LVCMOS33 } [get_ports segments[1] ]
        set_property -dict { PACKAGE_PIN K16   IOSTANDARD LVCMOS33 } [get_ports segments[2] ]
        set_property -dict { PACKAGE_PIN K13   IOSTANDARD LVCMOS33 } [get_ports segments[3] ]
        set_property -dict { PACKAGE_PIN P15   IOSTANDARD LVCMOS33 } [get_ports segments[4] ]
        set_property -dict { PACKAGE_PIN T11   IOSTANDARD LVCMOS33 } [get_ports segments[5] ]
        set_property -dict { PACKAGE_PIN L18   IOSTANDARD LVCMOS33 } [get_ports segments[6] ]
```

13.11
```verilog
module comparator(input [3:0] A, input [3:0] B, output EQ, GT, LT);
     assign EQ = (A == B)? 1 : 0;
     assign GT = (A  > B)? 1 : 0;
     assign LT = (A  < B)? 1 : 0;
endmodule
```

```
########## Constraints #########
##Switches
set_property -dict { PACKAGE_PIN J15   IOSTANDARD LVCMOS33 } [get_ports { B[0] } ];
set_property -dict { PACKAGE_PIN L16   IOSTANDARD LVCMOS33 } [get_ports { B[1] } ];
set_property -dict { PACKAGE_PIN M13   IOSTANDARD LVCMOS33 } [get_ports { B[2] } ];
set_property -dict { PACKAGE_PIN R15   IOSTANDARD LVCMOS33 } [get_ports { B[3] } ];
set_property -dict { PACKAGE_PIN R17   IOSTANDARD LVCMOS33 } [get_ports { A[0] } ];
set_property -dict { PACKAGE_PIN T18   IOSTANDARD LVCMOS33 } [get_ports { A[1] } ];
set_property -dict { PACKAGE_PIN U18   IOSTANDARD LVCMOS33 } [get_ports { A[2] } ];
set_property -dict { PACKAGE_PIN R13   IOSTANDARD LVCMOS33 } [get_ports { A[3] } ];
```

13.14
```verilog
module register_4bit(CLK, SW, Q);
input CLK;
input [3:0]SW;
output reg [3:0]Q;

always @ (posedge CLK)
Q <= SW;
endmodule
```

```
########## Constraints #########
set_property -dict { PACKAGE_PIN P17   IOSTANDARD LVCMOS33 } [get_ports
CLK]

set_property -dict { PACKAGE_PIN J15   IOSTANDARD LVCMOS33 } [get_ports  SW[0] ];
set_property -dict { PACKAGE_PIN L16   IOSTANDARD LVCMOS33 } [get_ports  SW[1] ];
set_property -dict { PACKAGE_PIN M13   IOSTANDARD LVCMOS33 } [get_ports  SW[2] ];
set_property -dict { PACKAGE_PIN R15   IOSTANDARD LVCMOS33 } [get_ports  SW[3] ];

set_property -dict { PACKAGE_PIN H17   IOSTANDARD LVCMOS33 } [get_ports  Q[0] ];
set_property -dict { PACKAGE_PIN K15   IOSTANDARD LVCMOS33 } [get_ports  Q[1] ];
set_property -dict { PACKAGE_PIN J13   IOSTANDARD LVCMOS33 } [get_ports  Q[2] ];

set_property -dict { PACKAGE_PIN N14   IOSTANDARD LVCMOS33 } [get_ports  Q[3] ];
```

APPENDIX B
GLOSSARY

Address: A unique identification number (or locator) for source or destination of data. An address specifies the register or memory location of an operand involved in the instruction.

Address Space: The number of storage location in a microcomputer's memory that can be directly addressed by the microprocessor. The addressing range is determined by the number of address pins provided with the microprocessor chip.

American Standard Code for Information Interchange (ASCII): An 8-bit code commonly used with microprocessors for representing alphanumeric codes.

Analog-to-Digital (A/D) Converter: Transforms an analog voltage into its digital equivalent.

AND Gate: The output is 1, if all inputs are 1; otherwise the output is 0.

Arithmetic and Logic Unit (ALU): A digital circuit which performs arithmetic and logic operations on two n-bit numbers.

ASIC: Application Specific IC. Chips designed for a specific, limited application. Normally reduces the total manufacturing cost of a product by reducing chip count.

Assembler: A program that translates an assembly language program into a machine language program.

Assembly Language: A type of microcontroller and microprossor programming language that uses a semi-English-language statement.

Asynchronous Operation: The execution of a sequence of steps such that each step is initiated upon completion of the previous step.

Asynchronous Sequential Circuit: Completion of one operation starts the next operation in sequence. Time delay devices (logic gates) are used as memory.

Barrel Shifter: A specially configured shift register that is normally included in 32-bit microprocessors for cycle rotation. That is, the barrel shifter shifts data in one direction.

Behavioral Modeling: Using hardware description languages such as Verilog and VHDL, a system can be described in terms of what it does and how it behaves rather than in terms of its components and their interconnections.

Binary-Coded Decimal (BCD): The representation of 10 decimal digits, 0 through 9, by their corresponding 4-bit binary number.

Bit: An abbreviation for a binary digit. A unit of information equal to one of two possible states (one or zero, on or off, true or false).

Boolean Algebra: A mathematical system that provides the basis for logic operations such as NOT, AND, and OR. George Boole, an English mathematician, introduced this theory of digital logic. The term *Boolean variable* is used to mean the two-valued binary digit 1 or 0.

Digital Logic with an Introduction to Verilog and FPGA-Based Design. First Edition. M. Rafiquzzaman and Steven A. McNinch. 389
© 2019 John Wiley & Sons, Inc. Published 2019 by John Wiley & Sons, Inc.

Buffer: A temporary memory storage device deigned to compensate for the different data rates between a transmitting device and a receiving device (for example, between a CPU and a peripheral). Current amplifiers are also referred to as buffers.

Bus: A collection of wires that interconnects computer modules. The typical microcomputer interface includes separate buses for address, data, control, and power functions.

Central Processing Unit (CPU): The brains of a computer containing the ALU, register section, and control unit. CPU in a single chip is called a microprocessor.

Chip: An Integrated Circuit (IC) package containing digital circuits.

Clock: Timing signals providing synchronization among the various components in a microcomputer system. Analogous to heart beats of a human being.

CMOS: Complementary MOS. Dissipates low power, offers high density and speed compared to TTL.

Combinational Circuit: Output is provided upon application of inputs; contains no memory.

Compiler: A program which translates the source code written in a high-level programming language into machine language that is understandable to the processor.

Condition Code Register: Contains information such as carry, sign, zero, and overflow based on ALU operations.

Control Unit: Part of the CPU; its purpose is to translate or decode instructions read (fetched) from the main memory into the Instruction Register.

CPLD: Complex PLD. This chip contains several basic PLDs along with all interconnections.

Data: Basic elements of information represented in binary form (that is, digits consisting of bits) that can be processed or produced by a microcomputer. Data represents any group of operands made up of numbers, letters, or symbols denoting any condition, value, or state. Typical microcomputer operand sizes include: a word, which typically contains 2 bytes or 16-bits; a long word, which contains 4 bytes or 32 bits; a quad word, which contains 8 bytes or 64 bits.

Dataflow Modeling: Behavioral modeling with concurrent statements.

Decoder: A chip, when enabled, selects one of 2n output lines based on n inputs.

Demultiplexer: Performs reverse operation of a multiplexer.

Digital to Analog (D/A) Converter: Converts binary number to analog signal.

Diode: Two terminal electronic switch.

Directly Addressable Memory: The memory address space in which the microprocessor can directly execute programs. The maximum directly addressable memory is determined by the number of the microprocessor's address pins.

Dynamic RAM: Stores data as charges in capacitors and therefore, must be refreshed since capacitors can hold charges for a few milliseconds. Hence, requires refresh circuitry.

EAROM (Electrically Alterable Read-Only Memory): Same as EEPROM or E²PROM. Can be programmed one line at a time without removing the memory form its sockets. This memory is also called read-mostly memory since it has much slower write times than read times.

EEPROM or E² PROM: Same as EAROM (see EAROM).

Encoder: Performs reverse operation of a decoder. Contains a maximum of 2^n inputs and n outputs.

EPROM (Erasable Programmable Read-Only Memory): Can be programmed and erased all programs in an EPROM chip using ultraviolet light. The chip must be removed from the microcomputer system for programming.

Equivalence: See Exclusive-NOR.

Exclusive-OR: The output is 0, if inputs are same; otherwise, the output is 1.

Exclusive-NOR: The output is 1, if inputs are same; otherwise, the output is 0.

Extended Binary-Coded Decimal Interchange Code (EBCDIC): An 8-bit code commonly used with microprocessors for representing alphanumeric codes. Normally used by IBM. Obsolete code.

Flag(s): An indicator, often a single bit, to indicate some conditions such as trace, carry, zero, and overflow.

Flash Memory: Utilizes a combination of EPROM and EEPROM technologies. Used in cellular phones and digital cameras.

Flip-Flop: One-bit memory.

FPGA: Field Programmable Gate Arrays. This chip contains several smaller individual logic blocks along with all interconnections.

Full adder: Adds three bits generating a sum bit and a carry bit.

Gate: Digital circuits which perform logic operations.

Half adder: Adds two bits generating a sum bit and a carry bit.

Handshaking: Data transfer via exchange of control signals between the microprocessor and an external device.

Hardware: The physical electronic circuits (chips) that make up the microcomputer system.

HCMOS: High speed CMOS. Provides high density and consumes low power.

Hexadecimal Number System: Base-16 number system.

High-Level Language: A type of programming language that uses a more understandable human-oriented language such as C.

HMOS: High-density MOS reduces the channel length of the NMOS transistor and provides increased density and speed in VLSI circuits.

Instruction: Causes the microprocessor or microcontroller to carry out an operation on data. A program contains instructions and data.

Instruction Cycle: The sequence of operations that a microprocessor has to carry out while executing an instruction.

Instruction Register (IR): A register storing instructions; typically 32 bits long for a 32-bit microprocessor.

Instruction Set: Lists all the instructions that the microcomputer can execute.

Inverting Buffer: Performs NOT operation. Current amplifier.

Karnaugh Map: Simplifies Boolean expression by a mapping mechanism.

Keyboard: Has a number of push button-type switches configured in a matrix form (rows x columns).

Large-Scale Integration (LSI): An LSI chip contains 100 to 1000 gates.

LED: Light Emitting Diode. Typically, a current of 10 ma to 20 ma flows at 1.7v to 2.4v drop across it.

Machine Code: A binary code (composed of 1's and 0's) that a microcomputer understands.

Machine Language: A type of microprocessor programming language that uses binary or hexadecimal numbers.

Mask ROM: Programmed by a masking operation performed on the chip during the manufacturing process; its contents cannot be changed by user.

Maskable Interrupt: Can be enabled or disabled by executing typically the interrupt instructions.

Memory: Any storage device which can accept, retain, and read back data.

Memory Access Time: Average time taken to read a unit of information from the memory.

Memory Address Register (MAR): Stores the address of the data

Microcomputer: Consists of a microprocessor, a memory unit, and an input/output unit.

Microcontroller: Typically includes a CPU, memory, Input/Output, timer, A/D (Analog to Digital) and D/A (Digital to Analog) converters in the same chip.

Microprocessor: The Central Processing Unit (CPU) of a microcomputer.

Multiplexer: A hardware device which selects one of n input lines and produces it on the output.

NAND: The output is 0, if all inputs are 1; otherwise, the output is 1.

Nibble: A 4-bit word.

Non-inverting Buffer: Input is same as output. Current amplifier.

NOR: The output is 1, if all inputs are 0's; otherwise, the output is 0.

NOT Gate: If the input is 1, the output is 0, and vice versa.

Object Code: The binary (machine) code into which a source program is translated by a compiler, assembler, or interpreter.

Octal Number System: Base 8-number system.

One's Complement: Obtained by changing 1's to '0's, and 0's to 1's of a binary number.

OR Gate: The output is 0, if all inputs are 0; otherwise, the output is 1.

Parity: The number of 1's in a word is odd for odd parity and even for even parity.

Peripheral: An I/O device capable of being operated under the control of a CPU through communication channels. Examples include disk drives, keyboards, CRT's, printers, and modems.

Personal Computer: Low-cost, affordable microcomputer normally used by an individual for word processing and Internet applications.

Processor Memory: A set of microprocessor or microcontroller registers for holding temporary results when a computation is in progress.

Program: A self-contained sequence of computer software instructions (source code) that, when converted into machine code, directs the computer to perform specific operations for the purpose of accomplishing some processing task. Contains instructions and data.

Program Counter (PC): A register that normally contains the address of the next instruction to be executed in a program.

Programmable Array Logic (PAL): Contains programmable AND gates and fixed OR gates. Similar to a ROM in concept except that it does not provide full decoding of the input lines. PAL's can be used with 32-bit microprocessors for performing the memory decode function.

Programmable Logic Array (PLA): Contains programmable AND and programmable OR gates.

Programmable Logic Device (PLD): Contains AND gates and OR gates.

PROM (Programmable Read-Only Memory): Can be programmed by the user by using proper equipment. Once programmed, its contents cannot be altered.

Random Access Memory (RAM): A read/write memory. RAMs (static or dynamic) are volatile in nature (in other words, information is lost when power is removed).

Read-Only-Memory (ROM): A memory in which any addressable operand can be read from, but not written to, after initial programming. ROM storage is nonvolatile (information is not lost after removal of power).

Register: A high-speed memory usually constructed from flip-flops that are directly accessible to the microprocessor. It can contain either data or a specific location in memory that stores word(s) used during arithmetic, logic, and transfer operations.

Sequential Circuit: Combinational circuit with memory.

Seven-Segment LED: Contains an LED in each of the seven segments. Can display numbers.

Single-chip Microcomputer: Microcomputer (CPU, memory, and input/output) on a chip.

Single-chip Microprocessor: Microcomputer CPU (microprocessor) on a chip.

Software: Programs in a microcomputer.

SRAM: See Static RAM.

Static RAM: Also known as **SRAM**. Stores data in flip-flops; does not need to be refreshed. Information is lost upon power failure unless backed up by battery.

Status Register: A register which contains information concerning the flags in a processor.

Structural Modeling: Using hardware description languages such as Verilog and VHDL, a schematic or a logic diagram can be described.

Synchronous Operation: Operations that occur at intervals directly related to a clock period.

Synchronous Sequential Circuit: The present outputs depend on the present inputs and the previous states stored in flip-flops.

Transistor: Electronic switch; performs NOT; current amplifier.

Tristate Buffer: Has three output states: logic 0, 1, and a high-impedance state. This chip is typically enabled by a control signal to provide logic 0 or 1 outputs. This type of buffer can also be disabled by the control signal to place it in a high-impedance state.

Two's Complement: The two's complement of a binary number is obtained by replacing each 0 with a 1 and each 1 with a 0 and adding one to the resulting number.

Verilog: Not an acronym. Hardware design language developed by Gateway Design Automation in 1984 and later acquired by Cadence Design Systems. Verilog syntax is based mostly on C and some Pascal. Used for programming CPLD and FPGA chips.

Very Large Scale Integration (VLSI): A VLSI chip contains more than 1000 gates. More commonly, a VLSI chip is identified by the number of transistors rather than the gate count.

VHDL: Stands for VHSIC (Very High Speed Integrated Circuit) Hardware Description Language. Developed by U.S. Department of Defense. Syntax is based on Ada. Can be used to program CPLD and FPGA chips.

Word: The bit size of a microprocessor refers to the number of bits that can be processed simultaneously by the basic arithmetic and logic circuits of the microprocessor. A number of bits taken as a group in this manner is called a word

APPENDIX C: STEP-BY-STEP TUTORIAL FOR DOWNLOADING AND INSTALLING XILINX VIVADO IDE

Appendix C provides a step-by-step procedure for downloading and installing Xilinx Vivado IDE.

<u>Installation</u>

1. Xilinx Vivado installer can be downloaded from the following location:
   https://www.xilinx.com/support/download.html

2. Download the web installer as it is much smaller than the full tool suite and will only install what is needed. You will need to create an account on Xilinx's website to download and install the Vivado IDE.

Vivado Design Suite - HLx Editions - 2018.3 Full Product Installation

Important

We strongly recommend to use the web installers as it reduces download time and saves significant disk space.

Please see Installer Information for details.

Note: Download verification is only supported with Google Chrome and Microsoft Internet Explorer web bowsers.

> Vivado HLx 2018.3: WebPACK and Editions - Windows Self Extracting Web Installer

⬇ Vivado HLx 2018.3: WebPACK and Editions - Windows Self Extracting Web Installer (EXE - 62.66 MB)

MD5 SUM Value : 92c535eb974e9ac0ecf0c278adeb1033

Download Includes	Vivado Design Suite HLx Editions (All Editions)
Download Type	Full Product Installation
Last Updated	Dec 10, 2018
Answers	2018.x - Vivado Known Issues
Documentation	Release Notes
Support Forums	Installation and Licensing

3. Log in with your Xilinx account information and click **Next**.

User Authentication

Please provide your Xilinx user account credentials to download the required files.
If you don't have an account, please create one. If you forgot your password, you can reset it here.

User ID	
Password	

⊙ Download and Install Now

Select your desired device and tool installation options and the installer will download and install just what is required. Downloaded installation files will be saved for future use. NOTE: Future installs using these downloaded files will be restricted to the options selected during this install. For access to all options later, choose "Download Full Image".

4.   Accept all three license agreements on the following page and click **Next**.

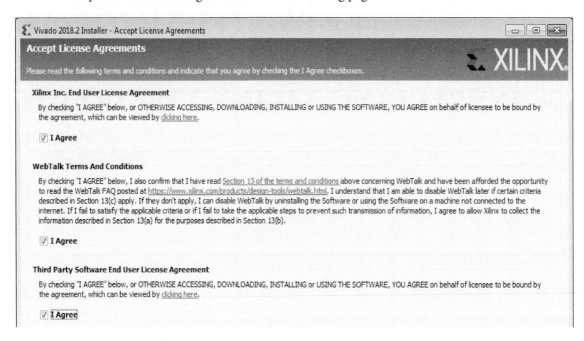

5.   Select the following installation options for a minimal install with what is needed. Click **Next** when done.

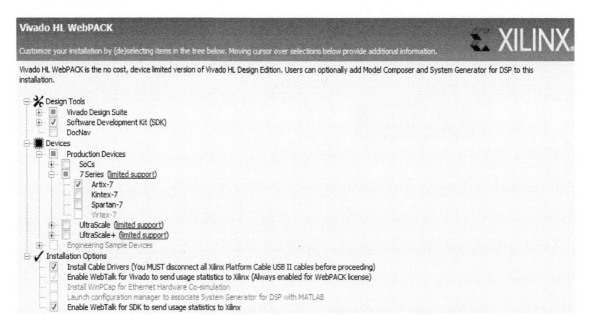

6. Select Vivado WebPACK install option and click **Next**.

7. Choose an install location (default location is recommended) and click **Next**.

8. Click **Install** on the last page to begin installation. Installation can take over 30 minutes. You will be shown an installation complete message when it finishes.

APPENDIX D: STEP-BY-STEP TUTORIAL FOR CREATING & SIMULATING A VERILOG DESIGN USING XILINX VIVADO IDE

Appendix D provides a step-by-step procedure for synthesizing a Verilog design for both combinational and sequential circuit using Xilinx Vivado IDE.

I   COMBINATIONAL CIRCUIT

The following circuit is to be implemented:

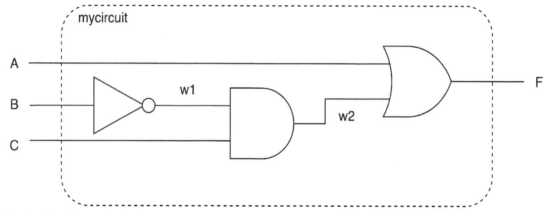

Step 1: Creating a Project

a) Launch the Vivado IDE

b) Select **Create Project** in the Quick Start pane or from the menu select File > Project > New.

c) Give the project a name and a save location on your computer.

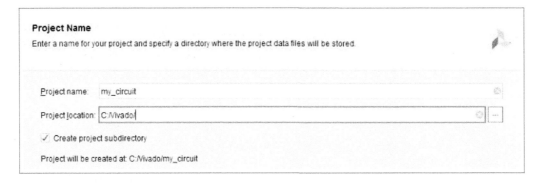

d) Select **RTL Project** and check the **Do not specify sources at this time** box.

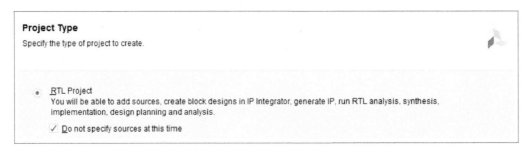

e) Search for device **xc7a100tcsg324-1** and select the FPGA part. Click **Finish** on the next page.

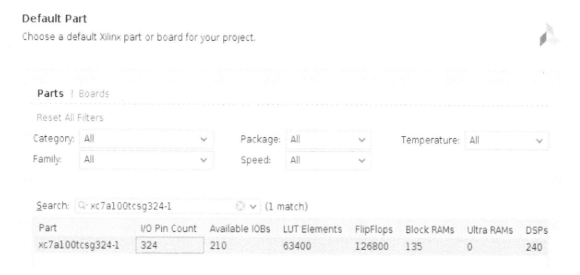

Step 2: Create Verilog Source File

a) To add a source, click **Add Sources** in the left pane.

b) Click **Next** to add a design source.

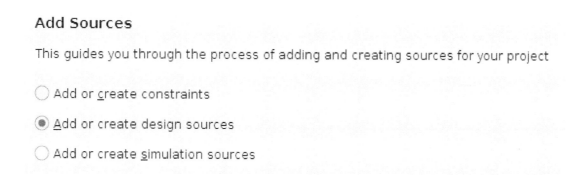

c) Click **Create File** and give your Verilog file a name.

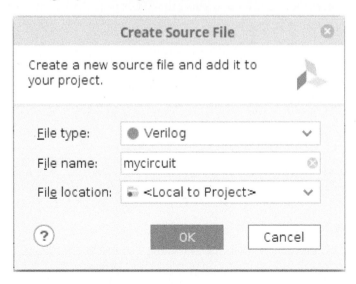

d) Click **OK** and then **Finish** to add the new source file to your project.

e) Click **OK** and then **Yes** to skip changing ports since they will be manually added later.

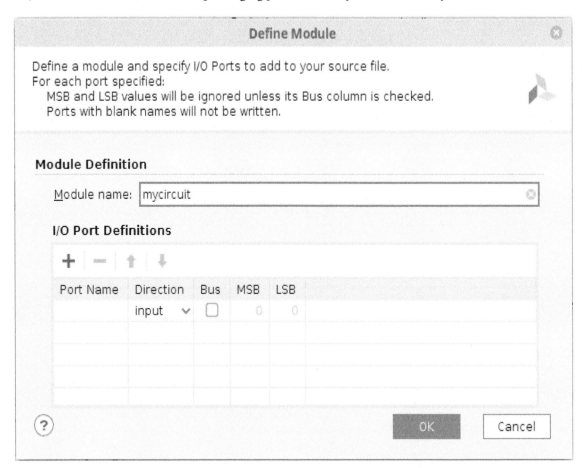

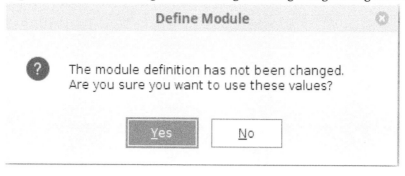

Step 3: Enter Verilog Code
a) Double click the mycircuit.v source file in the Sources Pane on the left.

Enter the Verilog design. It is usually good design practice to have one module per file.

```verilog
`timescale 1ns / 1ps

module mycircuit(input A, input B, input C, output F);
wire w1,w2;
not(w1,B);
and(w2,C,w1);
or(F,A,w2);
endmodule
```

b) After saving the file, the Messages pane at the bottom can be used to check for Verilog syntax errors.

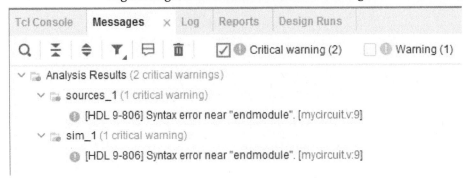

c)   Once any syntax errors are resolved, click "Run Synthesis" to compile the design.

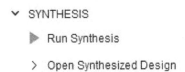

d)   If there are no errors, the synthesis step will complete successfully.

Step 4:   Verilog Test Bench and Simulation

a)   To add a simulation source, click **Add Sources** in the left pane.

b)   Select **Add or create simulation sources** and click **Next.**

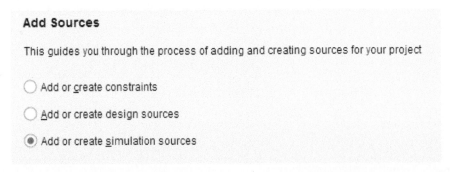

c)   Click **Next** to add a Simulation Source named **mycircuit_testbench** and follow the
instructions from Step 2 - Adding Sources section.

d)   Write the code for the Verilog test bench which instantiates the mycircuit module. Inputs to the
module to be tested need to be declared as reg, and outputs as wire. Note that "dut" in the
following is abbreviation for "device under test," and is used as the instance name for the module.
There must be space between module name and dut.

```
`timescale 1ns / 1ps

module mycircuit_testbench();
reg A, B, C;
wire F;

mycircuit dut(A,B,C,F);   // Positional association is used see
                          // Section 8.6

initial begin
        A = 0; B = 0; C = 0;
    #1  A = 0; B = 0; C = 1;
    #1  A = 0; B = 1; C = 0;
    #1  A = 0; B = 1; C = 1;
    #1  A = 1; B = 0; C = 0;
    #1  A = 1; B = 0; C = 1;
    #1  A = 1; B = 1; C = 0;
    #1  A = 1; B = 1; C = 1;
end
endmodule
```

e)   If everything is correct, the Sources panel should nest your Verilog module under the test bench
as shown below :

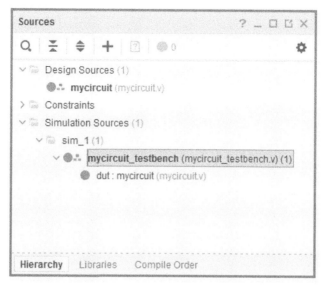

f)   To run the test bench and simulation, select the testbench file in the sources window and
click **Run Simulation** and select **Run Behavioral Simulation**. If there are multiple test
bench files in Simulation Sources, the one that is set as 'top' indicated by the ⁑ symbol. The top
module can be changed by right-clicking the desired module and selecting **Set as Top**.

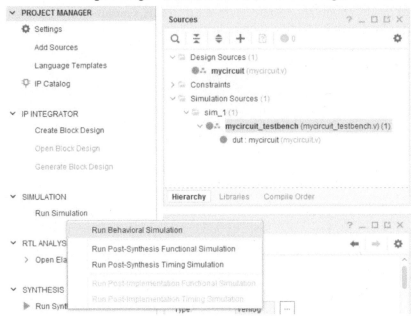

g)   Adjust the waveform window to show the appropriate waveform. The most useful controls are:

Button	Function
🔍➕ 🔍➖	Zoom In / Zoom Out
◀❘ ❘▶	Goto Beginning / End
⬅ ➡	Goto Next / Prev Edge

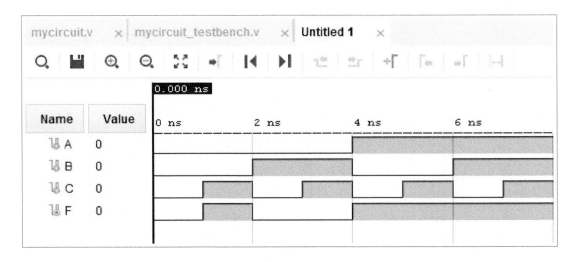

II   SEQUENTIAL CIRCUIT

The following 4-bit register is to be implemented:

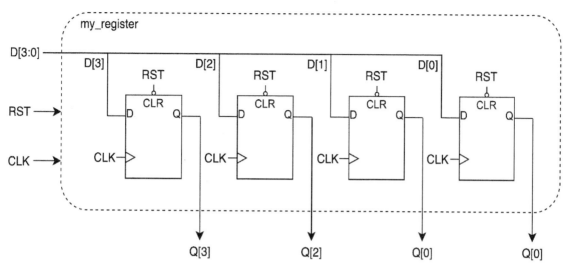

Step 1: Creating a Project
a) Launch the Vivado IDE

b) Select **Create Project** in the Quick Start pane or from the menu select File > Project > New.

c)   Give the project a name and a save location on your computer.

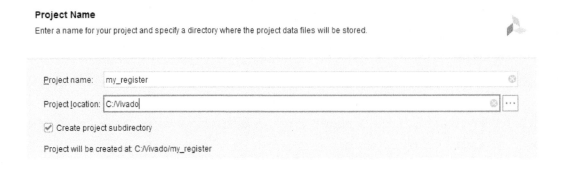

d)   Select **RTL Project** and check the **Do not specify sources at this time** box.

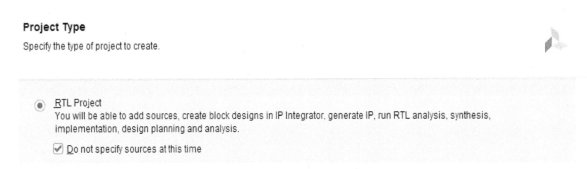

e)   Search for device **xc7a100tcsg324-1** and select the FPGA part. Click **Finish** on the next page.

Step 2: Create Verilog Source Files

To add a source, click **Add Sources** in the left pane.

b) Click **Next** to add a design source.

Add Sources

This guides you through the process of adding and creating sources for your project

○ Add or create constraints

◉ Add or create design sources

○ Add or create simulation sources

c) Click **Create Source File** and give your Verilog file a name.

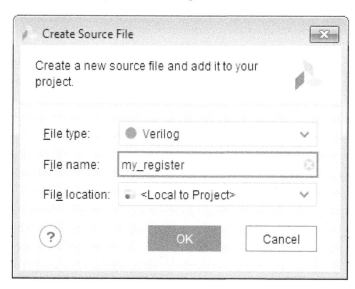

d) Click **OK** to add the source file to the project.

e) Repeat the steps (c) and (d) again add a second Verilog file named D_flipflop.

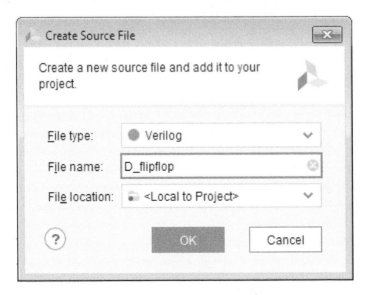

f) Once the two sources are added, click **Finish** to add the new source file to your project.

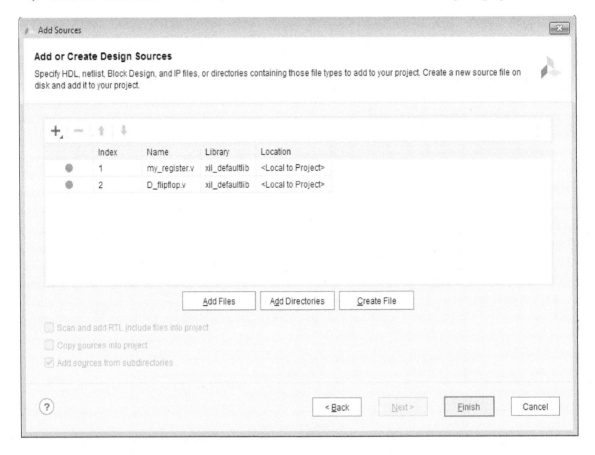

g) Once the window appears for the module ports, click **OK** and then **Yes** to skip changing ports since they will be manually added later.

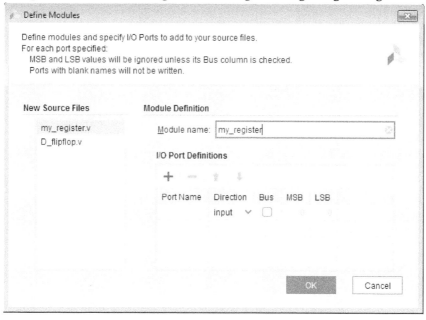

Step 3: Enter Verilog Code

a)   Double-click the D_flipflop.v source file in the Sources pane on the left.

Enter the Verilog design. It is usually good design practice to have one module per file.

```verilog
module D_flipflop(CLK, CLR, D, Q, Qnot);
input CLK, CLR, D;
output reg Q = 0;
output Qnot;

assign Qnot = ~Q;

always @ (posedge CLK or negedge CLR)
// Check if CLR == 0
if(CLR == 0)
 Q <= 1'b0;
// Posedge Clk and CLR not enabled.
else
 Q <= D;
endmodule
```

b)   Double-click the my_register.v source file in the Sources pane on the left.

c)   Type in the code below into my_register.v which instantiates the D_flipfop modules previous written, and connects the CLK, CLR, and D inputs to them. The Q outputs are also connected to the Q outputs of the D flipflops.

```verilog
`timescale 1ns / 1ps

module reg_4bit(
input CLK,
input CLR,
input [3:0]D,
output [3:0]Q
  );

D_flipflop DFF0(CLK,CLR, D[0],Q[0],);
D_flipflop DFF1(CLK,CLR, D[1],Q[1],);
D_flipflop DFF2(CLK,CLR, D[2],Q[2],);
D_flipflop DFF3(CLK,CLR, D[3],Q[3],);

endmodule
```

d)   Once saved, if everything is correct and any syntax errors are resolved, the Sources pane will show the module hierarchy of the design:

e) Click "Run Synthesis" to compile the design.

✓ SYNTHESIS

▷ Run Synthesis

> Open Synthesized Design

f) If there are no errors, the synthesis step will complete successfully.

Step 4: Verilog Test Bench and Simulation

a) To add a simulation source, click **Add Sources** in the left pane.

b) Select **Add or create simulation sources** and click **Next.**

Add Sources

This guides you through the process of adding and creating sources for your project

○ Add or create constraints

○ Add or create design sources

◉ Add or create simulation sources

c) Click **Next** to add a Simulation Source and follow the instructions from Step 2 parts (c) through (g) to add a simulation Verilog file named D_flipflop_sim. Double-click on the D_flipflop_sim.v file which will be listed in the Simulation Sources in the Sources pane.

d) Write the code for the Verilog testbench. Inputs to the module to be tested need to be declared as reg, and outputs as wire. As a first step, the D_flipflop module can be simulated. Type below code to create a test bench for the D flipflop:

Inputs to the module to be tested need to be declared as reg, and outputs as wire.

```
`timescale 1ns / 1ps

module D_flipflop_sim();
reg CLK=0, CLR, D;
wire Q, Qnot;

  D_flipflop dut(CLK,CLR,D,Q,Qnot);

initial forever #0.5 CLK = ~CLK;

initial begin
  #0   CLR = 1; D = 0;
  #1            D = 1;
  #1            D = 0;
  #1            D = 1;
  #1 CLR = 0;
  #1 CLR = 1;
  #1 ;
end
endmodule
```

e) If everything is correct, the Sources panel should nest your Verilog module under the test bench as shown below :

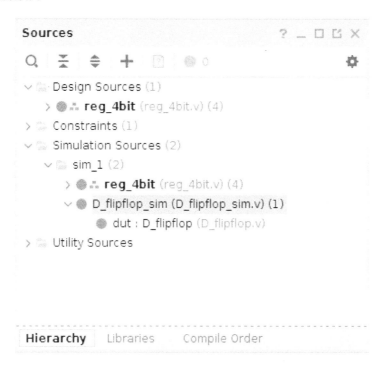

f) To run the test bench and simulation, Select the testbench file in the sources window and click **Run Simulation** and select **Run Behavioral Simulation.** If there are multiple test bench files in Simulation Sources, the one that is set as 'top' indicated by the ⚙ symbol. The top module can be changed by right-clicking the desired module and selecting **Set as Top**.

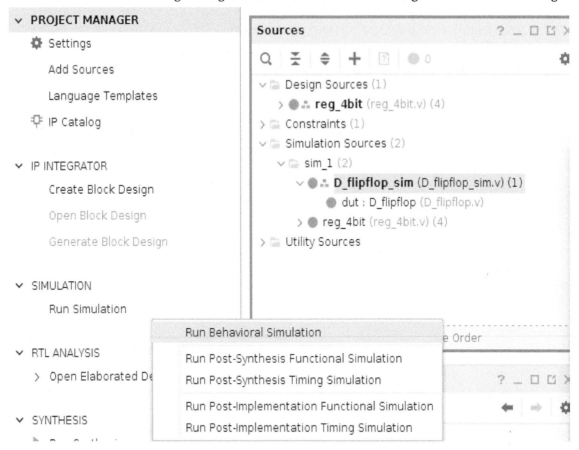

g) The simulation waveform will show once simulation is complete. In the below simulation, the clock toggles every 0.5ns. The D input is toggled to load the value of 1 and then 0, and then 1 again into the flop. At 4ns, the CLR is set to low which clears the flipflop asynchronously.

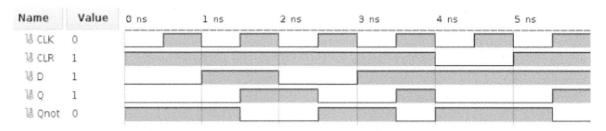

h) The simulation opens the window can be adjusted to show the appropriate waveform. The most useful controls are:

Button		Function
$\oplus$	$\ominus$	Zoom In / Zoom Out
$\vert\blacktriangleleft$	$\blacktriangleright\vert$	Go to Beginning / End
⇥	⇥	Go to Next / Prev Edge

i) Create another test bench, this time for the reg_4bit outer module. Follow steps (a) through (c) to add another simulation source named reg_4bit_sim using the following test bench code. Remember to right-click the reg_4bit_sim file in the Create Source File pane and select "Set as top". The simulation will only simulate the module which is designed as top by the ⬚⬚ symbol.

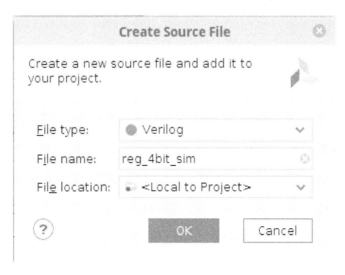

```verilog
`timescale 1ns / 1ps
module reg_4bit_sim();
reg CLK=0, CLR;
reg [3:0]D;
wire [3:0]Q;

   reg_4bit dut(CLK, CLR, D, Q);

   // Create clock
initial forever #0.5 CLK = ~CLK;

   // Input stimuli
initial begin
      D = 0; CLR = 1;
   #1   D = 5;
   #1   D = 9;
   #1   D = 15;
   #1   CLR = 0;
   #1   CLR = 1; D = 7;
end
endmodule
```

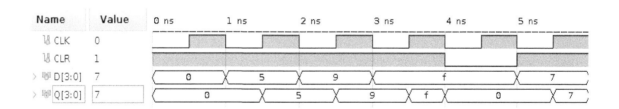

The register is initially loaded with a value of 0, followed by 5, 9 and finally 15 (F in hexadecimal). At 4ns, the CLR input is reset to 0, which clears the register and resets the value back to zero. Finally, the register is loaded with a value of 7 at 5.5ns when the clock toggles high.

APPENDIX E: STEP-BY-STEP PROCEDURE FOR IMPLEMENTING FPGA-BASED DESIGN USING VIVADO IDE & NEXYS A7 FPGA BOARD

Appendix E provides the step-by-step procedure for implementing FPGA-based design using Verilog and Xilinx Vivado IDE. FPGA-based implementation steps (Chapter 13) are listed below:

Step 1: **Create the Verilog module**
Step 2: **Create a test bench and run the simulation**
Step 3: **Assign signals to FPGA I/O pins by adding constraints**
Step 4: **Generate, Bitstream, Program, and Test**

I   COMBINATIONAL CIRCUIT

This appendix shows how to implement the combinational design shown in Appendix D on the Nexys A7 FPGA board. To implement the design on the FPGA board, the signals from the Verilog module need to be mapped to physical pins on the FPGA. Below shows how the Verilog design is mapped to switches and LEDs on the FPGA board.

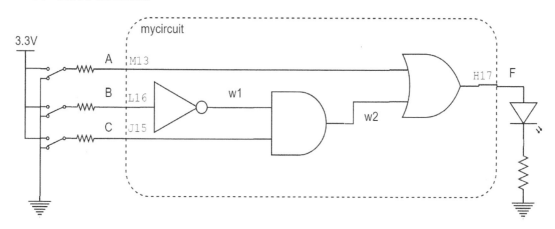

Step 1:   Create the Verilog Module

```
mycircuit.v
-----------------------------------------------------------------
module mycircuit(input A, input B, input C, output F);
    wire w1,w2;
    not(w1,B);
    and(w2,C,w1);
    or(F,A,w2);
endmodule
-----------------------------------------------------------------
```

Step 2: Create a test bench and run the simulation

mycircuit_testbench.v

```
------------------------------------------------------------------
module mycircuit_testbench();
reg A, B, C;
wire F;

mycircuit dut(A,B,C,F);

initial begin
        A = 0; B = 0; C = 0;
    #1  A = 0; B = 0; C = 1;
    #1  A = 0; B = 1; C = 0;
    #1  A = 0; B = 1; C = 1;
    #1  A = 1; B = 0; C = 0;
    #1  A = 1; B = 0; C = 1;
    #1  A = 1; B = 1; C = 0;
    #1  A = 1; B = 1; C = 1;
end
endmodule
------------------------------------------------------------------
```

Simulation result for mycircuit_testbench:

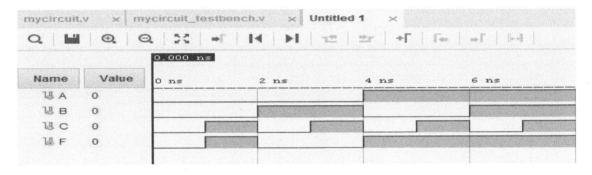

Step 3: Assign signals to FPGA I/O by adding constraints

a) **Add Sources** in the left pane as previously done with design and simulation sources.

b) Select **Add or create constraints** and click **Next.**

> **Add Sources**
>
> This guides you through the process of adding and creating sources for your project
>
> ● Add or create constraints
>
> ○ Add or create design sources
>
> ○ Add or create simulation sources

c) Click **Next** to add a Constraint Source, and follow the **Adding Sources** section.

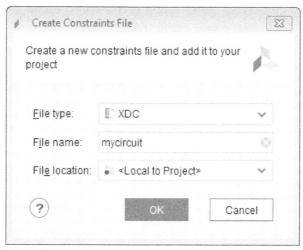

d) Click **OK** followed by **Finish** to add the constraint source to the project. Note: Using an FPGA development board which has a master XDC file provided, can save significant time since it already contains all the FPGA pins and voltages.

e) Double-click on the mycircuit.xdc file, now listed under the **Constraints** section of the **Sources** pane.

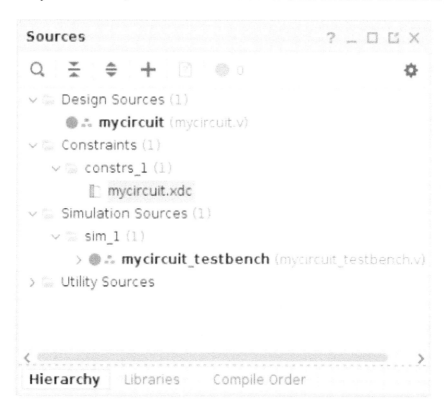

f) Type the following into the XDC file. These constraints connect signals A, B, and C to FPGA pins M13, L16, and J15 which are connected to switches on the board. H17 is set to the F output signal which is connected to a LED.

```
set_property -dict {PACKAGE_PIN M13  IOSTANDARD LVCMOS33} [get_ports A]
set_property -dict {PACKAGE_PIN L16  IOSTANDARD LVCMOS33} [get_ports B]
set_property -dict {PACKAGE_PIN J15  IOSTANDARD LVCMOS33} [get_ports C]
set_property -dict {PACKAGE_PIN H17  IOSTANDARD LVCMOS33} [get_ports F]
```

g) Save the constraints file and click "**Run Implementation**"

h) Once complete, the bitstream to program the FPGA needs to be generated.

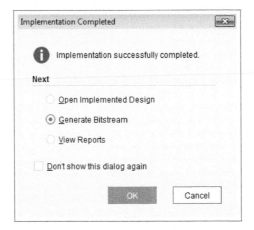

i) Click **OK** to start bitstream generation which can also be started from the left pane.

j) If successful, the FPGA is ready to be programmed with the generated bitstream.

Step 4: Generate Bitstream, program FPGA, and test.

a) Open the Vivado Hardware Manager.

b) Connect the Nexys A7 FPGA board to the computer using the micro-USB cable, and move the power switch located in the top left between the DC jack and the USB port to the 'ON' position. A red LED should illuminate indicating that board has power.

c) Click **Open Target** then **Auto Connect** and connect to the FPGA.

d) If an FPGA is found, it will be listed in the hardware pane.

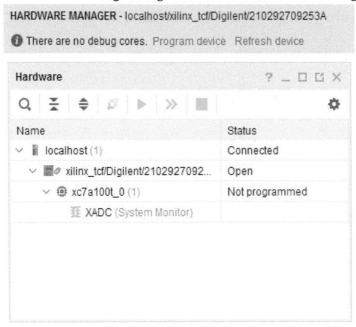

e) To program the FPGA, click **Program Device** from either the left panel or the green bar at the top.

f) On the last window, check that the bitstream file matches the top level Verilog module name, and click **Program Device.**

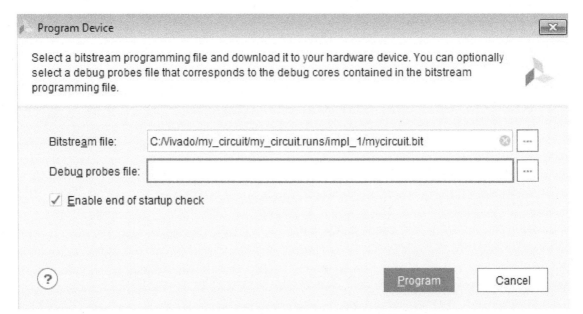

g) After programming completes, the FPGA will be configured with the Verilog design. The switches can be manipulated and the LED observed to confirm that the design functions as intended. In the image below, the values are set as A = 1, B = 0, and C = 1, therefore the output should be '1'. As expected, the LED connected to the F output is illuminated, indicating a value of 1.

SCREENSHOT:

II   **FPGA IMPLEMENTATION OF SEQUENTIAL CIRCUIT**

This appendix shows how to implement the sequential logic design shown in Appendix D on the Nexys A7 FPGA board. To implement the design, the *Clk*, and CLR inputs need to be connected to push buttons, and the D inputs to switches. The Q outputs will be connected to four LEDs on the board. The figure below shows the connections on the FPGA board:

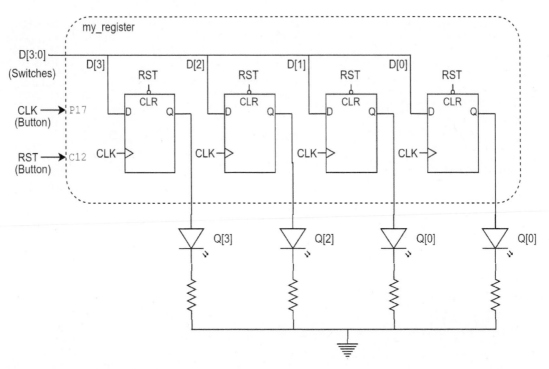

Step 1:   Create the Verilog Modules
D_flipflop.v

```verilog
module D_flipflop(CLK, CLR, D, Q, Qnot);
   input CLK, CLR, D;
   output reg Q = 0;
   output Qnot;

   assign Qnot = ~Q;

   always @ (posedge CLK or negedge CLR)
   // Check if CLR == 0
   if(CLR == 0)
       Q <= 1'b0;
   // Posedge Clk and CLR not enabled.
   else
       Q <= D;
endmodule
```

```
-----------------------------------------------------------------
D_flipflop.v
-----------------------------------------------------------------
module reg_4bit(
   input CLK,
   input CLR,
   input [3:0]D,
   output [3:0]Q
     );

D_flipflop DFF0(CLK,CLR, D[0],Q[0],);
D_flipflop DFF1(CLK,CLR, D[1],Q[1],);
D_flipflop DFF2(CLK,CLR, D[2],Q[2],);
D_flipflop DFF3(CLK,CLR, D[3],Q[3],);

endmodule
```

Step 2: Create a test bench and run the simulation:

```
D_flipflop_sim.v
-----------------------------------------------------------------
module D_flipflop_sim();
reg CLK=0, CLR, D;
wire Q, Qnot;

   D_flipflop dut(CLK,CLR,D,Q,Qnot);

initial forever #0.5 CLK = ~CLK;

initial begin
  #0   CLR = 1; D = 0;
  #1           D = 1;
  #1           D = 0;
  #1           D = 1;
  #1 CLR = 0;
  #1 CLR = 1;
  #1  ;
end
endmodule
```

Simulation result for D_flip-flop sim:

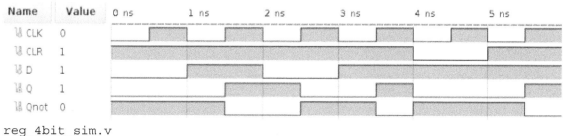

```
reg_4bit_sim.v
-----------------------------------------------------------------
module reg_4bit_sim();
```

```
reg CLK=0, CLR;
reg [3:0]D;
wire [3:0]Q;

  reg_4bit dut(CLK, CLR, D, Q);

  // Create clock
initialforever #0.5 CLK = ~CLK;

  // Input stimuli
initialbegin
      D = 0; CLR = 1;
  #1  D = 5;
  #1  D = 9;
  #1  D = 15;
  #1  CLR = 0;
  #1  CLR = 1; D = 7;
end
endmodule
```

Simulation result for reg_4bit_sim:

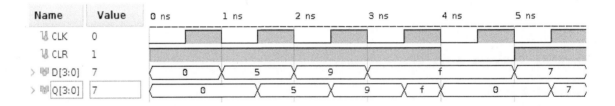

Step 3: Assign signals to FPGA I/O by adding constraints

a) **Add Sources** in the left pane as previously done with design and simulation sources.

b) Select **Add or create constraints** and click **Next.**

Add Sources

This guides you through the process of adding and creating sources for your project

◉ Add or create constraints

○ Add or create design sources

○ Add or create simulation sources

c) Click **Next** to add a constraint source, and follow the **Adding Sources** section.

d) Click **OK** followed by **Finish** to add the constraint source to the project. Using an FPGA development board which has a master XDC file provided, can save significant time since it already contains all the FPGA pins and voltages.

e) Double-click on the reg_4bit.xdc file now listed under the **Constraints** section of the **Sources** pane.

f) Type the following into the XDC file. These constraints connect signals A, B, and C to FPGA pins M13, L16, and J15 which are connected to switches on the board. H17 is set to the F output signal which is connected to a LED.

```
##Switches
set_property -dict { PACKAGE_PIN J15   IOSTANDARD LVCMOS33 } [get_ports D[0] ]
set_property -dict { PACKAGE_PIN L16   IOSTANDARD LVCMOS33 } [get_ports D[1] ]
set_property -dict { PACKAGE_PIN M13   IOSTANDARD LVCMOS33 } [get_ports D[2] ]
set_property -dict { PACKAGE_PIN R15   IOSTANDARD LVCMOS33 } [get_ports D[3] ]

##Buttons
set_property -dict { PACKAGE_PIN P17   IOSTANDARD LVCMOS33 } [get_ports CLK ]
set_property -dict { PACKAGE_PIN C12   IOSTANDARD LVCMOS33 } [get_ports CLR ]

## LEDs
set_property -dict { PACKAGE_PIN H17   IOSTANDARD LVCMOS33 } [get_ports Q[0]]
set_property -dict { PACKAGE_PIN K15   IOSTANDARD LVCMOS33 } [get_ports Q[1]]
set_property -dict { PACKAGE_PIN J13   IOSTANDARD LVCMOS33 } [get_ports Q[2]]
set_property -dict { PACKAGE_PIN N14   IOSTANDARD LVCMOS33 } [get_ports Q[3]]
```

g) Save the constraints file and click **Run Implementation**.

h) Once complete, the bitstream to program the FPGA needs to be generated.

i) Click **OK** to start bitstream generation which can also be started from the left pane.

j) If successful, the FPGA is ready to be programmed with the generated bitstream.

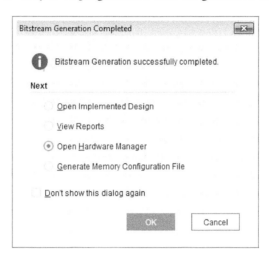

Step 4: Generate Bitstream, program FPGA, and test

a) Open the Vivado Hardware Manager

b) Connect the Nexys A7 FPGA board to the computer using the micro-USB cable, and move the power switch located in the top left between the DC jack and the USB port to the 'ON' position. A red LED should illuminate indicating that board has power.

c) Click **Open** then **Target Auto Connect** to connect to the FPGA.

d) If an FPGA is found, it will be listed in the hardware pane.

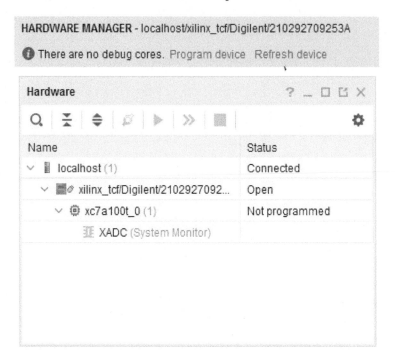

e) To program the FPGA, click **Program Device** from either the left panel or the green bar at the top.

f) On the last window, check that the bitstream file matches the top level Verilog module name, and click **Program.**

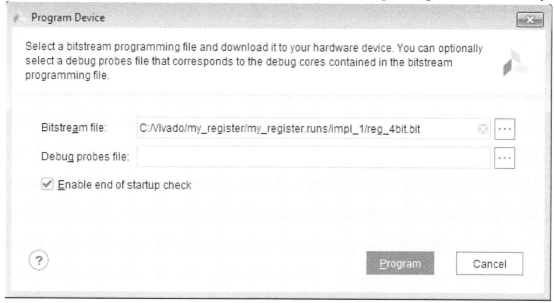

g) After programming completes, the FPGA will be configured with the Verilog design. The switches
   can be manipulated and the LED observed to confirm that the design functions as intended.
   The initial state of the register is zero. 4'b1100 or 12 in decimal is selected on the switches, and the
   CLK button is pressed, the value of 12 is loaded into the register and the value is displayed on the
   LEDs as shown below with an illuminated LED representing a 1 and OFF being 0.

SCREENSHOT:

When the CLR button is pressed, the value in the register is asynchronously cleared to zero, as indicated by all the LEDs connected to the Q outputs being off.

SCREENSHOT:

BIBLIOGRAPHY

Agarwal, Tarun, *Basic FPGA Architecture and Its Applications*, Edgefx Technologies Pvt-Ltd.

Arnold, M. G., *Verilog Digital Computer Design*, Prentice Hall, Upper Saddle River, NJ, 1999.

Breeding, K., *Digital Design Fundamentals*, 2nd ed., Prentice Hall, Upper Saddle River, NJ, 1992.

Brown, S. and Vranesic, Z., *Fundamentals of Digital Logic with Verilog Design*, McGraw-Hill, New York, 3rd ed., 2014.

Ciletti, M. D., *Advanced Digital Design with the Verilog HDL*, Prentice Hall, 2003.

Ciletti, M. D., *Modeling, Synthesis, and Prototyping with the Verilog HDL*, Prentice Hall, Upper Saddle River, NJ, 1999.

DIGICERT blog – "FPGA" blog.digilentinc.com.

Digilent. (n.d.). *Nexys A7 Reference Manual*. Retrieved from Digilent: https://reference.digilentinc.com/reference/programmable-logic/nexys-a7/reference-manual.

"Digital Circuits – Shift Registers". Tutorialspoint, 2019.

Floyd, T., *Digital Fundamentals*, Prentice Hall, 8th ed., 2003.

Fpga4fun.com, www.fpga4fun.com

Hamacher, V.C., Vranesic, Z. G., and Zaky, S.G., *Computer Organization*, McGraw-Hill, New York, 1978; 2nd ed., 1984; 3rd ed., 1990.

Harris, D. and Harris, S., *Digital Design and Computer Architecture*, 2nd ed., Elsevier, Inc., 2013.

Hayes, J., *Introduction to Digital Logic Design*, Addison-Wesley, Reading, MA, 1993.

History of Gates – Boolean Logic, http://wiki.sys.org.

"Johnson Ring Counter" www.electronic-turlab.us.

JTAG Interface – www.interfacebus.com.

Katz, R. *Contemporary Logic Design*, Benjamin/Cummings, San Francisco, 1994.

Mano, M., Computer Engineering, Prentice Hall, Upper Saddle River, NJ, 1988.

Mano, M., *Computer System Architecture*, Prentice Hall, Upper Saddle River, NJ, 1983.

Mano, M., *Digital Design*, 2nd ed., Prentice Hall, Upper Saddle River, NJ, 1991; 3rd ed., 2002.

Mano, M., and Kime, C., *Logic and Computer Design Fundamentals*, 2nd ed. updated, Prentice Hall, Upper Saddle River, NJ, 2001.

Mano, M. and Ciletti, M., *Digital Design with an Introduction to the Verilog HDL, VHDL, and System Verilog*, 6th ed., Pearson, 2018.

"Mealy and Moore Type Finite State Machines", faculty.kfupm.edu.sa.

"Moore and Mealy Machines", www.tutorialspoint.com.

National Semiconductor, *CMOS Logic Data Book*, National Semiconductor, Santa Clara, CA, 1988.

National Semiconductor, *Fast® Advanced Schottky TTL Logic Data Book*, National Semiconductor, Santa Clara, CA, 1990.

National Semiconductor, *LS/S/TTL Logic Data Book*, National Semiconductor, Santa Clara, CA, 1989.

National Semiconductor, *Programmable Logic Devices Data Book and Design Guide*, National Semiconductor, Santa Clara, CA, 1989.

Nelson, V. P., Nagle, H. T., Irwin, J. D., amd Carroll, B. D., *Digital Logic Circuit Analysis and Design*, Prentice Hall, Upper Saddle River, NJ, 1995.

Quora Digest, "JTAG", www.quora.com.

Rafiquzzaman M., *Fundamentals of Digital Logic and Microcomputer Design*, 5th Edition, Wiley, 2005.

Rafiquzzaman M., *Microcontroller Theory and Applications with the PIC18F*, Wiley, 2011.

Rafiquzzaman M., and Chandra R. *Modern Computer Architecture*, West/PWS, 1988.

Rafiquzzaman M., *Microprocessors and Microcomputer-based System Design*, 1st ed., CRC Press, 1990.

Rafiquzzaman M., *Microprocessors and Microcomputer-based System Design*, 2nd ed., CRC Press, 1995.

Roth, C., and Kinney, L., *Fundamentals of Logic Design*, 7th ed., Cengage Learning, 2014.

"Sequence Detector" Study.com.

"Serial Adder" by S. Shirani, McMaster University.

"Shift Registers" sanfoundry.com.

Texas Instruments, *Linear Circuits Data Book,* Texas Instruments, Dallas, TX. 1990.

Texas Instruments, *The TTL Data Book,* Vol. 1, Texas Instruments, Dallas, TX. 1984.

Texas Instruments, *The TTL Data Book for Design Engineers*, 2nd ed., Texas Instruments, Dallas, TX. 1976.

"The Shift Register" – Electronics Tutorial, Aspencore Inc., 2019.

Tocci. R. J., and Widmer, N. S., *Digital Systems*, 7th ed., Prentice Hall, Upper Saddle River, NJ, 1998.

University of Texas, Dallas. "Data Flow Modelling".

Vahid, F., *Digital Design with RTL Design, VHDL, and Verilog*, Wiley, 2nd ed., 2011.

Wakerly, J., *Digital Design Principles and Practices*, 3rd ed. updated, Prentice Hall,
        Upper Saddle River, NJ. 2001.

"What is JTAG", fpga4fun.com.

Wikipedia.org/wiki/Unicode, *"Unicode"*, 2014.

Wikipedia.org, *"Master Slave ff "*.

Wikipedia.org, *"Field Programmable Gate Array"*.

Wikipedia.org, *"Sequence Generator"*.

Wikiperdia.org. "Classical *Positive-Edge Triggered D Flip-Flop"*.

Wikipedia.org, *"Digital Electronics"*.

Wikipedia.org, *"Register-Transfer Level"*.

Wikipedia.org, *"JTAG"*.

Xilinx. (2018, August 20). *7 Series FPGAs Configuration UG470v1.13.1*. Retrieved from
        https://www.xilinx.com/support/documentation/user_guides/ug470_7Series_Config.pdf.

Xilinx. (2018, May 8). *Series FPGAs SelectIo Resources US471v1.10*. Retrieved from Xilinx.com:
        https://www.xilinx.com/support/documentation/user_guides/ug471_7Series_SelectIO.pdf.

INDEX

A

Adder, 139–147
  4-bit, 330–334
  behavioral modeling for, 196–197
  binary, 139–147, 155–156, 187–188
  carry look-ahead, 157–160
  carry propagate, 155–157
  dataflow modeling for, 194–195
  fast, 154–160
  full, 141–142, 154–155, 186–187
  half, 139–142, 185–186
  ripple carry, 141, 155–157
  serial, 240–242
Additive multiplier (AM), 162
Address, 2
Advanced Micro Devices, Inc. (AMD), 170
Alphanumeric codes, 31
Altera, 171, 301
ALU (Arithmetic Logic Unit), 152, 153, 154–164
  array multipliers, 160–162
  design, 162–164
  fast adders, 154–160
always block, 195–196, 281–283
and, reserved keyword, 176
AND gate, 160, 161
  PLD, 167–170
AND operation, 56–57
AOI (AND-OR-INVERT) implementation, 59–60, 98, 99
Arithmetic operations, 36–48
  BCD, 44–45
  binary, 36–44
  binary multiplication and division by shift operations, 46–48
  error correction and detection, 48–49
  multiword binary addition and subtraction, 45–46
Array multiplier, 160–162
ASCII (American Standard Code for Information Interchange), 31, 32
ASIC (Application Specific Integrated Circuit), 301
ASM (algorithmic state machines), 227, 246–254
  state machine design, 249–254
assign keyword, 189, 193, 194
Asynchronous sequential circuit, 228, 254–256

B

Barrel shifter, 152
Basic cell *S*, 275–276
BCD adder/subtractor, 139–147
BCD arithmetic, 44–45
  addition, 44–45

  subtraction, 45
BCD to seven-segment decoder, 112–114, 200
begin keyword, 195
begin-end statements, 197
Behavioral modeling, 176, 181, 195–201
  gated D latch, 353–355
BICMOS (Combination of Bipolar and HCMOS), 1, 17
Binary adder/subtractor, 139–147
  in ALU design, 162–163
  dataflow modeling for, 194–195
  four-bit, Verilog, 187–188
Binary arithmetic, 36–44
  addition, 36
  multiplication and division by shift operations, 46–48
  multiword binary addition and subtraction, 45–46
  signed division, 42–44
  signed multiplication, 41–42
  subtraction, 36–41
  unsigned division, 42
  unsigned multiplication, 41
Binary counter, 263–268
Binary digit, 2
Binary number system, 22
  converting to decimal, 23–24
  converting to hexadecimal, 25
  converting to octal, 24
Binary numbers, 1, 18
  signed/unsigned, 27–30
Binary to seven-segment converter, 324–328
Binary-coded-decimal (BCD) code, 30–31
Bipolar junction transistors (BJTs), 4, 5
Bit, 2
Bit size, 2
Bitfile, 311–312
Bitwise operations, 190–191
Blocking assignments, 282–289
Boards, FPGA, 315–320
Boole, George, 16
Boolean algebra, 63–71
Boolean function, 63
  complement of, 71
  Karnaugh maps, 81–95
  in PLAs, 167–169
  Quine-McCluskey method, 81, 95–96
  standard representations of, 77–80
Boolean identities, 64–69
Boolean logic, 16. *See also* Logic operations
Boolean variable, 53
Boundary-scan register, 313
Braun's multiplier, 162
Bus, 2
Byte, 2

C

CAD (computer-aided design), 16, 175
Cadence Design Systems, 175
Canonical forms, 77
Carry flag, 46–48
Carry look-ahead adder (CLA), 157–160
Carry propagate adder (CPA), 155–157
Carry propagation path, 161
Carry-save addition, 159–160
case statements, 195
case-endcase construct, 198–200, 289, 290
Characteristics table, 221
CLB (Configurable Logic Block), 308, 310, 311
Clear inputs, 219–220
Clock, 2
    forever loop, 293–294
    manual, 293–294
Clock generator, 227
Clocked sequential circuits. *See* Synchronous sequential
        circuits
CMOS (complementary MOS), 11–13, 16
    EEPROM, 171
Code converter, 113
Codes, 30–35
    alphanumeric, 31
    binary-coded-decimal, 30–31
    excess-3 code, 31–35
    Gray, 33–35
    Unicode, 35
Combination systems, 4
Combinational circuit, 227
    in ALU design, 162–164
    using Verilog, 175–209
Combinational circuits, 70–71
    analysis, 107–108
    basic concepts on, 107
    design, 108–112
    multiple-output, 113–117
Combinational logic components, 121–149
    BCD adder/subtractor, 139–147
    binary adders/subtractors, 139–147
    comparators, 121–123
    decoders, 124–130
    demultiplexers, 137–138
    design of, 121
    encoders, 130–133
    multiplexers, 133–137
Combinational shifter, 151–152
Comparator, 121–123
Compiler, 1, 175
Complement of a Boolean function, 71
Computer hardware, 1
Concatenation operators, 192–193, 195
conditional statements, 195
Configuration pins, 314
Consensus Theorem, 69–70
Constraint file, 320
Continuous assignment, 193
Control unit, 152, 153
Controller, 250, 251
Counters, 263–268
    4-bit with FPGA, 356–359
    Johnson, 273–275
    modulo-*n*, 271–273
    ring, 273, 275
    Shift register, 271–275

up-down, 290, 291
CPLD (Complex PLD), 16, 17, 170–171, 302
CPU, 152–154, 289
    defined, 1, 2
Cycle rotation, 152

D

D flip-flop, 220, 221, 222
D/A (digital-to-analog) converter chip, 18
Daisy chain loop, 313
Data processor, 250
Dataflow modeling, 176, 189–195
    sequential circuits, 282
Decimal number system, 21–22
    converting to binary, 23–24
    converting to hexadecimal, 25–26
    converting to octal, 25
Decoder, 124–130, 153
    4-to-16 binary, 329–330
    Verilog description for, 188–189
DeMorgan's Theorem, 71, 78, 89
Demultiplexer, 137–138
Design levels, 4
Device level, 4, 289
Digital circuits, 5
Digital logic, evolution of, 16–18
Diligent Nexys A7 FPGA trainer board, 315–319
Diodes, 5
    OR gate, 165, 166
DIP (dual in-line package), 15
Don't care conditions, 90–94
Dynamic hazard, 70–71

E

EBCDIC (Extended Binary-Coded Decimal Interchange
        Code), 31, 32
Edge-triggered D flip-flop, 214–216
EEPROM/E²PROM (Electrically Erasable Programmable
        ROM), 2–3, 167
Embedded controllers, 18
Encoder, 130–133
    active-high 4-to-2, 204–205
    priority, 334–337
end keyword, 195
endmodule keyword, 176, 180
    alignment of, 182
EPROM (Erasable Programmable ROM), 3, 167
Equality operators, 192
Equivalence, 61, 123
Error detection/correction, 48–49
Excess-3 code, 31–35
Excitation table, 221, 239–240
Execute, 154

F

Falling-edge flip-flop, 282
Fast adder, 154–160
Fetch, 153
Field programmable device (FPD), 170–171
Fixed-point representation, 35
Flash memory, 3, 315
Flip-flops, 155, 214–226
    in clocked sequential circuits, 227
    for counters, 263–268

D, 220, 221, 222, 229–230, 263–268, 338–340, 343–346
edge-triggered D, 214–216
falling-edge, 282
JK, 216–217, 220, 221, 222, 238–240, 264–266, 347–348
positive-edge triggered, 282
preset and clear inputs, 219–220
RS, 220
state analysis, 228–233
summary of, 220–223
T, 217–218, 221, 222, 263–264, 266–268, 341–343
timing parameters for edge-triggered, 218–219
Floating-point representation, 35
forever loop, 293–294
4-bit adder, 330–334
4-bit binary adder, 187–188
behavioral modeling for, 196–197
dataflow modeling for, 202–203
4-to-16 binary decoder, 329–330
Four-variable K-map, 84–87
FPDs (Field Programmable Devices), 170–171
FPGA (Field Programmable Gate Array), 3, 16, 17, 170–171,
263, 301–378
4-bit adder, 330–334
4-bit counter, 356–359
4-to-16 binary decoder, 329–330
8-bit shift register, 360–362
architecture, 311
basics, 301–302
boards, typical, 315–320
chips, typical, 312–314
CLBs, 308, 310
configuration pins, 314
CPLDs compared with, 302
D flip-flop, 338–340, 343–346
design, 320
examples, 322–373
gated D-latch, 350–355
general purpose register, 363–369
HDLs in designing, 175–176
implementation, 320–322
JK flip-flop, 347–348
LUTs, 302–307
power/ground pins, 315
priority encoder, 334–337
programmable switch matrix, 308
programming, 311–312
state diagram implementation, 369–373
T flip-flop, 341–343
user I/O pins, 315
XOR gate, 322–324
FPLAs (field programmable PLAs), 170–171
FSM (Finite State Machine), 293
Full adder, 141–142, 154–155, 185–186
behavioral modeling for, 196
dataflow modeling for, 194–195
Functional simulator, 175
Fundamental mode of operation, 254
Furnace temperature control, 18–19

G

Gated D latch, 213–214, 350–355
Gated SR latch, 213
Gates, 3, 53
combination circuit design with, 108–112
comparator, 121–123
feedback among, 228

for time delay, 228
XOR, 322–324
General Purpose Register. *See* GPR (General Purpose Register)
Glitches, 70–71
Glue logic, 17
GPR (General Purpose Register), 153, 275–276, 363–369
Gray code, 33–35

H

Half-adder, 139–142, 185–186
Half-subtractor, 143–146
Hamming code, 49
Hazards, 70–71
HCMOS (High Speed Complementary MOS), 1, 17
outputs, 13–14
HCT, 11–12
HDLs (Hardware Description Languages), 3, 16, 175–176.
See also Verilog
evolution of, 16–17
Hexadecimal number system, 22
converting to binary, 25
converting to decimal, 25–26
Hierarchical structural modeling, 176, 186–187

I

IC (Integrated Circuit), 14–16, 167
if-else statements, 195, 197, 289
initial block, 195
input keyword, 176, 182
Intel Corporation, 17
Inverter, 6
I/O (input/output)
defined, 1
interrupt, 133
programmable blocks, 311
I/O pins, 315

J

JK flip-flop, 216–217, 220, 221, 222
Johnson counter, 273–275
JTAG loop, 313
JTAG (Joint Test Action Group) port, 313

K

Karnaugh, Maurice, 16
Karnaugh maps, 16, 81–95
don't care conditions, 90–94
flip-flop, 221–222, 230–231
flip-flop input equations, 239–240
four-variable, 84–87
prime implicants, 87–89
product-of-sums form in, 89–90
three-variable, 82–84
Keywords, Verilog, 176
K-maps. *See* Karnaugh maps

L

Latches, 211–214
gated D, 213–214, 353–355
gated SR, 213

SR, 211–213
LED (light emitting diodes), 6–7
Logic block, configurable, 308, 310
Logic circuits
    NAND gates, 96–98
    NOR gates, 98–101
Logic gate. *See* Gates
Logic level, 4, 289
Logic operations
    AND, 56–57
    basic, 53–57
    Boolean algebra, 63–72
    NAND, 58
    NOR, 57–58
    NOT, 53–54
    OR, 54–55
    positive and negative, 62
    XNOR, 61–62
    XOR, 59–60
Logical operators, 191–192
Logical shift, 46–48
Logical shift operators, 192
LSB (Least Significant bit), 179, 268–269
LSI (large-scale integration), 14–15, 165
LUT (Look-Up Table), 301, 302–307

M

Maxterms, 77–80, 78
    decoders for, 144
M-bit, 165
Mealy circuit/machine, 232–234, 243
Memory, 1
    EEPROM/E²PROM, 2–3, 167
    EPROM, 3, 167
    flash, 315
    PROM, 166–170
    RAM, 3, 245–246
    ROM, 3–4, 165–167
Memory Address Register (MAR), 152–153
Microcomputer, 1, 3
Microcontroller, 2
    in ALU design, 162–163
    evolution of, 17–18
    typical applications of, 18–19
Microprocessor, 1
    in ALU design, 162–163
    evolution of, 17–18
Minimization of states, 235–237
Minterms, 77–80
    decoders for, 144
Mobius counter. *See* Johnson counter
MOD-4 counter, 252–253
Mode input, 162
Modeling
    behavioral, 176
    dataflow, 176, 189–195, 282
    hierarchical structural, 176, 186–187
    RTL, 289–297
    structural, 176, 181, 182–189
Module declarations, 177–180
Module items, 181
module keyword, 176, 180
    alignment of, 182
Modulo operator, 190
Modulo-*n* counter, 271–273
Moore circuit/machine, 232–234

MOS (metal oxide semiconductor), 1, 4, 11–14
    complementary, 11–13
    input switch, 14, 15
    operation as an inverter, 11
    outputs, 13–14
    in PLDs, 167–170
    transistors in ROM, 165
MSB (most significant bit), 48, 268–269
MSI (medium-scale integration), 14–15
Multiple-output combinational circuits, 113–117
Multiplex, register SUM (Sequential logic), 290
Multiplexer (MUX), 133–137
    2-to-1, 185
    in binary adders/subtractors, 139–147

N

Named association, 181
NAND gate, 96–98, 99
nand keyword, 176
NAND operation, 58
Negative logic, 62
negedge, 282
Nets, 178, 179
Nibble, 2
NMOS, 11–12
Noise margin, 9
Non-blocking assignments, 282–288
Non-overlapping sequence detector, 242
Nonvolatile storage device, 3–4
NOR gate, 98–101
NOR operation, 57–58
not keyword, 176, 182
NOT operation, 53–54
    in ALU design, 162
not reserved keyword, 176
Npn transistor, 5–6
Number systems, 21–30
    binary, 22, 27–30
    converting between, 22–26
    decimal, 21–22
    general number representation, 21–27
    hexadecimal, 22
    octal, 22

O

Octal number system, 22
    converting to binary, 24
    converting to decimal, 25
One's complement, 27–28
OR gate
    PLD, 167–170
    three-input diode, 165, 166
or keyword, 176
OR operation, 54–55
    in ALU design, 162
or reserved keyword, 176
output keyword, 176, 182
Overflow flag, 40, 48
Overlapping sequence detector, 242–244

P

PAL (Programmable Array Logic), 167–170
    SPLDs, 170–171
Parallel In-Parallel Out shift register, 268

Parallel In-Serial Out shift register, 268
parameter keyword, 283
Parity bit, 48–49
Parity checker, 291
Parity generation and checking, 72–73
Partial select, 179–180
PCB (printed-circuit board), 15, 315
PGA (pin grid array), 15
PLAs (Programmable Logic Arrays), 167–170
    commercially available field, 170–171
    state machine design, 253–254
PLDs (Programmable Logic Devices), 16, 167–170
PMOS, 11–12, 17
Pnp transistor, 5–6
Port declarations, 177–180
posedge, 282
Positive logic, 62
Power dissipation, 8
Power/ground pins, 315
Preset inputs, 219–220
Primary variable, 254
Prime implicants, 87–89
Primitive flow table, 255, 256
Primitives, 180
Priority encoder, 334–337
Procedural statement, 282–283
Product-of-sums (POS) form, 89–90
Program, 3
Programmable I/O blocks, 311
Programmable logic device (PLD). *See* PLDs (Programmable
        Logic Devices)
Programmable switch matrix, 308, 311
PROM (programmable ROM), 166–167
PLDs and, 167–170
Propagation delay, 8–9

Q

Quine-McCluskey method, 81, 95–96

R

RAM (random-access memory), 3
    sequential logic circuit, 245–246
    static, 245
Read-only memory. *See* ROM (read-only memory)
Reduction operators, 191
reg keyword, 178, 179, 195
Register SUM (Sequential logic), 290
Register transfer level. *See* RTL (Register Transfer Level)
        modeling
Registers, 4
    general-purpose, 152–154, 178, 275–276
    shift, 268–271
Ring counter, 273, 275
Ripple carry adder, 141, 155–156
ROM (read-only memory), 3–4, 165–167
    EEPROM, 167
    mask, 166
    programmable, 166–167
RS flip-flop, 220, 221
RTL (Register Transfer Level) modeling, 289–297

S

Schematic capture, 175
SECDED (Single Error Correction Double Error Detection),
        49
Secondary variable, 254
Sensitivity list, 196
Sequence generator/detector, 242–245
Sequential logic circuits, 107
    analysis of, 228–233
    ASM charts, 227, 246–254
    asynchronous, 228, 254–256
    design, 237–240
    HDLs for, 175
    introduction to, 227–228
    minimization of states, 235–237
    RAM, 245–246
    sequence generator/detector, 242–245
    serial adder, 240–242
    types of, 233–234
Sequential logic design, 281–300
    always blocks, 281–283
Sequential systems, 4
Serial adder, 240–242
Serial In-Parallel Out shift register, 268
Serial In-Serial Out shift register, 268
Seven-segment display, 6–7, 9
Shannon, Claude, 16
Shift operations, 46–48
Shift register, 240. *See also* Johnson counter
    8-bit, 360–362
Shift register counter, 271–275
Shifter, combinational, 151–152
Sign flag, 39
Signed division, 42–44
Signed multiplication, 41–42
Simple module, 180–181
Simulation, 201–206
    non-blocking assignment, 287–288
SOP (sum-of-products), 78, 167
Speed power product (SPP), 4
SPLD (Simple PLD), 170–171
SR (Set-Reset) latch, 211–213
    gated, 213
SRAM (static RAM), 245
    in LUTs, 302–303
SSI (small-scale integration), 14–15
State diagram, 230–233
    ASM charts and, 246–247
    FPGA implementation, 369–373
State machine design using ASM chart, 249–254
State machines. *See* Synchronous sequential circuits
State symbols, 246–247
State table, 228–231, 233
    sequence generator/detector, 242–244
States, minimization of, 235–237
Static hazard, 70–71
Static RAM. *See* SRAM (static RAM)
Structural modeling, 176, 181, 182–189
Subtractor
    full-, 143–144
    half-, 143–144
SUM (Sequential logic), 290
Sum-of-products. *See* SOP (sum-of-products)
Switch matrices, 301
    programmable, 308, 311
Switch-tail counter. *See* Johnson counter
Synchronous sequential circuits, 227–254
    analysis of, 228–233
    ASM charts, 227, 246–254
    counters, 263–268

design, 237–240
minimization of states, 235–237
RAM, 245–246
sequence generator/detector, 242–245
serial adder, 240–242
types of, 233–234
Synthesis, 175, 320
Systems level, 4, 289

T

T flip-flop, 217–218, 221, 222
TCK (Test Clock), 313
TDI (Test Data Input), 313
TDO (Test Data Output), 313
Test bench, 176, 201–206
parity checker, 292–293
Three-variable K-map, 82–84
$time function, 201
Time-delay devices, 228
Timing diagram, 232
TMS (Test Mode Select), 313
Totem-pole output circuit, 9–10
Transistors, 4, 5–6
OFF/ON status of, 1
operation as inverters, 6
Transition table, 253–254
Transmission gate, 11–12
Tristate, 10
Truth table, 63, 77, 79
ALU design, 164
flip-flop, 221–222
LUTs, 303–305, 307
ROM, 166
TTL (transistor transistor logic), 7–9
outputs, 9–10
switch inputs, 11
Twisted ring counter. *See* Johnson counter
2-to-1 MUX, 185, 194, 200
2-to-4 decoder, 183–185, 193
behavioral modeling for, 200–201
Two-bit comparator, 121–123
Two's complement, 28–29
Two-variable K-map, 81–82

U

Unicode, 35
Unsigned division, 42
Unsigned multiplication, 41
Up-down counter, 290, 291

V

Vending machine design, 294–297
Verilog, 16
basics of, 176–182, 281–283
behavioral modeling, 176, 181, 195–201
binary to seven segment converter, 324–328
blocking/non-blocking assignments, 282–289
case-endcase construct, 198–200
combinational circuit design using, 175–209
dataflow modeling, 176, 189–195
design flow to FPGA, 320–321
FPGA, 301–378
keywords, 176
modeling logical conditions in a circuit, 198

module and port declarations, 177–180
module items, 181
negedge, 282
operators, 191
posedge, 282
representing numbers in, 176–177
reserved keywords, 176
RTL modeling, 289–297
sequential logic design using, 281–300
simulation, 201–206
structural modeling, 176, 181, 182–189
test bench, 176, 201–206
typical segment in, 177–182
vending machine design, 294–297
VHDL (Very High Speed Description Language), 17, 175–176
VHSIC (Very High Speed Integrated Circuits), 175–176
VLSI (very large-scale integration), 14–15

W

wire keyword, 178, 179, 182
Word, 2, 165

X

Xilinx, 171, 301
Xilinx Artix 7, 312, 315–320
Xilinx Spartan 6, 306
Xilinx Vivado IDE, 281
XNOR implementations, 72–73
xnor keyword, 176
XNOR operation, 61–62, 123
XOR gate, 322–324
XOR implementations, 72–73
xor keyword, 176
XOR operation, 59–60